Japan's Nationalist Right in the Internet Age

Japan's nationalist right have used the internet to organize offline activism in increasingly visible ways.

Hall investigates the role of internet-mediated activism in Japan's ongoing historical and territorial disputes. He explores the emergence of two right-wing activist organizations, Nihon Bunka Channel Sakura and Ganbare Nippon, which have played a significant role in pressure campaigns against Japanese media outlets, campaigns to influence historical memorials, and campaigns to assert Japan's territorial claim to the Senkaku/Diaoyu Islands. Taking a multidisciplinary approach, he analyzes how activists maintained cohesion, raised funds, held protests that regularly drew hundreds to thousands of participants, and used fishing boats to land activists on disputed islands. Detailing events that took place between 2004 and 2020, he demonstrates how skilled social actors built cohesive grassroots protest organizations through the creation of shared meaning for their organization and its supporters.

A valuable read both for scholars seeking insight into the dynamics surrounding Japan's history disputes and territorial issues and for those seeking to compare Japanese right-wing internet activism with its counterparts elsewhere.

Jeffrey J. Hall is Assistant Professor and Junior Researcher at Waseda University's Organization for Regional and Inter-Regional Studies in Tokyo, Japan.

Routledge Contemporary Japan Series

Masculinity and Body Weight in Japan
Grappling with Metabolic Syndrome
Genaro Castro-Vázquez

New Frontiers in Japanese Studies
Edited by Akihiro Ogawa and Philip Seaton

Social Change in Japan, 1989-2019
Social Status, Social Consciousness, Attitudes and Values
Edited by Carola Hommerich, Naoki Sudo and Toru Kikkawa

Avant-Garde and Nondominant Thought in Postwar Japan
Image, Matter, and Separation
Kenichi Yoshida

Wildlife, Landscape Use and Society
Regional Case Studies in Japan
Ken Sugimura

Women and Political Inequality in Japan
Gender Imbalanced Democracy
Mikiko Eto

Somaesthetics and the Philosophy of Culture
Projects in Japan
Satoshi Higuchi

Japan's Nationalist Right in the Internet Age
Online Media and Grassroots Conservative Activism
Jeffrey J. Hall

For more information about this series, please visit: *www.routledge.com/Routledge-Contemporary-Japan-Series/book-series/SE0002*

Japan's Nationalist Right in the Internet Age

Online Media and Grassroots Conservative Activism

Jeffrey J. Hall

Routledge
Taylor & Francis Group
LONDON AND NEW YORK

First published 2021
by Routledge
2 Park Square, Milton Park, Abingdon, Oxon OX14 4RN

and by Routledge
605 Third Avenue, New York, NY 10158

Routledge is an imprint of the Taylor & Francis Group, an informa business

British Library Cataloguing-in-Publication Data
A catalogue record for this book is available from the British Library

Library of Congress Cataloging-in-Publication Data
Names: Hall, Jeffrey J. (Jeffrey James), author.
Title: Japan's nationalist right in the Internet age: : online media and grassroots conservative activism / Jeffrey J. Hall.
Description: Abingdon, Oxon ; New York, NY : Routledge, 2021. | Series: Routledge contemporary Japan series | Includes bibliographical references and index. |
Identifiers: LCCN 2020046641 (print) | LCCN 2020046642 (ebook) | ISBN 9780367558284 (hardback) | ISBN 9780367558437 (paperback) | ISBN 9781003095392 (ebook)
Subjects: LCSH: Right-wing extremists--Japan. | Nationalism--Japan. | Internet and activism--Japan. | Internet--Political aspects--Japan.
Classification: LCC HN730.Z9 R3236 2021 (print) | LCC HN730.Z9 (ebook) | DDC 320.540952--dc23
LC record available at https://lccn.loc.gov/2020046641
LC ebook record available at https://lccn.loc.gov/2020046642

ISBN: 978-0-367-55828-4 (hbk)
ISBN: 978-0-367-55843-7 (pbk)
ISBN: 978-1-003-09539-2 (ebk)

Typeset in Galliard
by Deanta Global Publishing Services, Chennai, India

Contents

Illustrations

Figures

Tables

Acknowledgments

I have many people to thank for helping make this book a reality.

This book began as research conducted for my master's thesis and doctoral dissertation at Waseda University in Tokyo, Japan. Therefore, my largest thanks go to the excellent professors who served as my advisors between 2009 and 2015: Shinohara Hatsue, Gracia Liu-Farrer, Stephen R. Nagy, J. Patrick Boyd, and Gotō Kenichi. With their guidance I was able to clarify my methodology, narrow down my case studies, and discover the academic theory that guided my writing.

It would have been impossible to find the time to finish this book without the stability and the resources provided by Waseda University in the immediate years after completing my doctoral program. I was hired first as a postdoctoral researcher at Waseda University's Graduate School of Asia-Pacific Studies (GSAPS), and then as a Junior Researcher at its Organization for Regional and Inter-Regional Studies (ORIS). I owe a debt of gratitude to all of the professors and faculty of those departments, including Umemori Naoyuki, Nakano Yoshihiro, Koyama Shukuko, Asano Toyomi, Kuroda Kazuo, and Katsuma Yasushi.

There are also many researchers whom I met when presenting my preliminary research at international conferences and whose questions, suggestions, comments, and research helped me gain a broader perspective of my research topic. To name a few: Kevin Doak, Tamara Fuchs, Natalie-Anne Hall, Kim Changho, Chris Kostov, Higuchi Naoto, Ayaka Loeschke, Fabian Schaefer, Vivian Shaw, Nathaniel Smith, and Watanabe Chihiro. Special thanks go to Ernils Larsson, who has helped influence my research (and my taste in beer) in the years since our days together at Waseda.

I am also grateful to private and public organizations in Japan for their financial support. As a master's and doctoral student, I was lucky enough to benefit from two private scholarships from Mitsubishi Corporation and Tonen General Group. My postdoctoral research was funded in part by a generous Grant-in-Aid for Young Scientists from the Japan Society for the Promotion of Science (Grant No: 17K13861).

During the final stages of my research, the Université libre de Bruxelles (ULB) was kind enough to invite me first as a participant to a research workshop and later as a Visiting Professor. These experiences were incredibly valuable in helping me complete this book. Thank you François Foret, Vanessa Frangville, Thierry Kellner, Frederik Ponjaert, and Chenchen Zhang.

Turning an unpolished dissertation into an academic book was no easy task. I benefitted greatly from the help of two GSAPS graduate students, Austin Smith and Roméo Marcantuoni, who assisted with background research and manuscript editing.

Finally, on a personal note, I would like to thank my wonderful family. My parents, Larry and Marni Hall, are most responsible for my interest in politics and history. Without the love and support of my entire family, I would have never made it this far. The greatest thanks go to my amazing wife and constant companion, Emi, whose kind heart and a good sense of humor helped me get through long months of writing in a tiny Tokyo apartment during the 2020 pandemic.

1 Introduction

A 21-year-old student arrived at a classroom at Waseda University, prepared for another day of one of his favorite literature courses. He had expected a normal day of study, but the events that day would mark a turning point in his life.

The professor arrived late. With a stunned look on his face, he informed the class that Mishima Yukio had just committed suicide. The shock was so great that he could not teach the class. Instead, he sent the students home, telling them to spend the rest of the day contemplating what had just happened.[1]

It was November 25, 1970. One of Japan's most famous novelists was dead. But it was no normal suicide. Mishima had killed himself after leading a private student militia into a military base, taking a Japanese general hostage, and calling on Japan's Self-Defense Forces to carry out a coup d'état.

The student returned to his apartment and watched Japanese television news coverage of Mishima's failed coup. Cameras had been present when Mishima spoke to a group of soldiers who had assembled in response to the hostage-taker's demands. Standing on the balcony of the army headquarters building, Mishima attempted to deliver an impassioned plea for them to rise up and restore Japan's emperor and military to its rightful place. Instead, his speech was drowned out by the jeering and shouting of annoyed and angry soldiers. Overhead, television news helicopters added to the noise. Having failed to inspire a military uprising, Mishima went back inside the building and committed ritual suicide with one of his student militiamen.

It was difficult to hear what Mishima was saying in the clips that aired on television. The noise, especially the noise of the news helicopters, was too loud. It made the student reach a conclusion about the state of postwar Japan: a patriotic man's voice could not be heard. When the student later sought out and read one of Mishima's last articles, the following passage deeply impacted him:

> I cannot have much hope for the future of Japan. As days pass, I feel more and more deeply that if things should proceed this way, "Japan" might end up disappearing. Japan might disappear, and in its place, a large economic country, which is inorganic, vacant, neutral, medium colored, wealthy, and shrewd, would remain at one corner of the Far East. I don't feel like conversing with those people who think that that is all right.[2]

Thirty-four years later, the former literature student – Mizushima Satoru – would meet someone else whose life had been touched by Mishima. Together, they would create an alternative media outlet that would try to break through what they considered to be the noise of the mainstream media. They wanted to prevent the "disappearance" of Japan that Mishima had warned was coming. Their message would be one of nationalistic pride battling against the "anti-Japanese" forces inside and outside Japan. Anyone with an internet connection would be able to view their programs and hear their message.

I moved to Japan in August 2005, months after the founding of a website that would become globally significant as a platform for alternative media: YouTube.com. In those early years of YouTube, it was quite easy to find popular English-language content representing both the political left and the right, but my attempts to consume Japanese-language content met with different results. The most-viewed video rankings on YouTube Japan's news category were largely dominated by the political right. When searching in Japanese for videos on historically controversial topics, the only videos with thousands of views seemed to be those expressing the nationalist viewpoints. Although some Japanese left-leaning voices have since established popular channels on YouTube, the videos of the right remain more popular today.

When I began my research in 2008, there were few studies on right-wing activism in Japan and even fewer that examined events taking place in the internet era. An important early work, the 2003 book *Japanese Cybercultures*, included a valuable case study of activist groups' use of the internet during the 2001 history textbook affair, in which Isa Ducke noted that traditional methods had "only been slightly enhanced by basic internet features" such as e-mail.[3] She also observed that the fact that many of the activists were of middle or older age was a contributing factor to a lack of internet use. For most of the non-state actors studied in the volume, it could be generally stated that they lacked access to the "finance, facilities, and expertise" necessary to truly exploit the potential of the internet.[4]

Another notable work, from 2010, explored how several small independent progressive media organizations used video sharing sites such as YouTube to expand the distribution of their news content. Gabriele Hadl observed that the emergence of these citizen media outlets created an opportunity for civic groups to create forums in which misunderstood social issues could be discussed and addressed.[5] Similar developments on the right remained unexplored.

The emergence of Japan's nativist right in the mid-2000s, a new collection of extreme hate groups that used the internet for recruitment and organization, has led to a new focus of academic and journalistic attention on right-wing activism in Japan. Most of this new research has centered on the largest and most infamous of the new nativist groups, the Association of Citizens against the Special Privileges of the Zainichi, commonly known as Zaitokukai, a contraction of its Japanese name. The fieldwork-based research of Higuchi Naoto, Yasuda Koichi, Asahina Yuki, and Nathaniel M. Smith has greatly contributed to a rich understanding of these xenophobic groups and their participants. While I discuss their findings in Chapter 2 of this book, the focus of this book is on less extreme conservative activists who have a larger following, have achieved more for their cause, but have been largely ignored as a subject of detailed academic research.

This book examines the phenomenon of internet-mediated grassroots conservative activism through an exploration of the activism of Nihon Bunka Channel Sakura (Japanese Culture Channel Sakura: hereafter referred to as Channel Sakura), an alternative media outlet founded by Mizushima Satoru. Since its creation in 2004, Channel Sakura and its activist wing, Ganbare Nippon, have been an influential force in the activism of Japan's nationalist right. Mizushima and his fellow activists use their media outlet to bring together a variety of right-leaning organizations, holding some of the largest right-wing demonstrations in postwar Japanese history. While some of their campaigns have failed to achieve any of their goals, others have been remarkably successful.

Channel Sakura's campaigns have goals that many readers would consider very far from the mainstream of Japanese society. In its discussion of historical issues, it does not trust the international consensus of historians regarding Japan's conduct in World War II. For example, it aired many programs denying well-documented war atrocities, such as the Nanjing Massacre. It also called out media organizations that reported on those atrocities as "anti-Japanese." In accordance with this view, its activists held demonstrations demanding the complete dissolution of NHK, Japan's national broadcaster. Objectionable films, books, television programs, and news reports were attributed to Chinese communist infiltration of Japanese society.

In the 16 years since its founding in 2004, Channel Sakura has experienced far more setbacks than successes, yet it has remained strong and well-organized while rival organizations faded into obscurity. How do we make sense of this phenomenon? How can one explain its ability to maintain cohesion, raise funds, and regularly hold protests that draw hundreds or even thousands of participants? Why did it thrive while other organizations, such as Zaitokukai, fizzled out?

This book answers these questions by arguing that social actors within Channel Sakura (and its protest wing, Ganbare Nippon) skillfully took advantage of structural shifts to create new opportunities for activist campaigns. As a part of Japan's assertive conservative right, Channel Sakura tapped into an existing niche of the Japanese population that found value in a worldview that treated pre-1945 history as something worthy of pride. It also distributed its videos for free on YouTube, making it easier for newcomers to discover the viewpoints of Japan's right. Existing near the fringes of mainstream Japanese society, the activists of Channel Sakura were ever-watchful for new opportunities to challenge the existing order and advocate on behalf of their views.

Analytical framework

My analysis of Channel Sakura's emergence and participation in several major protest campaigns is guided by Fligstein and McAdam's general theory of Strategic Action Fields (SAFs). This theoretical approach is aimed at overcoming the "balkanization" of social scientific research on social/political activism that leads to analyses that place too much or too little emphasis on political and economic structures or on non-material culture and existential motivations.[6] SAFs are conceived as "mesolevel social orders" in which

> actors (who can be individual or collective) are attuned to and interact with one another on the basis of shared (which is not to say consensual) understandings about the purposes of the field, relationships to others in the field (including who has power and why), and the rules governing legitimate action in the field.[7]

All forms of collective actors, whether they are organizations, government systems, or social movements, are created from SAFs. Some fields can be inside other fields in a hierarchical manner, which Fligstein and McAdam compare to the image of Russian nesting dolls. In other cases, fields are positioned in a different manner. The connections between different fields generally indicate conditions of interdependence or the potential to effect change in one another.

Strategic Action Fields have no clear formalized boundaries, making them broader and more fluid than other sociological approaches to the organization. Actors and groups can move across and between different SAFs, positions and arrangements within and between SAFs can be created or altered, and through a range of processes, an SAF can be either stabilized or de-stabilized. Social actors and organizations place themselves within SAFs and act based on the influence of "power and culture."[8]

Social skill, the "ability to induce cooperation in others," is a major element of understanding how and why events occur within Strategic Action Fields.[9] A skilled social actor is one that is particularly skilled at creating a positive sense of meaning for themselves and others by tailoring their actions to the current state of a given field. They create *stories* that appeal to the "identity and interests" of their audience, aiming to gain their cooperation. The same *stories* are also used to induce actions against their opponents.[10] Skilled social actors are constantly seeking to maintain or improve their position within fields.

While I employ the term *skilled social actors* throughout this book, this concept is not far from what Alexander Bukh has referred to as *national identity entrepreneurs*, that is, "non-state actors (individuals, civic groups, or any other entity that is not part of the state and has a capacity for agency) who create and actively promote a certain narrative … that invokes the nation."[11] There is considerable overlap in these concepts, especially when it comes to Channel Sakura's activism regarding territorial disputes (discussed in Chapter 7).

Strategic Action Fields are composed of incumbents and challengers. Incumbents are actors with a privileged place within the field, having claim to most of the material and status rewards. The rules within a field tend to favor the incumbents, and prevailing shared meanings tend to legitimate their higher position. In contrast, challengers are actors who have less influence over a field. As part of the field, the challengers recognize their position relative to the incumbents, and while they recognize "the dominant logic of incumbent actors, they can usually articulate an alternative vision of the field in their position in it." Within a stable field, challengers seek out new opportunities to shift the balance in their favor.[12]

My analysis of Channel Sakura is guided by a "realist" approach to Strategic Action Fields, meaning that the concepts of SAFs are used to illustrate and explain a particular phenomenon of interest. Using an SAF framework will produce "research that contains a kind of sociological history in which the goal is to use concepts to make sense of how a particular set of actors get organized, stay in power, or perhaps find themselves supplanted by other actors."[13] In other words, this book has an empirical focus on social actors within specific activist campaigns, noting their place within particular field, and how they have acted in periods of instability or change within fields. In the interest of readability, I have used the terms "fields of contestation" or "fields" when describing Strategic Action Fields in the three case study chapters (5, 6, and 7).

Research methods

This book combines research I conducted in Japan between 2008 and 2020, employing a variety of methods. My key source of information was programs produced and uploaded by Channel Sakura – hundreds of hours of primary source material on the views of activists and how their campaigns were playing out. Secondary material, such as newspaper reporting on demonstrations, helped to verify claims. This was supplemented by online and offline ethnographic fieldwork.

In early 2008 I created a YouTube account for the purpose of consuming Channel Sakura's video content. My daily routine included watching Channel Sakura's latest programs and marking the more interesting ones as "favorites" to be watched later. In some instances in which programs were not available on YouTube, I would turn to Nico Nico Douga or Channel Sakura's own, very slow, website. I would read some of the comments on videos, particularly the most popular comments. I would buy books recommended by the videos and watch films that were introduced in the programs. I was a "lurker" within their cyber community. While I did not participate directly in comment threads or make use of voting buttons to rate comments and videos, I became very familiar with the viewpoints expressed by users. Through this experience, I was regularly updated on the progress of numerous concurrent activist campaigns, three of which are detailed in later chapters of this book.

In order to understand the online community of Channel Sakura viewers, I also gathered data through non-participant observation of Channel Sakura's website, its web forums, and the comment threads of its YouTube videos. I did not engage with users on these sites or participate directly in their online activities. Popularly known as "lurking" on the internet, this approach to gathering data is used by anthropologists who conduct unobtrusive ethnographies of virtual communities (netnography).[14] I also engaged in non-participant observation of several offline demonstrations organized by Channel Sakura between 2009 and 2020. Although most of this book is not written as an ethnography, sections of Chapter 4 about the meaning-making methods of activists are based on this fieldwork.

The study of internet activism is a study of ephemeral data. It is not rare for online content, whether it be a blog post, news article, or YouTube video, to disappear from the internet. Sometimes, this is a case of websites going out of business, while at other times, the deletion of data is a choice made by the original content creator. While it is technically possible for researchers to download backups of YouTube videos, such an action violates YouTube's terms of service and may violate copyright laws.[15] Many of the videos and websites I cite in this book have disappeared from the internet, necessitating that I work on the basis of previously recorded notes. Nonetheless, whenever possible I have cited the original titles and URLs of these websites and videos in question. It is possible that some of this disappeared content could be re-uploaded to other sites, making it accessible to future researchers.

Another issue is how one should address the claims and arguments of individuals who aim to spread conspiracy theories and/or to deny or downplay well-documentary historical events. Many readers of this book will no doubt, like many Japanese people, find the viewpoints of these activists to be reprehensible. Researchers of other right-wing movements have warned of the danger that writing about the views of such individuals could increase their visibility and amplify their objectionable ideas.[16] Giving extremist groups and ideas attention could be, as Whitney Philips has argued, like giving them "oxygen."[17] This book is not, however, focused on the arguments of Japanese nationalists. In instances where details are provided, they are done so to better understand the motivations of social actors and their meaning-making practices within fields of contestation. My analysis considers online videos in the context in which they would likely be consumed – by people who are part of a subculture that makes sense of reality quite differently from mainstream society. To better understand how activists function as skilled social actors, the sense-making or meaning-making function of media for certain audiences needs to be taken seriously, even if the content of that media is objectionable or wrong.[18] Historians have devoted decades to providing extensive documentation of the Nanjing Massacre, the abuse of the "comfort women," and Imperial Japan's oppressive rule of its colonies.[19] Thus, rather than re-writing what other scholars have written, I have written about how activists have used their own version of the "truth" within specific campaigns.

Although the social actors studied in this book are often referred to as "right-wing" or "far-right" in English-language news reports and in some academic papers, I prefer to use terms such as "conservative," "nationalist," "conservative right," or "assertive conservative right." When reading about the worldview of these groups, some may question why they are not simply referred to as "right-wing." This is a choice made not to downplay their views but rather to differentiate them from the more well-known "right-wing" (uyoku) of Japan. It is a term associated with a specific form of extreme right-wing activism, involving intimidation, violence, and loud, black vans, with frequent ties to the criminal underworld. Many of the right-leaning activist groups that rose out of post-1990s

Japan are very different, so I use the different terms to avoid confusion with the more extreme forms of right-wing activism found in Japan.

The structure of this book

This book consists of eight chapters, including this introduction.

Chapter 2 introduces the landscape of nationalist activism in postwar Japan. Because Channel Sakura was created by people with roots in both the traditional postwar right-wing and the post-1990s assertive conservative right, the historical and social context behind these movements will be explored. It also provides a detailed picture of the different organizations and individuals who make up the assertive conservative right in postwar Japan, something that has until now been lacking in academic studies of Japan's history disputes.

Chapter 3 details how a confluence of skilled social actors from different conservative backgrounds came together to found Channel Sakura. It also provides basic information about Channel Sakura's fundraising, programming, and conception of grassroots activism. This information is especially important for understanding how this organization maintained financial stability and social cohesion. In addition, it discusses how allied organizations, including Taiwanese and Uyghur groups, benefit from cooperation with Channel Sakura. A picture emerges of an organization that helped propel the ideas of the assertive conservative right from niche magazines and books to the wider world of the internet.

Chapter 4 looks into the ways that Channel Sakura created shared meaning for its supporters. This includes the use of historical stories and slogans to link their activism to a lineage of Japanese patriots who worked to save their country in times of crisis. The use of patriotic symbols, including decorations and images, is also noted. There is also an interactive dimension to this meaning-making, in which viewers send edible gifts to Channel Sakura, with some of them being consumed during livestreamed virtual drinking parties. The use of powerful symbols and rituals in offline activities is discussed as well, focusing on the activists' annual flag march to the Yasukuni Shrine.

Chapters 5 through 9 detail Channel Sakura's role in three activist campaigns. I selected these because each involved distinctly different types of targets, different types of tactics, and differing outcomes.

The first campaign (Chapter 5) was against NHK for the airing of a "biased" historical documentary about the colonization of Taiwan in 2009. The campaign took place within a field in which the right has fought to influence the programming of Japan's public broadcaster, which they see as left-leaning and "anti-Japanese." I discuss in detail how activists obtained the help of Taiwanese, including members of the aboriginal Paiwan people, to create videos outlining complaints against NHK. Protest marches and petitioning were supplemented by a class-action lawsuit against NHK, in which thousands of supporters sought monetary compensation. Although the lawsuit ultimately failed, it can be seen as a significant contribution to the Japanese right's ongoing efforts to weaken NHK's independence.

The second campaign (Chapter 6), which took place in 2011, aimed to remove descriptions of "comfort women" and the massacre of civilians from a proposed historical signboard in Okinawa. Channel Sakura's opponents in this field were academics and progressive citizens' groups. Unlike the other campaigns I discuss, this one resulted in a swift and clear outcome. The signboard's contents were censored, and opponents failed to convince the Okinawa Prefectural Government to reverse its decision. Although very short and limited in scope, this protest campaign represented a significant and tangible victory for conservative activists.

The third campaign (Chapter 7) I discuss is Channel Sakura and Ganbare Nippon's activities related to the Senkaku Islands territorial dispute. In this case, which includes events from 2009 until 2020, conservative activists took advantage of destabilizing events to successfully organize major street demonstrations, raise money to buy a fishing boat, and carry out landings on the islands. The fishing boats were also used to catch fish, which was served to Japanese lawmakers and Channel Sakura viewers. Within this international field of contestation, these activists carried out actions that drew considerable attention from the outside world and contributed to the increasingly tense state of the dispute between Japan and China.

The final chapter of this book looks at developments that occurred after the key events discussed in the previous chapters. The first is the 2014 Tokyo gubernatorial campaign of General Tamogami Toshio, a key figure within the conservative right and a frequent participant in the actions described in other chapters of this book. Although Tamogami's campaign received over 600,000 votes and widespread media attention, it led to the second event – his arrest and conviction for campaign finance violations. In the aftermath of this scandal, there was a major split among Channel Sakura supporters and allied groups. Some of the activists who sided with Tamogami eventually gravitated around new online activist and media organizations, most notably DHC Television. The creation and popularity of DHC and other well-funded right-wing media platforms signals disunity, but viewer numbers have not dropped. I close with a discussion of the future prospects for organizations like Channel Sakura, including how online crackdowns on overseas far-right movements, such as the American alt-right, could threaten the survival of alternative media outlets that use the internet to spread viewpoints that could be classified as "hate speech."

Notes

1 "【水島総】三島由紀夫・森田必勝両烈士四十八年祭 [桜H30/11/29]" ["Mizushima Satoru" Mishima Yukio – Morita Masakatsu, the 48th Anniversary of Two Patriots (Sakura Heisei 30/11/29)], Nihon Bunka Channel Sakura, November 29, 2018, https://www.nicovideo.jp/watch/so34243752.

2 Yukio Mishima, 文化防衛論 [In Defense of Culture] (Tokyo: Chikuma Bunko, 2006), quoted in Joseph Verbovszky, "Overcoming Modernity in Yukio Mishima," *Discussions* 9, no. 2 (2013), http://www.inquiriesjournal.com/articles/797/overcoming-modernity-in-yukio-mishima.

3 Isa Ducke, "Activism and the Internet: Japan's 2001 History-Textbook Affair," in *Japanese Cybercultures*, ed. Nanette Gottlieb and Mark McLelland (New York: Routledge, 2003), 216.
4 Nanette Gottlieb and Mark McLelland, "The Internet in Japan," in *Japanese Cybercultures*, ed. Nanette Gottlieb and Mark McLelland (New York: Routledge, 2003), 14.
5 Gabriel Hadl, "Media and Civic Engagement in Japan," in *Civic Engagement in Contemporary Japan. Nonprofit and Civil Society Studies*, ed. Henk Vinken, Yuko Nishimura, Bruce L.J. White and Masayuki Deguchi (New York: Springer, 2010), https://doi.org/10.1007/978-1-4419-1504-7_9.
6 For example, Resource Mobilization Theory has been criticized for neglecting socially constructed meaning-based motivations for activism (see: Andrea Hemetsberger, "Understanding Consumers' Collective Action on the Internet – A Definition and Discussion of Relevant Concepts for Research," *Advances in Consumer Research* 30 (2003)). New Social Movement Theory and Framing Theory have also been criticized for placing too much emphasis on culture and social meaning, while ignoring material and structural factors (see: Ann Mische, "Cross-Talk in Movements: Reconceiving the Culture-Network Link," in *Social Movements and Networks: Relations Approaches to Collective Action*, ed. Mario Diani and Douglas McAdam (Oxford University Press, 2002), 279; and Lauren Langman, "Occupy: A New Social Movement," *Current Sociology* 61, no. 4 (2013)).
7 Neil Fligstein and Doug McAdam, *A Theory of Fields* (New York: Oxford University Press, 2012), 2.
8 Neil Fligstein and Doug Mcadam, "Toward a General Theory of Strategic Action Fields*," *Sociological Theory* 29, no. 1 (2011), 22, https://doi.org/10.1111%2Fj.1467-9558.2010.01385.x.
9 Neil Fligstein, "Social Skill and the Theory of Fields," *Sociological Theory* 19, no. 2 (2001), https://doi.org/10.1111%2F0735-2751.00132.
10 Fligstein and Mcadam, "Toward a General Theory of Strategic Action Fields*," 14.
11 Alexander Bukh, *These Islands Are Ours* (Stanford University Press, 2020), Kindle Edition, Location 294.
12 Fligstein and McAdam, *A Theory of Fields*, 5–11.
13 Ibid.
14 In regard to ethnical concerns about this kind of methodology, I have leaned in the direction of scholars who choose to protect the anonymity of research subjects. See: Tuikka Anne-Marie, Nguyen Chau, and K. Kimppa Kai, "Ethical Questions Related to Using Netnography as Research Method," *ORBIT Journal* 1, no. 2 (2017), https://doi.org/10.29297/orbit.v1i2.50.
15 Nicolas Legewie and Anne Nassauer, "YouTube, Google, Facebook: 21st Century Online Video Research and Research Ethics," *Forum Qualitative Sozialforschung/Forum: Qualitative Social Research* 19, no. 3 (2018), http://dx.doi.org/10.17169/fqs-19.3.3130.
16 Thomas Colley and Martin Moore, "The Challenges of Studying 4chan and the Alt-Right: 'Come on in the Water's Fine,'" *New Media & Society* (2020), https://doi.org/10.1177%2F1461444820948803.
17 Whitney Phillips, "The Oxygen of Amplification: Better Practices for Reporting on Extremists, Antagonists and Manipulators," *Data & Society*, May 22, 2018, https://datasociety.net/output/oxygen-of-amplification/
18 Alan McKee, *Textual Analysis: A Beginner's Guide* (London: Sage Publications, 2003), 48–49.
19 For example: Yuki Tanaka, *Japan's Comfort Women: Sexual Slavery and Prostitution During World War II and the US Occupation* (New York: Routledge,

2002); and Joshua A. Fogel, *The Nanjing Massacre in History and Historiography* (Berkeley: University of California Press, 2000); Andrew D. Morris, *Japanese Taiwan: Colonial Rule and its Contested Legacy* (London: Bloomsbury, 2015).

Bibliography

Colley, Thomas, and Moore, Martin. "The Challenges of Studying 4chan and the Alt-Right: 'Come on in the Water's Fine'." *New Media & Society* (2020). https://doi.org/10.1177/1461444820948803.

Ducke, Isa. "Activism and the Internet: Japan's 2001 History-Textbook Affair." In *Japanese Cybercultures*, ed. Nanette Gottlieb and Mark McLelland, 205–221. New York: Routledge, 2003.

Fligstein, Neil. "Social Skill and the Theory of Fields." *Sociological Theory* 19, no. 2 (2001): 105–125. https://doi.org/10.1111/0735-2751.00132.

Fligstein, Neil, and McAdam, Doug. "Toward a General Theory of Strategic Action Fields*." *Sociological Theory* 29, no. 1 (2011). https://doi.org/10.1111/j.1467-9558.2010.01385.x.

Fligstein, Neil, and McAdam, Doug. *A Theory of Fields*. New York: Oxford University Press, 2012.

Fogel, Joshua A. *The Nanjing Massacre in History and Historiography*. University of California Press, 2000.

Gottlieb, Nanette, and McLelland, Mark. "The Internet in Japan." In *Japanese Cybercultures*, ed. Nanette Gottlieb and Mark McLelland, 1–16. New York: Routledge, 2003.

Hadl, Gabriel. "Media and Civic Engagement in Japan." In *Civic Engagement in Contemporary Japan. Nonprofit and Civil Society Studies*, ed. Henk Vinken, Yuko Nishimura, Bruce L..J. White and Masayuki Deguchi, 153–169. New York: Springer, 2010. https://doi.org/10.1007/978-1-4419-1504-7_9.

Hemetsberger, Andrea. "Understanding Consumers' Collective Action on the Internet – A Definition and Discussion of Relevant Concepts for Research." *Advances in Consumer Research* 30 (2003). https://flosshub.org/sites/flosshub.org/files/hemetsberger3.pdf.

Langman, Lauren. "Occupy: A New New Social Movement." *Current Sociology* 61, no. 4 (2013): 510–524. https://doi.org/10.1177/0011392113479749.

Legewie, Nicolas, and Nassauer, Anne. "YouTube, Google, Facebook: 21st Century Online Video Research and Research Ethics." *Forum Qualitative Sozialforschung/Forum: Qualitative Social Research* 19, no. 3 (2018). http://dx.doi.org/10.17169/fqs-19.3.3130.

McKee, Alan. *Textual Analysis: A Beginner's Guide*. London: SAGE, 2003.

Mische, Ann. "Cross-Talk in Movements: Reconceiving the Culture-Network Link." In *Social Movements and Networks: Relations Approaches to Collective Action*, ed. Mario Diani and Douglas McAdam. Oxford University Press, 2003. https://doi.org/10.1353/sof.2005.0041.

Mishima, Yukio. 文化防衛論 [In Defense of Culture]. Tokyo: Chikuma Bunko, 2006, quoted in Verbovszky, Joseph. "Overcoming Modernity in Yukio Mishima." *Discussions* 9, no. 2 (2013).

Morris, Andrew D. *Japanese Taiwan: Colonial Rule and Its Contested Legacy*. London: Bloomsbury, 2015.

Nihon Bunka Channel Sakura. "【水島総】三島由紀夫・森田必勝両烈士四十八年祭[桜H30/11/29]" ['Mizushima Satoru' Mishima Yukio – Morita Masakatsu, the 48th Anniversary of Two Patriots (Sakura Heisei 30/11/29)]. November 29, 2018. https://www.nicovideo.jp/watch/so34243752

Phillips, Whitney. "The Oxygen of Amplification: Better Practices for Reporting on Extremists, Antagonists and Manipulators." *Data & Society*, May 22, 2018. https://datasociety.net/output/oxygen-of-amplification/.

Smith, Nathaniel M. "Fights on the Right: Social Citizenship, Ethnicity, and Postwar Cohorts of the Japanese Activist Right." *Social Science Japan Journal* 21, no. 2 (Summer 2018): 235–257. https://doi.org/10.1093/ssjj/jyy015.

Tanaka, Yuki. *Japan's Comfort Women: Sexual Slavery and Prostitution During World War II and the US Occupation*. New York: Routledge, 2002.

Tuikka, Anne-Marie, Nguyen, Chau, and Kimppa, Kai K. "Ethical Questions Related to Using Netnography as Research Method." *ORBIT Journal* 1, no. 2 (2017): 1–11. https://doi.org/10.29297/orbit.v1i2.50.

2 The landscape of postwar Japanese nationalist activism

When one encounters terms like "Japan's right-wing" or "Japanese nationalists," it often brings to mind men in military-style uniforms who drive around in black vans with loudspeakers, shouting slogans over wartime propaganda songs. Those people do exist and make themselves visible, but they are a tiny subsection of Japan's right. A wide variety of nationalistic groups with differing agendas, goals, and styles of activism emerged on the political right of Japan after World War II. In this chapter, I provide a brief overview of this diverse landscape of conservative and right-wing groups.

Old uyoku organizations

Japan's traditional or "old" radical right-wing organizations of the postwar era, the uyoku, emerged in the immediate years after Japan's defeat in World War II. Many of these groups and their founders had ties to pre-1945 ultranationalist and right-wing organizations, which had dissolved or been banned after the war. Over 200 radical right-wing groups were banned by US Occupation authorities from participation in politics, and many politicians and businessmen who were associated with prewar militarism were also purged from their positions.[1] New organizations were founded in their place, and previously banned individuals re-engaged in politics as the Occupation ended. In that same period, organized crime – Japan's yakuza gangs – grew in power, with some forming links with the radical right.

Cold War fears of communism, the rise of left-wing political organizations, and increasing labor union activism helped these groups build ties with Japan's conservative political elites. To control the situation, politicians turned to yakuza-affiliated uyoku groups to provide muscle for the status quo. Throughout the 1950s, uyoku and yakuza were used to break up strikes and demonstrations. In these incidents, police often looked the other way when right-wing violence occurred.[2] Yakuza-affiliated uyoku groups were also highly visible in 1960, when hundreds of right-wingers were used to violently clash with striking coal miners in Miike and break up protests against the US–Japan Security Treaty.[3]

Another pivotal event in 1960 was the assassination of Japan Socialist Party chairman Asanuma Inejirō, which occurred on stage during a nationally televised political debate. The sword-wielding assassin was 17-year-old Yamaguchi Otoya, a former member of the rightist group Dai Nippon Aikokutō (Greater Japan Patriotic Party), who resigned his membership shortly before the attack. Although Yamaguchi would become a hero to many supporters of Japan's far-right, to others his crime and subsequent suicide in prison were shocking reminders of prewar right-wing terrorism.[4]

The violence of 1960 led to a decline in the influence of uyoku organizations. Mainstream society was appalled by what they had seen. Conservative politicians began to shy away from the use of what Eiko Maruko Siniawer has referred to as political "violence specialists." Japanese voters widely disapproved of political violence, and they were making their voices heard in elections.[5] Police tolerance for right-wing violence also decreased, meaning that illegal acts committed by uyoku groups were taken much more seriously.[6]

Some uyoku groups were set up by yakuza gangs in order to facilitate bribery, extortion, and other forms of corruption under the guise of legitimate political activities.[7] In more recent years, new laws cracking down on organized crime have forced many uyoku organizations to close their doors.[8] Groups that heavily relied on money from extortion and gang activities found their old sources of income drying up. Few managed to survive into the 21st century.

One surviving group was Dai Nippon Aikokutō, founded in 1951 by prewar ultranationalist politician Akao Bin. Like other old uyoku organizations, Dai Nippon Aikokutō was anti-communist and pro-American in its political outlook. Although it did not have open ties to the yakuza and considered itself a political party, it was not above acts that threatened editors of magazines that published works deemed disrespectful to the emperor.[9] Such extreme acts, as well the violent act committed by former member Yamaguchi Otoya, caused it to be categorized as "particularly radical and dangerous" by Japanese police.[10] Throughout the postwar decades, founder Akao Bin used the party to promote himself as a candidate for Japan's National Diet. A lack of public support for uyoku groups meant that he never came close to electoral success.[11] Dai Nippon Aikokutō lived on after Akao's death in 1990, and its loudspeaker vans can still be seen around Tokyo.

Another noteworthy survivor is Nihon Seinensha (Japan Youth Association), founded as an anti-communist patriotic group in 1961 by Kobayashi Kusuo, vice chairman of the Sumiyoshi-kai yakuza syndicate. Boasting over 2,000 members, it is one of the largest uyoku in Japan. It gained infamy in the 1970s for its attacks on ultra-leftist groups and also helped fund anti-communist militants who were fighting against the Soviet invasion of Afghanistan in the 1980s.[12] Of particular relevance to this book is Nihon Seinensha's construction of lighthouses on the disputed Senkaku Islands, which is discussed in Chapter 7.

Uyoku have become a noticeable part of life in major cities of Japan, such as Tokyo. They are known for driving menacing-looking trucks, buses, and vans emblazoned with nationalistic slogans, imperial chrysanthemums, and Japanese flags. Their vehicles are fitted with loudspeakers, which they use to shout slogans and denounce their enemies. These vehicles often parade around the embassies of opposing countries such as Russia or China. Their history of sudden and violent acts of protest means that they often have police officers following them, ready to intervene when any radical actions take place.

The right's reaction to left-wing student movements

The 1960s and 1970s witnessed very large left-wing movements at Japan universities. Thousands of Japanese students took part in demonstrations and strikes at campuses. Universities would often call in police to regain control of their campuses, resulting in violent clashes between students and police. In 1968, over 6,000 student protesters were arrested in Japan.[13]

This period saw a conservative answer in the formation of "anti-radical" student organizations that "devoted themselves to normalizing the chaotic campuses or to countering left-wing activities." The students in these organizations represented a political spectrum from the center to the extreme right. When writing about Japan's conservative student movements in 1972, Karl Dixon noted that the groups sought to distance themselves from prewar nationalist ideologies and the old uyoku:

> it is not entirely correct to refer to them collectively as "rightists," implying extremism, or even "nationalists" in the context of the prewar kokka shugi. They have called themselves the mizoku-ha, students of the racialist (Japanist) school or the nationalist faction. The minzoku-ha students themselves generally object to being identified with the prewar-type "rightists" and "nationalists" and maintain that the "genuine" rightist youths are usually not university students. Perhaps the most important differentiation in practical terms, however, is simply that they are strangers to the kind of fanaticism that characterized the prewar nationalist youths.[14]

The largest of these student organizations was Nihon Gakusei Dōmei (Japan Student Alliance – hereafter referred to by its shortened name, Nichigakudō), which had somewhere between 300 and 1,500 activists in September 1971. Nichigakudō subscribed to an ideology that it called "neo-nationalism" (*shin minzoku shugi*). It rejected the expansionistic nationalism of prewar Japan in favor of an "inward-looking" type of nationalism. Dixon argued that their approach matched well with public opinion in Japan and rated "their prospects for continued existence and growth following the post-university struggle slump as good if they can continue to eschew violence."[15] Many important future figures on the Japanese right were involved in this movement, including Issuikai founder Suzuki Kunio and Nippon Kaigi secretary general Kabashima Yūzō.[16]

An influential force in the formation of these student groups was Seichō no Ie (House of Growth), one of Japan's so-called "new religions." Since its founding in the 1930s, it gained hundreds of thousands of Japanese followers in Japan and overseas. Among its teachings is a nationalistic love of Japan's emperor and the Japanese flag, which is placed to the side of its altars.[17] Beginning in the 1950s, it became very active in supporting conservative political causes and right-wing politicians within the ruling Liberal Democratic Party (LDP).[18] Throughout the Cold War and into the 2000s, Seichō no Ie continued to play an important role as a base of support for nationalist politicians and organizations in Japan.[19] In the 1960s and 1970s, it operated dormitories for its members, who were strongly encouraged to join in the above-mentioned student organizations.[20]

Another organization that recruited conservative students was the Tate no Kai (Shield Society), a private militia organized by novelist Mishima Yukio in 1968. Although they gained considerable attention because of their celebrity leader and visually impressive military-style uniforms, they never numbered more than 100 members. Their ideology was a non-xenophobic nationalism that focused on restoring Japan's samurai spirit and the veneration of the emperor. On November 25, 1970, Mishima and four Tate no Kai members seized control of the Tokyo headquarters of Japan's Self-Defense Forces (JSDF), took a general hostage, and tried to convince the JSDF to carry out a coup d'état. When soldiers were forced to assemble before Mishima and listen to his speech, many openly mocked him. Mishima and Morita Masakatsu of Tate no Kai then committed ritual suicide, and the two other members were arrested. Mishima and his co-conspirators were aware that their coup had no chance of success, and the political meaning of their act has been widely debated.[21] Tate no Kai was completely disbanded two years later. However, many surviving right-wing and conservative organizations honor his memory, treating him as a national hero (see Chapter 4).[22]

The New Right

The New Right (*shin uyoku*) emerged out of the conservative student activism of the 1970s. Unlike the "old" uyoku, the New Right was extremely critical of Japan's alliance with the United States.[23]

The most well-known New Right organization is Issuikai (First Wednesday Association – named after the day it originally held meetings), founded in 1972 by Suzuki Kunio. Suzuki and its other founders were members of the postwar generation, who had been involved in conservative campus activism. Suzuki had known Morita Masakatsu, and Morita's death alongside Mishima inspired him to give up a newspaper job and return to the world of political activism.[24] Issuikai's fiercely critical stance of American foreign policy and globalism, publishing of ideological literature, and willingness to acknowledge common ground with some left-wing groups earned it a degree of respect from progressive media and intellectuals in Japan.[25] This openness to interaction with the left[26] made its leaders de facto spokesmen for nationalist issues in the Japanese and international media.[27]

Issuikai also stood out for its international outlook. In 2010, Issuikai hosted an international congress of nationalist political groups in Tokyo, drawing leaders from Britain, Hungary, Belgium, Italy, France, Bulgaria, and Ukraine. The keynote address at the gathering was delivered by Marine Le Pen, leader of France's National Front party. The goal of the congress, according to Issuikai, was to discuss "how we can protect the national identity in our respective countries and co-operate to win the battle against globalization."[28] Prior to the American invasion of Iraq, Issuikai was supportive of the regime of Saddam Hussein, whom they celebrated as a nationalist standing up against American imperialism. Its leadership made 20 visits to Iraq between the Gulf War and the 2003 American invasion.[29] Thus, it can be said that Issuikai carries out transnational forms of activism in support of what they see as protecting Japan's national identity.

New Right groups such as Issuikai tend to shun the sound truck parading tactics used by the traditional uyoku. Instead, loudspeakers are used for speechmaking in front of busy train stations.

Old uyoku and new uyoku – the "politics of futility"

Although there are considerable differences between the old uyoku and New Right, both utilize similar tactics that alienate the general public. There is an unwillingness to embrace moderate viewpoints and forms of activism that would be more attractive to the general public. Nathaniel M. Smith has argued that the extreme actions of the old uyoku and the New Right function as a form of empowerment, a way for them to feel a connection to an idealized Japan.

> Their alienating activism flies in the face of expectations of public life and comportment, thereby reasserting their status as outsiders. This quickly turns into a tricky recursive loop, since it is their very status as "outsiders" that lets them recognize the failings of contemporary society and that motivates them to act. Their attempt to chastise society embodies an intrusive, disruptive form. But the intrusive and disruptive are understood as a way to properly express alarm and offer redress as a committed patriot to a nation gone astray.[30]

Through noisy speeches, radical acts of violence, and other disruptive or threatening actions, they feel a connection to other heroes of Japan, such as Mishima Yukio, the Kamikaze pilots of World War II, Yamaguchi Otoya, or other postwar rightists who died carrying out acts of patriotism. They see themselves as "bearers of an ethno-religious identity grounded in the figure of the Japanese emperor," not as subjects of the postwar juridical state. When they commit violent and illegal acts, these rightists are performing "acts of fealty" to "an imagined sovereign and the imagined purity of an ethnic nation."[31]

The uyoku create meaning for themselves and members of their organizations through their aggressive and disruptive acts. Their activism forms an "action-based conduit from a lived reality to an imagined totality." Acts of violence may also be a means of proving one's commitment to a group. Young members sometimes earn financial sponsorship after being arrested for illegal displays of patriotism.[32] Some members of these groups are full-time activists, often living on a meager income from part-time work so they can devote as much time as possible to their organizations' activities.

Although Smith described their view as "ethnic" nationalism, this should not be confused with the racism of more recent nativist groups. It is not an ethnic nationalism based on xenophobic hatred of non-Japanese races or ethnic groups. Their imagined Japan is one similar to the ideal of the pre-1945 multi-nation empire, in which imperial subjects could be of different ethnic and racial backgrounds, all of them honoring the nation and the emperor.

This relative lack of racism may also be influenced by the fact that uyoku groups include members who are ethnic Koreans or Burakumin. Since the early postwar period, the uyoku have existed on the margins of society, co-existing with other "outsiders" in Japan, whether they be Koreans, Burakumin, and/or gangsters.[33]

History as a major issue after the 1990s

The 1990s witnessed the emergence of a new type of conservative activism in Japan. This activism arose out of disputes over historical remembrance. The 50th anniversary of World War II, together with a combination of various geopolitical and cultural factors, had set the stage for a re-examination of the past. Emperor Hirohito, who reigned throughout the war and continued to reign into the postwar period, died in 1989, triggering a wave of recollection about war responsibility. Political changes occurred outside of Japan as well, with South Korea becoming more democratic, the Berlin Wall coming down, and the Soviet Union collapsing soon afterward.

The end of the Cold War marked a huge shift in the geopolitical and military landscape of Asia and the world. The Cold War made cooperation against Soviet communism a top priority, delaying regional discussion of Japan's wartime conduct. Now that it was over, it became fair game to pursue issues that had been shelved for decades. Topics such as the Nanjing Massacre and the so-called "comfort women" were raised as major issues by Japan's Asian neighbors. For Japan's political right, its principal enemy, the Soviet Union, would be replaced with the Asian nations that raised these "anti-Japanese" issues, namely Korea and China.[34]

Japan's role in the world and the appropriateness of its pacifist constitution came into question as its participation was sought in the Gulf War and in UN peacekeeping missions. Whereas the Cold War period had brought with it a stable order in which Japan had a relatively clear role and could experience prosperous economic growth, the post–Cold War period brought political and economic uncertainty. This led to confusion and anxiety among many Japanese people.[35]

It was the beginning of a new era, one in which Japanese society would continue to undergo a "structural lull" in both an economic and a societal sense. As Minoru Iwasaki and Steffi Richter described it:

> So-called readjustment and structural reform policies began to threaten the corporate, school, and family systems that were important pillars of Japan's postwar community as well as the material basis of middle-class consciousness

> in its support of welfare-society and livelihood guarantees. Together with the neoliberal reorganization of society, efforts were made to operate these systems on the basis of completely different principles. The problems accompanying an aging society, along with the changes that emerged through the direct linking of the domestic labor market with the international labor market, confronted people daily with a truly material reality. Added to this were the legal and illegal flows of international labor, as well as the loss of Japanese industries caused by their relocation to countries able to produce cheaper products. One by one, these problems heightened the confused sense of anxiety among people.[36]

When people are faced with such a crisis, "existing assumptions and interpretive models become the object of skepticism."[37] Among these was the interpretation of history. Japanese society was poised for new disputes over how to make sense of the past.

This time of uncertainty brought major changes to Japan's political leadership. For most of the postwar period, the political power in Japan had been in the hands of the conservative LDP. Official stances on history took a generally conservative viewpoint, with relatively few reflections on Japan's history of imperialism. However, Japanese society's views on history were not uniformly in favor of a single dominant historical narrative. From the 1970s onward, accounts of war atrocities were published. The liberal perspective of influential organizations such as the Japan Teacher's Union also helped turn the tide of Japanese public opinion in favor of a view that Imperial Japan had waged wars of aggression and should express remorse for its past conduct. The political situation in the early 1990s reflected this trend.[38]

During the same period the "comfort women" issue gained international attention. In response to domestic and international pressure, the Japanese government issued an official apology acknowledging that the Japanese military authorities had been directly involved in coercing Asian women against their will into working as prostitutes for the Imperial Japanese military (see Chapter 6 for more discussion of this topic).[39]

Public opinion polls at the time showed that a sizable majority of the Japanese people were in favor of the apology statements.[40] Gavan McCormack has argued that these polls, together with other data, suggested a "national consensus in favor of apology, admission of the aggressive and colonial character of the war, and compensation to the victims."[41] The 1990s was the "golden age of reconciliation" for Japan.[42] Although the conservative LDP would fully regain power a few years later, subsequent prime ministers continued to endorse apology statements issued in the 1990s, including the 1995 apology by socialist prime minister Murayama Tomiichi (1994–1996).

The assertive conservative right

While there was widespread public support for the official apologies issued by the Japanese government in the 1990s, there were also a considerable number of people in Japan who were very unhappy with these developments. For decades, conservative groups within Japan had been working to resist what they saw as left-wing and foreign attempts to spread a distorted view of history. Following protests about textbook content from Korea and China in the 1980s and the Japanese apologies of the 1990s, descriptions of wartime atrocities were on the rise in public school history textbooks. Dissatisfaction with the new atmosphere of apology led to the growth of a new nationwide conservative movement.

Togo Kazuhiko has called this movement the assertive conservative right, defining it as having three major characteristics:

> First, the breadth and depth of the assertive conservative right's justification for prewar activities creates an impression that they believe virtually everything Japan did before the war was just. If this statement goes too far for some, they will at least concede that though Japan's actions were not perfect, Japan committed the same mistakes as other major imperial powers, so there is nothing especially egregious in Japan's wartime conduct. Others argue that Japan's past apologies are sufficient for whatever wrong it has done, and that there is no need to apologize [further].
>
> Second, the assertive conservative right spares no words in lambasting those Japanese whom they consider to be dishonoring prewar Japan. The assertive conservative right severely criticizes those who view the majority verdict of the Tokyo Trials as a "judgment of civilization," support the Kono Statement of 1993 on "comfort women," support the 1995 Murayama apology, or other events that the assertive conservative right refers to as the Asahi Shimbun culture of remaining remorseful for prewar wrongdoings.
>
> Third, they spare no words against foreign countries they perceive as criminalizing prewar Japan. The assertive conservative right's anger is usually directed at China and Korea, or at Chinese or Koreans who continue to assert that prewar Japan was a criminal country, and claim that Japan has yet to sufficiently apologize.[43]

In advancing the concept of an assertive conservative right, Togo selected "assertive" instead of "extreme" because the latter term could cause readers to confuse the assertive conservative right with "those fanatic rightwing activists who go around with loudspeakers and who might be inspired to commit violence as a manifestation of their political beliefs." The assertive conservative right was completely different from the old and new uyoku groups discussed earlier in this chapter. Although both might hold similar beliefs about prewar history and foreign policy, the assertive conservative right differs from uyoku in "the way they manifest their views": they are non-violent in nature, do not rely on sound truck parades, and generally do not commit illegal acts.[44]

The following sections will describe major organizations that constitute the assertive conservative right and what scholars have written about the motivations behind their supporters. As we will see in the next chapter, several of these organizations played an important role in the founding of the organization that the later chapters of this book focus on – Nihon Bunka Channel Sakura.

Conservative politicians

When the conservative LDP was out of power in 1993, a group of its Diet members founded the History Review Committee (Rekishi Kentō Iinkai). Steered by some of the party's most right-leaning members, it organized sessions at which conservative historians spoke and questioned the official view that was found in textbooks and government apology statements. It disbanded in 1995 after reaching and publishing its conclusions about history. Among these were that Imperial Japan had not engaged in "aggressive" wars and that famous war atrocities such as the Nanjing Massacre were fabrications.[45] The committee included future prime ministers Hashimoto Ryūtarō, Mori Yoshirō, and Abe Shinzō.

The LDP returned to power in 1994 as part of a coalition government with the Japan Socialist Party and New Party Sakigake, and the three parties agreed to adopt a resolution marking the 50th anniversary of the end of World War II. Socialists wanted the resolution to include a clear apology, but there was considerable dissent within the LDP. A group of LDP lawmakers founded the Diet Member's Council of the 50th Anniversary of the War (Shūsen Gojūshūnen Giin Renmei) in December 1994 and fought to stop the plan. Abe Shinzō served as a deputy secretary general for the council. Eventually, it was able to recruit about half of the serving LDP lawmakers into its ranks. Although it did not have the votes to fully block the resolution, it did succeed in having its language toned down. The success of conservative groups in toning down this resolution did not, however, stop Prime Minister Murayama from issuing his own strongly worded apology.[46]

When the LDP regained its position as a majority party, its prime ministers nonetheless ended up endorsing the Murayama apology. It marked a "consolidation of the conservative center with the left" that was a shock to some of the more conservative politicians in the party.[47] Frustration over this new status quo provoked further nationalistic backlashes.

The right fought back against the trend of apologies through groups such as the Young Diet Member's Committee to Consider the Future of Japan and History Education (Nihon no Zento to Rekishi Kyōiku wo Kangaeru Wakate Giin no Kai), founded in 1997. Like the other groups mentioned, it fought in favor of a revisionist view of history that downplayed Japan's war atrocities and war responsibility. This committee was well known for including Abe Shinzō and Nakagawa Shōichi as members, but they were also joined by Hagiuda Kōichi, Nishikawa Kyoko, Nakayama Nariaki, and Etō Seiichi. It held study sessions and worked to support grassroots campaigns to reform history education in Japan. These campaigns were led by Tsukurukai, a private activist organization (see below).[48]

Politicians also formed groups in support of the controversial Yasukuni Shrine, the largest of which is the Association of Diet Members Who Visit Yasukuni

Shrine (Minna de Yasukuni Jinja ni Sanpai Suru Kokka Giin no Kai), which in 2014 had members from six different parties. Notable members included Abe Shinzō (LDP), Inada Tomomi (LDP), Aisawa Ichiro (LDP), Inoue Shinji (LDP), and Hiranuma Takeo (Japan Restoration Party).

Under Prime Minister Koizumi Junichirō (2001–2006), history disputes gained a new level of importance in Japan's international relations. Koizumi's visits to the Yasukuni Shrine caused anger in China and Korea, despite his public statements repeating Murayama-esque historical views.[49] There were also controversies regarding a new history textbook approved by the Japanese Ministry of Education during Koizumi's term (see the Tsukurukai section below). Koizumi may not have held views that fully matched those of the assertive conservative right, but the events during his tenure helped the assertive conservative right gain attention. It has been argued that Koizumi's use of nationalist issues was part of a populist political strategy to gain public support for his economic reforms, rather than nationalism as a goal in itself.[50] In Koizumi's last cabinet, Abe Shinzō was appointed chief cabinet secretary and became prime minister when Koizumi retired in 2006.

Given his prior support for historical revisionism, the assertive conservative right had high hopes in Abe's leadership, but his first term as prime minister (2006–2007) ended as a disappointment.[51] As prime minister, he moderated his views on history, taking a cautious stance that included acknowledging previous official apologies. After only one year, Abe resigned, citing poor health. It seemed like the end of the assertive conservative right's aspirations for national political leadership.

However, during the LDP's years as an opposition party from 2009 to 2012, Abe made a comeback. Part of that comeback involved securing the right-wing of his party through active engagement with the assertive conservative right.[52] Aided by his improved health and the heightened tensions with China, Abe regained the leadership of his party. In the 2012 election, he led the LDP to a landslide victory. The election campaign had much to do with public dissatisfaction with the ruling Democratic Party of Japan (DPJ)'s perceived inability to live up to expectations, and the historical views of the assertive conservative right were not a major campaign issue for Abe. Riding a new wave of support for the LDP, Abe became prime minister again.

After returning to the office, Abe was relatively popular and served until 2020, becoming the longest-serving prime minister in postwar Japanese history.[53] In his later terms, Abe proved to be more supportive of the assertive conservative right's agenda. Unlike Koizumi, it could be argued that Abe saw nationalist objectives as a goal in themselves, rather than as a means of mobilizing support for other policies. Among his actions were a visit to Yasukuni in 2013, the appointment of conservatives to the board of Japan's public broadcasting channel (NHK), taking a firm stance on the Senkaku Islands dispute, and successfully pushing through a re-interpretation of the pacifist clauses of the Japanese Constitution. These actions did not have a major negative impact on public support for the Abe administration.[54] However, it was just a fraction of the policy changes that were sought by the assertive conservative right. Abe continued to support the official apologies of the 1990s and did not enact major changes to history education. When Abe gave a speech on the 70th anniversary of the war's end in August 2015, he repeated key phrases acknowledging that Japan waged aggressive wars. Although it was not as directly apologetic as Murayama's 1995 statement, it was still a far cry from what outspoken nationalists would have said about the war.[55]

Tsukurukai

A central issue for the assertive conservative right was how their nation's pre-1945 history should be depicted in public school history textbooks. A central force in this debate was the Japanese Society for History Textbook Reform (Rekishi Kyōkasho wo Tsukurukai, commonly referred to as Tsukurukai), founded in 1996. Its leaders were a collection of conservative scholars who believed that the existing textbooks used in Japanese history classes taught a distorted and masochistic version of history. They aimed to create their own history textbook, which could be used to teach junior high schoolers across Japan a version of history that would make them proud to be Japanese.

It had its origins in earlier efforts to sway historical remembrance. In the early 1990s, academics who favored a revisionist view of history had regularly appeared before study sessions organized by conservative lawmaker groups such as the History Review Committee. These meetings served as a venue in which like-minded scholars and politicians formed a network with the goal of influencing history education in Japan. The participants in these sessions went on to found and support Tsukurukai.[56]

Tsukurukai's founders included Fujioka Nobukatsu of Tokyo University, Nishio Kanji of the University of Electro-Communications, Takahashi Shirō of Meisei University, and popular comic book author Kobayashi Yoshinori. Fujioka was a professor of education who founded the conservative Association for the Advancement of the Liberalist View of History (Jiyūshugi Shikan Kenkyūkai) in 1995 and authored several bestselling books criticizing Japanese public school history education. Kobayashi was the author of many extremely popular comic strips and books that tackled historical issues from a conservative perspective.[57]

The Ministry of Education certified Tsukurukai's first textbook in 2001. Although it had undergone numerous government-ordered revisions that softened its ideological stance, it nonetheless ignited protests within Japan, China, and Korea. The campaign against Tsukurukai's book proved to be a success, and only a tiny percentage of Japanese schools adopted the textbook.[58] The controversy did, however, increase public interest in the textbook's contents and a version of it sold relatively well at bookstores.

The motivations of people who participated in Tsukurukai's campaigns were investigated by sociologists Oguma Eiji and Uno Yoko in their book "A Nationalism of Healing."[59] Through detailed interviews with attendees of Tsukurukai meetings, they found it to be a genuine grassroots movement containing many people with no past experience of political activism. Some, such as a 23-year-old woman, were introduced to the issue of textbooks through the comics of Kobayashi Yoshinori. Others, such as a 76-year-old man, were already members of conservative organizations such as Nippon Kaigi. Most of the members were interested in Tsukurukai's political issues, but another major motivation for continued participation in the movement was the sense of community and solidarity that it generated. For people living in an era of globalism in which traditional societal bonds had weakened, participation in a grassroots movement such as Tsukurukai allowed them to experience a comforting sense of community while feeling like patriotic citizens.

In the early 2000s, ideological disagreements within Tsukurukai caused two of its founders – Nishio Kanji and Kobayashi Yoshinori – to leave the organization. Nishio and Kobayashi were dissatisfied with what they saw as the organization's pro-American view of history. The splintering of the organization led to a decline in its membership.[60]

Kobayashi Yoshinori

Comic book author Kobayashi Yoshinori has been widely credited as a major influence on the growth of the assertive conservative right. Comics form a major portion of book sales for adults in Japan, and he was one of Japan's most well-known authors of political comics.

Kobayashi's first book-length comic book on the Pacific War, *Sensōron*, sold over 420,000 copies in its first few months of sales in 1998.[61] He went on to release more comics, covering a wide range of conservative viewpoints on history and Japan's relations with its neighbors. The popularity of Kobayashi's works inspired numerous copycats who have sought to capitalize on the market that Kobayashi seems to have created.

Kobayashi's works introduce readers to the idea that Japan's education system unfairly teaches a masochistic view of history that only informs young people that their nation has done horrible things. This has caused modern Japanese people to be unable to take pride in their country, and the entire country has lost its way as a result.

According to Barak Kushner, Kobayashi's work appealed to a meaning-hungry segment of the Japanese population who felt that Japan had lost its sense of mission in the world:

> Kobayashi's strain of nationalist identity, which he claims was shaped during Japan's imperial era, imparts the sense of belonging that contemporary Japanese fear has been lost: his works tie that absence to the longing for a time when Japan's power reached its zenith and had a clear purpose in empire building ...The consumption of manga dealing with history and identity results from the perception within Japan that the nation, having lost an empire, has yet to define an alternative role. Japanese read Kobayashi because he offers them a nostalgic, affirmative identity that they, as a community, can adopt.[62]

In other words, his comics helped create meaning for readers who were seeking out a shared sense of identity in an uncertain nation.

As a founding member of Tsukurukai, Kobayashi helped attract younger followers to its campaigns. However, following the previously mentioned ideological disagreements within the organization, Kobayashi left Tsukurukai in 2002.[63] He has continued to write nationalist comic books but does so outside of a formal activist organization.

Nippon Kaigi

Nippon Kaigi (Japan Conference) is one of Japan's largest and most influential conservative advocacy organizations. Its membership includes the political, business, and religious elite, giving it considerable financial resources and connections to the highest levels of Japanese government.[64] It also has thousands of grassroots members who are "not traditional right-wing types" – students, workers, housewives, and members of religious groups.[65]

Nippon Kaigi was formed in 1997, around the same time that Tsukurukai came into existence, but it was a merger of two older conservative organizations. The first of these, the National Conference to Defend Japan (Nihon wo Mamoru Kokumin Kaigi), was founded in 1981 as an organization of conservative politicians, intellectuals, business leaders, and former military officers. The second, the Society to Protect Japan (Nihon wo Mamoru Kai), was an association of conservative religious groups founded in 1974 that included the Association of Shintō Shrines (Jinja Honchō), Buddhist group Reiyūkai, as well as the "new religions" Sūkyō Mahikari and Seichō no Ie.

Nippon Kaigi's core leadership consisted of former members of 1970s student activist groups. The most well-known figure among them is Kabashima Yūzō, who led a Seichō no Ie–affiliated student group at Nagasaki University in the 1970s and continued work as a professional conservative activist into the 1990s and 2000s.[66] Although leadership changes within Seichō no Ie caused it to halt its support of political causes, Kabashima's continued leadership has led some to characterize Nippon Kaigi in terms of a Seichō no Ie conspiracy. These kind of claims could be found in Sugano Tamotsu's 2016 bestseller "A Study on the Japan Conference" (*Nippon Kaigi no Kenkyū*), which highlighted the network of former Seichō No Ie members within Nippon Kaigi as proof that the religious group, through its senior member Ando Iwao, was a kind of puppet master pulling the strings behind right-wing Japanese politics.[67] This theory, which was not strongly supported by evidence, downplays the important role that other groups, such as Shintō organizations, have played in the movement.[68]

Nippon Kaigi has aimed to generate "grassroots movements" (kokumin undō) toward the achievement of a variety of goals, ranging from constitutional revision, the implementation of more nationalistic history textbooks and moral education, the protection of traditional gender roles, the promotion of greater respect for the imperial family, and taking stronger stances on territorial disputes.[69] Among the grassroots movements launched by Nippon Kaigi was a protest group that successfully advocated for the removal of references to Japanese wartime atrocities from the Peace Osaka museum in 1997.[70] Nippon Kaigi activists have also been credited with the campaign that led to a 1999 law officially recognizing the Hinomaru flag and national anthem as state symbols.

Nippon Kaigi's predecessor organization, the Society to Protect Japan, led a project to create a nationalistic history textbook in the early 1980s. Due to South Korean and Chinese protests, the book was heavily censored by the Education Ministry in 1987. The approved version of their textbook did not sell well.[71] Nippon Kaigi later abandoned its own independent efforts and became a backer of Tsukurukai's textbook campaigns.

Another important feature of Nippon Kaigi is its associations of national and regional legislators, which include many important figures within the Liberal Democratic Party, as well as members of opposition parties. Nearly every outspokenly nationalistic politician since 1997 has been a member of Nippon Kaigi, but there are also many others who listed themselves as members without strongly advocating for its goals. While this may point to the existence of growing support for Nippon Kaigi, it has also been argued that many LDP politicians joined during the prime ministership of Abe Shinzō (2012–2020) to signal support for the prime minister and the overall party platform or to network with other politicians.[72] If this is the case, it could experience a decline in lawmaker membership after 2020.

Internet Right-Wingers

As organizations such as Tsukurukai and Nippon Kaigi were emerging, internet forums were becoming an increasingly popular form of communication. Japan's largest internet forum, the textboard 2channel (2ch.net), gave rise to a subculture of virulently xenophobic nationalists known as the Net Right-Wingers (netto uyoku). In the popular imagination, they are isolated, frustrated young men who use the anonymity of the internet to post hateful and xenophobic messages online.

However, this anonymity has made it particularly difficult to gather reliable information about who the Net Right-Wingers are, how large their subculture actually is, and what motivates them. The website on which they emerged and continue to be a major presence, 2channel, is a place where all users can post anonymously (without pseudonyms). When studying posts on 2channel, it is impossible to know how many different individuals are actually participating in a discussion. What could appear to be a conversation between two or three individuals could in fact be just one person fooling around (something called "sock puppetry" in English internet slang). Moreover, anonymous internet forums are a fertile ground for trolling, a practice through which users entertain themselves by posting socially disruptive and offensive messages.[73] Researchers who read unmoderated anonymous websites and treat offensive postings as serious expressions of ideology run the risk of making skewed observations.

Nonetheless, considerable progress has been made toward understanding the Net Right-Wingers. One of the leading researchers on this topic, Tsuji Daisuke, used 2008 survey data to argue that slightly over 1% of internet users in Japan could be classified Net Right-Wingers (based on: disliking China/Korea, holding conservative/nationalistic political views, and actively sharing those views online).[74] Nagayoshi Kikuko has argued that Tsuji's emphasis on conservative views of political issues was too restrictive, and if one focuses on xenophobia rather than politics, the figure would be closer to 3%.[75] Furthermore, Yamaguchi Tomomi has argued that current definitions of Net Right-Wingers may need to be expanded to include those that hold discriminatory attitudes toward other minority groups, such as the LGBT community.[76] The degree to which Net Right-Wingers are passive or active participants in the subculture is also a matter of debate, with one 2013 estimate claiming that there could be 50,000–100,000 users who actively post online and over a million passive Net Right-Wingers.[77]

While they may be numerous, the degree to which the Net Right-Wingers can function as a cohesive group has been questioned. Sakamoto Rumi has argued, based on analysis of thousands of 2channel posts about political issues, that Net Right-Winger nationalism is "aggressive and shrill, but fragmentary." There was little doubt about the hostility of 2channel users toward Koreans, but Sakamoto noted that posters tended to avoid association with established right-wing and nationalist organizations.[78] On the other hand, Kaigo Muneo analyzed popular 2channel aggregation blogs and found that such sites reflect Net Right-Winger tones of arguments but language that is supportive of conservative LDP politicians.[79] Other research has suggested that Net Right-Wingers have aligned themselves with the agenda of the LDP and Nippon Kaigi, "potentially forming an enormous online support army" for the nationalist agenda of Prime Minister Abe.[80]

Tsuji, Nagayoshi, and other researchers have argued that there is a correlation between online consumption of news and the holding of Net Right-Winger political beliefs.[81] Whether or not one subscribes to the view that the Net Right-Wingers can be organized as a support base for conservative politicians and political causes, they are clearly a support base for internet media. In conducting research on the later chapters of this book, it was hard to find 2channel threads about right-wing topics that did not include numerous links to online media platforms. It would be hard to imagine the success of right-wing YouTube channels without the existence of a large subculture of right-leaning internet users who distrusted traditional media outlets.

The nativist movement of the 2000s

The mid-2000s witnessed the emergence of a new category of conservative groups – extreme nativist organizations that drew upon the online gathering places of the Net Right-Wingers to organize hate demonstrations. The most common Japanese academic term for these groups is the Action Conservative Movement (kōdō suru hoshu undo), sometimes shortened to "ACM" in English scholarship.[82] Higuchi Naoto, on the other hand, has referred to them as Japan's "nativist" (haigaishugi) movement.[83] As these groups are aggressively focused on hatred of Korean and Chinese immigrants rather than other conservative political issues, I prefer Higuchi's term.

The largest, most well-known, and most researched of these groups is the Citizens against the Special Privileges of the Zainichi (Zainichi Tokken wo Yurusanai Shimin no Kai: commonly referred to as Zaitokukai). Founded in 2007 by Sakurai Makoto, it aimed to highlight the alleged threat posed by the "special privileges" enjoyed by Japan's special permanent resident visa holders.[84]

While the arguments laid out on the organization's website suggested a peaceful and calm approach to activism, Zaitokukai's offline events took on an entirely different character. Demonstrations organized by Zaitokukai stood out for the extreme nature of the signs and words expressed by participants. For example, here is a description of a Zaitokukai-sponsored protest, quoted from a 2014 report on racism compiled by the Korean Residents Union in Japan (Mindan):

> They parade around the Korean residential area with over 100 participants as they yell remarks like the following: "Leave Japan!" "Stop running Pachinko parlors!" "Shoot Koreans!" "Turn Seoul into a sea of fire!" "Pursue the lawless Koreans to death!" "Send the Koreans to the gas chamber!" "Koreans aren't even human!" "Cockroaches!" "Calling them cockroaches is an insult to cockroaches!" "They stink!" "Die!" "Get out!" "Knock them out!" "Perverts!" "Criminals!" "Construct gas chambers for them!" "Burn them alive!" "Don't breathe the same air as us!" "Crawl on your bellies!" Among the protest crowd, there have been some confirmed to be carrying placards inscribed with, "Fuck Korea" "Kill the anti-Japanese" "Good or Bad Koreans, it doesn't matter, kill them all!" In addition, they would also jeer at passerbys, whether they be Korean or Japanese, "Do you like Korea? We don't need Japanese like that. Leave!"[85]

The use of racist and threatening language led to a debate on freedom of expression in Japan. This resulted in the creation of the country's first laws aimed at restricting so-called "hate speech."[86] Nativist demonstrations were also frequently challenged by anti-racist activists whose counter-demonstrations often outnumbered the nativists.[87] New local ordinances restricting hate speech and social media crackdowns on hateful content created further problems for the offline and online activities of nativist organizations.[88] These factors, combined with the election of a conservative government, led to a decline in the size and frequency of nativist demonstrations.[89]

Journalist Yasuda Kōichi's 2012 book "The Internet and Nationalism" (*Netto to Aikoku*) is the best-known Japanese book about this phenomenon, and won the 2012 Kodansha Non-Fiction Prize and Japan Congress of Journalists Prize. In his book, Yasuda portrays Zaitokukai as a product of feelings of economic uncertainty among the working classes of Japanese society. In other words, they feel socially and economically isolated, and can experience positive emotions by channeling their ill feelings into hatred of Koreans.

Sociologist Higuchi Naoto conducted interviews with Zaitokukai participants and came to very different conclusions. Instead of finding social or economic anxiety as influences on joining the movement, Higuchi found that many of his interviewees had been raised in politically conservative households or had been involved in conservative political activities for the year.[90] The idea that they are just "ordinary" people who, due to anxiety, join nativist groups was misleading. Most of Higuchi's interviewees were already ideologically on the right:

> There are, in this sense, specific problems with Yasuda's opinion that Zaitokukai is made up of "your neighbors." There are certainly many activists in the nativist movement who are "ordinary people" with jobs, but ideologically they are not "neutral or apolitical"; they are conservative.[91]

People who are already subscribed to a conservative worldview are more receptive to how nativist groups frame and introduce information. Higuchi sees these nativists as an outgrowth of the existing nationalist and revisionist movement of the 1990s and a conservative establishment that already encouraged hostility toward Korea and China.[92] He also argued that the geopolitical situation in Asia has aided in their rise.[93] Issues such as war responsibility, the abduction of Japanese citizens by North Korea, and ongoing territorial disputes fueled hatred toward people from Korea and China. Higuchi found that the attitudes of Zaitokukai members toward immigrants from countries such as the Philippines and Brazil, who tend to have a lower socioeconomic status than Korean and Chinese immigrants, were not particularly negative. This is very different from the observations of scholars of the far-right in Europe and the United States, for whom the perceived economic or cultural threats from immigrant laborers, or demographic replacement, are central ideas.

Other research has highlighted the importance of emotion in the process of becoming an active member of nativist organizations. Yuki Asahina found through interviews with activists that experiences of shock, anger, disgust, or fear – often in the form of exposure to negative information about immigrants – helped trigger an emotional process that led to participation in the nativist movement. Engagement with the movement, both online and offline, turned short-term emotional responses into a long-term obligation to a movement they believed was fighting against immoral "others." The "others" they focus on are specific groups – Chinese and Koreans – that they believe are geopolitical enemies of Japan. As one interviewee stated, "when it comes to the anti-Japan states, I think my idea is close to that of the far-right. But I do not have the same idea for all foreigners. I don't think like 'fuck Americans' so I think I am not exactly the far-right."[94]

Higuchi contrasts the nativist right with the ultra-right groups in Europe in America, which have drawn upon specific subcultures as a cultural base for their movements, such as soccer hooligans, skinheads, or the religious right. The internet community on 2channel is Japan's "functional equivalent" of these subcultures.[95] Yasuda's book also identifies 2channel as a major source of support for Zaitokukai. Similarly, Asahina has found that interviewees were often first introduced to nativist issues through posts on 2channel or by online video clips.[96]

The extreme and hateful language of the nativist right in many ways mirrored the kind of Net Right-Winger posts one could regularly encounter on 2channel, Yahoo Answers, YouTube, Twitter, and other social media platforms. This could represent a change in the "cosmetic and ideology" of Japan's right,[97] but the decline of the Nativist movement in recent years suggests that the transfer of online hate speech into the world of offline demonstrations has fizzled out.

As the nativist right dwindled in size, other new political organizations that had emerged in the mid-2000s did not. In the following chapters of this book, I will explore activism of one such organization – Nihon Bunka Channel Sakura – which, like Zaitokukai, utilized the internet to organize and promote offline events. However, unlike Zaitokukai, it was an organization that could build coalitions with other activist organizations, organize demonstrations involving thousands of people, and actually achieve tangible results.

Notes

1 Masayuki Hayashi, "The Emperor's Legions: A History of Japan's Right Wing," *AMPO Japan-Asia Quarterly Review* 23, no. 2 (1988).
2 Alex Gibney, "How Burly Men with Missing Digits Influence Japanese Politics: Yakuza: Once Brotherhoods of Cast-offs Guided by Grisly Rituals, Japan's Gangs Are Now Businessmen Looking for Market Share," *Los Angeles Times*, December 27, 1992, http://articles.latimes.com/1992-12-27/opinion/op-4908_1_japanese-politics.
3 Eiko Maruko Siniawer, *Ruffians, Yakuza, Nationalists* (Ithaca: Cornell University Press, 2015), 167–170; and Nick Kapur, *Japan at the Crossroads* (Cambridge, MA: Harvard University Press, 2018), 248–254.
4 Siniwer, *Ruffians, Yakuza, Nationalists*, 170–173.
5 Ibid., 173.
6 Peter J. Katzenstein and Yutaka Tsujinaka, *Defending the Japanese State: Structures, Norms and the Political Responses to Terrorism and Violent Social Protest in the 1970s and 1980s* (Ithaca: Cornell University Press, 1991), 30–33.
7 Kenneth Szymkowiak and Patricia G. Steinhoff, "Wrapping up in Something Long: Intimidation and Violence by Right-Wing Groups in Postwar Japan," *Terrorism and Political Violence* 7, no. 1 (1995), doi:10.1080/09546559508427292
8 Nathaniel Smith, "Facing the Nation: Sound, Fury, and Public Oratory among Japanese Right-Wing Groups," in *Sound, Space and Sociality in Modern Japan*, ed. Joseph D. Hankins and Carolyn S. Stevens, 37–56 (New York: Routledge, 2013).
9 Kapur, *Japan at the* Crossroads, 256–258.
10 J. A. A. Stockwin, *Collected Writings of J.A.A. Stockwin* (London: Japan Library, 2004), 175.
11 J. Wayne Sabey, "Akao Bin (1898-1990)," entry in *Modern Japan: An Encyclopedia of History, Culture, and Nationalism*, ed. James L. Huffman (London: Routledge 1997), 7.
12 Hayashi, "The Emperor's Legions: A History of Japan's Right Wing," 26–31.
13 Patricia G. Steinhoff, "Student Protest in the 1960s," *Social Science Japan* 15 (1999), 3. http://newslet.iss.u-tokyo.ac.jp/ssj15/ssj15.pdf.

14 Karl Dixon, "Recent Shift in Japanese Right-Wing Student Movements: The 'Minzoku-Ha' Students," *Asian Survey* 12, no. 11 (1972).
15 Ibid.
16 Shigeki Yamadaira, ドキュメント 新右翼——何と闘ってきたのか [Document: The New Right – What Are They Fighting Against?], (Tokyo: Shodensha, 2017), 90–91.
17 Birgit Staemmler, "Seichō No Ie," in *Handbook of East Asian New Religious Movements*, ed. Lukas Pokorny, Franz Winter and Brigit Staemmler (Leiden: Brill, 2018), 97–99.
18 Robert Kisala, *Prophets of Peace* (University of Hawaii Press, 1999), 81.
19 Gavan Mccormack, "Nationalism and Identity in Post-Cold War Japan," *Pacifica Review: Peace, security & global change* 12, no. 3 (2000), doi:10.1080/713604486
20 Yamadaira, ドキュメント 新右翼——何と闘ってきたのか [Document: The New Right – What Are They Fighting Against?], 33.
21 William Andrews, *Dissenting Japan* (London: Hurst, 2016), 60.
22 Daiki Shibuichi, "The 'Uyoku Rōnin Dō': Assessing the Lifestyles and Values of Japan's Contemporary Right Wing Radical Activists," *Electronic Journal of Contemporary Japanese Studies*, November 28, 2007.
23 Gwan-ja Jo, "The Revival of Japanese Right-Wing Thought and the Coincidental Collaboration of the Left and Right," *Journal of Japanese Studies* 1, no.1 (2015), doi:10371/94439
24 Andrews, *Dissenting Japan*, 279.
25 "POINT OF VIEW/ Mitsuhiro Kimura: Mindless Patriotism Ravages Today's Japan," *Asahi Shimbun*, August 9, 2013, http://ajw.asahi.com/article/views/opinion/AJ201308090016.
26 "「今会いたい、今話しをしたい」一水会の鈴木邦男さんと語る" ["I Want to Meet Them, Speak to Them" Speaking with Issuikai's Suzuki Kunio], *Fukushima Mizuho*, September 19, 2013, https://www.youtube.com/watch?v=5keIhR_5Ycc.
27 "Old Habits Die Hard," *Economist*, May 19, 2007, http://www.economist.com/node/9205495
28 Katie Englehart, "The Rise of the Far Right in Europe – Macleans.ca," *Macleansca*, November 30, 2013, http://www.macleans.ca/news/world/rise-of-the-far-right-in-europe
29 Shibuichi, "The 'Uyoku Rōnin Dō': Assessing the Lifestyles and Values of Japan's Contemporary Right Wing Radical Activists."
30 Nathaniel Michael Smith, "Right Wing Activism in Japan and the Politics of Futility," PhD diss., Yale University (2011), 20.
31 Ibid., 22–23.
32 Ibid.
33 Ibid., 238
34 Naoto Higuchi, *Japan's Ultra-Right*, trans. Teresa Castelvetere (Tokyo: Trans Pacific Press, 2016), 25.
35 Yoshiko Nozaki, *War Memory, Nationalism, and Education in Postwar Japan, 1945–2007: The Japanese History Textbook Controversy and Ienaga Saburo's Court Challenges* (London: Routledge, 2009), 137.
36 M. Iwasaki and S. Richter, "The Topology of Post-1990s Historical Revisionism," *Positions: East Asia Cultures Critique* 16, no. 3 (2008), 525–526.
37 Ibid.
38 Philip A. Seaton, *Japan's Contested War Memories: The 'memory Rifts' in Historical Consciousness of World War II* (London: Routledge, 2007), 44–50.
39 "Statement by the Chief Cabinet Secretary Yohei Kono on the Result of the Study on the Issue of 'Comfort Women,'" *Ministry of Foreign Affairs in Japan*, August 4, 1993. http://www.mofa.go.jp/policy/women/fund/state9308.html.

40 Jane W. Yamazaki, *Japanese Apologies for World War II: A Rhetorical Study* (London: Routledge, 2006), 84.
41 Gavan McCormack, "The Japanese Movement to 'Correct' History," *Bulletin of Concerned Asian Scholars* 30, no. 2 (1998), 16.
42 Sven Saaler, "Is Japan Drifting Toward Isolation?" *Nippon.com*, January 23, 2014, https://www.nippon.com/en/column/g00145/.
43 Kazuhiko Togo, "The Assertive Conservative Right in Japan: Their Formation and Perspective," *SAIS Review* 30, no. 1 (2010).
44 Ibid., 81.
45 Xiaohua Ma, "Constructing a National Memory of the War: War Museums in China, Japan, and the United States," in *The Unpredictability of the Past: Memories of the Asia-Pacific War in U.S./East Asian Relations*, ed. Marc S. Gallicchio (Durham: Duke University Press, 2007), 171–172.
46 Hiro Saito, *The History Problem: The Politics of War Commemoration in East Asia* (Honolulu: University of Hawai'i Press, 2017), 88–91.
47 Togo, "The Assertive Conservative Right in Japan: Their Formation and Perspective," 81.
48 Muneo Narusawa, "Abe Shinzo: Japan's New Prime Minister a Far-Right Denier of History," *Asia-Pacific Journal* 11, no. 1 (2013).
49 Togo, "The Assertive Conservative Right in Japan: Their Formation and Perspective," 83.
50 Stephen R. Nagy, "Nationalism, Domestic Politics and the Japan Economic Rejuvenation," *East Asia* 31, no. 1 (2014).
51 Togo, "The Assertive Conservative Right in Japan: Their Formation and Perspective," 85.
52 Jonathan Soble, "Shinzo Abe's Nationalistic Streak under Scrutiny," *Financial Times*, April 28, 2013, http://www.ft.com/intl/cms/s/0/b65cb4aa-afe5-11e2-acf9-00144feabdc0.html
53 "Japan's PM Abe to Step Down Due to Health Concerns after Record-Long Tenure," *Mainichi Shimbun*, August 28, 2020. https://mainichi.jp/english/articles/20200828/p2g/00m/0na/092000c.
54 Kazuya Fukuoka, "Commemorating and Othering: A Study of Japanese Public Opinion on Prime Minister Abe's 2013 Yasukuni Pilgrimage," *East Asia* 36 (2019). https://doi.org/10.1007/s12140-019-09322-w; and Maeda Yukio, "Public Opinion and the Abe Cabinet: Alternating Valence and Position Issues," in *Japan Decides 2017*, ed. Ethan Scheiner, Robert Pekkanen, Daniel M. Smith and Steven Reed (London: Palgrave Macmillan, 2018), https://doi.org/10.1007/978-3-319-76475-7_8.
55 Andrew Gordon, "The Abe Statement: A Balancing Act That Leaves Work to Be Done," *Nippon.com*, August 18, 2015. https://www.nippon.com/en/column/g00305/.
56 Yoojin Koo, "The Tsukurukai's Networking with Politicians: Conservative Diet Members Groups in Japanese Interest Group Politics," *Journal of East Asian Students, Yamaguchi University* 12 (2014).
57 Charles Nuckolls, "The Cartoon Nationalism of Contemporary Japan," in *Something Wicked This Way Comes*, ed. Colette Balmain and Lois Drawmer (Leiden: Brill, 2009). doi:10.1163/9789042028791_006.
58 Shinbun Akahata, 中学教科書採択　育鵬社激減 [Junior High School Textbook Adoption – Ikosha Declines Drastically]. September 22, 2020. https://www.jcp.or.jp/akahata/aik20/2020-09-22/2020092201_01_1.html
59 Eiji Oguma and Yōko Ueno, "癒し"のナショナリズム—草の根保守運動の実証研究 [A Nationalism of "Healing" – An Empirical Study of the Grassroots Conservative Movement] (Tokyo: Keiō Gijuku Daigaku Shuppankai, 2003).

60 Tsuyoshi Hasegawa and Kazuhiko Togo, *East Asia's Haunted Present: Historical Memories and the Resurgence of Nationalism* (Westport, CT: Praeger Security International, 2008), 87.
61 Rebecca Clifford, "Cleansing History, Cleansing Japan: Kobayashi Yoshinori's Analects of War and Japan's Revisionist Revival," *Nissan Occasional Paper Series* 35 (2004).
62 Barak Kushner, "Nationality and Nostalgia: The Manipulation of Memory in Japan, Taiwan, and China since 1990," *International History Review* 29, no. 4 (2007).
63 Yangmo Ku, "Japan's Postwar Historical Narrative and Textbook Policy: Diplomatic Pressure, Transnational Activism, and Conservative Reaction" (Paper presented at the annual meeting of the International Studies Association Annual Conference Global Governance: Political Authority in Transition, Le Centre Sheraton Montreal Hotel, MONTREAL, QUEBEC, CANADA, March 16, 2011).
64 Jun Okumura, "Most of You Have Not Heard of Nippon Kaigi," *GlobalTalk 21 Blog*, January 02, 2008, http://son-of-gadfly-on-the-wall.blogspot.com/2008/01/most-of-you-have-not-heard-of-nippon.html
65 Jennifer Ellen Robertson, *Politics and Pitfalls of Japan Ethnography: Reflexivity, Responsibility, and Anthropological Ethics* (London: Routledge, 2009), 66.
66 Tamotsu Sugano, 日本会議の研究 [A Study of the Japan Conference] (Tokyo: Fushōsha, 2016), 39–49; and "As I See It: Nippon Kaigi and the Debate Over Constitutional Revision," *Mainichi Shimbun*, December 17, 2016, https://mainichi.jp/english/articles/20161217/p2a/00m/0na/001000c.
67 Sugano, 日本会議の研究 [A Study of the Japan Conference], 283–284, 290–292.
68 Thierry Guthmann, "Nationalist Circles in Japan Today: The Impossibility of Secularization," *Japan Review* 30, Special Issue (2017), doi:10.15055/00006739; and Ernils Larsson, "Jinja Honchō and the Politics of Constitutional Reform in Japan," *Japan Review* 30, Special Issue (2017), doi:10.15055/00006740.
69 Keita Takayama, *Right Turn in Japan's Third Great Education Reform: A Critical, Globalization Approach to the Studies of Japanese Education* (Ann Arbor, MI: UMI, 2007), 141; and Etsuko Toyoda and David Chapman, "Family Matters: Nippon Kaigi and Keeping Things Normal," *Japanese Studies* 39, no. 3 (2019), doi:10.1080/10371397.2019.1646097.
70 Akihiro Ogawa, "Peace, a Contested Identity: Japan's Constitutional Revision and Grassroots Peace Movements," *Peace & Change* 36, no. 3 (2011).
71 Yoshiko Nozaki and Mark Selden, "Japanese Textbook Controversies, Nationalism, and Historical Memory: Intra- and Inter-national Conflicts," *Asia-Pacific Journal* 7, no. 5 (2009).
72 Daiki Shibuichi, "The Japan Conference (Nippon Kaigi): An Elusive Conglomerate," *East Asia* 34 no. 3 (2017). doi:10.1007/s12140-017-9274-1.
73 Madelyn R. Sanfilippo, Pnina Fichman and Shengnan Yang, "Multidimensionality of Online Trolling Behaviors," *Information Society* 34, no. 1 (2018).
74 Daisuke Tsuji, "インターネットにおける「右傾化」現象に関する実証研究" [Empirical Study on the Rightward Shift Occurring on the Internet], *Tsuji Daisuke's Seminar* (Blog), September 10, 2008, http://d-tsuji.com/paper/r04/index.htm.
75 Kikuko Nagayoshi, "ネット右翼とは誰か——ネット右翼の規定要因" [Who Are the Net Right? - - Factors Among the Net Right], in ネット右翼とは何か [What Is the Net Right?] (Tokyo: Seikyusha, 2019), 19.
76 Yamaguchi Tomomi, "ネット右翼とフェミニズム" [The Net Right and Feminism], in ネット右翼とは何か [What Is the Net Right?] (Tokyo: Seikyusha, 2019), 167, 189–182.

77 Daisuke Tsuda, Rika Kayama and Kōichi Yasuda (Eds.), 安倍政権のネット戦略 [The Internet strategy of the Abe administration] (Tokyo: Tsukuru shuppan, 2013).
78 Rumi Sakamoto, "'Koreans, Go Home!' Internet Nationalism in Contemporary Japan as a Digitally Mediated Subculture," *Asia-Pacific Journal* 9, no. 10 (2011), 2.
79 Muneo Kaigo, "Internet Aggregators Constructing the Political Right Wing in Japan," *JeDEM-eJournal of eDemocracy and Open Government* 5, no. 1 (2013).
80 Fabian Schäfer, Stefan Evert and Philipp Heinrich, "Japan's 2014 General Election: Political Bots, Right-Wing Internet Activism, and Prime Minister Shinzō Abe's Hidden Nationalist Agenda," *Big Data* 5, no. 4 (2017). doi:10.1089/big.2017.0049.
81 Daisuke Tsuji and Satoshi Kitamura, "Exposure to Online News and Polarization of Xenophobic Attitudes: A Quantitative Analysis of Survey Data in Japan and the US," *Osaka Human Sciences* 6 (2020): 1–17; and Nagayoshi, "ネット右翼とは誰か——ネット右翼の規定要因" [Who Are the Net Right? – Factors Among the Net Right], 34–35.
82 Tom Gill, "The Nativist Backlash: Exploring the Roots of the Action Conservative Movement," *Social Science Japan Journal* 21, no. 2 (2018). doi:10.1093/ssjj/jyy023.
83 Higuchi, *Japan's Ultra-Right*.
84 Daiki Shibuichi, "Zaitokukai and the Problem with Hate Groups in Japan," *Asian Survey* 55, no. 4 (2015). doi:10.1525/as.2015.55.4.715.
85 "Report on the Issue of Racism and Hate Speech in Japan," *Korean Residents Union in Japan*, July 18, 2014, http://tbinternet.ohchr.org/Treaties/CERD/Shared Documents/JPN/INT_CERD_NGO_JPN_17699_E.pdf.
86 Koji Higashikawa, "Japan's Hate Speech Laws: Translations of the Osaka City Ordinance and the National Act to Curb Hate Speech in Japan," *Asian-Pacific Law & Policy Journal* 19, no. 1 (2017); and Ayako Hatano, "The Internalization of International Human Rights Law: The Case of Hate Speech in Japan," *New York University Journal of International Law and Politics* 50, no. 2 (Winter 2018).
87 Vivian Shaw, "Strategies of Ambivalence: Cultures of Liberal Antifa in Japan," *Radical History Review* 2020, no. 138 (2020); and Daiki Shibuichi, "The Struggle Against Hate Groups in Japan: The Invisible Civil Society, Leftist Elites, and Anti-Racism Groups," *Social Science Japan Journal* 19, no. 1 (2016); and Nathaniel M. Smith, "Vigilante Video: Digital Populism and Anxious Anonymity Among Japan's New Netizens," *Critical Asian Studies* 52, no. 1 (2020); and Ayako Hatano, "Can Strategic Human Rights Litigation Complement Social Movements: A Case Study of the Movement against Racism and Hate Speech in Japan," *University of Pennsylvania. Asian Law Review* 14 (2019), 228.
88 Jeffrey J. Hall, "Japan's Right-Wing YouTubers: Finding a Niche in an Environment of Increased Censorship," *Asia Review* 8 no. 1 (2018). doi:10.24987/SNUACAR.2018.08.8.1.315.
89 Gill, "The Nativist Backlash: Exploring the Roots of the Action Conservative Movement."
90 Higuchi, *Japan's Ultra-Right*, 21–22.
91 Ibid., 66.
92 Naoto Higuchi, "The 'Pro-Establishment' Radical Right," in *Civil Society and the State in Democratic East Asia*, ed. David Chiavacci, Simona Grano and Julia Obinger (Amsterdam University Press, 2020).
93 Naoto Higuchi, "Japan's Far Right in East Asian Geopolitics: The Anatomy of New Xenophobic Movements," *University of Tokushima, Social Sciences Research* 28 (2014).

94 Yūki Asahina, "Becoming Right-Wing Citizens in Contemporary Japan," *Contemporary Japan* 31, no. 2 (2019), doi:10.1080/18692729.2019.1655618.
95 Higuchi, *Japan's Ultra-Right*, 69.
96 Asahina, "Becoming Right-Wing Citizens in Contemporary Japan."
97 Andrews, *Dissenting Japan*, 285.

Bibliography

Andrews, William. *Dissenting Japan*. London: Hurst, 2016.

Asahi, Shimbun. "POINT OF VIEW/ Mitsuhiro Kimura: Mindless Patriotism Ravages Today's Japan." August 9, 2013. http://ajw.asahi.com/article/views/opinion/AJ201308090016.

Asahina, Yūki. "Becoming Right-Wing Citizens in Contemporary Japan." *Contemporary Japan* 31, no. 2 (2019): 122–140. https://doi.org/10.1080/18692729.2019.1655618.

Clifford, Rebecca. "Cleansing History, Cleansing Japan: Kobayashi Yoshinori's Analects of War and Japan's Revisionist Revival." *Nissan Occasional Paper Series* 35 (2004).

Dixon, Karl. "Recent Shift in Japanese Right-Wing Student Movements: The 'Minzoku-Ha' Students." *Asian Survey* 12, no. 11 (1972): 953–959. https://doi.org/10.2307/2643116.

Economist. "Old Habits Die Hard." May 19, 2007. http://www.economist.com/node/9205495

Englehart, Katie. "The Rise of the Far Right in Europe – Macleans.ca." *Macleansca*, November 30, 2013. http://www.macleans.ca/news/world/rise-of-the-far-right-in-europe

Fukuoka, Kazuya. "Commemorating and Othering: A Study of Japanese Public Opinion on Prime Minister Abe's 2013 Yasukuni Pilgrimage." *East Asia* 36 (2019): 349–368. https://doi.org/10.1007/s12140-019-09322-w.

Fukushima, Mizuho. "「今会いたい、今話しをしたい」一水会の鈴木邦男さんと語る" ["I Want to Meet Them, Speak to Them" Speaking with Issuikai's Suzuki Kunio"]. September 19, 2013. https://www.youtube.com/watch?v=5keIhR_5Ycc.

Gibney, Alex. "How Burly Men with Missing Digits Influence Japanese Politics: Yakuza: Once Brotherhoods of Cast-offs Guided by Grisly Rituals, Japan's Gangs Are Now Businessmen Looking for Market Share." *Los Angeles Times*, December 27, 1992. http://articles.latimes.com/1992-12-27/opinion/op-4908_1_japanese-politics.

Gill, Tom. "The Nativist Backlash: Exploring the Roots of the Action Conservative Movement." *Social Science Japan Journal* 21, no. 2 (2018): 175–192. https://doi.org/10.1093/ssjj/jyy023.

Gordon, Andrew. "The Abe Statement: A Balancing Act That Leaves Work to Be Done." *Nippon.com*, August 18, 2015. https://www.nippon.com/en/column/g00305/.

Guthmann, Thierry. "Nationalist Circles in Japan Today: The Impossibility of Secularization." *Japan Review* 30, Special Issue (2017): 207–225. https://doi.org/10.15055/00006739.

Hall, Jeffrey J. "Japan's Right-Wing YouTubers: Finding a Niche in an Environment of Increased Censorship." *Asia Review* 8, no. 1 (2018): 315–347. https://doi.org/10.24987/SNUACAR.2018.08.8.1.315.

Hasegawa, Tsuyoshi, and Togo, Kazuhiko. *East Asia's Haunted Present: Historical Memories and the Resurgence of Nationalism.* Westport, CT: Praeger Security International, 2008.

Hatano, Ayako. "The Internalization of International Human Rights Law: The Case of Hate Speech in Japan." *New York University Journal of International Law and Politics* 50, no. 2 (Winter 2018): 637–654.

Hatano, Ayako. "Can Strategic Human Rights Litigation Complement Social Movements: A Case Study of the Movement against Racism and Hate Speech in Japan." *University of Pennsylvania. Asian Law Review* 14 (2019).

Hayashi, Masayuki. "The Emperor's Legions: A History of Japan's Right Wing." *AMPO Japan-Asia Quarterly Review* 23, no. 2 (1988): 26–31.

Higashikawa, Koji. "Japan's Hate Speech Laws: Translations of the Osaka City Ordinance and the National Act to Curb Hate Speech in Japan." *Asian-Pacific Law & Policy Journal* 19, no. 1 (2017): 1–22.

Higuchi, Naoto. "Japan's Far Right in East Asian Geopolitics: The Anatomy of New Xenophobic Movements." *University of Tokushima, Social Science Research* 28 (2014): 163–183.

Higuchi, Naoto. *Japan's Ultra-Right.* Translated by Teresa Castelvetere. Tokyo: Trans Pacific Press, 2016.

Higuchi, Naoto. "The 'Pro-Establishment' Radical Right." In *Civil Society and the State in Democratic East Asia*, ed. David Chiavacci, Simona Grano, and Julia Obinger, 117–140. Amsterdam: Amsterdam University Press, 2020.

Jo, Gwan-ja. "The Revival of Japanese Right-Wing Thought and the Coincidental Collaboration of the Left and Right." *Journal of Japanese Studies* 1, no. 1 (2015): 29–56. https://doi.org/10371/94439.

Kaigo, Muneo. "Internet Aggregators Constructing the Political Right Wing in Japan." *JeDEM: eJournal of eDemocracy and Open Government* 5, no. 1 (2013): 59–79. https://doi.org/10.29379/jedem.v5i1.184

Kapur, Nick. *Japan at the Crossroads.* Cambridge, MA: Harvard University Press, 2018.

Katzenstein, Peter J., and Tsujinaka, Yutaka. *Defending the Japanese State: Structures, Norms and the Political Responses to Terrorism and Violent Social Protest in the 1970s and 1980s.* Ithaca: Cornell University Press, 1991.

Kisala, Robert. *Prophets of Peace.* Honolulu: University of Hawaii Press, 1999.

Koo, Yoojin. "The Tsukurukai's Networking with Politicians: Conservative Diet Members Groups in Japanese Interest Group Politics." *Journal of East Asian Students*, Yamaguchi University 12 (2014): 21–42.

Korean Residents Union in Japan. "Report on the Issue of Racism and Hate Speech in Japan." July 18, 2014. http://tbinternet.ohchr.org/Treaties/CERD/Shared Documents/JPN/INT_CERD_NGO_JPN_17699_E.pdf.

Ku, Yangmo. "Japan's Postwar Historical Narrative and Textbook Policy: Diplomatic Pressure, Transnational Activism, and Conservative Reaction." Paper presented at the annual meeting of the International Studies Association Annual Conference Global Governance: Political Authority in Transition, Le Centre Sheraton Montreal Hotel, MONTREAL, QC, CANADA, March 16, 2011.

Kushner, Barak. "Nationality and Nostalgia: The Manipulation of Memory in Japan, Taiwan, and China since 1990." *International History Review* 29, no. 4 (2007): 793–820. https://doi.org/10.1080/07075332.2007.9641141.

Larsson, Ernils. "Jinja Honchō and the Politics of Constitutional Reform in Japan." *Japan Review* 30, Special Issue (2017): 227–253. https://doi.org/10.15055/00006740.

Ma, Xiaohua. "Constructing a National Memory of the War: War Museums in China, Japan, and the United States." In *The Unpredictability of the Past: Memories of the Asia-Pacific War in U.S./East Asian Relations*, ed. Marc S. Gallicchio, 155–200. Durham: Duke University Press, 2007.

Mainichi Shimbun. "As I See It: Nippon Kaigi and the Debate Over Constitutional Revision." December 17, 2016. https://mainichi.jp/english/articles/20161217/p2a/00m/0na/001000c.

Mainichi Shimbun. "Japan's PM Abe to Step Down Due to Health Concerns after Record-Long Tenure." August 28, 2020. https://mainichi.jp/english/articles/20200828/p2g/00m/0na/092000c.

Maruko Siniawer, Eiko. *Ruffians, Yakuza, Nationalists.* Ithaca: Cornell University Press, 2015.

McCormack, Gavan. "The Japanese Movement to 'Correct' History." *Bulletin of Concerned Asian Scholars* 30, no. 2 (1998): 16–23. https://doi.org/10.1080/14672715.1998.10411039.

McCormack, Gavan. "Nationalism and Identity in Post-Cold War Japan." *Pacifica Review: Peace, Security & Global Change* 12, no. 3 (2000): 247–263. https://doi.org/10.1080/713604486.

Nagayoshi, Kikuko. "ネット右翼とは誰か——ネット右翼の規定要因" [Who Are the Net Right? – Factors Among the Net Right]. In ネット右翼とは何か [What Is the Net Right?], 13–43. Tokyo: Seikyusha, 2019.

Nagy, Stephen R. "Nationalism, Domestic Politics and the Japan Economic Rejuvenation." *East Asia* 31, no. 1 (2014): 5–21. https://doi.org/10.1007/s12140-014-9204-4.

Narusawa, Muneo. "Abe Shinzo: Japan's New Prime Minister a Far-Right Denier of History." *Asia-Pacific Journal* 11, no. 1 (2013).

Nozaki, Yoshiko. *War Memory, Nationalism, and Education in Postwar Japan, 1945-2007: Japanese History Textbook Controversy and Ienaga Saburo's Court Challenges.* London: Routledge, 2009.

Nozaki, Yoshiko, and Selden, Mark. "Japanese Textbook Controversies, Nationalism, and Historical Memory: Intra- and Inter-national Conflicts." *Asia-Pacific Journal* 7, no. 5 (2009). https://apjjf.org/-Mark-Selden/3173/article.html

Nuckolls, Charles. "The Cartoon Nationalism of Contemporary Japan." In *Something Wicked This Way Comes*, ed. Colette Balmain, and Lois Drawmer, 61–78. Leiden: Brill, 2009. https://doi.org/10.1163/9789042028791_006.

Ogawa, Akihiro. "Peace, a Contested Identity: Japan's Constitutional Revision and Grassroots Peace Movements." *Peace & Change* 36, no. 3 (2011): 373–399. https://doi.org/10.1111/j.1468-0130.2011.00703.x.

Oguma, Eiji, and Ueno, Yōko. 癒し"のナショナリズム—草の根保守運動の実証研究 [A Nationalism of "Healing" – An Empirical Study of the Grassroots Conservative Movement]. Tokyo: Keiō Gijuku Daigaku Shuppankai, 2003.

Okumura, Jun. "Most of You Have Not Heard of Nippon Kaigi." *GlobalTalk 21 Blog*, January 02, 2008, http://son-of-gadfly-on-the-wall.blogspot.com/2008/01/most-of-you-have-not-heard-of-nippon.html.

Robertson, Jennifer Ellen. *Politics and Pitfalls of Japan Ethnography: Reflexivity, Responsibility, and Anthropological Ethics.* London: Routledge, 2009.

Saaler, Sven. "Is Japan Drifting Toward Isolation?" *Nippon.com*, January 23, 2014. https://www.nippon.com/en/column/g00145/.

Sabey, J. Wayne. "Akao Bin (1898–1990)." In *Modern Japan: An Encyclopedia of History, Culture, and Nationalism*, ed. James L. Huffman. London: Routledge 1997.

Saito, Hiro. *The History Problem: The Politics of War Commemoration in East Asia*. Honolulu: University of Hawai'i Press, 2017.

Sakamoto, Rumi. "'Koreans, Go Home!' Internet Nationalism in Contemporary Japan as a Digitally Mediated Subculture." *Asia-Pacific Journal* 9, no. 10 (2011). https://apjjf.org/2011/9/10/Rumi-SAKAMOTO/3497/article.html.

Sanfilippo, Madelyn R., Fichman, Pnina, and Yang, Shengnan. "Multidimensionality of Online Trolling Behaviors." *Information Society* 34, no. 1 (2018): 27–39. https://doi.org/10.1080/01972243.2017.1391911.

Schäfer, Fabian, Evert, Stefan, and Heinrich, Philipp. "Japan's 2014 General Election: Political Bots, Right-Wing Internet Activism, and Prime Minister Shinzō Abe's Hidden Nationalist Agenda." *Big Data* 5, no. 4 (2017): 294–309. https://doi.org/10.1089/big.2017.0049.

Seaton, Philip A. *Japan's Contested War Memories: The "Memory Rifts" in Historical Consciousness of World War II*. London: Routledge, 2007.

Shaw, Vivian. "Strategies of Ambivalence: Cultures of Liberal Antifa in Japan." *Radical History Review 2020* 138 (2020): 145–170. https://doi.org/10.1215/01636545-8359482.

Shibuichi, Daiki. "The 'Uyoku Rōnin Dō': Assessing the Lifestyles and Values of Japan's Contemporary Right Wing Radical Activists." *Electronic Journal of Contemporary Japanese Studies* (November 28, 2007). http://japanesestudies.org.uk/discussionpapers/2007/Shibuichi.html.

Shibuichi, Daiki. "Zaitokukai and the Problem with Hate Groups in Japan." *Asian Survey* 55, no. 4 (2015): 715–738. https://doi.org/10.1525/as.2015.55.4.715.

Shibuichi, Daiki. "The Struggle Against Hate Groups in Japan: The Invisible Civil Society, Leftist Elites, and Anti-Racism Groups." *Social Science Japan Journal* 19, no. 1 (2016): 71–83. https://doi.org/10.1093/ssjj/jyv035.

Shibuichi, Daiki. "The Japan Conference (Nippon Kaigi): An Elusive Conglomerate." *East Asia* 34, no. 3 (2017): 179–196. https://doi.org/10.1007/s12140-017-9274-1.

Shinbun, Akahata. 中学教科書採択　育鵬社激減 [Junior High School Textbook Adoption – Ikuhosha Declines Drastically]. September 22, 2020. https://www.jcp.or.jp/akahata/aik20/2020-09-22/2020092201_01_1.html.

Smith, Nathaniel M. "Right Wing Activism in Japan and the Politics of Futility." PhD dissertation, Yale University, 2011.

Smith, Nathaniel M. "Facing the Nation: Sound, Fury, and Public Oratory among Japanese Right-Wing Groups." In *Sound, Space and Sociality in Modern Japan*, ed. Joseph D. Hankins and Carolyn S. Stevens, 37–56. New York: Routledge, 2013.

Smith, Nathaniel M. "Vigilante Video: Digital Populism and Anxious Anonymity among Japan's New Netizens." *Critical Asian Studies* 52, no. 1 (2020): 67–86. https://doi.org/10.1080/14672715.2019.1687315.

Soble, Jonathan. "Shinzo Abe's Nationalistic Streak under Scrutiny." *Financial Times*, April 28, 2013. http://www.ft.com/intl/cms/s/0/b65cb4aa-afe5-11e2-acf9-00144feabdc0.html

Staemmler, Birgit. "Seichō No Ie." In *Handbook of East Asian New Religious Movements*, ed. Lukas Pokorny, Franz Winter, and Brigit Staemmler, 88–108. Leiden: Brill, 2018.

Steinhoff, Patricia G. "Student Protest in the 1960s." *Social Sciences Japan* 15 (1999): 3–6, http://newslet.iss.u-tokyo.ac.jp/ssj15/ssj15.pdf.

Stockwin, J.A.A. *Collected Writings of J.A.A. Stockwin*. London: Japan Library, 2004.

Sugano, Tamotsu. 日本会議の研究 [A Study of the Japan Conference]. Tokyo: Fushōsha, 2016.

Szymkowiak, Kenneth, and Steinhoff, Patricia G. "Wrapping up in Something Long: Intimidation and Violence by Right-Wing Groups in Postwar Japan." *Terrorism and Political Violence* 7, no. 1 (19945): 265–298, https://doi.org/10.1080/09546559508427292

Takayama, Keita. *Right Turn in Japan's Third Great Education Reform: A Critical, Globalization Approach to the Studies of Japanese Education*. Ann Arbor, MI: UMI, 2007.

Togo, Kazuhiko. "The Assertive Conservative Right in Japan: Their Formation and Perspective." *SAIS Review* 30, no. 1 (2010): 77–89. https://doi.org/10.1353/sais.0.0078.

Tomomi, Yamaguchi. "ネット右翼とフェミニズム" [The Net Right and Feminism]. In ネット右翼とは何か [What is the Net Right?], 164–195. Tokyo: Seikyusha, 2019.

Toyoda, Etsuko and Chapman, David. "Family Matters: Nippon Kaigi and Keeping Things Normal." *Japanese Studies* 39, no. 3 (2019): 371–390, https://doi.org/10.1080/10371397.2019.1646097.

Tsuda, Daisuke, Kayama, Rika, and Yasuda, Kōichi (eds.), 安倍政権のネット戦略 [The Internet Strategy of the Abe Administration]. Tokyo: Tsukuru Shuppan, 2013.

Tsuji, Daisuke. "インターネットにおける「右傾化」現象に関する実証研究" [Empirical Study on the Rightward Shift Occurring on the Internet]. *Tsuji Daisuke's Seminar* (Blog), September 10, 2008. http://d-tsuji.com/paper/r04/index.htm.

Yamadaira, Shigeki. ドキュメント 新右翼——何と闘ってきたのか [Document: The New Right – What Are They Fighting Against?]. Tokyo: Shodensha, 2017.

Yamazaki, Jane W. *Japanese Apologies for World War II: A Rhetorical Study*. London: Routledge, 2006.

Yukio, Maeda. "Public Opinion and the Abe Cabinet: Alternating Valence and Position Issues." In *Japan Decides 2017*, ed. Ethan Scheiner, Robert Pekkanen, Daniel M. Smith, and Steven Reed, 127–147. London: Palgrave Macmillan, 2018. https://doi.org/10.1007/978-3-319-76475-7_8.

3 Channel Sakura takes flight

Creating a grassroots internet media organization for Japan's conservative right

The founders

On August 14, 1945, Warrant Officer Tagata Takeo was ready to die. He was 29 years old, married with a child, and one of the Japanese Imperial Army's top fighter pilots. Tagata had served for 9 years, flying over 200 combat missions over Burma, China, and Taiwan.[1] During his time in Taiwan in 1944, Tagata had been one of the first flight instructors for the young pilots of Japan's new Special Attack Force, a suicide attack force commonly known in English as the Kamikaze.[2] More than half of the 90 young men Tagata trained had already died on suicide missions.[3] Japan's war situation was getting so bad that its Army determined it necessary to also sacrifice skilled pilots such as Tagata. On that August day, Tagata was told by his superiors that he should expect orders within the next few days for a suicide mission against the Soviet navy in Vladivostok.[4]

The orders never came. Japan announced its surrender to the Allied Powers one day later, sparing Tagata from the fate suffered by so many of his students. Over the next decades, Tagata would be a leading voice against the popular idea that Kamikaze pilots were tragic victims forced to die by a fanatical militarist regime. His efforts would bring him into contact with various elements of Japan's political right, almost all of whom were receptive to his view of history.

In the last few years of his life, Tagata became an important figure in the creation of an alternative media platform for Japan's conservative right: Nihon Bunka Channel Sakura (Japanese Culture Channel Sakura, commonly referred to as Channel Sakura). It would become important in organizing grassroots activist campaigns from 2004 until the publication of this book in 2021. Its birth, and its ability to survive in the precarious world of online media, came about through the cooperation of various social actors, including Tagata, within the field of Japan's right and through the creation of a loyal viewer base willing to donate funds and labor.

This chapter will explore the creation of Channel Sakura and the important factors that contributed to its survival. This includes a discussion of its methods of funding, the types of programs it creates, how programs are distributed and consumed, and the popularity of its programs. There will also be an examination of how Channel Sakura has presented itself as an inclusive organization – building grassroots campaigns that avoid the alienating tactics of lawbreaking and hate speech. Allied organizations were offered a chance to use Channel Sakura's platform for spreading their messages, networking with other conservative organizations, and promoting the sale of conservative literature.

The story of Channel Sakura's creation cannot be told without first telling the story of its three key founding figures: Tagata Takeo, Matsuura Yoshiko, and Mizushima Satoru. Their life experiences, their connections to other members of the conservative right, and the circumstances under which they first met are important for understanding Channel Sakura. Each was a skilled social actor bringing important resources together and filling a nationalist niche.

Tagata Takeo – Kamikaze pilot activist

As mentioned at the beginning of this chapter, Tagata Takeo was a veteran pilot of the Imperial Japanese Army. The end of the war saved Tagata from having to carry out his own suicide mission, but it also left his life directionless. He had spent almost all of his adult life in the Army, an institution that no longer existed. Moreover, American Occupation authorities severely restricted Japanese aviation, rendering useless his over 4,000 hours of flying experience.

What did Tagata do with his life? According to *Kamikaze: Japan's Suicide Gods*, a 2002 English language book co-authored by British writer Albert Axell and Japanese conservative journalist Kase Hideaki, Tagata returned to his family farm in Kyushu, bringing along two of his friends – young Army pilots from Korea and Taiwan. His family welcomed and hosted the two men until they could arrange transport back to their homelands, which were no longer a part of the Japanese empire. Axell and Kase topped-off this feel-good story of international friendship by noting that Tagata spent the postwar years a humble "dirt farmer," working the fields of his family farm:

> Tagata farmed for 15 years, growing rice, wheat, sweet potatoes, potatoes, cucumbers and spinach. He also harvested pears and persimmons. He sold rice and wheat on the market but kept the other produce for the family's consumption.
>
> "Farming is the most honest toil there is," he says. Perhaps he felt this way because, as he was fond of saying, farming "was in my blood." After all, he came from an old farming family.[5]

While it may be true that Tagata worked on his family farm, the book left out another aspect of his life: his involvement in ultra-nationalistic political activism.

In the early postwar years, Tagata became a leader of a far-right uyoku group known as the Nihon Kakumei Kikuhata Dōshikai (The Japan Revolutionary Chrysanthemum Flag Association: hereafter referred to as the Kikuhata Dōshikai). Founded in 1947, it was one of Japan's largest right-wing organizations in the late 1940s, having an estimated 6,000 members in 1949.[6]

Writing in 1950, Nobutaka Ike of Stanford University described the Kikuhata Dōshikai as the "National Socialists" of Japan, a fiercely anti-communist organization following an ideology that closely resembled the views of German Nazism. However, there were significant differences from older forms of such ideologies. Ike described how the shock of defeat in the war had changed the right in Japan, and "Kikuhata-ism" had developed traits that set it apart from Japan's prewar right:

1. Renunciation of force: In view of the long tradition of militarism and violence in politics, this is striking. It may be a reflection of the current unpopularity of militarism and militarists.
2. Use of democratic symbols: This underscores the tremendous appeal of democratic ideals in contemporary Japan. It stands in sharp contrast to the open rejection of democracy by prewar Rightists.
3. Appeal for mass support: Before the war Japanese Right-wing groups carefully avoided enlisting mass support. This was one of the distinguishing features of Japanese "fascism."[7]

The Kikuhata Dōshikai's literature set a 300-year timetable for revolution. It would require an initial period of several decades to peacefully overtake Japan through electoral victories and then would move on to spread its ideology around the world.[8] However, their attempts at electoral politics did not meet with success. For example, in the 1952 House of Councilors election, Tagata and the Kikuhata Dōshikai received only 20,966 votes – 0.0007% of voters. This placed them in the 140th place in an election that awarded only 75 seats.[9]

Like other uyoku groups in early postwar Japan, the Kikuhata Dōshikai was employed as muscle against left-wing labor demonstrations.[10] This included helping break up a coal miners' strike in Kyushu and battling pro-communist groups during the Toho film studio strikes of 1946.[11] This kind of activity was viewed by Japan's political elites and their American backers as a contribution to the struggle against communism.[12]

Writing in 1960, Ivan Morris highlighted the danger posed by the Kikuhata Dōshikai's deceptive use of democratic slogans. He argued that it was actually "determined to pursue nationalist objectives by forceful means."[13] In a nation that had just suffered tremendous losses in war, violent ultra-nationalists lacked mass appeal, so many groups, including the Kikuhata Dōshikai, focused on "forming links with established power circles, becoming elite-oriented 'patriotic cliques.'"

Having played a pivotal role in the creation and maintenance of Japan's Kamikaze force, Tagata also became involved in postwar veterans' organizations that sought to promote a positive remembrance of the Kamikaze pilots who died in the war. He wanted the pilots to be seen by the public as brave heroes instead of pitiful victims, he told the Association for Retention of the Great Memorial of the Greater East Asian Holy War (Dai Tōa Seisen Taihi) in 2003:

> After the war, many people say ridiculous things such as kamikaze pilots were victim of militarism, or kamikaze pilots died tragically. Kamikaze pilots died bravely for their beloved homeland and their family as true Japanese. We shouldn't forget to be thankful to those kamikaze pilots.[14]

In other writings and interviews, Tagata emphasized how the pilots, himself included, thought of their families and their country before their flights. Kamikaze tactics were depicted as a legitimate act of warfare that was not the same as suicide. Describing his own decision to volunteer, he said it "came naturally" from his sense of duty to his nation. It was not something that was forced upon the pilots:

> I believe that no Kamikaze pilot thought he himself was committing an act of suicide. For them it was not a case of suicide at all. A sortie that would end in self-destruction was looked upon as a noble, a calculated act. Actually, in battle, you are often asked to sacrifice your life voluntarily. Such a norm is not restricted to the Japanese ... We pilots were allowed to choose our own fate. A Special Attack pilot heads towards his last moment by himself, of his own free will. However dire the situation faced by the nation, it was the pilot's decision to end his life in order to help the nation.[15]

Tagata spread his view of the Kamikaze pilots through numerous interviews with journalists and authors. He also wrote several books in Japanese about his life and about aerial combat in the Pacific War – "The Eternal Ki-91" (Eien no Hien – 1967), "Air Battle – Ki-91 vs. Grumman" (Kūsen Hien tai Guraman – 1989), and "Farewell Note to Japan" (Nihon e no Isho – 1996). In depicting the dead pilots as heroic volunteers, rather than young men forced to kill themselves by a cruel militaristic system, there was no need to seek out and blame individuals who had contributed to that system.

A longtime friend of Tagata was film director Watanabe Kunio. In the postwar years he worked with Shintōhō, a film studio created to separate itself from the left-wing strikes that Watanabe, Tagata, and the Kikuhata Dōshikai had opposed in the late 1940s. Tagata had long hoped to make a Kamikaze-themed film with Watanabe, and the director was receptive to the idea.[16] However, Tagata lacked experience as a screenwriter, and when Watanabe passed away in 1981, the project had not advanced beyond the initial planning stages. The realization of Tagata's plan would have to wait until he met several activists from a younger generation.

Matsuura Yoshiko – a student of Mishima and Japan's New Right

Matsuura Yoshiko, born in 1948, was a member of Japan's first postwar generation. Her involvement in political activism began in the late 1960s during her years as a student at Tokyo Kasei Gakuin Junior College. At the time, Japanese universities were a hotbed of left-wing activism, but Matsuura instead opted for the right-wing anti-communist activism.

Matsuura was a member of a student association of Seichō no Ie believers. Seichō no Ie (House of Growth) is a Shintō-influenced monotheistic spiritual movement with beliefs that are a mix of Japanese spiritualism and American New Thought. Founded in 1930, it supported the Japanese government during the war and became known in the postwar period for its involvement in conservative student movements and the founding of Nippon Kaigi (see Chapter 2).

In addition to her involvement with Seichō no Ie–affiliated student organizations, Matsuura was a secretary for Tate no Kai, a private right-wing militia founded and led by novelist Mishima Yukio. Her fiancé at the time (and future husband), Mochimaru Hiroshi, was a student leader of Tate no Kai.[17] Mochimaru was an "instrumental" figure in the founding of the militia, but both he and Matsuura left the organization one year before Mishima's dramatic death.[18] Despite their organizational split with Mishima, the couple remained admirers of the novelist, even after his death. Until Mochimaru's passing in 2013 the couple regularly conducted speaking events honoring Mishima and co-wrote a book praising the novelist's patriotism.[19]

Matsuura successfully ran for a seat in Tokyo's Suginami ward Assembly in 2003. Her campaigning and her political activities focused on nationalistic issues, such as promoting "patriotic" history education. One of her most notable achievements in that regard was her role in influencing the Suginami ward to adopt Tsukurukai's revisionist history textbook in its junior high schools in 2005.[20] Given that most school districts across Japan rejected the nationalistic textbook, the Suginami ward's decision has been called one of the organization's biggest successes.[21] Before stepping down to allow her son to take her place in 2019, Matsuura was re-elected three times, once as a member of the Liberal Democratic Party (LDP) and twice as a member of the Party for Future Generations. She also served as the leader of the Tokyo branch of Nippon Kaigi, an organizer of the Association of Regional Lawmakers Opposing the Installation of Comfort Women Statues (Ianfu Zō Secchi ni Kōgi Suru Zenkoku Chihō Giin no Kai), and the president of the Association of Local Lawmakers Who Protect Tsushima (Tsushima wo Mamoru Zenkoku Chihō Giin no Kai).

Through her participation in a variety of organizations and events related to Japan's right, Matsuura built a wide network of social contacts. This included Tagata Takeo, whom she met for the first time in 2000 when he was a guest speaker at an event sponsored by constitutional scholar Mitsuma Shingo. After the lecture, she was invited to join Tagata for tea at the home of another Suginami ward politician, where they talked at length about politics, religion, and history. Tagata told her about his wish to make a film preserving the history of Kamikaze pilots so he could teach younger generations about their sacrifice. He asked for her help in putting the project together, and she agreed.[22]

Despite having decades of experience with Japan's nationalist right, in YouTube videos of her retelling the story of her meeting with Tagata, Matsuura portrayed herself as a member of the ignorant postwar generation. She claimed that she didn't really know much about Kamikaze pilots in 2000, other than the negative things she had learned growing up. According to her story, Tagata taught her about the pure patriotism of the pilots. Given Matsuura's past, it is hard to believe this claim. Nonetheless, her story places her in a position that would likely be familiar to potential viewers. As I mentioned in Chapter 2, some of the people who joined the post-1990s grassroots movements were "ordinary" individuals with no experience in previous forms of political activism.[23]

Lacking the necessary skills to make such a film, they searched for a director. Yamamoto Takuma (president of Kaikosha and vice chairman of Nippon Kaigi) and Kase Hideaki (chairman of the Society for the Dissemination of Historical Fact and co-author of the earlier-mentioned book on Kamikaze) introduced them to Mizushima Satoru, an experienced director and screenwriter. Their first meeting was held at Kase's office.[24]

Mizushima Satoru – activist filmmaker

In a freelance career that spanned several decades, Mizushima Satoru participated in the production of over 300 television dramas, documentaries, and films. Many of the productions were unrelated to political or historical issues. For example, Mizushima wrote and directed *Haru-chan: Machikutabireta Onna* (Haru, the Woman Who Was Tired of Waiting) in 1987 and *Koimachi* (Waiting for Love) in 1999, two romance drama series that aired on Fuji TV, one of Japan's major broadcast networks.[25] There were, however, some films among his directing credits that reflected conservative views of history, such as the 1995 film *Minami No Shima Ni Yuki Ga Furu* (Snow Falls in the South Seas), depicting Japanese soldiers bravely fighting and dying for their country in the Pacific War.[26] Mizushima also founded a financially successful satellite TV channel that broadcasted television programs for the Filipino community in Japan.

Mizushima was enthusiastic about making a Kamikaze film for Tagata Takeo and Matsuura Yoshiko, but they would need additional support in their effort. A committee was formed with advisors consisting mainly of conservative academics, activists, war veterans, and business leaders. Notable members were: Takahashi Shirō (co-founder of Tsukurukai), Umezawa Shigeo (president of the Japan Aviation Academy), Nakamura Akira (co-founder of the Friends of Lee Teng-Hui Japan), Uematsu Kazuko (local law maker from Shizuoka prefecture), and Momochi Akira (Nippon Kaigi member).[27] The film was paid for through a fundraising campaign aimed at war veterans and members of conservative organizations.[28]

After raising the necessary funds, Tagata, Matsuura, and Mizushima traveled with a crew to the Philippines to film battlefields where Kamikaze pilots lost their lives. They successfully completed a documentary film in 2001 – *Tokkō Shōgen Shū: Kuni Yaburetemo Kuni ha Horobizu* (Kamikaze Testimony: Even If the Country Is Defeated, It Shall Not Perish).[29]

From this successful collaboration they came upon a grander idea – why not create an entire television channel devoted to their worldview? The committee formed for their Kamikaze documentary had shown that Matsuura and Tagata had access to a network of conservative groups. Mizushima brought practical television and film industry know-how that could make their idea a reality. In April 2002, Matsuura created a formal plan for the organization. Takahashi Shirō, Uematsu Kazuko, and Umezawa Shigeo joined them as leaders of the project.[30]

Utilizing Uematsu Kazuko's local connections, Mizushima visited business executives throughout Shizuoka prefecture to raise the necessary funds for the establishment of a TV channel. Uematsu also raised money from her own family. Mizushima sold his Philippine-themed satellite channel and contributed most of the proceeds to the new project.[31] Eventually, 100 million yen was gathered and used as the starting funds for Channel Sakura's incorporation.

Channel Sakura was officially launched on August 15, 2004, with Mizushima Satoru as its president. As the anniversary of Japan's defeat in World War II, it was a symbolic date. A flier announcing its creation declared that "postwar Japan was going to change." The flier's description of programming introduced a collective meaning-making experience in which viewers, together with Channel Sakura, would work to preserve and promote traditional culture. Programs would also look back on the history of "our country" and help "us" rediscover the true spirit of Japan.

Key individuals who contributed to the founding of Channel Sakura were listed on its official website. Among the 90 names are important figures in the conservative right, including Fujioka Nobukatsu (founder of Tsukurukai and Professor at Tokyo University), Itagaki Tadashi (former National Diet lawmaker, head secretary of Japan War-Bereaved Families Association, board member of Nippon Kaigi), Kabashima Yūzō (secretary general of Nippon Kaigi), Kase Hideaki (chairman of the Society for Dissemination of Historical Fact), Matsumura Toshiaki (executive director of Nippon Kaigi), Momochi Akira (board member of Nippon Kaigi), Nakamura Akira (professor at Dokkyo University), and Nishio Kanji (founder of Tsukurukai). There were also more than a dozen business executives, a similar number of academics, and several retired officers of the Japan Self-Defense Forces.

It was a list that represented a cross-section of Japan's nationalist right and its support network. Fourteen of the people on the list held leadership positions within Nippon Kaigi, the country's largest nationalist advocacy organization. Eleven were members of Tsukurukai. In addition, seven were members of the Lee Teng-Hui Association in Japan, an organization that maintains ties to the Taiwan independence movement. The "culture" part of Japanese Culture Channel Sakura is also reflected in the support of several professional calligraphers. By drawing on the social and financial connections of its 90 founders, Channel Sakura had impressive resources at its disposal.

Funding Channel Sakura

Since its founding, Channel Sakura has struggled to stay afloat. It was not, like its later rival discussed in the final chapter of this book (DHC Television), funded by the wealth of one of the country's richest businessmen. Instead, it initially sought to survive through satellite TV subscription fees. When this proved inadequate, it eventually settled on a risky but successful business model based on voluntary contributions.

The original funding plan for the network was not very different from many other satellite television channels. Subscribers to Sky Perfect satellite dish services would need to pay an 880-yen monthly fee to watch Channel Sakura on their television sets. Channel Sakura started by airing programs for 24 hours a day on Sky Perfect channel 767. However, by April 2007 funds were running low, and Channel Sakura cut back its programming to only a few hours a week. For several weeks in October 2008, financial difficulties forced it to temporarily stop satellite broadcasting. It returned to satellite television a month later through a deal to rent time on another company's satellite channel. From November 2008 to November 2017, Channel Sakura programs aired for several hours at night on Mondays through Saturdays.

Two years after its founding, in May 2006, Channel Sakura began distributing programs on the internet. It started with an on-demand system in which users could purchase and then watch individual programs. A year later, it changed to a new system through the launch of the subscription-based So-TV website. A subscription to So-TV was 3,150 yen a month and included access to live broadcasts and high-quality copies of Channel Sakura's entire archive of programming.

A far more accessible option for internet viewers was YouTube.com. Channel Sakura began to offer its content for free on the site in March 2008, making it possible for anyone with a broadband internet connection to view their content. Videos were also made available on the Japanese video sharing site Nico Nico Douga. It was, however, not the entire archive of their programming, and some videos were available for a limited time only.

Offering programming without a subscription fee required a new means of funding. Although YouTube did have a built-in advertising system that generated revenue for content creators, the fact that many of Channel Sakura's videos at that time received less than 20,000 views made it unlikely that ads ever came close to covering its expenses. Unlike many YouTube channels, it was not a single person filming at home. Not only did Channel Sakura maintain an office and studio in Tokyo's Shibuya neighborhood, but it also had paid staff members.

The solution was a form of crowdfunding. On September 10, 2008, Mizushima Satoru and Matsuura Yoshiko established the Two-Thousand Member Committee. Its goal was to recruit 2,000 members, all of whom would pledge to donate 10,000 yen a month. Membership included free access to the So-TV website, a subscription to a printed newsletter, and the autograph from any of Channel Sakura's newscasters.[32] They compared this system to the subscription fees that every television owner in Japan must pay to support Japan's public broadcaster, NHK. However, unlike the NHK system, viewers did not have a legal obligation to pay fees to Channel Sakura. With most of its new programs available for free on YouTube, there was no absolute need to join the Two-Thousand Member Committee. Basing their survival on voluntary donations represented a considerable risk. If enough viewers decided to free-ride, it would have been the end of their channel.

Within one month, they had recruited 819 members. The number of people in the Two-Thousand Member Committee gradually increased, reaching a peak of 1,863 in September 2009. Between September 2009 and September 2010, the number fluctuated between 1,600 and 1,800.[33] Channel Sakura stopped reporting the number of members after September 2010, citing problems with getting an accurate count of membership. People who joined the Two-Thousand Member Committee were expected to pay on a voluntary basis, payment schedules were irregular, and many members had difficulty keeping up with pledged payments.[34]

A monthly payment of 10,000 yen is quite a large sum for the average person, especially for a single television channel. To provide an option for individuals who wanted to offer a lesser level of monthly support, they established the Friends of Channel Sakura (Tomo no Kai). This lower tier was 2,000 yen a month and provided members with an original Channel Sakura mobile phone strap and special DVDs twice a year. Channel Sakura also accepted one-time donations.

In a 2013 program marking the ninth anniversary of Channel Sakura's creation, Mizushima Satoru discussed this funding system. He admitted that the original funding system, which was based on his Philippine satellite channel's subscription system, "was a total failure." The success of the alternative funding system was entirely thanks to the internet. A model based on free distribution of programs had increased their audience and led to greater fundraising. Mizushima expressed optimism that Channel Sakura's viewership would continue to increase.[35] In some more recent longer programs, Channel Sakura has displayed partial lists of the Two-Thousand Member Committee scrolling across the screen. Some of the names were displayed as full names of people and companies, while others were online usernames such as "KUMO" and "KU." From the inclusion of company names on the list, it would seem that corporate persons can count toward the 2,000-person goal of the Committee.[36]

Although part of its mission statement is to avoid reliance on "big business" (ōte kigyō), some Channel Sakura programs do contain small advertisements. Starting at 10,000 yen, viewers can put either their name or the name of their small business on the screen in the end credits of video programs. There are also occasional advertisements for politics and history books, as well as books seemingly unrelated to politics, such as books offering general business advice.[37]

Channel Sakura is a private corporation that does not make its financial records available to the general public. Although it presents itself as not seeking profit, it is not an NPO, meaning that it does not have a legal requirement to be transparent about its financial situation.[38] Coupled with the lack of information about the actual number of people paying 2,000 Member Committee dues, this means that the exact details of Channel Sakura's funding were unclear.

This naturally gives rise to speculation about Channel Sakura's backers. How much of its operating costs originates from grassroots supporters, and how much of it is from corporations or wealthy business persons? Given Channel Sakura's relatively small size, simple production value of its programs, and its inability to financially maintain 24-hour satellite broadcasting, it may not need a huge amount of money to survive. It is conceivable that a slightly under 2,000 people paying 10,000 yen a month, together with occasional advertisement fees, could keep Channel Sakura operating in the black.

Channel Sakura's programming

As its full name suggests, some of Japanese Culture Channel Sakura's programming is focused on expressing pride and appreciation of Japanese cultural practices and traditions. However, most of its programs deal with topics of greater interest to Japan's nationalists, such as historical disputes, territorial disputes, and fear of left-wing or foreign enemies. If one defined "culture" in terms of a culture war of the conservative right against its political and ideological enemies, then it very much could be categorized as a culture-focused channel.

Its programs were filmed in professional studios, with sets resembling what one might see on a low budget television channel. The studio used for its regular news program, "Sakura Project," featured large flatscreen televisions in the background, which were used for the display of video or images. Other programs, such as the casual talk show *Hi Izuru Kuni Yori* (From the Land of the Rising Sun), were filmed on a set resembling a talk show, with comfortable chairs and a coffee table.

Channel Sakura uploads videos to YouTube under the account name SakuraSoTV. As of August 2014, Channel Sakura had uploaded over 13,000 videos to its YouTube page. The total number of video views was about 164 million. This means that Channel Sakura videos received an average of about 12,500 views per video. More recently, in April 2020, Channel Sakura deleted many of its older clips on YouTube, pruning its contents down to programs that aired within a 3-month period, with a few exceptions made for popular videos uploaded years earlier. As of October 2020, Channel Sakura hosted 1,100 video clips with a total view count of 81 million, which came to an average of about 73,600 views per video.

There was also a steady increase in the number of YouTube accounts subscribed to Channel Sakura's videos. It has gained between several hundred and several thousand subscribers each week, rising from 160,000 in August 2014 to 502,000 in October 2020. This meant that several hundred thousand users received updates on the latest Channel Sakura videos when they logged in to their YouTube account. However, view counts on individual videos rarely came close to channel's subscriber count, indicating that most subscribers are not watching every video. It was quite common for uploaded videos to receive less than 10,000 views.

Channel Sakura's most popular videos tended to be longer format programs on very specific topics. Here is an example of popular topics, from a ranking of Channel Sakura's six most-viewed videos of all time as of August 9, 2014:

1. "Special Report: Japan Is being destroyed by Pachinko" (Hōdō Tokuban Pachinko de Kowareru Nippon) uploaded on February 12, 2009 – 649,142

views – A video exploring the pachinko industry's financial links to North Korea.

2. "Inoue Kazuhiko – Thorough Analysis of South Korea's Real Military Power!" (Inoue Kazuhiko Kankokugun no Jitsuryoku wo tettei bunseki!) uploaded on June 24, 2010 – 549,557 views – A critical evaluation of South Korea's military strength.
3. "Kō Bunyū – Chinese and Koreans are really this different from Japanese" (Kō Bunyū Nihonjin to ha Konnani Chigau Chugokujin to Kankokujin) uploaded on October 19, 2012 – 422,719 views – A video in which the reasonable Japanese are contrasted with the supposedly irrational and rude Chinese and Koreans.
4. "Tamogami's Speech – Doubting Hiroshima's Peace! Full Version" (Tamogami Kōenkai Hiroshima no Heiwa wo Utagau Kanzenhan) uploaded on August 11, 2009 – 411,577 views – A speech by Tamogami Toshio held in Hiroshima on the anniversary of the atomic bombing. He attacked pacifists as a threat to the peace of Japan, and called for a nuclear-armed Japan.
5. "Murata Haruki – Should this be apologized for too? The Truth About South Korea's Anti-Japanese Museums" ([Murata Haruki] Koredemo Shazai Shimasuka? Kankoku Hannichi Kinenkan no Jittai) August 31, 2010 – 334,352 views – Murata Haruki speaking about "anti-Japanese" museums in South Korea as an example of "brainwashing" the country's population to hate Japan.
6. "Sakuraji #50 – Very Popular! Mitawaki Junko Lectures: Challenge Korea?!" (Sakuraji #50 Daininki! Mitawaki Junko Koen, Kankoku ni Idomu!?) uploaded on September 12, 2012 – 368,203 views – Mitawaki Junko of the Tokyo University of Foreign Studies discussed how the mainstream media, China, and Korea were not telling the "truth" about numerous historical and political issues.

Each of the above videos is over 20 minutes in length. Longer videos tended to receive more views, especially if they had a topic that was not specific to a single short-term news story. Each of these five videos was arguably as relevant in 2014 as they were a few years earlier. Channel Sakura uploaded many shorter videos, which usually covered single short-term news events. Such videos tended to receive less than 10,000 views.

A new military figure – Tamogami Toshio

Tagata Takeo, the Kamikaze pilot co-founder of Channel Sakura, passed away in March 2008. Recalling Tagata's funeral in 2010, co-founder Matsuura Yoshiko noted that she had seen a set of flowers donated by General Tamogami Toshio, a name that did not ring any bell in her head at the time.[39] In early 2008 Tamogami was the chief of staff of Japan's Air Self-Defense Force, making him one of the top military officials in the country but certainly not a household name. It would not be until later in 2008 that Tamogami would out himself as a historical revisionist, end his military career, and enter the world of conservative activism.

Tamogami's rebirth as an activist was in part due to the actions of an eccentric right-wing billionaire, Motoya Toshio.[40] Motoya, a real estate developer and CEO of APA Group hotels, was a well-known figure in historical revisionist circles and had known Tamogami since the late 1990s. In May 2008, Motoya organized an essay contest on the theme of "The True Outlook for Modern and Contemporary History," to which Tamogami submitted an essay entitled, "Was Japan an Aggressor Nation?" (Nihon wa Shinryaku Kokka de Atta no Ka?). The essay, which argued that Japan was not an aggressor nation in World War II, won the top price, which included a 3-million-yen cash prize (about 30,000 USD).[41]

The essay was a rehashing of common claims made by Japan revisionists. In its six pages it only referenced four sources, three of which were by prominent historical revisionists who contributed to Channel Sakura programs (Sakurai Yoshiko, Kō Bunyū, and Fukui Yoshitaka). Two of the judges of the 2008 essay contest, journalist Hanaoka Nobuaki and Watanabe Shōichi, were also founding supporters of Channel Sakura and frequent contributors to its programs.[42] The contest organizer, Motoya, was also a good friend of Channel Sakura co-founder Umezawa Shigeo.[43]

The essay was widely reported by the media because it was a direct contradiction of the Japanese government's official positions on historical responsibility. It was a deliberate act of insubordination, leading to Tamogami's demotion and forced retirement. Instead of retreating from the public stage, Tamogami sought to expand on his fame through the publication of a book, *Mizukara no Mi ha Kaerimizu* (I Don't Repent), and through involvement in nationalist causes. He found his way to Channel Sakura in 2009, hosting a weekly program called *Tamogami Juku* (Tamogami's Cram School). Much of the program's focus was on Japan's current defense policy, as well as explorations of historical issues.

In some respects, Tamogami filled a void left by Tagata Takeo's passing. Tamogami, like Tagata, was an outspokenly nationalistic former soldier with many admirers on the political right. Tagata had served as an honorary figurehead for Channel Sakura and its activists but had been too advanced in age to take an active role in its activities. Tamogami, on the other hand, was still in his sixties and capable of energetically taking on a leadership role. Mizushima Satoru would provide him the opportunity to do so.

Ganbare Nippon

The defeat of Japan's conservative LDP and formation of a new government under the Democratic Party of Japan (DPJ) provided the stimulus for the 2010 birth of a new conservative activist organization, Ganbare Nippon Zenkoku Kōdō Iinkai (Let's Go Japan – National Action Committee). Channel Sakura's

Mizushima Satoru was the prime mover behind the organization. Mizushima asked Tamogami Toshio to serve as its leader, and the former general accepted.[44]

Ganbare Nippon's Leadership consisted of Channel Sakura regulars and conservative politicians:

- Chairman – Tamogami Toshio
- Managing director – Mizushima Satoru (president of Channel Sakura)
- Secretary general – Uematsu Kazuko (Shizuoka local lawmaker, co-founder of Channel Sakura)
- Cultural Committee chairman – Ijiri Kazuo (Tsukurukai, Nippon Kaigi, Channel Sakura newscaster)
- Osaka Branch counselor – Nishimura Shingo (conservative lawmaker, House of Representatives)
- Osaka Branch representative – Miyake Hiroshi (Japan Restoration Party lawmaker, House of Representatives)

Activists saw the DPJ government in power at that time, under Hatoyama Yukio and Ozawa Ichirō, as a corrupt and pro-China regime. Ganbare Nippon was created to organize conservatives across Japan to fight against DPJ policies that they believed were a threat to the integrity of the Japanese nation.

Ganbare Nippon's inaugural event was held in Tokyo on February 2, 2010. In the weeks leading up to it, Channel Sakura and conservative media such as the *Sankei Shimbun* published reports advertising the time and place of the event.[45] Over 2,000 people attended. In addition to speeches by Mizushima and Tamogami, former (and future) prime minister Abe Shinzō delivered a speech signaling support for their cause.[46] Other conservative lawmakers such as Inada Tomomi, Yamatani Eriko, Hiranuma Takeo, Furuya Keiji, Takaichi Sanae, and Etō Seiichi also attended the event. A photo of the event can be seen in Figure 3.1.

Ganbare Nippon would function as an activist wing to the already existing network of Channel Sakura contributors and supporters. Mizushima envisioned it as a base at which conservative people from various organizations and political parties could come together as allies. He hoped that Ganbare Nippon's grassroots power would help return a conservative government to power in the next general election.[47] Channel Sakura had encouraged protests and worked together with other groups in the past, but now it would set up its own organization of activists who could be called upon to organize demonstrations.

As a national organization, Ganbare Nippon had local chapters across Japan. Most of them were centered on regionally important conservative lawmakers and activists. For example, while LDP lawmaker Inada Tomomi pursued nationalistic policies in Tokyo, her father, Tsubakihara Yasuo, headed the Kyoto branch of Ganbare Nippon. The organizing efforts of regional branches were amplified by Channel Sakura's internet broadcasts, which regularly shared photos and video clips of devoted grassroots activists throughout the country.

Figure 3.1 Tamogami Toshio delivers a speech at Ganbare Nippon's inaugural meeting on February 2, 2010. Large banners proclaim that it is a national grassroots organization that will prevent the dissolution of Japan and oppose the granting of voting rights to non-citizens. (Public Domain, Wikipedia)

Channel Sakura's grassroots vision of the Japanese people

Channel Sakura officially described itself as a "grassroots TV channel of the Japanese people, by the Japanese people, and for the Japanese people" (nippon kokumin no nippon kokumin ni yoru nippon kokumin no tame no sōmō terebi kyoku). This phrase takes a famous line from Abraham Lincoln's Gettysburg Address and modifies it into something reflecting a particular brand of Japanese nationalism. As Kevin Doak has argued, the Japanese language contains several words that can be used when describing nationalism and the people of a nation, and one's choice of wording can represent an ideological stance. Channel Sakura frequently used the word ***kokumin*** to describe the people of Japan, reflecting a civil and political conception instead of an ethnic (***minzoku***) conception of nationhood.[48] Among recent Japanese prime ministers, the dominant term for referring to Japanese citizens has also been ***kokumin***.[49]

The language of civic nationalism was present throughout Channel Sakura programs and the offline demonstrations by Ganbare Nippon. It referred to its movement as a *kokumin undō* (national citizen's movement, or grassroots movement). As mentioned in Chapter 2, this was the same term used by Nippon Kaigi in its plans for starting grassroots movements. Because Channel Sakura's founders and regular guests included Nippon Kaigi members, it is not surprising that these organizations were on the same page on this matter.

Activism in postwar Japan has often been called *shimin undō*, which like *kokumin undō*, can be translated into English "citizen activism." However, there is an important distinction between the two when it comes to the relationship between the state and the citizen. Nathaniel Smith has argued that new conservative activists of the 1990s and 2000s act "from a position as a citizen (kokumin) of the postwar state ... although their activism is classifiable as *shimin* in that it is organized outside the realm of the state, the baseline assumptions of the right and legality with which they frame their activist program is state-based." This is in contrast to the more extreme uyoku groups, which act based on "the definitional space of the *minzoku*," allowing them to justify illegal and disruptive acts by denying the legitimacy of the postwar legal state.[50]

Mizushima Satoru's choice of terminology also reflected his desire to unify ideologically diverse conservatives under an inclusive umbrella organization. Mizushima made a distinction between *shimin undō*, which he saw as small and narrowly focused, and Channel Sakura's *kokumin undō*, which is meant to be broad and inclusive. His activism was meant to bring together anyone who "loves Japan."[51] This inclusiveness could be seen in Channel Sakura's embrace of both the scholars who left Tsukurukai due to ideological disputes and those who stayed with the organization. Channel Sakura's debate programs allowed for conservatives to disagree without being forced into supporting a narrowly focused platform.

This inclusiveness included a welcoming attitude to certain foreign-born people who naturalized and became Japanese citizens. Several regular Channel Sakura guests fell into this category, such as Ilham Mahmut of Japan Uyghur Association (formerly a Chinese citizen), Pema Gyalpo (formerly a Chinese citizen), and Professor Oh Seon-hwa of Takushoku University (formerly a South Korea citizen). Although called upon as experts of their former homelands, they were often recognized as Japanese. For example, indignation at the mistreatment of a "Japanese person" (*nihonjin*) was expressed in the aftermath South Korea's refusal of an entry visa for Oh Seon-hwa.[52]

One 2013 Channel Sakura program provided a particular insight into its activists' opinions on Japanese-ness. The discussion centered on a recently published article by Kevin Doak about Prime Minister Abe Shinzō's conception of *kokumin*. Doak's article argued that this conception rejected the idea of Japaneseness being based on ethnicity and accepted people, such as soccer player Ruy Ramos, who became Japanese citizens because they loved Japan and wanted to help the country. Channel Sakura's newscasters proclaimed the article to be an accurate analysis of Abe's inclusive and correct view of Japan. Doak was praised as a person who understood Japan "100 times more than the average Japanese person."[53]

However, when discussing the issue of voting rights for non-citizens, Channel Sakura programs expressed doubts about the loyalty of some naturalized Japanese citizens. Commentators criticized Japan's naturalization laws for not making it more difficult for foreigners to become Japanese citizens.[54] Chinese were depicted as naturalizing for selfish reasons like making money in Japan, and viewers were told that trust in Japanese passports would be reduced worldwide if too many Chinese are allowed to become Japanese citizens.[55] Thousands of Chinese who naturalized and became Japanese citizens were treated as still owing their allegiance to mainland China.[56] Mizushima and other Channel Sakura guests argued that Japan needed to counter this problem by following America's example and requiring an oath of loyalty in its naturalization process.[57]

Channel Sakura and the mainstream media

Channel Sakura depicted itself as the grassroots media alternative to Japan's mainstream media. While it told the "truth" to viewers, mainstream media outlets were considered to be under the influence of harmful business, religious, or foreign influences.

Left-leaning media outlets such as the Asahi Shimbun were regularly described as "anti-Japanese" in their reporting. Channel Sakura and Ganbare Nippon also held frequent demonstrations in front of the Asahi Shimbun offices in Tokyo, announcing over loudspeakers that its newspaper was full of reporters who distort the truth and hate Japan.

Even mainstream conservative media outlets were targeted as "anti-Japanese" at times. Although the *Yomiuri Shimbun* is generally regarded as a conservative-leaning newspaper, Channel Sakura denounced its printing of articles favorable to female imperial succession and demonstrations were held outside of Yomiuri's Tokyo headquarters.[58] Among major newspapers, the *Sankei Shimbun* is viewed most favorably by Channel Sakura. This is because the Sankei is the most right-leaning of Japan's major papers, and it frequently devoted positive coverage to events organized by Channel Sakura and Ganbare Nippon.

However, Fuji TV, a network owned by the same parent company as the *Sankei Shimbun*, has also been targeted for protest because of its alleged "anti-Japanese" obsession with South Korean popular culture.[59] At one demonstration I attended in September 2011, Channel Sakura commentator Miwa Kazuo began his speech to Ganbare Nippon members with praise of the Sankei newspapers, which he considered to be quite fair. By explaining that the television network, but not the newspaper, had fallen into the grips of "anti-Japanese" forces, they could justify consuming one Sankei Group's product while boycotting another.

Channel Sakura's worldview, and the worldview of many within the Japan's conservative right, rested upon the idea that much of the mainstream media in Japan has a left-wing bias that distorts the truth about historical issues and foreign policy. This perception was the justification for Channel Sakura's existence. The conservative right felt that their views were not reflected in the mainstream media, so they made their own channel that could bypass left-wing gatekeepers of the media and transmit information directly to viewers.[60]

Non-violence and legal protest

Channel Sakura's brand of grassroots activism was one that aimed to respect the law and not commit acts of violence. In keeping with this goal, offline demonstrations were organized in advance with the permission of authorities. During protest marches, participants walked in organized lines, taking care to follow the instructions of their police escorts. Larger demonstrations were split into segments to avoid the possibility of causing disruptions to traffic. Police officers, who are present at demonstrations for crowd and traffic control, were treated with respect.

This has made Channel Sakura and Ganbare Nippon demonstrations very different from the popular conception of right-wing protest – that is to say gatherings of loud, angry, and dangerous men. In some of the larger Channel Sakura demonstration marches, it was not rare to observe young participants and female participants with small children and even baby carriages. While it is quite common for Japanese police to dispatch large numbers of officers to maintain order at demonstrations, these events were not as confrontational in nature as other demonstrations I observed, such as marches by extreme nativist groups, uyoku sound truck parades, or demonstrations by left-wing anti-imperial groups.

However, offline events and demonstrations were often quite loud. Ganbare Nippon regularly used vans with loudspeakers as well as megaphones. Marchers were encouraged to join in and shout slogans. Other forms of disruptive behavior were usually frowned upon.

A notable exception took place in September 2011, when Channel Sakura and Ganbare Nippon were carrying out a demonstration against Fuji TV's headquarters in Tokyo. The demonstrators noticed that the Japanese flag flying in front of the Fuji TV building was dirty and ragged in appearance. Mizushima Satoru, having brought many flags along with his demonstration, offered to give a clean new flag to Fuji TV, so that it could replace what he considered a disgracefully dirty flag. After some chanting from demonstrators, Fuji TV personnel agreed to change the flag but said they did not need one of Mizushima's flags. Just as a fresh flag was brought to the scene, an order was received from higher-ups reversing the decision to replace the flag. This ignited anger among the demonstrators, who forcefully took down the ragged flag and replaced it with one of their own. Mizushima argued that the act was justifiable because the "national flag of Japan is not something that Fuji TV could own."[61] A scuffle broke out between protesters and security guards, with one protester allegedly tearing Fuji TV's flag. Mizushima denied these claims, but a police investigation into the incident was launched a year later, and police sent documents to prosecutors about the involvement of one Ganbare Nippon activist. Prosecutors ultimately decided not to press charges.[62]

Similarly, in 2012 Mizushima and several activists illegally landed on the Senkaku Islands after their application to land had been rejected by Japanese authorities. Mizushima justified his actions on the basis of a higher authority – the need to protect the islands when the government was failing to protect them (see Chapter 7).

It is notable that both of these exceptions did not involve acts meant to harm other human beings. In this respect, one can see a major difference from the lawbreaking activism of the old uyoku, which included violent acts such as arson, ramming vehicles into barricades, and death threats.

Mizushima has said that it is of crucial importance to produce programs and carry out "activism that one would not be embarrassed to carry out in the presence of the Emperor."[63] These ideals do not just dictate acceptable forms of action. They have also been applied to speech.

As part of their mission to be a non-extremist grassroots movement, Channel Sakura and Ganbare Nippon have sought to prevent the use of so-called hate speech at their events. This can be a difficult task, especially when organizing anti-Chinese, anti-Korean, or anti-immigration protests. Focus has been placed on avoiding base and crude language, as well as potentially offensive banners or flags.

The term "hate speech" entered the mainstream consciousness of Japanese thanks in part to Channel Sakura. In the early years of Channel Sakura's broadcasting Mizushima Satoru allowed an up-and-coming blogger and activist named Sakurai Makoto to use its programs as a platform to discuss anti-Korean conspiracy theories and the alleged existence of "special privileges" granted to Japan's Zainichi Korean community.[64] Sakurai's vision for acceptable activism, however, was very different from Mizushima's. Zaitokukai, founded by Sakurai in 2005, became infamous across Japan and the world for the extreme hate spouted at its demonstrations, ranging from racial slurs to calls for outright genocide. The "hate speech" issue was widely discussed in the media and led the Japanese authorities to pass anti-hate speech laws.

Amid public concern about this issue, Mizushima took a strong stance against what he considered hate speech and racist language. At events organized by Ganbare Nippon, participants were told they must carry out protests that any Japanese person can be proud of, rather than using base and crude language. Mizushima and Sakurai severed ties between their organizations and videos of Sakurai's previous appearances on Channel Sakura were deleted from online archives. They became bitter enemies, denouncing each other as harmful to the cause of Japanese nationalism. For example, when Sakurai ran for governor of Tokyo in 2016, Channel Sakura strongly opposed him, reminding viewers of the reprehensible statements he made in 2012 calling for killing all Korean people. Reacting to a flood of angry pro-Sakurai trolls posting comments on Channel Sakura videos, Mizushima repeated his view that characterizing the entire Korean race as bad was reprehensible. Blanket statements denouncing an entire race did not fit with Mizushima's ideas of the "basic principles of people involved in political activism."[65]

Rank and file members of organizations like Zaitokukai were not completely banned from Channel Sakura and Ganbare Nippon events. If they wished to join an event, they could do so as individuals, following the rules set by Mizushima. However, any official cooperation with Zaitokuai or "sound truck uyoku" (gaisen uyoku) groups was out of the question.

Another measure taken to distance themselves from more extreme groups was the creation of rules regarding flags used at demonstrations. The national flag of Japan was allowed, but the rising sun flag was not allowed. Although the rising sun flag has often been associated with militarism and prewar Japan, Mizushima did not prevent its use on those grounds. Instead, he argued that it was a flag of the Japanese military, so its use in political demonstrations was disrespectful to the military.[66] My observation of demonstrations found that this flag rule was generally obeyed but was limited in its enforcement to actual flags. It was not rare to see participants with rising sun t-shirts or pins. Depending upon the issue addressed by demonstrations, Tibetan, Uyghur, and World Taiwanese Congress flags were also allowed.

Channel Sakura's discussions of hate speech have not taken place within a right-leaning echo chamber. In some notable cases, it has invited commentary from its ideological opponents. For example, a November 2013 panel discussion on the "Zainichi Issue" (*Zainichi mondai*) featured a three-hour debate between four Channel Sakura regulars and four left-leaning activists/journalists, including Noma Yasumichi and Kim Nobukatsu of the Counter-Racist Action Collective (C.R.A.C.). Although the participants disagreed strongly on many issues, the discussion was generally calm and civil, even after Noma pointed out that Mizushima and Channel Sakura had helped Sakurai Makoto spread "lies" about Zainichi Koreans.[67] As was customary with such programs, the recent books by each panel discussant, including books that supported the left-leaning activists, were displayed on the screen.

Opposition to hate speech, however, does not equate to support for laws against it. Since the beginning of legal efforts to combat the rise in hate speech, Mizushima and other Channel Sakura regulars have strongly opposed such actions as attacks on freedom of expression. As a result, organizations that seek to strengthen anti-hate laws and bring lawsuits against offenders, such as the International Network to Overcome Hate Speech and Racism (Heito Supīchi to Reishizumu wo Norikoeru Kokusai Nettowāku),[68] have been condemned as "anti-Japanese" on Channel Sakura programs.[69]

It should also be pointed out that not approving of overtly racist language and other crudely hateful language does not mean that Channel Sakura's programs or Ganbare Nippon's offline demonstrations are free of what many would consider xenophobic hate. While not condemning Koreans or Chinese as racially inferior or inherently bad, conspiracy theories about segments of those populations have been frequently introduced, and comment responses to Channel Sakura videos often contained racial slurs against those groups. Activism that insists on using moderate language can still encourage hate. As I argue in the final chapter of this book, shifting definitions of hate speech have come to pose a threat to Channel Sakura.

Cooperation with international activists

From its very start, Channel Sakura was meant to bring together various elements of Japan's conservative right. Its founders and leaders had ties to a variety of important activist organizations and drew upon those groups to provide panelists and participants for its numerous programs. This included domestic organizations such as Nippon Kaigi and Tsukurukai, but there were also significant ties to international activist organizations.

Pro-Taiwan independence activists

Pro-Taiwan independence organizations in Japan have been a key ally of Channel Sakura. Taiwanese independence activists wanted to assert that Taiwan had a separate identity from China and thus should be treated as an entirely different country. To achieve this, they looked back on Taiwan's history as a colony of Japan. They advanced the view that Japan liberated Taiwan from oppressive colonial Chinese domination and helped nurture Taiwan's uniquely non-Chinese society. The postwar acts of oppression committed by Nationalist Chinese authorities against the population of Taiwan are contrasted with what they see as the less oppressive colonization by Japan. This view merged well with the views of Japan's conservative right, which sought out positive appraisals of Japan's pre-1945 history and condemned mainland China as an aggressive threat to the region.

Former Taiwanese President Lee Teng-hui was a leader of the pro-independence movement and a dear friend of Japan's assertive conservative right. Lee grew up and was educated during the period of Japanese colonial rule, attending Kyoto University in the 1940s. His older brother served in the Japanese Imperial Navy was killed in the war. During and after serving as president, Lee expressed favorable views of Japan's colonial rule of Taiwan. As Barak Kushner has pointed out, this was part of Lee's support for a distinct non-Chinese Taiwan:

> Promoters of Taiwan's independence, including Lee and the business tycoon Xu Wenlong, welcome Japan's nationalist rhetoric because they, too, deny Taiwan's Chinese identity. They emphasize Taiwan's colonial inheritance to promote the idea that it does not belong to China, that it does not share a history with China, and that it should be considered a sovereign state.[70]

Lee also partnered with Kobayashi Yoshinori, the popular nationalist comic book author, to produce a 2001 bilingual manga that depicted Japanese colonialism as positive for Taiwan and demonized mainland China.[71] He drew further support from Japan's right by visiting the controversial Yasukuni Shrine in Tokyo and offering prayers to the spirits of his brother and Japan's other war dead. Furthermore, Lee voiced support for Japan's territorial claim to the Senkaku Islands.[72] Taking Japan's side in that territorial dispute can be interpreted as another denial of Taiwan's Chinese identity, because these territorial claims are linked to the idea that the Republic of China government in Taiwan is the legitimate government for all of China, rather than a separate island country.

Therefore, it should come as no surprise that the Japan chapter of the Friends of Lee Teng-Hui Association, an organization devoted to Japan–Taiwan friendship and Taiwanese independence, is associated with Japan's conservative right. Founded in 2002, its leadership positions were dominated by conservative Japanese political figures, including Kase Hideaki, Nakanishi Terumasa of the Yasukuni Shrine Reverence Association and Tsukurukai, and Nippon Kaigi leaders Odamura Shirō and Takubo Tadae.

Another notable board member of the Lee Teng-Hui Association in Japan was Nagayama Hideki. Nagayama ran his own organization, called the Taiwan Research Forum (Taiwan Kenkyū Forum), which aimed to promote good relations with Taiwan and spread awareness about counterpoints to Chinese viewpoints. Nagayama has been an active member of Channel Sakura's newscaster team since 2004, as well as a board member of the Ganbare Nippon organization since 2010. Starting in 2013, he has hosted his own "Taiwan Channel" weekly program on Channel Sakura. It was a bilingual program aimed at Japanese and Taiwanese viewers, featuring a Taiwanese co-anchor who translated Nagayama's statements about Japan–Taiwan issues.[73]

Uyghur activists

What do activists from other organizations gain through cooperation with Channel Sakura? A specific example can be found in the Yu-Wen Chen's research on the Uyghur Lobby. Chen follows the case of Ilham Mahmut, founder of the Japan Uyghur Association (JUA).[74]

Shortly after founding the JUA in 2008, Mahmut met Nagayama Hideki at a Falun Gong event in Tokyo. He came to know that Nagayama was a host of Channel Sakura television programs and an activist involved in pro-Taiwan organizations such as the Friends of Lee Teng-Hui. Through Nagayama, Mahmut was introduced to Channel Sakura and its allies within Japan's conservative right. Chen's analysis of communications found that the JUA developed a relatively intimate relationship with Ganbare Nippon. Thanks to Nagayama, the JUA was connected to a network of pro-Taiwan independence groups, Free Tibet groups, and other anti-China groups. Connections were also formed to Nippon Kaigi.

Ilham Mahmut has been a regular guest on Channel Sakura programs – having appeared over 40 times since 2009. His appearances included programs that spread awareness about the situation of Uyghur people in China, as well as programs on entirely different topics. In programs that attacked China, Mahmut could be relied upon to deliver negative statements about the Chinese government. He also enthusiastically supported Ganbare Nippon's efforts to carry out boat activism around the Senkaku Islands (discussed in Chapter 7), going as far as traveling to the islands himself and waving their organizations banners.

Mahmut's claims about human rights abuse and Chinese massacres of Uyghurs are used for two purposes: one that directly benefits Mahmut and another that benefits the historical views of the Japanese conservative right. By painting a picture of a China that has committed and is still committing atrocities against the Uyghur people, Mahmut brings awareness to what he sees as the suffering of his people at the hands of a foreign occupier. Yet, at the same time, this view of China aids Japanese conservatives who seek to deny or downplay Chinese claims of atrocities committed by the Japanese in World War II. China is depicted as an immensely dishonest state: one that denies ongoing atrocities against the Uyghurs while telling the world "false" stories about Japanese atrocities that took place in the 1930s and 1940s. While spreading awareness about wrongdoing against his own people, Mahmut aided activists who seek to deny their own nation's wrongdoing.

Examples of Mahmut's appearances on Channel Sakura include:

- June 16, 2009 – During Channel Sakura's anti-NHK campaign discussed in Chapter 5, Mahmut appeared on a program to denounce the public broadcaster's coverage of the Uyghur issue. Agreeing with Channel Sakura's claim that NHK is pro-China, Mahmut argued that it was deliberately underreporting the mistreatment of his people.[75]
- July 8, 2009 – Mahmut provided most of the commentary to a program about the ongoing unrest involving the Uyghur population in China. The Chinese government was blamed for causing the problem through its discriminatory policies, and the international media was criticized for failing to blame China for the massacres of Uyghur people.[76]
- November 9, 2010 – As a participant in the anti-Chinese demonstrations that took place after the Senkaku Island boat collision incident, Mahmut praised the many Japanese who came out to support the marches. He tied the Senkaku issue to China's own "aggression" against his own homeland.[77]
- August 18, 2011 – Mahmut was a guest in a video report highlighting a JUA demonstration held in Hiroshima on the anniversary of its atomic bombing. He sought to draw awareness to the thousands of Uyghurs who allegedly died because of Chinese nuclear testing and denounced China for failing to recognize and take responsibility for its crimes.[78]
- April 9, 2012 – In a special program on the "Free Uyghur" issue, Mahmut was joined by Dolkun Isa, secretary general of the World Uyghur Congress. They spoke about the importance of the World Uyghur Congress meeting that would be held in Tokyo the next month. Mahmut served as an interpreter for Isa, who could not speak Japanese.[79] Channel Sakura devoted additional programs to covering the WUC meeting and the speeches delivered there.
- June 10, 2013 – A special episode of "Sakura Project" was devoted to the cruelty of modern China. Mahmut was one of the six guests on the show. The other guests were mostly members of pro-Taiwan independence groups. The discussion blamed China for territorial aggression, economic dishonesty, corruption, racism, and militarism. Mahmut was given roughly 10 minutes of the one-hour program to speak, using about two-thirds of it to criticize

> Japanese and American diplomacy toward China, and one-third to highlight the discrimination against Uyghur people in China.[80]

Within three years of coming into contact with Channel Sakura, Mahmut had formed his own relationships with various conservative organizations and conservative politicians and had the confidence to act independently: "Now that they know me, I can phone the offices of Diet members without Nagayama's help."[81] Despite having only 30 members in his organization, Mahmut formed connections that allowed him to have twice-monthly meetings with national lawmakers. Cooperating with Nagayama and Channel Sakura had clear benefits for the JUA.

Cooperation with Channel Sakura could also be profitable for activists and intellectuals who were seeking to promote books. Many of Channel Sakura's programs followed a format in which a guest or a panel of guests is invited to discuss a certain historical or political issue. At the beginning of the program, there was usually an introduction of recent or upcoming books written by the guests. Throughout the program, the books were prominently displayed. In this respect, Channel Sakura could serve as an important part of a promotional tour for a new book, especially when it happens to appeal to a niche market of conservative readers.

Conclusion

Channel Sakura was born through the efforts of highly motivated and skilled social actors within Japan's assertive conservative right. Tagata Takeo was an old-school rightist who had built ties to both veteran's groups and post-1990s conservative organizations. Matsuura Yoshiko brought her connections to a variety of conservative activist groups and politicians. Uemura Kazuko and several other well-connected patrons secured funding. Finally, Mizushima Satoru had the know-how to run a television channel, write scripts, create sets, and direct television programs. Technical skills, social connections, and a willingness to embrace unorthodox forms of funding helped Channel Sakura maintain itself for over 15 years.

The plan to launch an alternative media outlet did not threaten the influence of already-existing activist groups. Its co-founders included members of two of the largest organizations in Japan's assertive conservative right: Nippon Kaigi and Tsukurukai. A grassroots television network that encouraged grassroots conservative protests fit snugly into Nippon Kaigi's own goals for creating such movements. For Tsukurukai, Channel Sakura provided an outlet for its members to lecture viewers on history and encourage activism in support of its textbooks. International activist organizations, such pro-Taiwan independence organizations and the Japan Ugyhur Association, also found benefits in cooperation with Channel Sakura. For many of these groups, which had limited or no digital presence, Channel Sakura's online videos helped take their message from the old world of printed pamphlets, right-wing magazine articles, and books to the wider world of YouTube. As former Channel Sakura contributor put it, Channel Sakura functioned as "the bridge across which the ideas of the postwar political right, previously confined to a few outlets in the print media, found their way into cyberspace."[82]

The skilled social actors among Channel Sakura and its allies helped create an inclusive gathering of conservatives. By stipulating acceptable tactics and forms of protest, they kept their activism free of extreme hate speech, violence, and criminal acts. They avoided connections to Japan's old uyoku and its new hate groups, cultivating a non-extremist identity that was meant to make their grassroots campaigns attractive to normal people.

Notes

1 Albert Axell and Hideaki Kase, *Kamikaze: Japan's Suicide Gods* (Harlow: Longman, 2002), 94–100.
2 Ibid., 40.
3 Takeo Tagata, "Tokkotai and Me," *Kamikaze*, July 21, 2003, https://web.archive.org/web/20190224065109/http://www.geocities.jp/kamikazes_site_e/tokkotaiandMe.html.
4 Axell and Kase, *Kamikaze: Japan's Suicide Gods*.
5 Ibid., 219–220.
6 Ray Falk, "Seed of Dragons," *Pathfinder* 56, no. 25 (1949): 24.
7 Nobutaka Ike, "National Socialism in Japan," *Pacific Affairs* 23, no. 3 (1950): 311–314.
8 Ibid.
9 "昭和３１年７月８日執行(第４回）" [Shōwa 31/7/8 Results (Fourth Time)], *Kamo City* (Homepage), last accessed September 8, 2020, http://www.city.kamo.niigata.jp/section/senkyo/senkyo.data/sangi/S31.07.08.htm
10 "秋ふかき　隣はなにを……" [Autumn Deepens, My Neighbor …], *Nihon Bunka Channel Sakura* (Homepage), September, 2009, http://www.ch-sakura.jp/mizushima/1296.html.
11 Joseph L. Anderson and Donald Richie, *The Japanese Film: Art and Industry* (Clarendon: C.E. Tuttle Company), 166–171, http://www.eiganokuni.com/kimata/08.html
12 Robert P. Martin, "Japanese Ultra-Nationalists Reorganizing Forces," *The Gazette and Daily* (York, PA), June 22, 1950, p. 19.
13 Ivan I. Morris, *Nationalism and the Right Wing in Japan; a Study of Postwar Trends* (London: Oxford University Press, 1960).
14 Brian J. McVeigh, *Nationalisms of Japan: Managing and Mystifying Identity* (Lanham: Rowman & Littlefield Publishers, 2003), 53.
15 Axell and Kase, *Kamikaze: Japan's Suicide Gods*, 214.
16 Stuart Galbraith, *The Toho Studios Story: A History and Complete Filmography* (Lanham: Scarecrow Press, 2008), x.
17 "【持丸博】「楯の会」初代学生長が語る在りし日の三島由紀夫[桜H22/11/20]" ['Mochimaru Hiroshi' The First Student Leader of the Tatenokai Speaks About His Memories of Mishima Yukio], *Nihon Bunka Channel Sakura*, November 20, 2010, https://www.youtube.com/watch?v=uzh2CEhHmwo; and John Nathan, *Mishima: A Biography* (Tokyo: Tuttle, 1981), 225.
18 Yoshiko Sakurai, "A Thought on True Patriotism and Japan's Search for Strategic Direction," *Yoshiko Sakurai Official Web Site*, December 21, 2010, http://en.yoshiko-sakurai.jp/2010/12/21/2264.
19 Yoshiko Matsuura, 今よみがえる三島由紀夫—自決より四十年 [Mishima Yukio Remembered Today – 40 Years Since His Suicide] (Tokyo: Takagi Shobō, 2010).

20 "Suginami Adopts Contentious History Text," *Japan Times*, August 13, 2005, last accessed August 9, 2014, http://www.japantimes.co.jp/news/2005/08/13/national/suginami-adopts-contentious-history-text/ - .U73qo_mSzB0.

21 Philip A. Seaton, *Japan's Contested War Memories: The 'Memory Rifts' in Historical Consciousness of World War II* (London: Routledge, 2007), 52; and Yoko Watanabe, "Behind the Adoption of Tsukurukai Textbook," http://www.geocities.jp/lumokurago/english.htm.

22 Yoshiko Matsuura, "地方議員の出番です" [It's Time for Local Legislators to Take the Charge], *Nippon Kaigi Local Assembly League* (Homepage), January 1, 2007, http://prideofjapan.blog10.fc2.com/blog-entry-608.html.

23 "【追悼】田形竹尾先生を偲んで[桜H24/3/27]" ["Memorial" In Honor of Tagata Takeo (Sakura Heisei 24/3/27)]. *Nihon Bunka Channel Sakura*, March 27, 2012, https://www.youtube.com/watch?v=kpGp-WbF-ug

24 "【水島総】田形竹尾先生を偲んで[桜H25/3/7]" ["Mizushima Satoru" In Honor of Tagata Takeo (Sakura Heisei 25/3/7)]. *Nihon Bunka Channel Sakura*, March 7, 2013, https://www.youtube.com/watch?v=D4FqXBZHBbU

25 A list can be found on the Japanese equivalent of IMDB: http://www.tvdrama-db.com/name/p/type-ENSHUTSU=keyex-%E6%B0%B4%E5%B3%B6%E3%80%80%E3%80%80%E7%B7%8F

26 "【特別公開】映画「南の島に雪が降る」[桜H25/8/10]" ["Special Opening" Film: Snow Falls in the South Seas (Sakura Heisei 25/8/10)]. *Nihon Bunka Channel Sakura*, August 10, https://www.youtube.com/watch?v=O2_izEaxxVw

27 "【追悼】田形竹尾先生を偲んで[桜H24/3/27]" ["Memorial" In Honor of Tagata Takeo (Sakura Heisei 24/3/27)]. *Nihon Bunka Channel Sakura*, March 27, 2012, https://www.youtube.com/watch?v=kpGp-WbF-ug

28 "1-2【松浦芳子】 & 【植松和子】 ﾁｬﾝﾈﾙ桜の原点を語る" ["Matsuura Yoshiko" & "Uematsu Kazuko" Speaking about the Origins of Channel Sakura], seityannkoina1, December 22, 2010, https://www.youtube.com/watch?v=ZqH3Q-WhaqI

29 Yoshiko Matsuura, "誇りある日本をつくる会" [Association for Building a Japan That Has Pride] November 18, 2003, http://www.matsuura-yoshiko.com/nippon.html

30 "【追悼】田形竹尾先生を偲んで[桜H24/3/27]" ["Memorial" In Honor of Tagata Takeo (Sakura Heisei 24/3/27)]. *Nihon Bunka Channel Sakura*, March 27, 2012, https://www.youtube.com/watch?v=kpGp-WbF-ug

31 Satoru Mizushima, "映画「南京の真実（仮題）」製作と日本文化チャンネル桜の放送形態変更について" [Regarding "The Truth of Nanjing" Film and the Nihon Bunka Channel Sakura's Broadcasting Changes], *The Truth of Nanjing* (Blog), March 2007, http://www.nankinnoshinjitsu.com/blog/2007/03/.

32 "【草莽崛起】チャンネル桜二千人委員会へのご加入のお願い[桜H25/8/6]" ["The People Rise Up" Appeal to Subscribe to the Channel Sakura 2,000 Member Committee], *Nihon Bunka Channel Sakura*, August 6, 2013, https://www.youtube.com/watch?v=JJH9IZf_FYg

33 Data is available at: "日本文化チャンネル桜二千人委員会" [Nihon Bunka Channel Sakura's 2,000 Member Committee], *Basic Knowledge of Communication Terminology*, http://www.wdic.org/w/WDIC/%E6%97%A5%E6%9C%AC%E6%96%87%E5%8C%96%E3%83%81%E3%83%A3%E3%83%B3%E3%83%8D%E3%83%AB%E6%A1%9C%E4%BA%8C%E5%8D%83%E4%BA%BA%E5%A7%94%E5%93%A1%E4%BC%9A.

34 "【水島総】二千人委員会、感謝とご報告[桜H24/7/19]"["MizushimaSatoru" 2,000 Member Committee, Our Gratitude and Announcements], *Nihon Bunka Channel Sakura*, July 19, 2012, https://www.youtube.com/watch?v=czXiXp6ZaOg

35 "【感謝】10回目の開局記念日、「言志13」メルマガ化など[桜H25/8/15]" ["Our Gratitude" Tenth Anniversary, Genshi 13, Pivot to E-Zine (Sakura Heisei 25/8/15)]. *Nihon Bunka Channel Sakura*, August 15, 2013, https://www.youtube.com/watch?v=Sa343wYahms.

36 "【討論】パチンコとＩＲ[桜H30/7/28]" ["Discussion" Pachinko and Integrated Resorts (Sakura Heisei 30/7/28)]. *Nihon Bunka Channel Sakura*, June 28, 2018, https://www.youtube.com/watch?v=UmVJquHjieA

37 "【特別番組】「李承晩ＴＶ」特集[R1/9/26]" ["Special Broadcast" Syngman Rhee TV Compilation 'Reiwa 1/9/26)]. *Nihon Bunka Channel Sakura*, September 26, 2019, https://www.youtube.com/watch?v=WCxIQCBdj34

38 Robert Pekkanen, "Japan's New Politics: The Case of the NPO Law," *Journal of Japanese Studies* 26, no. 1 (January 01, 2000), https://doi.org/10.2307/133393.

39 "【追悼】田形竹尾先生を偲んで[桜H24/3/27]" ["Memorial" In Honor of Tagata Takeo (Sakura Heisei 24/3/27)]. *Nihon Bunka Channel Sakura*, March 27, 2012, https://www.youtube.com/watch?v=kpGp-WbF-ug

40 His estimated net worth was 1.5 billion USD in August 2020. "Toshio Motoya," *Forbes*, https://www.forbes.com/profile/toshio-motoya/#5d4dd70c2bb6.

41 Christopher Hughes, "Chapter Three: The Transformation of Civilian Control," *The Adelphi Papers* 48, no. 403 (April 2008): 53–66, https://doi.org/10.1080/05679320902955245.

42 "【訃報】花岡信昭氏ご逝去[桜H23/5/16]" ['Obituary' Hanaoka Nobuaki Has Passed Away (Sakura Heisei 23/5/16)]. *Nihon Bunka Channel Sakura*, May 16, 2011, https://www.youtube.com/watch?v=AgfR_-A1BUI.

43 Toshio Motoya, "By Becoming a Country of Freedom and Responsibility, Japan Will Regain Its Spirit," *APA Group Big Talk 229*, 2010, http://www.apa.co.jp/appletown/bigtalk/bt1008/bt1008_english.html.

44 "【直言極言】頑張れ日本！全国行動委員会結成大会＆全国総決起集会のご案内[桜H22/1/22]" ["Frank and Direct" Ganbare Nippon! National Action Committee and General Kick-Off Assembly Information (Sakura Heisei 22/1/22)]. *Nihon Bunka Channel Sakura*, January 22, 2010, https://www.youtube.com/watch?v=DazqFsn1nZM.

45 "【お知らせ】頑張れ日本！全国行動委員会結成大会＆　全国総決起集会[桜H22/2/1]" ["Announcement" Ganbare Nippon! National Action Committee and General Kick-Off Assembly (Sakura Heisei 22/2/1)]. *Nihon Bunka Channel Sakura*, February 1, 2010, https://www.youtube.com/watch?v=euWCEYTsuRM.

46 "「頑張れ日本！」安倍元総理の演説です！"[Ganbare Nippon! Prime Minister Abe's Speech], *Yamato Press*, February 20, 2010, https://www.nicovideo.jp/watch/sm9781378.

47 "【直言極言】頑張れ日本！全国行動委員会[桜H22/2/12]" ["Frank and Direct" Ganbare Nippon! National Action Committee (Sakura Heisei 22/2/12)]. *Nihon Bunka Channel Sakura*, February 12, 2010, https://www.youtube.com/watch?v=0wG1dgqBlL0.

48 Kevin Michael Doak, *A History of Nationalism in Modern Japan: Placing the People* (Leiden: Brill, 2007).

49 James Patrick Boyd, "States of the Nations: Nationalism, Narratives and Normative Change in Postwar Japan," PhD diss., Massachusetts Institute of Technology (2012), 346.

50 Nathaniel Michael Smith, "Right Wing Activism in Japan and the Politics of Futility," PhD diss., Yale University (2011), 207.

51 "【直言極言】国民運動・保守の在り方[桜H22/12/24]" ["Frank and Direct" The State of Civic Movements and Conservatism (Sakura Heisei 22/12/24)].

Nihon Bunka Channel Sakura, December 24, 2010, https://www.youtube.com/watch?v=n0c42t4vyV4.

52 "【ファシスト国家】人権蹂躙！韓国の呉善花氏入国拒否問題[桜H25/7/29]" ["Fascist State" Trampling on Human Rights! South Korea and the O Sonfa Entry Refusal Incident (Sakura Heisei 25/7/29)]. *Nihon Bunka Channel Sakura*, July 29, 2013, https://www.youtube.com/watch?v=Mgm7Wi9VQM8.

53 "【感々学々】長崎の鐘と、ケヴィン・ドーク氏の日本論[桜H25/8/9]" ['Feel and Learn' The Bells of Nagasaki and Kevin Doak's Nihonron (Sakura Heisei 25/8/9)]. *Nihon Bunka Channel Sakura*, August 9, 2013, https://www.youtube.com/watch?v=z5xcezh_qLk.

54 "【赤池誠章】今、国籍法を再び考える！[桜H25/6/18]" ["Akaike Masaaki" Let's Rethink Naturalization Laws Now! (Sakura Heisei 25/6/18)]. *Nihon Bunka Channel Sakura*, June 18, 2013, https://www.youtube.com/watch?v=PQ3QthHyv0E.

55 "【魔都見聞録】問題だらけの移民関連法案、日本のパスポートを守れ！[桜H26/6/30]" [Travels in the Devil's City Nothing but Issues with the Immigration Law Proposal, Protect Japanese Passports! (Sakura Heisei 26/6/30)]. *Nihon Bunka Channel Sakura*, June 30, 2014, https://www.youtube.com/watch?v=D_gg9UwdE4M.

56 "【村田春樹】外国人の「帰化・永住権」最新動向レポート[桜H22/12/27]" ["Murata Haruki" Report of the Newest Movements in Naturalization and Permanent Residency for Foreigners (Sakura Heisei 22/12/27)]. *Nihon Bunka Channel Sakura*, December 27, 2010, https://www.youtube.com/watch?v=VA8pQBqDEXQ.

57 "2/3【討論！】決定版！在日問題を考える[桜H25/11/16]" [2/3 "Discussion!" The Last Word! Thinking about the Zainichi Problem (Sakura Heisei 25/11/16)]. *Nihon Bunka Channel Sakura*, November 16, 2013, https://www.youtube.com/watch?v=PcbA77rSE1g.

58 "【【草莽崛起】皇統の断絶阻止！読売新聞糾弾！緊急国民行動[桜H24/1/23] " ["The People Rise" Prevent the Break-Up of the Imperial Line! Emergency Civic Action (Sakura Heisei H24/1/23)]. *Nihon Bunka Channel Sakura*, January 23, 2012, https://www.youtube.com/watch?v=PmZKD36h0Ow.

59 "【古谷経衡】「フジテレビデモに行ってみた！」に関しての声明[桜H24/3/1]" ["Kotani Tsunehira" Statement Regarding "We Visited Fuji Television!" (Sakura Heisei 24/3/1)]. *Nihon Bunka Channel Sakura*, March 1, 2012, https://www.youtube.com/watch?v=pFOej-55tM0.

60 "【1/3【討論！】国防としての反日メディア解体[桜H25/2/2]" [1/3 "Discussion!" Dismantling Anti-Japanese Media as a Matter of National Security (Sakura Heisei 25/2/2)]. *Nihon Bunka Channel Sakura*, February 2, 2013, https://www.youtube.com/watch?v=_P5iIKmJbdI.

61 "【草莽崛起】フジデモ書類送検の詳細と、反撃の抗議デモ[桜H24/9/12]" ["The People Rise" Details of the Fuji Protest Documentation Sent to Prosecutor and Counter-Protest (Sakura Heisei 24/9/12)]. *Nihon Bunka Channel Sakura*, September 12, 2012, https://www.youtube.com/watch?v=2cJD0h4JN5Y.

62 "【水島総】１年前のフジテレビデモでの書類送検について[桜H24/9/11]" ["Mizushima Satoru" Regarding the Documentation Sent to Prosecutor for Last Year's Fuji Television Protest (Sakura Heisei 24/9/11)]. *Nihon Bunka Channel Sakura*, September 11, 2012, https://www.youtube.com/watch?v=43cBQJz4iFc.

63 "【感謝】10回目の開局記念日、「言志13」メルマガ化など[桜H25/8/15]" ["Our Gratitude" Tenth Anniversary, Genshi 13, Pivot to E-Zine (Sakura Heisei 25/8/15')]. *Nihon Bunka Channel Sakura*, August 15, 2013, https://www.youtube.com/watch?v=Sa343wYahms.

64 Kōichi Yasuda, ネットと愛国　在特会の「闇」を追いかけて [The Internet and Patriotism: Pursuing the Darkness of the Zaitokukai] (Tokyo: Kodansha, 2015), 515–517. Kindle.
65 "【水島総】視聴者の問いに答える[桜H28/7/29]" ["Mizushima Satoru" Answering Viewer Questions (Sakura Heisei 28/7/29']. *Nihon Bunka Channel Sakura*, July 29, 2016, https://www.nicovideo.jp/watch/so29342550.
66 "8.28チャンネル桜水島総社長記者会見（主催：自由報道協会）" [August 28, Channel Sakura – Mizushima Satoru Press Conference (Held by the Journalists Association of Japan)]. *Kuukonuko*, August 29, 2012, https://www.youtube.com/watch?v=AVbBQc8Cd64.
67 "1/3【討論！】決定版！在日問題を考える[桜H25/11/16]" [1/3 "Discussion!" The Last Word! Thinking about the Zainichi Problem (Sakura Heisei 25/11/16)]. *Nihon Bunka Channel Sakura*, November 16, 2013, https://www.nicovideo.jp/watch/so22261372; and "【チャンネル桜 】2007年9月18日【281kg爆弾！】誰も知らない在日特権" [(Channel Sakura) September 18, 2007 "281 kg Explosive!" Zainichi Privileges That No One is Aware of]. *Teera_*, November 18, 2018, https://www.youtube.com/watch?v=-dTfdtPArjU.
68 For more discussion on this group, see: Ayako Hatano, "Can Strategic Human Rights Litigation Complement Social Movements? A Case Study of the Movement Against Racism and Hate Speech in Japan," *University of Pennsylvania Asian Law Review* 14, no. 2 (2019).
69 "【ヘイトスピーチ】京都地裁の政治判決、頭をもたげる人権擁護法案[桜H25/10/10]" ["Hate Speech' Kyoto Court's Political Decision, Human Rights Proposal Rears its Head (Sakura Heisei 25/10/10]." *Nihon Bunka Channel Sakura*, October 10, 2013, https://www.youtube.com/watch?v=9jfQ5NgqQdM.
70 Barak Kushner, "Nationality and Nostalgia: The Manipulation of Memory in Japan, Taiwan, and China since 1990," *The International History Review* 29, no. 4 (2007): 794, https://doi.org/10.1080/07075332.2007.9641141.
71 Hayata Takefumi, "Japanese Must Look beyond Lee Teng-hui," *Taipei Times*, May 28, 2001, http://www.taipeitimes.com/News/editorials/archives/2001/05/28/0000087621.
72 "Taiwan Ex-leader Lee Draws Fire over Islands," *AFP News – Yahoo Singapore*, September 13, 2012, https://sg.news.yahoo.com/taiwan-ex-leader-lee-draws-fire-over-islands-143320937.html.
73 "【新節目】台湾チャンネル　日台交流頻道[桜H25/10/10]" ["New Critical Juncture" Taiwan Channel, The Way to a Prosperous Exchange Between Japan and Taiwan (Sakura Heisei 25/10/10)]. *Nihon Bunka Channel Sakura*, October 10, 2013, https://www.youtube.com/watch?v=H7pvCrI7prM.
74 Yu-wen Chen, *The Uyghur Lobby: Global Networks, Coalitions and Strategies of the World Uyghur Congress* (New York: Routledge, 2014), 94–100.
75 "【イリハム・マハムティ】ＮＨＫ報道とウイグル問題[桜 H21/6/16]" ["Ilham Mahmut" NHK Broadcasting and the Uyghur Problem (Sakura Heisei 21/6/16)]. *Nihon Bunka Channel Sakura*, June 16, 2009, https://www.youtube.com/watch?v=RC_lZFAO8p0.
76 "1/3【イリハム・マハムティ】今、ウイグルで何が起こっているか[H21/7/8]" ["Ilham Mahmut" What is Happening in Uyghur Right Now? Heisei 21/7/8)]. *Nihon Bunka Channel Sakura*, July 8, 2009, https://www.youtube.com/watch?v=Wv0eFBjKSwM.
77 "【イリハム・マハムティ】尖閣、ウイグル問題をAPECに問う[桜H22/11/10]" ["Ilham Mahmut" Inquiring about the Senkaku and Uyghur Problems at APEC (Sakura Heisei 22/11/10)]. *Nihon Bunka Channel Sakura*, November 9, 2010, https://www.youtube.com/watch?v=n3FxamhkbEE.

78 "【原爆忌】ヒロシマは、ウイグルの被爆にも目を向けて[桜H23/8/19]" ["Nuclear Taboo" Hiroshima Should Also Be Aware of the Radiated Uyghur People (Sakura Heisei 23/8/19)]. *Nihon Bunka Channel Sakura*, August 19, 2012, https://www.youtube.com/watch?v=mT0nJBWZZjo.

79 "【Free Uyghur】拡大するアジアの人権危機、ウイグルから日本へ[桜H24/4/9]" ["Free Uyghur" The Expanding Asian Human Rights Crisis, From the Uyghur to Japan 7 Sakura Heisei 24/4/9)]. *Nihon Bunka Channel Sakura*, April 9, 2012, https://www.youtube.com/watch?v=pzjePYj3G-w.

80 "1/2【桜プロジェクトSP】中国の行っている残酷な現実[桜H25/6/10]" [1/2 "Sakura Project Special" The Reality of the Cruelties Occurring in China (Sakura Heisei 25/6/10)]. *Nihon Bunka Channel Sakura*, June 10, 2013, https://www.youtube.com/watch?v=RPSo4ct2-Co.

81 Chen, *The Uyghur Lobby: Global Networks, Coalitions and Strategies of the World Uyghur Congress*, 94–100.

82 Furuya Tsunehira, "The Roots and Realities of Japan's Cyber-Nationalism," *Nippon.com*, January 21, 2016. https://www.nippon.com/en/currents/d00208/the-roots-and-realities-of-japan%E2%80%99s-cyber-nationalism.html?pnum=2.

Bibliography

AFP News – Yahoo Singapore. "Taiwan Ex-leader Lee Draws Fire over Islands." September 13, 2012. https://sg.news.yahoo.com/taiwan-ex-leader-lee-draws-fire-over-islands-143320937.html.

Anderson, Joseph L., and Richie, Donald. *The Japanese Film: Art and Industry*. Clarendon: C.E. Tuttle Company. http://www.eiganokuni.com/kimata/08.html.

Axell, Albert, and Kase, Hideaki. *Kamikaze: Japan's Suicide Gods*. Harlow: Longman, 2002.

Basic Knowledge of Communication Terminology. "日本文化チャンネル桜二千人委員会" [Nihon Bunka Channel Sakura 2000-Person Committee]. http://www.wdic.org/w/WDIC/%E6%97%A5%E6%9C%AC%E6%96%87%E5%8C%96%E3%83%81%E3%83%A3%E3%83%B3%E3%83%8D%E3%83%AB%E6%A1%9C%E4%BA%8C%E5%8D%83%E4%BA%BA%E5%A7%94%E5%93%A1%E4%BC%9A.

Boyd, James Patrick. "States of the Nations: Nationalism, Narratives and Normative Change in Postwar Japan." PhD Diss., Massachusetts Institute of Technology, 2012.

Chen, Yu-wen. *The Uyghur Lobby: Global Networks, Coalitions and Strategies of the World Uyghur Congress*. New York: Routledge, 2014.

Doak, Kevin Michael. *A History of Nationalism in Modern Japan: Placing the People*. Leiden: Brill, 2007.

Falk, Ray. "Seed of Dragons." *Pathfinder* 56, no. 25 (1949).

Forbes. "Toshio Motoya." https://www.forbes.com/profile/toshio-motoya/#5d4dd70c2bb6.

Furuya, Tsunehira. "The Roots and Realities of Japan's Cyber-Nationalism" *Nippon.com*, January 21, 2016. https://www.nippon.com/en/currents/d00208/the-roots-and-realities-of-japan%E2%80%99s-cyber-nationalism.html?pnum=2

Galbraith, Stuart. *The Toho Studios Story: A History and Complete Filmography*. Lanham: Scarecrow Press, 2008.

Hatano, Ayako. "Can Strategic Human Rights Litigation Complement Social Movements? A Case Study of the Movement Against Racism and Hate Speech in Japan." *University of Pennsylvania Asian Law Review* 14, no. 2 (2019): 228–274.

Hughes, Christopher. "Chapter Three: The Transformation of Civilian Control." *The Adelphi Papers* 48, no. 403 (April 2008): 53–66. https://doi.org/10.1080/05679320902955245.

Ike, Nobutaka. "'National Socialism' In Japan." *Pacific Affairs* 23, no. 3 (1950): 311–314.

Japan Times. "Suginami Adopts Contentious History Text." August 13, 2005. Last Accessed August 09, 2014. http://www.japantimes.co.jp/news/2005/08/13/national/suginami-adopts-contentious-history-text/ - .U73qo_mSzB0.

Kamo City. "昭和３１年７月８日執行(第４回）" [Shōwa 31/7/8 Results (Fourth Time)]. Homepage, Last Accessed September 8, 2020. http://www.city.kamo.niigata.jp/section/senkyo/senkyo.data/sangi/S31.07.08.htm.

Kushner, Barak. "Nationality and Nostalgia: The Manipulation of Memory in Japan, Taiwan, and China since 1990." *The International History Review* 29, no. 4 (2007): 793–820. https://doi.org/10.1080/07075332.2007.9641141.

Martin, Robert P. "Japanese Ultra-Nationalists Reorganizing Forces." *The Gazette and Daily*, June 22, 1950.

Matsuura, Yoshiko. "誇りある日本をつくる会" [Association for Building a Japan That Has Pride]. November 18, 2003, http://www.matsuura-yoshiko.com/nippon.html.

Matsuura, Yoshiko. "地方議員の出番です" [It's Time for Local Legislators to Take the Charge]. *Nippon Kaigi Local Assembly League (Homepage)*, January 1, 2007, http://prideofjapan.bloghttp://10.fc2.com/blog-entry-608.html.

Matsuura, Yoshiko. 今よみがえる三島由紀夫—自決より四十年 [Mishima Yukio Remembered Today - 40 Years Since His Suicide]. Tokyo: Takagi Shobō, 2010.

McVeigh, Brian J. *Nationalisms of Japan: Managing and Mystifying Identity*. Lanham: Rowman & Littlefield Publishing Group, 2003.

Mizushima, Satoru. "映画「南京の真実（仮題）」製作と日本文化チャンネル桜の放送形態変更について" [Regarding "The Truth of Nanjing" Film and the Nihon Bunka Channel Sakura's Broadcasting Changes]. *The Truth of Nanjing (Blog)*, March 2007. http://www.nankinnoshinjitsu.com/blog/2007/03/.

Morris, Ivan I. *Nationalism and the Right Wing in Japan; a Study of Postwar Trends*. London: Oxford University Press, 1960.

Motoya, Toshio. "By Becoming a Country of Freedom and Responsibility, Japan Will Regain Its Spirit." *APA Group Big Talk 229*, 2010. http://www.apa.co.jp/appletown/bigtalk/bt1008/bt1008_english.html.

Nathan, John. *Mishima: A Biography*. Tokyo: Tuttle, 1981.

Nihon Bunka Channel Sakura. "秋ふかき　隣はなにを……" [Autumn Deepens, My Neighbor …]. Homepage, September, 2009. http://www.ch-sakura.jp/mizushima/1296.html.

Pekkanen, Robert. "Japan's New Politics: The Case of the NPO Law." *Journal of Japanese Studies* 26, no. 1 (January 01, 2000): 111–148. https://doi.org/10.2307/133393.

Sakurai, Yoshiko. "A Thought on True Patriotism and Japan's Search for Strategic Direction." *Yoshiko Sakurai Official Web Site*, December 21, 2010. http://en.yoshiko-sakurai.jp/2010/12/21/2264.

Seaton, Philip A. *Japan's Contested War Memories: The 'Memory Rifts' in Historical Consciousness of World War II.* London: Routledge, 2007.

Smith, Nathaniel M. "Right Wing Activism in Japan and the Politics of Futility." PhD diss., Yale University, 2011.

Tagata, Takeo. "Tokkotai and Me." *Kamikaze*, July 21, 2003. https://web.archive.org/web/20190224065109/http://www.http://geocities.jp/kamikazes_site_e/tokkotaiandMe.html.

Takefumi, Hayata. "Japanese Must Look beyond Lee Teng-hui." *Taipei Times*, May 28, 2001. http://www.taipeitimes.com/News/editorials/archives/2001/05/28/0000087621.

Watanabe, Yoko. "Behind the Adoption of Tsukurukai Textbook." http://www.geocities.jp/lumokurago/english.htm.

Yamato Press. "「頑張れ日本！」安倍元総理の演説です！"[Ganbare Nippon! Prime Minister Abe's Speech]. February 20, 2010. https://www.nicovideo.jp/watch/sm9781378.

Yasuda, Kōichi. ネットと愛国　在特会の「闇」を追いかけて [The Internet and Patriotism: Pursuing the Darkness of the Zaitokukai]. Tokyo: Kodansha, 2015. Kindle.

4 Rallying around the flag

Heroes, symbolism, and rituals

For over a decade, at the height of Japan's intense mid-August heat, hundreds of Japanese people have gathered to silently march through the streets of Tokyo carrying Japanese flags to the Yasukuni Shrine. Although they said nothing while they marched, a banner and an audio recording informed onlookers that they were carrying out a march to honor Japan's "heroic war dead" (eirei). Each year one man stands at the head of the marching columns, carrying a huge Japanese flag – Mizushima Satoru, the founder and president of Nihon Bunka Channel Sakura, an online broadcaster representing the views of Japan's assertive conservative right.

The march is carried out under the banner of Ganbare Nippon, an activist organization that Mizushima founded to facilitate demonstrations and protest campaigns promoted by Channel Sakura's programs. In his earlier career, Mizushima had decades of experience as a film director, a screen writer, and a set designer. He was a professional storyteller, well-versed in the importance of symbols and images. These skills, along with those of his fellow activists, came together to plan and create elaborate events like the silent flag march.

Successful political movements and organizations are sustained through the efforts of skilled social actors who strive to build solidarity through the creation of meaning for themselves and their followers.[1] In this chapter I will explore examples of Channel Sakura's meaning-making, which came in the form of references to familiar heroes, the use of patriotism-inspiring images, online activities that promoted a sense of virtual community, and participation in ritual performances such as the flag march. The shared meaning created through these processes helped Channel Sakura's activists and their supporters make sense of the world around them and relate their actions to the inspiring actions of previous generations of Japanese nationalists.

Patriotic heroes and men of action

In his research on Japan's far-right organizations, the uyoku, Nathaniel M. Smith described an extremist form of activism that alienated the general public. While these acts placed them on the fringes of society, Smith noted that the uyoku actually found a form of empowerment in them. They saw themselves as modern-day equivalents of famous Japanese patriot heroes, awakened to the truth and surrounded by masses of people who haven't yet realized it. Even if their deeds proved futile, they were living the life of an ideologically and morally pure patriot.[2] If they were on the right side of an issue, there was nothing admirable about compromising with those who were wrong.

It would be fair to say that Channel Sakura's use of historical heroes plays a similar role. Indeed, some, such as Mishima Yukio, are also venerated by uyoku activists. However, when Mizushima Satoru and his fellow Channel Sakura hosts talk about historical heroes, they do so in a way that relates them to peaceful grassroots activism. They link their ongoing activist campaigns to the long struggles faced by patriotic heroes. Channel Sakura's message is not one of futility. They do not think that they will forever be alienated from mainstream society. Rather, they look to small victories and paint a picture of sustained struggle that will eventually change the face of Japan. Like the heroes they idealize, they may not live to see the day that their vision is achieved, but there is a belief that success will come someday in the future.

Yoshida Shōin

On almost every Channel Sakura program and in almost every Channel Sakura and Ganbare Nippon street demonstration, there have been banners or text featuring the words "Sōmō Kukki" (草莽崛起). This can be roughly translated to "grassroots uprising." It is most commonly associated with the writings of Yoshida Shōin (1830–1859), a 19th-century samurai intellectual who helped spark the movement that overthrew the Tokugawa Shogunate and brought Japan into the modern world. Yoshida was executed by Tokugawa authorities before his dream could be realized and has since been considered a patriotic martyr.[3]

In his writings, Yoshida argued that Japan had fallen into a state of selfishness, with both commoners and the elites choosing personal comfort over confrontation with foreign threats to their nation:

> Nowadays all people live selfishly and seek only leisure in which to indulge their own desires ... The common man thinks of his life and his own and refuses to perform his duty to his lord. The samurai regards his household as his own private possession and refuses to sacrifice his life for his state. The feudal lords regard their domains as their own and refuse to serve king and country. Unwilling to serve king and country, at home they cherish only the objects of desire, and abroad they willingly yield to the foreign barbarians, inviting defeat and destruction. Thus the scenic beauties they enjoy will not long remain in their possession.[4]

As a solution to this problem, Yoshida introduced the idea of "grassroots heroes" who would be needed to act:

> Neither the lords nor the shogun can be depended on [to save the country], and so our only hope lies in grassroots heroes.[5]

The heroes would, if necessary, have to abandon their traditional loyalty to lords and act on their own:

> When I consider the state of things in our fief, I found that those who hold official positions and receive official stipends are incapable of the utmost in loyalty and patriotic service. Loyalty of the usual sort, perhaps, but if it is true loyalty and service you seek, then you must abandon this fief and plan a grassroots uprising.[6]

Yoshida's "grassroots heroes" carrying out a "grassroots uprising" were not peaceful. Their uprising did not consist of activists carrying placards and collecting signatures for petitions. Samurai inspired by Yoshida writings instead used political assassination and armed revolt to bring down the Tokugawa Shogunate. Later, in the 20th century, Yoshida's writings would be used to formulate an imperial bushidō ideology used to indoctrinate Japanese soldiers to loyally fight for the emperor in World War II.[7]

Channel Sakura and its activists have chosen a gentler interpretation of Yoshida's life and ideas. Emphasis is placed on an idealized view of Yoshida and his followers as middle- and low-ranking samurai who played a major role in the movement to overthrow the unjust Tokugawa Shogunate. They were "grassroots heroes" who placed their loyalty to the nation above all other things, helping to push Japan toward modernization.[8] In borrowing Yoshida's term for a grassroots uprising, Channel Sakura linked the situation of present-day Japan to the crisis Japan faced in the 1850s. Like Yoshida, they were among the first to discover a state of danger that the rest of the country was failing to realize, so they were trying to push their country into action.[9] Under banners bearing Yoshida's slogan, Channel Sakura's supporters were offered a chance to feel as if they are the modern non-violent version of Yoshida's patriotic samurai followers.

Saigō Takamori

Channel Sakura's second official slogan was Keiten Aijin (敬天愛人), meaning "revere heaven, love mankind." It was the favorite motto of Saigō Takamori (1828–1877), another samurai who achieved heroic status in the turmoil of the late 19th century. Like Yoshida, Saigō played an important role in bringing down the Tokugawa Shogunate and replacing it with an Imperial government. Both men advocated violent revolt in their lifetimes, were treated as martyrs after their deaths, and inspired later violent and non-violent political action.

The historical Saigō was a skilled military leader who, after resigning from his position in a regime he helped establish, grew disillusioned with its reforms and ultimately became the leader of a revolt against it. In the resulting conflict, the Satsuma Rebellion, Saigō's army of former samurai seeking to regain their once-privileged status, was defeated by the new Imperial Japanese Army. Tens of thousands of Japanese died in the process, including Saigō, who committed ritual suicide.

Saigō's final war has been viewed by some as a class war, in which the former oppressor class, the samurai, were fighting against the modern state, which had given various rights to commoners.[10] Saigō and the men who had fought alongside him were treated like criminals by the Japanese government at the time, and as such their souls were denied enshrinement as heroic war dead at Tokyo's Yasukuni Shrine.[11]

In the popular imagination, however, Saigō was quickly rehabilitated into a heroic figure. Both the earlier events in his life and his violent end as a rebel were celebrated as the actions of a selfless patriot. He became "a symbol for all forms of principled resistance" and "alternative to a statist, bureaucratic, and centralizing vision of modern Japan."[12] As years passed and memories of the negative aspects of the samurai era faded, the nostalgic idealization of the Saigō and the samurai virtues he represented were also embraced by the Japanese state, which pardoned him in 1889.[13]

Channel Sakura and Ganbare Nippon sought to emulate the virtues and political skills of the idealized Saigō Takamori. Saigō had a reputation of being liked by almost everyone he met, and his dedicated patriotism and respectable personality helped bring different groups together to fight for the emperor against the Tokugawa Shogunate. By drawing on this example, Channel Sakura encouraged viewers to see themselves as morally-upright individuals working with political organizations towards a common goal.[14] Just as Saigō fought alongside samurai patriots from different backgrounds, Channel Sakura saw itself as dealing with a diverse group of 21st-century Japanese patriots. In both cases, there was a need to put aside minor differences and band together to protect Japan.

Mishima Yukio

As I mentioned in Chapter 2, the novelist Mishima Yukio was an important figure in postwar Japanese right-wing activism. His suicide after an attempted coup d'état shocked many Japanese people, but it also inspired others. Several of Channel Sakura's founders were students at the time of Mishima's death, with some participating in right-wing student organizations, including Mishima's own Tate no Kai group. Therefore, it is not surprising that they would honor him as an inspirational hero.

Channel Sakura has produced programs to commemorate the anniversary of Mishima's death each year in November. These included the filming and broadcasting of anniversary ceremonies held by third party groups,[15] as well as programs in which Channel Sakura panelists discuss their views of Mishima.[16]

In one such program, filmed in November 2015, journalist Miyazaki Masahiro argued that there are crucial moments in Japanese history that occur once every 100 or 200 years in which one individual's actions shake the entire nation, producing a "spark of vitality." These important people may not have been honored at the time of their deaths, but later Japanese recognized their importance. The three most recent figures on Miyazaki's list were Yoshida Shōin, Saigō Takamori, and Mishima Yukio. Although mainstream Japanese society had not yet recognized Mishima as such a figure, Miyazaki predicted that things would change in 100 or 200 years and that Mishima would one day be revered as a holy figure with his own Shintō shrine.[17] Other panelists did not go so far as to claim that a Mishima Shrine would be built, but they expressed similar views about how Mishima was a great figure who had inspired people in Japan and the world.

Shortly after forming Ganbare Nippon, Mizushima Satoru shared his recollections of the day Mishima died. He was a third-year university student, and hearing about the SDF soldiers laughing at Mishima's speech and seeing Mishima's ultimate failure, Mizushima was moved to think about the state of postwar Japan. He was also influenced by Mishima's novels. When launching the Ganbare Nippon movement 40 years after Mishima's death, Mizushima said he was deeply influenced by the author. However, in contrast to the Tate no Kai, Mizushima saw his own movement as more like the patriotism of "rural samurai"– acting at a grassroots level.[18]

On numerous occasions Mizushima has commented on his memory of watching Mishima on television as the sound of news helicopters made it impossible for people to hear Mishima's speech. For Mizushima, it was an analogy of postwar Japan, in which the masses aren't exposed to the patriotic truth because of the interference of the mainstream media.[19] That media was, in his view, intentionally making Japan weaker.

Current events were also interpreted through the lens of Mishima's death. In a November 2019 editorial program commemorating Mishima, Mizushima tied the pro-democracy protests in Hong Kong to the teachings of Mishima. The events in Hong Kong were a reflection of Mishima's warnings that a comfortable lifestyle could not make up for a loss of national spirit. Just as the protesters in Hong Kong were risking everything to protect their national spirit from mainland China, Japanese people needed to look to Mishima's willingness to die in defense of his country. Mishima also called on supporters to attend Ganbare Nippon demonstrations supporting the brave Hong Kong protesters who were fighting for their country.[20]

In its videos, Channel Sakura portrayed its movement as a successor to the patriotic spirit of Mishima. Like Mishima, they were deeply concerned about the state of postwar Japan and worried that their country faced a dangerous future. Although they did not advocate a Mishima-style coup d'état, they appreciated Mishima's ideology and devoted themselves to protecting Japan. They saw themselves as trying to save the nation for which Mishima had given his life.

Japanese heroes during the Holocaust

In contrast to far-right nationalist movements in Europe and North America, anti-Semitism is not a major part of the ideology of Japanese nationalists. Rather than deny the Holocaust alongside its denial of Japan's wartime atrocities, Channel Sakura has used recognition of the Holocaust to its advantage.[21] The German genocide of the Jews is treated as a real historical event that cannot be denied and should be commemorated, in contrast to Chinese commemorations of events that

Japan's nationalist right believes did not happen, such as the Nanjing Massacre. Recognition of the Holocaust also provides a chance to tell viewers that pre-1945 Japan was a friend of the Jewish people and an opponent of racist ideologies.

The most famous historical figure used in these arguments is Sugihara Chiune, who served as a diplomat in wartime Lithuania and used his position to issue transit visas that helped Jewish refugees escape to Asia.[22] In a period in which Japan is internationally regarded as an enthusiastic friend of Nazi Germany, Sugihara serves as a useful example for those who want to argue that Japan did not support Nazi racism. In one Channel Sakura program from 2010, Sugihara was introduced as a perfect example of a Japanese hero that should be brought up when one travels abroad and gets into a discussion about wartime history.[23] International recognition of Sugihara's heroism has also been repeatedly emphasized as proof that Japan is receiving much-needed respect. Lithuania, which has turned its former Japanese consulate into a Sugihara memorial museum, has been described as a "pro-Japanese country."[24]

Channel Sakura has also introduced several wartime Imperial Japanese Army officers, Higuchi Kiichirō, Yasue Norihiro, and Inuzuka Koreshige, as heroic figures who rescued Jews from the Holocaust.[25] These military men, members of an army that has been demonized for wartime aggression and atrocities in Asia, were introduced as figures who have unfairly not received the level of attention that the world has given Sugihara.[26] Their actions, along with Sugihara's, have been contextualized as in line with Japan's Racial Equality Proposal of 1919, which was rejected by the other Great Powers and could have supposedly prevented the Holocaust if it has passed.[27]

This attempt to portray Japan as an anti-racist power that tried to protect the Jews was clouded by other programs, which have promoted anti-Semitic conspiracy theories. For example, in calling for resistance to a globalist world order that is under the control of powerful international financial organizations, Mizushima Satoru has claimed that Jews are at the center of such organizations.[28] Another example could be found in an August 2017 episode of Channel Sakura's news discussion program, Front Japan. It was co-hosted by former diplomat Mabuchi Mutsuo, who provided commentary on the "Jewish problem" (yudayajin no mondai). Mabuchi compared the efforts by American groups to remove statues of Christopher Columbus to Japanese revisionists' own fight against the historical perspectives forced on the world by Western powers. The view of Columbus as a heroic discoverer, rather than a villainous invader who stole native lands, was part of the untrue pro-Western history that was pushed on Japan and the rest of the world. Noting that the term "revisionist" has had a negative connotation, Mabuchi stated that these recent developments represented a big trend toward recognizing that revisionists are right. He then proceeded to discuss his own revisionist views about Soviet communism being a creation of Jewish revolutionaries who massacred countless Russians and how Hitler's Holocaust of the Jews was unfairly propped up as worse than the far larger atrocities committed by communism. This included the Nanjing Massacre, which Mabuchi believed was heavily publicized by China, as well as by Jewish historians in America, as a means of covering up the bad deeds of communist regimes. This was not Holocaust denial, but it did downplay the Holocaust while advancing an anti-Semitic interpretation of history.

Practical heroes

Several of the previously mentioned patriotic heroes were known for sticking to their ideals and choosing death, or career-suicide, over compromise. Their stories can be inspirational, but they do not constitute a model for successfully achieving one's results in a timely manner. They are extremely important and influential, but it is also important to note that Channel Sakura and its activists have often looked to examples of historical heroes who used diplomacy and compromise to attain their goals. Such figures are not the typical heroes one thinks of when hearing about Japanese nationalists. For example, in March 2012, Mizushima Satoru sought to inspire activists with a retelling of the stories of two historical figures – Komura Jutarō and Michael Collins.[29]

Komura Jutarō was a Japanese statesman and diplomat who served as foreign minister during the Russo-Japanese War. As the leader of the Japanese delegation at the Portsmouth Peace Conference of 1905, Komura was responsible for negotiating the treaty that ended the war on favorable terms for Japan. However, when the treaty was announced in Japan, public anger about the terms of the treaty led to city-wide rioting in Tokyo. The people expected a much more favorable treaty than the one Komura had delivered. According to Mizushima, Komura was a patriotic man with strongly held ideals, but he was faced with the reality that Japan's military and financial resources were nearly exhausted. Komura needed to agree to a settlement and was unfairly condemned as a traitor because of it. The Japanese who condemned him had expectations that did not fit with reality.

Mizushima used a non-Japanese example for his second story. Having recently viewed the 1996 film *Michael Collins*, he saw a parallel to Komura's situation in the life of the famous Irish independence fighter. Recalling the later part of the film, when Collins helped bring about negotiations with the British, Mizushima saw an example of another patriotic idealist who had to face reality. Despite being a "terrorist" who had taken extreme acts for the sake of his country, at the negotiations of the 1921 Anglo-Irish Treaty Collins accepted terms that granted Ireland independence but made the new Irish state a member of the British Commonwealth. In Collins, Mizushima saw a man who history had later judged as a hero, even though he was condemned at the time as a "traitor" who had compromised his ideals.

The two stories are used by Mizushima to explain the importance of realistic expectations. In their grassroots movement, they must expect to achieve change by "small steps," and that requires that they face the gap between the ideal and the realistic. That is how things really work in the "grown-up world."[30]

Symbols on the set

The programs of Channel Sakura were mostly filmed at its studios in Tokyo, where Mizushima Satoru's years of experience as a set designer have translated into visually pleasing newsrooms. These sets often included symbols and images tied to Channel Sakura's historical heroes, ongoing activism campaigns, and the natural beauty of Japan.

Channel Sakura's main slogan, Sōmō Kukki, was often prominently displayed on the set. While programs discussed a grassroots revolution, one saw the visual representation of such an idea in the background. For example, in a 2013 panel discussion program about the economic threats posed by China and South Korea, large banners bearing the calligraphy of slogan were placed along the walls of the room. Directly behind the discussion moderator was a television screen that cycled through images of beautiful Japanese nature, such as cedar trees, mountains, and streams. The screen also displayed quotations from texts by patriotic historical figures, such as Kusaka Genzui, a famous samurai who followed Yoshida Shōin's teachings.[31]

Channel Sakura news programs typically followed a format in which two or three people sat in front of large television screens. After Channel Sakura began its boat activism around the Senkaku Islands (discussed in Chapter 7), it became common to display footage of the Senkakus during every news program, regardless of whether or not the islands were being discussed. For example, in a December 2013 program focused on the Yasukuni Shrine's winter festival, the screen behind Mizushima and his co-anchor cycled through footage of the Senkaku Islands. Channel Sakura's fishing boat, the Daiichi Sakura Maru, was shown crossing in front of the largest of the islands, with text in the upper corner of the screen displaying Yoshida Shōin's "grassroots uprising" slogan. Desks were often decorated with Japanese traditional seasonal decorations. In this program it was a kadomatsu display of bamboo and pine for the coming New Year's holiday.[32]

A display of presents from viewers has also been a prominent feature of Channel Sakura programs. Every week, viewers from across Japan sent gifts to Mizushima and his news anchors, and the display of such gifts along with messages of gratitude became a ritual at the start or end of programs. The gifts were usually famous regional Japanese food products, such as premium rice, sweets, fruit, or sake. There are many videos of this kind, with such a wide variety of presents representing viewers in different regions of Japan. Such videos reinforce the idea that there is a nationwide grassroots community supporting Channel Sakura.

Virtual drinking parties

Not only are gifts from viewers proudly displayed on the camera, but some programs also feature the consumption and discussion of food. The food is very much presented in a way that propagates what Takeda Hiroko has referred to as the nationalist notion of "delicious food in a beautiful country."[33] Just like the displays of cedar trees and patriotic slogans on program sets, food is used to assert the wonderfulness of Japan, the nation that Channel Sakura and its activists see themselves as fighting to protect.

One of the most striking examples of this is the creation of a program in which viewers can join a live dinner with Channel Sakura president Mizushima Satoru.

Since 2015 Channel Sakura has used the live streaming features of both YouTube and NicoNico to air *Yozakura* (Cherry Blossoms at Night), a biweekly program in which special guests are interviewed by hosts Asano Kumi and singer/songwriter Saya. Upon the conclusion of each episode and the departure of the guest, an "After" program would be streamed in which Mizushima joined Asano and Saya to answer viewer questions over the course of an hour-long meal. The questions, which are taken from viewers watching the live broadcast, range from serious questions about the state of activist campaigns to asking Mizushima whether he prefers cucumbers or eggplant (he liked both if prepared as traditional Japanese tsukemono).[34] A live chatroom allowed viewers to communicate with the program hosts and with each other. Chatroom participants often mentioned that they were also having food and drinks while watching the program, engaging in a form of virtual *nomikai* (drinking party).

The sense of community in these virtual gathering was further reinforced in the choice of food and drink consumed. Mizushima and his co-hosts often drank beer, rotating between Japan's three major brands – Asahi, Kirin, and Sapporo. This selection of mass market beer reflected not only what average viewers would probably drink at home but also an assertion of Japanese identity through nationally iconic product consumption.[35] All three of Japan's iconic beer brands were recognized as delicious. Japanese sake was also frequently consumed during live broadcasts, with the hosts enjoying bottles donated by fellow activists and viewers.[36]

An example of this could be seen in an episode that aired on September 21, 2019, which began with the reading of a letter from Ageno Masahiro, a viewer in Kumamoto prefecture. Ageno identified himself as a member of the Friends of Channel Sakura (Tomo no Kai – discussed in Chapter 3) and announced that he has sent them bottles of Kohro, a high-quality sake produced in Kumamoto. He expressed a desire to see Mizushima, Asano, and Saya drink the sake on their program, noting that he would be wearing his Friends of Channel Sakura t-shirt and drinking his own glass while watching it on his computer screen. Ageno also sent them organic vegetables from his own garden, which were displayed alongside the sake in between Mizushima and his co-hosts. After finishing his letter, they thanked him for his generosity and applauded his hard gardening work. The bottle was poured into glasses, and after an initial toast, they sipped the sake while answering viewer questions. The viewers asked Mizushima about his views on typhoon relief efforts in Chiba prefecture, the upcoming Rugby World Cup, drone attacks in Saudi Arabia, his support for Taiwan's Formosa Television station, opposition to a consumption tax increase, and his annoyance at how younger Japanese people seem to laugh in a loud and phony manner. The discussion, which became more animated after several glasses of Ageno's sake, closed with thanks to viewers and a call of them to attend Saya's upcoming concerts and a Ganbare Nippon demonstration against tax increases.[37]

As mentioned in the previous chapter, members of Channel Sakura's Two-Thousand Member Committee, who donated 10,000 yen a month, are invited to offline social gatherings where they can drink and interact with Mizushima and other program hosts, but the membership and participation fees for such events are quite high. The virtual drinking party experience offered by Yozakura was completely free and offered a chance to have one's questions answered on air. Although viewers' faces were invisible to each other, the program may have provided the feeling of being at a social gathering. The chat room offered an opportunity for viewers to share their thoughts with each other and with Channel Sakura's hosts. Moreover, those who donated food and drinks had their letters read aloud and are thanked not only by Mizushima and his co-hosts but also by dozens of users in the live chatroom.

The COVID-19 pandemic forced a temporary suspension of the Yozakura program in the early April of 2020, as health guidelines strongly recommended against indoor social gatherings. The show resumed again in late June, with Mizushima and his co-hosts drinking a bottle of sake donated by a viewer in Hokkaido and eating sushi prepared from fish caught by their activists in the sea around the disputed Senkaku Islands (discussed in Chapter 7).[38] The concept of virtual drinking parties, which may have seemed odd to many people when Yozakura began its live-streamed broadcasts, had since become an increasingly accepted reality of the post-COVID life.[39]

Rallying around the flag at Yasukuni

As I mentioned in Chapter 3, Channel Sakura and Ganbare Nippon's offline demonstrations prohibited the carrying of flags that were not the Japanese national flag. This rule serves a double purpose – it prevents the use of potentially offensive flags and banners, and, perhaps more importantly, it gave protest marches a strong visual impact. Hundreds of people marching down the street can create a sea of Japanese flags – a striking display of unity (see Figure 4.1).

Between 2009 and 2020 I observed dozens of demonstrations promoted and organized by Channel Sakura, and the most visually impressive of these were their annual marches to the Yasukuni Shrine in Tokyo. These marches have been held on a symbolically important date – August 15 – the anniversary of Japan's surrender in the Pacific War and the anniversary of Channel Sakura's launch. For many of the participants, it was an event they attended after already visiting the shrine earlier in the day to offer prayers and offerings. A lot of preparation goes into the event, particularly the work of dozens of Ganbare Nippon volunteers who spend hours attaching hundreds of flags to flagpoles. The flags are distributed in a park about 15 minutes away from the shrine, where participants gather to listen to speeches from Mizushima and other Ganbare Nippon leaders, who stress the importance of the march. August 15 is the day when they describe themselves as becoming one with Japan's "heroic war dead," and the march is meant to show appreciation for those who died in World War II. The speeches also included references to the other activist campaigns taking place, such as the Senkaku Islands boat missions and the marches against mainstream media outlets.[40]

At the conclusion of the speeches, the participants stood at attention for Japan's national anthem and then began to file out of the park in pre-determined

Figure 4.1 Ganbare Nippon activists march around the corner in front of the Yasukuni Shrine on August 15, 2012. Every participant is carrying a Japanese flag. (Photo by Kaztima109)

groups. Led by Mizushima, they headed toward the Yasukuni Shrine in a four-person-wide column that stretched back for several blocks. A van with a loudspeaker preceded them, playing the instrumentals to "Umi Yukaba," a patriotic song from 1937 that was popular during the war. Every 30 seconds or so, a recording announced that they were the members of Ganbare Nippon, and they were coming to Yasukuni to express their gratitude to the heroic war dead.

Aside from the sound coming out of the loudspeaker, it was a silent march. Participants were not allowed to speak or shout slogans. They also did not carry signs, but many of the participants in the marches wore t-shirts identifying themselves as members of Ganbare Nippon, Kunimorishu, or other Channel Sakura–affiliated organizations, or t-shirts and caps with Japanese flags on them. Although the marches I observed did include some women and younger people, the majority of participants appeared to be men in their 40s or 50s. A very small number of participants, sometimes supported by younger relatives, were old enough to have lived during the war.

The march, which passed down the wide streets of Yasukuni-dōri through Jimbōchō and Kudanshita, often drew the attention of onlookers. Unlike other demonstrations held by right-wing and left-wing groups on the same day, it was very peaceful and did not involve clashes with police escorts or attempts to breach police barriers. This contrast was intentional. As I mentioned in the previous chapter, Channel Sakura has aimed to portray itself as leading a non-violent and law-abiding grassroots movement of ordinary Japanese people. Compared to the frighteningly loud uyoku, who dress in paramilitary uniforms and hold their own events near Yasukuni, the flag marchers appeared very normal.

This did not seem to be lost on onlookers, either. When observing the 2020 flag march, I overheard two construction workers commenting on the passing activists. One remarked that "this is peaceful and better [than the others]" (hei-wateki de kochi no hō ga ii). I also witnessed positive reactions from pedestrians, including applause and expressions of thanks to the marchers. In 2014 and 2015, I witnessed two separate instances of people on the street asking to join the march after it began and being given extra flags to wave. Given that many of the people who gather in the neighborhood around the Yasukuni Shrine on August 15 were traveling there to make offerings at the shrine, this kind of positive reception is not entirely surprising. I did not witness similar spontaneous responses of support from non-participants when observing other Channel Sakura demonstrations held in different neighborhoods of Tokyo.

After reaching another park closer to the shrine, the marching portion of the event officially ended. Participants were asked to gather again directly in front of Yasukuni's giant iron gate. They gradually trickled in and re-formed into a column. Standing at the front of the column, Mizushima and other Ganbare Nippon figures give short speeches thanking the participants. They also held a communal singing of Japan's national anthem, followed by "Umi Yukaba." Many of the participants knew the lyrics to the song:

> *Umi yukaba (If I go away to the sea)*
> *Mizuku kabane. (I shall be a corpse washed up.)*
> *Yama yukaba (If I go away to the mountain)*
> *Kusa musu kabane. (I shall be a corpse in the grass.)*
> *Okimi no he ni koso shiname (But if I die for the Emperor)*
> *Kaerimi wa seji. (It will not be a regret.)*

Umi Yukaba functioned much like a second national anthem for wartime Japan. It was played before the NHK radio broadcast announcing Japan's attack on Pearl Harbor.[41] As Japan lost the war, soldiers and Kamikaze pilots would sing it before heading out on suicidal missions. Through the song, the marchers were both honoring and connecting themselves with the Japanese who sacrificed themselves for the Japanese Empire. They were in the physical place where many Japanese soldiers, sailors, and airmen gathered to pray before going off to war, and it is also the place where the souls of those who never returned are enshrined. At the end of the song, they engaged in another act that Japanese soldiers were known to perform, "banzai" cheers for the emperor. These acts connected them to an imagined past and reinforced their commitment to continue activism for a country that they believed should better honor those who died in the war.

John Breen has written that the Yasukuni Shrine is a place of social importance for living people both to honor the war dead and to utilize their memory for modern meaning-making. Rites performed at Yasukuni generate "a sense of time collapsing: Japan is once more an Imperial Japan, a glorious empire, united in a spirit of loyalty and self-sacrifice." The organizations that worship there are working to help Yasukuni recreate an idealized past through the glorification of those who died in the war.[42] Ganbare Nippon's flag march is certainly an example of such a ritual. The participants in the march were born after the war and have no direct memory of the past they are commemorating. Akiko Takenaka has argued that members of these "postmemory generations" of Japanese have used revisionist narratives of the Yasukuni Shrine to come to terms with perceived trauma by recreating and taking "ownership of this inherited past that was never a part of their own experience."[43] The organizers of the event, however, would describe it as a natural act of patriotic gratitude to Japanese who fought and died for their nation.

The flag marches were emotionally powerful communal events, held at a symbolically important place on a symbolically important day. For those who could not physically attend the event, Channel Sakura produced video compilations which were distributed online. Throughout the march, Channel Sakura cameramen were running back and forth (see Figure 4.2), taking the best footage possible. When marchers sang, there were cameras on hand to get close-up shots. There was also a

Figure 4.2 Ganbare Nippon activists march down the street near the Yasukuni Shrine on August 15, 2020. A Channel Sakura camera films their progress. (Photo by Author)

camera placed on top of the van leading the march, providing a sweeping view of the marchers as they turned around corners. In post-production Channel Sakura superimposed photos of Kamikaze pilots over scenes of the march.

Mizushima, who marched alone at the front of the column with a large Japanese flag, was always being filmed by at least one of the cameras. Although other key figures in Ganbare Nippon marched behind a banner that lead the rest of the participants, there could be no question that Mizushima was their leader.

The viewers were given an audio-visual experience in honoring the war dead, and Mizushima ended the video by thanking the viewers for their continued support for Channel Sakura and Ganbare Nippon. The online response by viewers was overwhelmingly positive. For example, the 2013 video was viewed over 29,000 times and received 619 thumbs-up votes on YouTube (compared to just 17 thumbs-down votes).[44] Seven years later, after considerable growth in their subscriber count, their 2020 video received over 141,000 views, with over 6.3 thousand thumbs-up votes and only 146 down votes.[45] Many user comments complimented the beauty of the flags and the songs.

Conclusion

In this chapter, I introduced examples of how symbols, heroes, and rituals have been used to create meaning for Nihon Bunka Channel Sakura's activists and supporters. Their activism was tied to historical heroes; visual symbols of patriotism were ever-present in their programs; a sense of online community was re-enforced through gift-giving and virtual drinking parties; and their solidarity and commitment to the Japanese nation was reinforced through rituals such as the Yasukuni flag march.

In the following chapters, I will move on to detailed accounts of protest campaigns. In each of these campaigns, I will highlight how the skilled social actors within Channel Sakura and Ganbare Nippon sought out opportunities within fields of contestation, employing tactics that were meant to improve their position within each field while further creating a shared sense of mission and meaning for participants.

Notes

1 Charles Kurzman, "Meaning-Making in Social Movements," *Anthropological Quarterly* 81, no. 1 (2008), http://www.jstor.org/stable/30052738.
2 Nathaniel M. Smith, "Right Wing Activism in Japan and the Politics of Futility," PhD diss., Yale University (2011), 95–96.
3 Marius B. Jansen, *The Cambridge History of Japan Volume 5, The Nineteenth Century* (Cambridge: Cambridge University Press, 1989), 336.
4 *Yoshida Shoin Zenshu* vol. 4, 175, translated in William Theodore De Bary, Carol Gluck, Arthur E. Tiedemann, Willem Boot, William M. Bodiford, Andrew E. Barshay, and Yōngho Chōe, *Sources of East Asian Tradition: The Modern Period* (New York: Columbia University Press, 2008), 366

5 *Yoshida Shoin Zenshu* vol. 5, 315, translated in William Theodore De Bary, Carol Gluck, Arthur E. Tiedemann, Willem Boot, William M. Bodiford, Andrew E. Barshay, and Yōngho Chōe, *Sources of East Asian Tradition: The Modern Period* (New York: Columbia University Press, 2008), 366.

6 *Yoshida Shoin Zenshu* vol. 9, 239, translated in William Theodore De Bary, Carol Gluck, Arthur E. Tiedemann, Willem Boot, William M. Bodiford, Andrew E. Barshay, and Yōngho Chōe, Sources of East Asian Tradition: The Modern Period (Introduction to Asian Civilizations) 2008 (New York: Columbia University Press), 366.

7 Oleg Benesch, *Inventing the Way of the Samurai* (Oxford: Oxford University Press, 2016), 175–213.

8 "【倉山満】吉田松陰に学ぶ平成国防論[桜H22/10/27]" ["Kurayama Mitsuru" Learning about Heisei Defense Theories through Yoshida Shōin (Sakura Heisei 22/10/27)]. October 28, 2010, https://www.youtube.com/watch?v=TWX4wJgFEoo.

9 "【御礼】視聴者の方からの贈り物と吉田松陰の箴言[桜H24/5/24]" ["Our Thanks" Gifts from our Listeners and Yoshida Shōin's Book of Proverbs (Sakura Heisei 24/5/24)]. May 24, 2012, https://www.youtube.com/watch?v=foI8zuCUHEo.

10 Donald Calman, *The Nature and Origins of Japanese Imperialism: A Reinterpretation of the Great Crisis of 1873* (London: Routledge, 1992), 141–143; and Benesch, *Inventing the Way of the Samurai*, 37–38.

11 Akiko Takenaka, *Yasukuni Shrine: History, Memory, and Japan's Unending Postwar* (University of Hawaii Press, 2015), 47.

12 Mark J. Ravina, "The Apocryphal Suicide of Saigō Takamori: Samurai, Seppuku, and the Politics of Legend," *The Journal of Asian Studies* 69, no. 3 (2010), https://www.jstor.org/stable/40929189.

13 Benesch, *Inventing the Way of the Samurai*, 44–45.

14 "【藤井厳喜】保守運動・出よ、平成の西郷隆盛[桜H22/4/7]" ["Fujii Genki" The Conservative Movement: Come Forth, Heisei's Saigō Takamori (Sakura Heisei 22/4/7)]. April 7, 2010, https://www.youtube.com/watch?v=o-icUpJdvBQ.

15 "【三島由紀夫】没後41年、憂国忌・野分祭・四十一年祭[桜H23/11/28]" ["Mishima Yukio" 41 Years Since His Passing, Yūkokuki – Nowaki Festival, 41st Anniversary Memorial (Sakura Heisei 23/11/28)]. November 28, 2011, https://www.youtube.com/watch?v=UE4i6Bfmpy4; and "【松浦光修】三島由紀夫・森田必勝両烈士42年祭[桜H24/11/28]" ["Matsuura Mitsunobu" The Martyrs Mishima Yukio and Morita Masakatsu's 42th Anniversary (Sakura Heisei 24/11/28)]. November 28, 2012, https://www.youtube.com/watch?v=VYZrziJDZdc.

16 "【野分祭】三島・森田両烈士の遺した憂国の情[桜H22/11/25]" ["Nowaki Festival" The Patriotism the Martyrs Mishima and Morita Left Behind (Sakura Heisei 22/11/25)]. November 25, 2010, https://www.youtube.com/watch?v=hcG6h8AzZ-0.

17 "【討論！】三島由紀夫が伝えたかったこと[桜H27/11/28]" ["Discussion!" What Mishima Yukio Wanted to Say (Sakura Heisei 27/11/28)]. November 28, 2015, https://www.nicovideo.jp/watch/so27678179.

18 "【直言極言】「憂国忌」と「草莽崛起」[桜H22/10/29]" ["Frank and Direct" Yūkokuki and the Grassroots Uprising (Sakura Heisei 22/10/29)]. November 29, 2010, https://www.youtube.com/watch?v=z-6uXd7k1Lc.

19 "【直言極言】三島由紀夫の自決に思う[桜H23/11/25]" ["Frank and Direct" Thinking about Mishima Yukio's Suicide (Sakura Heisei 23/11/25)]. November 24, 2011, https://www.youtube.com/watch?v=EVVGAmsC06M.

20 “【直言極言】政治運動に己が命を懸けられるか？三島由紀夫「憂国忌」を前に考える[桜R1/11/22]” [“Frank and Direct” Could You Risk Your Life For a Political Movement? Thoughts Before Mishima Yukio’s Yūkokuki (Sakura Reiwa 1/11/22)]. November 22, https://www.nicovideo.jp/watch/so35988259.

21 Jeffrey J. Hall, “The Uses of the Holocaust in Japanese Conservative Internet Media,” *Journal of Asia-Pacific Studies* (Waseda University) 26 (March 2016).

22 J.M. Law, “Remembering Sugihara, Re-framing Japan in Europe: Holocaust Era Altruism and the Politics of Cultural Memory,” *Acta Orientalia Vilnensia* 7, no. 1–2 (2006), https://doi.org/10.15388/AOV.2006.3769.

23 “【感々学々】史実が語る日本の魂・ユダヤ人救出物語[桜H22/8/27]” [“Feeling and Learning” What Historical Facts Tell Us About the Japanese Spirit – A Story About Saving Jews (Sakura Heisei 22/8/27)]. August 27, 2010, https://www.youtube.com/watch?v=_TJw48y9nkc.

24 “【早い話が・・・】国家の存立、リトアニア帰朝報告[桜H22/5/7]” [“In short …” The Continued Existence of the State, Returning from Lithuania – Announcement]. May 6, 2014, https://www.youtube.com/watch?v=TbvJTo95Qog.

25 “【感々学々】史実が語る日本の魂・ユダヤ人救出物語その２[桜H22/9/3]” [“Feeling and Learning” What Historical Facts Tell Us About the Japanese Spirit – A Story About Saving Jews Part 2 (Sakura Heisei 22/9/3)]. September 3, 2010, https://www.youtube.com/watch?v=qqYxEoAWzf0; and Randolph L. Braham, *Contemporary Views on the Holocaust* (Boston: Kluwer-Nijhoff, 1983), 82–84.

26 “【ch桜北海道】杉原千畝の皆さんの知識はデマ[R1/5/13]” [“Channel Sakura Hokkaido” Everything You know About Sugihara Chiune Is False (Sakura Reiwa 1/5/13)]. May 13, 2019, https://www.youtube.com/watch?v=lARURRqVFiI.

27 “【魔都見聞録】日本の提案が受け入れられていたならば、ホロコーストは起こらなかったかもしれない[桜H26/3/17]” [“Travels in the Devil’s City” Had Japan’s Proposal Been Accepted the Holocaust May Not Have Occurred (Sakura Heisei 26/3/17)]. March 17, 2014, https://www.youtube.com/watch?v=tL2vIpwJUNA.

28 “【直言極言】草莽運動　何のために、誰が、どうやって[桜H25/5/31]” [“Frank and Direct” Grassroots Uprising: Who Can Participate and What Can You Do (Sakura Heisei 25/5/31)]. May 31, 2013, https://www.youtube.com/watch?v=mConU-s8XVU.

29 “【直言極言】国民運動、原理主義と現実主義の狭間で[桜H24/3/2]” [“Frank and Direct” Civic Movement: Between Fundamentalism and Realism (Sakura Heisei 24/3/2)]. March 2, 2012, https://www.youtube.com/watch?v=LEMeGeljnO4.

30 Ibid.

31 “2/3【討論！】中国・韓国経済の実態[桜H25/2/16]” [2/3 “Discussion!” The State of the Chinese and Korean Economy (Sakura Heisei 25/2/16)]. February 16, 2013, https://www.youtube.com/watch?v=SBNnb-IxWsA.

32 “【緊急告知】総理の靖国参拝に応え、明日官邸前で「ありがとう！」を[桜H25/12/26]” [“Emergency Announcement” In response to the PM’s visit to Yasukuni shrine let us go to the PM Office and Say our Thanks (Sakura Heisei 25/12/26)]. *Nihon Bunka Channel Sakura*, December 26, 2013, https://www.youtube.com/watch?v=tXdFrCbfn9s.

33 Takeda Hiroko, “Delicious Food in a Beautiful Country: Nationhood and Nationalism in Discourses on Food in Contemporary Japan,” *Studies in Ethnicity and Nationalism* 8, no. 1 (2008). HYPERLINK "https://doi.org/10.1111/j.1754-9469.2008.00001.x" https://doi.org/10.1111/j.1754-9469.2008.00001.x.

34 "【夜桜亭日記 #93 after】水島総が視聴者の質問に答えます！[桜H31/3/30]" ["Yaōtei Diaries #93 After" Mizushima Satoru Answers Listeners' Questions (Sakura Heisei 31/3/30)]. March 30, 2019, https://www.nicovideo.jp/watch/so34879000.

35 Nathalie Spielmann, Jennifer Smith Maguire and Steve Charters, "Product Patriotism: How Consumption Practices Make and Maintain National Identity," *Journal of Business Research* (2018). https://doi.org/10.1016/j.jbusres.2018.05.024.

36 "【夜桜亭日記　#103after】水島総が視聴者の質問に答えます！[桜R1/8/24]" ["Yaōtei Diaries #103 After" Mizushima Satoru Answers Listeners' Questions (Sakura Reiwa 1/8/24)]. August 24, 2019, https://www.nicovideo.jp/watch/so35579057.

37 "【夜桜亭日記　#105after】水島総が視聴者の質問に答えます！[桜R1/9/21]" ["Yaōtei Diaries #105 After" Mizushima Satoru Answers Listeners' Questions (Sakura Reiwa 1/9/21)]. September 21, 2019, https://www.nicovideo.jp/watch/so35710022.

38 "【夜桜亭日記 #118after】お久しぶりに、水島社長が視聴者の御質問に答えます！[桜R2/6/27]" ["Yaōtei Diaries #118 After" CEO Mizushima Answers Listeners' Questions for the First Time in a While (Sakura Reiwa 2/6/27)]. June 26, 2020, https://www.youtube.com/watch?v=wNdb_IB6uuw.

39 Kim Kyung Hoon and Akira Tomoshige, "Virtual Cheers! Japan's 'Nomikai' Goes Online for Coronavirus Time," *Reuters*, May 13, 2020, https://www.reuters.com/article/us-health-coronavirus-japan-online-drink/virtual-cheers-japans-nomikai-goes-online-for-coronavirus-time-idUSKBN22P04F.

40 "【海ゆかば】英霊に感謝し、靖國神社を敬う国民行進[桜H26/8/18]" ["Umi Yukaba" Citizen's March of Gratitude for the War Dead and Saving Yasukuni Shrine (Sakura Heisei 26/8/18)]. August 18, 2014, https://www.youtube.com/watch?v=nfAfOb1R5Ok.

41 Orbaugh, Sharalyn, "The Properly Feminine Nationalist Body in the Propaganda Kamishibai of Suzuki Noriko," *U.S.-Japan Women's Journal* 45, no. 1 (2013). https://doi.org/10.1353/jwj.2013.0017.

42 John Breen, "The Dead and the Living in the Land of Peace: A Sociology of the Yasukuni Shrine," *Mortality* 9, no. 1 (2004).

43 Takenaka, *Yasukuni Shrine: History, Memory, and Japan's Unending Postwar*, 168.

44 "【海ゆかば】英霊に感謝し、靖國神社を敬う国民行進[桜H25/8/16]" ["Umi Yukaba" Citizen's March of Gratitude for the War Dead and Saving Yasukuni Shrine (Sakura Heisei 25/8/16)]. August 16, 2013, https://www.youtube.com/watch?v=IdJxvxbsjMo.

45 "【戦後75年】令和2年8月15日・沈黙の日の丸行進～英霊に感謝し、靖國神社を敬う国民行進[桜R2/8/16]" ["75 Years After the War" Reiwa 2/8/15 – Silent Hinomaru Demonstration – Civic Action to Give Thanks to the War Dead and Respect the Yasukuni Shrine (Sakura Reiwa 2/8/16)]. *Nihon Bunka Channel Sakura*, August 16, 2020, https://www.youtube.com/watch?v=bA7v1c0eYrY.

Bibliography

Benesch, Oleg. *Inventing the Way of the Samurai*. Oxford: Oxford University Press, 2016.

Braham, Randolph L. *Contemporary Views on the Holocaust*. Boston: Kluwer-Nijhoff, 1983.

Breen, John. "The Dead and the Living in the Land of Peace: A Sociology of the Yasukuni Shrine." *Mortality* 9, no. 1 (2004): 76–93. https://doi.org/10.1080/13576270410001652550.

Calman, Donald. *The Nature and Origins of Japanese Imperialism: A Reinterpretation of the Great Crisis of 1873*. London: Routledge, 1992.

Hall, Jeffrey J. "The Uses of the Holocaust in Japanese Conservative Internet Media." *Journal of Asia Pacific Studies* (Waseda University) 26 (March 2016): 249–260. https://core.ac.uk/reader/286942950.

Hiroko, Takeda. "Delicious Food in a Beautiful Country: Nationhood and Nationalism in Discourses on Food in Contemporary Japan." *Studies in Ethnicity and Nationalism* 8, no. 1 (2008): 5–30. https://doi.org/10.1111/j.1754-9469.2008.00001.x.

Hoon, Kim Kyung, and Tomoshige, Akira. "Virtual Cheers! Japan's 'Nomikai' Goes Online for Coronavirus Time." *Reuters*, May 13, 2020. https://www.reuters.com/article/us-health-coronavirus-japan-online-drink/virtual-cheers-japans-nomikai-goes-online-for-coronavirus-time-idUSKBN22P04F.

Jansen, Marius B. *The Cambridge History of Japan Volume 5, Nineteenth Century*. Cambridge: Cambridge University Press, 1989.

Kurzman, Charles. "Meaning-Making in Social Movements." *Anthropological Quarterly* 81, no. 1 (2008): 5–15. http://www.jstor.org/stable/30052738.

Law, J.M. "Remembering Sugihara, Re-framing Japan in Europe: Holocaust Era Altruism and the Politics of Cultural Memory." *Acta Orientalia Vilnensia* 7, no. 1–2 (2006): 13–26. https://doi.org/ 10.15388/AOV.2006.3769.

Orbaugh, Sharalyn. "The Properly Feminine Nationalist Body in the Propaganda Kamishibai of Suzuki Noriko." *U.S.-Japan Women's Journal* 45, no. 1 (2013): 50–68. https://doi.org/10.1353/jwj.2013.0017.

Ravina, Mark J. "The Apocryphal Suicide of Saigō Takamori: Samurai, Seppuku, and the Politics of Legend." *Journal of Asian Studies* 69, no. 3 (2010): 691–721. https://doi.org/10.1017/S0021911810001518.

Smith, Nathaniel M. "Right Wing Activism in Japan and the Politics of Futility." PhD dissertation, Yale University, 2011.

Spielmann, Nathalie, Maguire, Jennifer Smith, and Charters, Steve. "Product Patriotism: How Consumption Practices Make and Maintain National Identity." *Journal of Business Research* (2018). https://doi.org/10.1016/j.jbusres.2018.05.024.

Takenaka, Akiko. *Yasukuni Shrine: History, Memory, and Japan's Unending Postwar*. Honolulu: University of Hawaii Press, 2015.

Yoshida Shoin Zenshu vol. 4, translated in William Theodore De Bary, Carol Gluck, Arthur E. Tiedemann, Willem Boot, William M. Bodiford, Andrew E. Barshay, and Yōngho Chōe, *Sources of East Asian Tradition: The Modern Period*. New York: Columbia University Press, 2008.

Yoshida Shoin Zenshu vol. 5, translated in William Theodore De Bary, Carol Gluck, Arthur E. Tiedemann, Willem Boot, William M. Bodiford, Andrew E. Barshay, and Yōngho Chōe, *Sources of East Asian Tradition: The Modern Period*. New York: Columbia University Press, 2008.

Yoshida Shoin Zenshu vol. 9, translated in William Theodore De Bary, Carol Gluck, Arthur E. Tiedemann, Willem Boot, William M. Bodiford, Andrew E. Barshay, and Yōngho Chōe, *Sources of East Asian Tradition: The Modern Period*. New York: Columbia University Press, 2008.

5 The 2009 anti-NHK protest campaign

In April 2009, Japan's public broadcasting channel, NHK, aired a documentary about Japan's imperialist "debut" through its colonization of Taiwan (1895–1945). The documentary was not a celebration of Japanese colonial achievements. Instead, it highlighted the oppressiveness of Japanese rule and the suffering it caused among the people of Taiwan. Information from historians was backed up by emotional interview footage of elderly Taiwanese people.

Although the documentary would receive critical acclaim, some members of Japan's conservative right believed it to be a biased and unfair portrayal of Japanese history. A coalition of right-leaning political groups organized a protest campaign against the public broadcaster. Utilizing internet media, they spread their criticism of the documentary, organized offline demonstrations, and gathered participants for what would be the largest class-action lawsuit in Japanese history.

This chapter explores this protest campaign, which stretched from 2009 until 2016, through an examination of one key organization – internet broadcaster Nihon Bunka Channel Sakura (Japanese Culture Channel Sakura, hereafter referred to as Channel Sakura). Under the leadership of its founder and president, Mizushima Satoru, Channel Sakura acted as a major player in a field of contestation over how Japan's public broadcasting network should portray history. Although activists did not achieve their stated goals and lost their lawsuit, Channel Sakura and its allies nonetheless carried out a remarkable aggressive campaign that put considerable pressure on Japan's public broadcaster and its documentary filmmakers. Together with other events that have occurred since 2009, this protest campaign may have contributed to a subsequent rightward shift in NHK's programming.

I begin this chapter with some background on past disputes over Japan's public broadcaster, demonstrating that a field of contestation exists in which different state and non-state actors seek to exert influence over its "unbiased" programming. I then go into detail about the 2009 documentary, the protest methods used by activists, and the results of their campaign. I close with an examination of more recent developments and the question of whether NHK has undergone a rightward shift since 2009.

Background – NHK, bias, and protest activities prior to 2009

Japan's national broadcasting organization is known by its acronym, NHK (Nihon Hōsō Kyōkai). Much like Britain's BBC, NHK is a publicly owned corporation that is primarily funded through the nationwide collection of license fees from television owners. As such, it is required by law to maintain political impartiality in its programming. In principle, this means that NHK should maintain editorial independence and not allow political pressure from the government or private groups to influence the content it produces. However, in recent decades, NHK's adherence to this principle has been challenged by groups on both the left and the right of Japanese politics.

Criticism from the political left often focuses on what they see as a reluctance by NHK to present strong criticism of the Japanese government, which for most of the period up to 2009 was under the conservative Liberal Democratic Party (LDP). While this may appear as an attempt to avoid political bias, it arguably results in pro-government reporting. This style of reporting could be influenced by the fact that despite having the appearance of total political independence, NHK must still receive parliamentary approval of annual budgets and subscription fee increases. In addition, NHK's board of directors consists of political appointees. While this may look like a recipe for complete political control of NHK, Ellis Krauss argued that this was a two-way street in which NHK desk reporters and NHK's large employee union could resist political pressure.[1] NHK does occasionally report news in a manner that displeases ruling party politicians, but the end result is self-censorship that produces a "news process designed to ensure a non-controversial news product that only informs but almost never explicitly offends."[2] This rather dull form of reporting stands out when viewed alongside the more critical news reports of private news outlets.

NHK's documentaries, however, are a different matter. Matsuda Hiroshi has argued that the Program Production Department of NHK, unlike the "pro-government" News Department, creates documentaries with "very liberal" views that often contradict government positions.[3] A prominent example of this occurred in the 1990s, when NHK produced a series of documentaries that were highly critical of the Japanese government's response to the redress demands of surviving wartime forced laborers.[4] Carrying out a wider overview of programs about war remembrance, Philip Seaton noted in 2007 that NHK programming had an "overall progressive leaning stance."[5]

Japan's conservative right views NHK as having a left-wing bias, not only in its documentaries but also in its news reporting. Conservatives have been publishing attacks on the NHK since at least the 1980s. Seaton has argued that "the sustained ferocious criticisms of NHK by nationalists" are indicative of NHK's overall left-leaning stance.[6] An example of this was Okada Shinichi's 1983 book *Questions for Biased NHK*, which attacked NHK's coverage of the 1982 history textbook dispute, accusing the network of "ignoring the national interest" and "distorting the facts," as well as being "traitorous" through its alleged violation of broadcasting law.[7] The conservative magazine *Seiron* has been a leading force of attacks on NHK, running 153 "NHK Watching" columns by revisionist academic Nakamura Akira from 1997 until his passing in 2010.[8]

The 2001 NHK Affair

The most well-known dispute over NHK's impartiality took place in 2001, involving *Towareru Senji Seibōryoku* (Questioning Sexual Violence in War), a documentary that addressed the "comfort women" issue as a war crime. The documentary, the second part of a four-part series on war responsibility, featured footage of the Women's International War Crimes Tribunal, a mock war crimes tribunal organized by left-wing activists of the NGO Violence Against Women in War Network Japan (VAWW-NET Japan). After a presentation of evidence, the tribunal ruled "that Japan's military sexual slavery, known as the comfort women system, was not only a war crime, but a crime against humanity." It found "the Showa Emperor Hirohito guilty, and the Japanese government to have incurred state responsibility."[9] However, when NHK aired the documentary about the tribunal, the final verdict was not included and scenes of the tribunal were "cut in an unnatural way, so that the line of argument they wished to present was not communicated to the viewers."[10] Moreover, NHK included an interview with conservative historian Hata Ikuhiko, an opponent of the tribunal. In a protest letter to NHK, VAWW-NET complained that the documentary was "completely different from what we were expecting" and did not present what they considered "a fair and balanced account" of their activities.[11]

The topic of the documentary was known to the public before it aired, attracting protests from the right. During the editing stage of the film product, NHK faced a "state of semi-siege, as rightists mobilized and sound trucks circled the NHK building blaring hostile messages and employees were jostled and abused as they entered or left the premises."[12] Left-leaning critics of NHK argued that the pressure from these protests directly caused NHK to make last-minute changes to the documentary and add interview footage of Hata, who was well known for his view that comfort women were not systematically coerced into sexual slavery by the Japanese military. Hata, who attended just one day of the tribunal's proceedings, criticized it as a one-sided endeavor. Recalling the tribunal in a later book, Hata compared its participants to a fanatical religious cult and dismissed its ruling as a "kangaroo court" with no one present to defend the accused, all of whom were dead.[13]

VAWW-NET activists had agreed to the documentary filming with the expectation that their tribunal would be fairly depicted. They were shocked to find that the final cut of the documentary had instead failed to communicate the tribunal's ruling and included statements from such a harsh critic.

In response, VAWW-NET took NHK to court. A lawsuit was filed against NHK and the subcontractors that created the documentary, arguing that the parties had violated VAWW-NET's trust by bowing to right-wing political pressure and making fundamental alterations to the program without prior consultation or explanation. The activists sought 20 million yen in damages. Initial court decisions were favorable. In 2001, a Tokyo District Court ruling found that a subcontractor had committed a violation of trust and ordered that 1 million yen in compensation be paid. The same ruling upheld NHK's freedom to edit programming and concluded that the edits had not been made as a result of political pressure. NHK and the subcontractor appealed to the Tokyo High Court, hoping to have the compensation ruling thrown out.

In the interval between the appeal and the Tokyo High Court decision, journalists uncovered new information. The *Asahi Shimbun* broke a story based on interviews with an NHK whistleblower, alleging that the documentary had, in fact, been edited in direct response to political pressure. The whistleblower named two prominent LDP Diet lawmakers, Deputy Chief Cabinet Secretary Abe Shinzō and Nakagawa Shōichi, as having visited and pressured NHK the day before the documentary aired.[14] The meeting took place at a time when NHK's budget would soon be going up for an approval vote in the Diet, so it was arguably a period in which NHK could be politically pressured by important figures in the ruling party. NHK, however, denied the content of the article, claiming that Nakagawa had not visited their offices and that a meeting with Abe had taken place but not influenced the decision to edit the documentary.[15] Abe also acknowledged that the meeting took place, claiming that he voiced his concern about NHK upholding its commitment to unbiased programming but denying that he had pressured the broadcaster into censoring the documentary. The *Asahi Shimbun* later announced that its report about the meeting had contained "uncertain" information.[16]

In a more recent retelling of these events, Michael Cucek has argued that too much attention has been given to Abe and Nakagawa. Many accounts have ignored another politician's influence, Katayama Toranosuke, Minister for Public Management, Home Affairs, Posts, and Telecommunications. Katayama made a similar visit to NHK a few days earlier to express his own concerns about the documentary. As the cabinet minister most directly responsible for telecommunications, Katayama may have actually been as influential, if not more so, than Abe and Nakagawa.[17]

When the appeal reached the Tokyo High Court in 2007, its ruling seemed to reflect the new revelations about political pressure. It found that both NHK and its subcontractor were at fault for failing to provide an explanation before editing the documentary, and they were ordered to pay 2 million yen in damages. This was, however, only a temporary cause of celebration for the VAWW-NET activists. The defendants once again appealed the case, this time to the Supreme Court.

The final decision on this case, issued by the Supreme Court in 2008, was a legal victory for NHK and its production company. The Court favored NHK's explanation that broadcasters have the right to freely edit their productions and that the trust and expectations of the plaintiffs were not subject to legal protection. Moreover, because no "enormous burdens" had been placed on the VAWW-NET activists, there was no justification for monetary compensation.

Although it was a legal loss for the activists, it has been argued that the court case helped spread awareness about both the tribunal and the degree to which politicians were attempting to intervene in NHK's nominally independent production process. [18]

The 2001 NHK Affair has been described as an example of a public broadcaster being pressured by rightists into censoring a documentary that focused on Japanese war crimes. It may have also led NHK and the *Asahi Shimbun* to tone down later coverage of the "comfort women" issue.[19] Tessa Morris-Suzuki and Nakano Kōichi have both cited this incident as an example of how language about the need for "fair" and "balanced" reporting can be used to intimidate and hinder journalists who criticize the status quo or report on controversial topics.[20]

When the 2001 NHK Affair came to a conclusion with the 2008 Supreme Court Ruling, the stage was set for a new round of contention. It was clear that the public broadcaster's "neutral" programming could be influenced by outside actors. In addition, the progressive organization that had filed the lawsuit against NHK had demonstrated the potential benefits of legal action – both in terms of putting pressure on NHK and in terms of drawing public attention to issues of political bias.

Although the above-mentioned studies argued that the 2001 NHK Affair was a victory for the right, it did not mean that NHK's progressive-leaning filmmakers and producers stopped making programs that angered nationalists. Documentaries about war history, a major topic of political controversy in Japan, continued to be made and continued to reflect non-nationalistic viewpoints. NHK's Program Production Department had suffered a blow with the "comfort women" documentary but was still punching back with serious programming. Thus, a field of contestation over NHK's programming remained, with various actors fighting to influence the nature of the national broadcaster's take on historical issues.

Progressive, left-leaning groups and the assertive conservative right were in conflict over contradicting conceptions of "bias" and "truth." To the left, NHK should have made documentaries reflecting a progressive view of history (in line with mainstream academic research) because such documentaries would represent a true account of history and fulfill NHK's obligations to viewers. To the right, documentaries that reflected a progressive view of history are biased and untruthful. Each side viewed its historical perspective as the truth, and the other side's perspective as not grounded in truth and harmful to Japan.

Within this field of contestation, the challengers on the right sought out opportunities to improve their position. In the 2001 case, conservative challenges to the documentary caused an alteration in favor of their historical viewpoints. However, left-leaning activists, who constituted actors within the field fighting to defend NHK's filmmakers from conservative influence, employed a lawsuit to further their cause. In the following sections of this chapter I will detail the 2009 anti-NHK campaign, in which the conservative right appeared to have learned from the left's use of a lawsuit to increase public attention to a cause. The challengers also had access to internet media, using Channel Sakura as a platform to spread awareness and organize their campaign in absence of attentive mainstream media reporting on their cause.

Launching the *Japan Debut* protest campaign

On April 5, 2009, NHK aired the first in the *Japan Debut* series of documentaries, a subsection of *Project Japan* that was meant to explore Japan's modernization and quest for great power status from the opening of the port of Yokohama in 1859 to the end of the Pacific War in 1945. This documentary, entitled *A First-Rate Asian Power* (*Ajia no Ittō Koku*), focused on Japan's colonization of Taiwan. Utilizing historical documents, interviews with international scholars, and the personal testimony of Taiwanese people who had lived under Japanese rule, it explained the motivations that led Japan to become a colonial power and the impact of its policies on Taiwanese people.

The documentary's portrayal of the negative aspects of colonialism – political suppression, racial and ethnic discrimination, the mistreatment of indigenous peoples, military conscription, and policies that suppressed local culture and religion – angered Japan's right and pro-Taiwan independence groups. A coalition of organizations, including Channel Sakura, launched a protest campaign against NHK, accusing the public broadcaster of violating its legal obligation to produce politically neutral programs. They accused NHK of selectively editing interviews, intentionally using incorrect or misleading terminology, and presenting false information as if it was factual. In their judgment, NHK's "biased and fabricated" documentary was created with the intent of convincing viewers that Japanese rule of Taiwan was evil and that the Taiwanese people felt deep resentment toward Japan.[21]

The first group to respond to the documentary was the Friends of Lee Teng-Hui Association in Japan, a chapter of a network of organizations that supported former Taiwanese president Lee Teng-Hui. As Lee was often regarded as one of the most pro-Japanese leaders of Taiwan and a friend of Japanese conservatives, the Japan chapter of this organization counted several prominent conservative figures among its members. The Association's president in 2009 was Odamura Shirō, vice-chairman of the Nippon Kaigi, as well as head of Meiseisha, the publishing company that specialized in nationalist literature and had published an internationally controversial history textbook for Japanese schools.[22] Included among the Association's vice-presidents and directors were Okazaki Hisahiko of Tsukurukai and Kase Hideaki of the Society for the Dissemination of Historical Fact. According to Wikipedia, it had 20 chapters in Japan and a membership of about 1,500 people.[23] Its e-magazine, which was sent out about three times a week during the protest campaign, had over 2,900 e-mail subscribers.[24] The Association sent a protest letter to NHK on April 10, five days after the program aired. It was also joined by the Taiwan Research Forum, an organization headed by Nagayama Hideki. Nagayama was also a member of the Friends of Lee Teng-Hui Association in Japan, the secretary of Ganbare Nippon, and a regular contributor to Channel Sakura programs.[25]

As explained in Chapter 3, pro-Taiwan independence groups aligned themselves with Japanese nationalists because both groups benefited from a view of history that shows Taiwan as a separate entity from China. By highlighting Japanese colonialism as a period of improvement for Taiwan, rather than as a period of Japanese invaders taking over a piece of Chinese territory, Taiwanese independence activists could emphasize that Taiwan has developed an identity that sets it apart from mainland China. This view is in harmony with the Japanese conservative right's favored view of history. In addition, Taiwanese independence activists and Japan's conservative right shared intensely negative views of mainland China's government and foreign policy. Thus, the membership and leadership of organizations such as the Friends of Lee Teng-Hui overlapped considerably with that of Japanese nationalist organizations.

It is particularly noteworthy that Kase Hideaki was the director of the Association. In Chapter 3, I noted that Kase helped bring together the original founders of Channel Sakura. It was in Kase's office that Mizushima Satoru, president of Channel Sakura, was introduced to co-founders Matsuura Yoshiko and Tagata Takeo. Just one day after the Friends of Lee Teng-Hui Association in Japan sent their first protest letter to NHK, Channel Sakura began making programs attacking the documentary.[26]

First responses

On April 16, 2009, Channel Sakura aired a 3-hour discussion panel about the documentary.[27] The panelists represented both Channel Sakura and the pro-Taiwan independence groups that would ally with it in the coming protest campaign. They included:

- **Odamura Shirō** – former president of Takushoku University, vice-chairman of Nippon Kaigi, and head of the Friends of Lee Teng-Hui Association in Japan
- **Koh Se-kai** – former de facto Taiwanese ambassador to Japan (2004–2008) and Taiwanese independence activist
- **Nishimura Shingo** – a House of Representatives lawmaker involved in conservative history causes
- **Matsuura Yoshiko** – an assemblywoman for Tokyo's Suginami ward, member of Nippon Kaigi, and co-founder of Channel Sakura
- **Yūhara Masataka** – board member of the Friends of Lee Teng-Hui Association in Japan
- **Lin Jianliang** – a Taiwanese resident of Japan, leader of the Voice of Taiwan, and member of the Friends of Lee Teng-Hui Association in Japan. In the early 2000s, he led the Name Rectification Movement that successfully allowed Taiwanese residents of Japan to have "Taiwan" listed as their nationality on Japanese documents[28]
- **Nagayama Hideki** – head of the Taiwan Research Forum

One could call this program a very early reaction to the documentary. So early, in fact, that many of the panelists hadn't yet seen it. This program took the form of collaborative storytelling, with each person sharing reactions to the documentary. Unable to really dig into the content of the documentary, most of the panelists instead focused on criticizing negativity about the colonization of Taiwan. They took turns sharing their own experiences visiting Taiwan or living in Taiwan, using those stories as proof that Taiwanese people did not resent Japan. They spoke of their personal anger or sense of victimization when seeing the documentary or when they were told about the documentary.

For example, Matsuura Yoshiko recalled a recent visit to Taiwan as part of a group of politicians on a fact-finding and cultural exchange mission. Her experience was one of meeting many Taiwanese who loved Japan. Displaying tourist photos, she told viewers about visiting a university campus in Tainan, where she found a Taisho Era monument that commemorated a visit by the then Crown Prince of Japan. It was in a remarkably good state, meaning that the Taiwanese had maintained and protected it over the years. She contrasted it to another of her tourist photos, depicting a statue of Chiang Kai-shek that was overgrown with grass and in a sad state of disrepair. The second statue was apparent proof that Chiang's postwar regime was viewed as worse than Japanese colonial rule.

Matsuura also told the panel about her experience hosting a Taiwanese exchange student at her Tokyo home. Although ten years had since passed, she remembered well how the Taiwanese girl was so happy to be doing a home stay in Japan. This personal experience was more proof that Taiwanese people did not hate Japan. Why, she asked, was NHK trying to convince Japanese viewers that Taiwan hated them?

Lin Jianliang told everyone that he had been looking forward to the documentary because it was about his country. However, a few minutes into the broadcast he determined it was "not the Taiwan I know" – instead, it was the exact opposite. It was a Taiwan that existed only inside an NHK documentary. Lin was angered to see a program that was so different from the "truth" that he knew. He even claimed that it was worse than the kind of "brainwashing" propaganda documentaries that would air on Taiwanese TV during the era of the Nationalist Chinese dictatorship.

Lin also presented anecdotes about how Taiwanese appreciated Japanese colonialism and loved Japan. His father, who had grown up under Japanese rule, warmly welcomed Japanese guests to their home in the postwar years. Lin also noted that author Ka Tokuzō, who had experienced life in colonial Taiwan, loved Japan's language and culture. The NHK documentary had featured Ka making negative comments about the colonial period. Lin went on to discuss scenes from recent Taiwanese films that were set in the colonial era. One example included a scene in which Taiwanese women encountered a Japanese soldier in their village and, witnessing his kindness, concluded that Japanese are polite and respectful.

Lin shared these stories as a representation of how modern Taiwanese held feelings of friendless and nostalgia toward Japan.

The other Taiwanese panelist, Koh Se-kai, expressed his displeasure about how the documentary put Taiwan on the same level as "anti-Japanese" China and North Korea. The documentary, he argued, was destroying the positive image of Taiwan that exists in Japan. As a Taiwanese he agreed that there were some bad aspects of Japanese colonial rule of Taiwan but felt the NHK documentary had absolutely no balance. He accused NHK of selectively editing interviews with elderly Taiwanese to only show negative things that they said.

Nishimura Shingo hadn't seen the documentary, so he based his commentary on secondhand information he'd obtained from friends who watched it. He also mentioned his suspicions about the general nature of NHK, which had a long history of propaganda-making. In fact, he claimed, NHK was involved in making propaganda for America during the postwar US Occupation of Japan. Nishimura then asserted that the same kind of thing was happening in 2009; only this time NHK was part of a Chinese communist "information war." In his view, the documentary was part of a secret plan to draw Taiwan away from Japan and into communist China's orbit.

Yūhara Masataka agreed that the documentary was "propaganda" produced from a pro-China standpoint. He expressed confidence that it did not represent the true voice of Taiwanese people. To illustrate the damage that the documentary had done to Japan–Taiwan relations, Yūhara told a story about a phone call he received the day after it aired. The caller, whose father had been a Japanese colonial official in Taiwan, was distraught after watching the documentary. NHK's historical account, which emphasized the racism and cruelty of Japanese rule, made the caller uneasy about what their father may have done in Taiwan. The caller was convinced that Taiwanese people must resent and hate Japan. Yūhara argued that the documentary, which was based on "fabrications," was tricking Japanese into thinking Taiwan was their enemy.

The program ended with moderator Mizushima Satoru calling on viewers to voice their displeasure directly to NHK. On-screen instructions were provided on how to e-mail NHK and officially lodge complaints.

Channel Sakura gathered together people in the room and the viewers at home to share stories and spin together a narrative that would drive their protest campaign. Their own encounters with Taiwanese and their own retelling of stories from Taiwanese people were presented as evidence of both NHK's distortion of the truth and their shared sense of moral indignation. Their stories, all of which aimed in the same direction, built solidarity between their respective organizations and reinforced their collective dislike of NHK.

In studying how human beings make sense of anomalous situations, psychologists have demonstrated the importance of storytelling. Stories help us make sense of the unknown, help elicit and channel emotional responses, and help sustain identities at an individual and group level. They are important form of meaning-making that contributes to collective action[29]. And it could be said that they were fulfilling such a role in this Channel Sakura program.

Through YouTube the action spread to an online space, where viewers also engaged in the form of meaning-making through leaving comments on the video program. For example, one user posted this about the NHK "traitors" in response to part 5 of the video:[30]

> I welcome friendship between Japan and Taiwan! Both countries should kick out the traitors and work together – the people and the government – towards prosperity and good relations. Let's send protest e-mails and calls about NHK's distortion of the truth. And let's punish NHK by spreading the movement to stop paying NHK fees.

Another wrote in response to part 1:

> NHK is forgetting that its sponsors are the Japanese people. This is a great crime.

The majority of comments posted in response to the video program expressed similar sentiments.

Issues of contention within the documentary

Although Channel Sakura's initial program about the documentary lacked in specifics, activists quickly devoted great time and effort to documenting every point they found to be unfair or inaccurate. Channel Sakura and its activist reporters would go on to produce many hours of programs devoted to attacking the one-hour documentary. In this section, I review several of the major complaints they had about the documentary and how they collected and spread information supporting their cause. I follow up each description with a summary of NHK's official responses, which were posted online in June and July 2009.

Deceptive editing of interviews with elderly Taiwanese

A major point of complaint for activists was the documentary's numerous scenes of elderly Taiwanese recalling negative aspects of Japanese rule. This portrayal flew in the face of the conservative right's beliefs about history and Taiwan's status as a pro-Japanese nation. An effort was thus undertaken by Channel Sakura to travel to Taiwan and create in-depth reports that discredited the documentary.

On April 21, 2009 – a mere two weeks after the original program aired on NHK – Channel Sakura aired its first report from Taiwan. Its reporters were determined to track down each of the elderly Taiwanese people who had appeared in the documentary, interview them, and demonstrate that they had positive views of the colonial period. This time-consuming effort produced remarkable success.

Channel Sakura's interviews put elderly Taiwanese on the record as having extremely positive views of Japan and their life under Japanese rule. Its reporters showed Taiwanese clips of themselves as they appeared on NHK, explained activists' complaints about the nature of the documentary, and asked the Taiwanese for comments. Many of the interviewees claimed to have mentioned both the positives and negatives of Japanese rule when interviewed by NHK and expressed agreement with Channel Sakura that more positive quotes should have been included in the documentary.[31]

The first few minutes and the ending of *A First-Rate Asian Power* included remarkable footage of elderly Taiwanese men gathered at Taipei's Bangka Park, all of whom were eager to demonstrate their Japanese language ability and talk about the colonial period. Several of the men could still recall the lyrics to popular wartime songs and slogans. As they performed the "Senjinkun no Uta" (Song of the Senjinkun), "Taiwangun no Uta" (Song of the Taiwan Army), and "Gunkan Kōshinkyoku" (Gunkan March), NHK's narrator noted that many young Taiwanese were sent off as Japanese soldiers to die in the Pacific War. One particularly vocal man in the group told the NHK cameras that he and the other Taiwanese had loyally fought for Japan, but Japan treated them "like orphans and threw them away" at the war's end. Channel Sakura's Inoue Kazuhiko traveled to Bangka Park and was able to find several of the men who appeared on NHK, including the man who had delivered the soundbite about being mistreated. Rather than express regret about having lived under Japanese rule, the man told Channel Sakura that he was sorry that Japan lost the war. He seemed proud of his wartime military service, saying that one can go to Yasukuni Shrine and confirm how hard the Taiwanese fought. The man was eager to demonstrate that he could still recite the Imperial Rescript on Education and liked to read Japanese novels. Joined by a few other men in the park, he stated that they had wanted to remain a part of Japan. Another man exclaimed that they all wanted to be Japanese, while others said they wanted Japan to support Taiwanese independence. The men, who had gathered around the Channel Sakura camera just as they had gathered around NHK's camera, applauded when Inoue thanked them for their service to Japan. Inoue's report was used by Channel Sakura and allied activities to argue that the men, as well as Taiwanese people in general, were far more positive about the colonial period than NHK had shown.[32]

Some of NHK's interviewees were willing to sit down for extended Channel Sakura interviews and express direct support for the protest movement. One was Ka Tokuzō, an 87-year-old Taiwanese man whose comments about ethnic discrimination had featured prominently in the NHK documentary. Ka looked back fondly on his days growing up and living in pre-1945 Taiwan and had even authored a book in Japanese that had been published in 2005 as part of Sakura no Hana Publishing Company's nationalistic *Nihonjin no Hokori* (Japanese Pride) series.[33] After he was contacted by groups that objected to the documentary, Ka joined the protest movement and provided statements for anti-NHK news articles and internet videos. Ka felt that NHK had maliciously included only his negative remarks about Japan. In his interviews with Channel Sakura he noted that he agreed with the protesters on almost every point of complaint about the documentary.[34]

Another Taiwanese interviewee that was depicted by activists as a supporter of the anti-NHK protests was 97-year-old Chiang Sung-hui. NHK's documentary had used interview footage of Chiang speaking about his father, Chiang Wei-shui, a major leader of the Taiwanese resistance movement against Japanese rule. In an extended interview with Channel Sakura, Inoue Kazuhiko presented a list of activists' major complaints about the documentary and asked Chiang to comment on each point. Chiang, speaking in fluent Japanese, expressed agreement with the list and detailed the reasons why he thought NHK was wrong.[35]

There was considerable confusion as to whether these men actually supported the anti-NHK protest movement. Despite Ka Tokuzō's contribution to articles and video reports criticizing the documentary, a June 6, 2009, explanation letter from NHK to LDP lawmakers stated that NHK had spoken to Ka and confirmed that he did not intend to file an official protest with the broadcaster.[36] However, on June 22, NHK sent a director and producer of the documentary to Taiwan for the purpose of meeting with Ka and the other Taiwanese who had made public statements against it. The purpose of the meeting was apparently to explain NHK's positions and convince the Taiwanese not to participate in the protest campaign. An October 2009 article in the conservative magazine *Sapio* alleged that the chief director of the documentary, Hamasaki Kenichi, tearfully told Ka Tokuzō that he had received death threats against his children from anti-NHK protesters. It was also reported that Hamasaki came to Ka's house equipped with printed statements from some 50 scholars who supported the documentary.[37] Under this pressure, Ka allegedly signed a statement retracting the statements he made against NHK.[38] However, even after that date, protesters still regularly made use of Ka's earlier remarks. When Ka passed away in February of 2010, Channel Sakura eulogized him as an important figure in the anti-NHK movement.[39] Channel Sakura videos about NHK produced in the several years after Ka's death continued to use footage of Ka speculating that the Chinese Communist Party exerted influence over NHK programming.

NHK's official response to the complaints about this issue acknowledged that it had the interview footage used in the documentary was cut from much longer interviews. However, NHK denied accusations of biased or unfair editing. NHK noted that even though Ka Tokuzō and Chiang Sung-hui made negative statements about its documentary in interviews with conservative journalists, NHK had not received any direct complaints from them.

Addressing the complaints about Ka Tokuzō's depiction in the documentary, NHK stated that time constraints had compelled it to use only 10 minutes of a 5-hour interview. However, cuts were not made on the basis of being positive or negative toward Japan. Some portions of that 5-hour interview were praise of Japanese colonialism, but NHK claimed it had also cut scenes of Ka criticizing Japan's economic exploitation of Taiwan.

NHK further backed up its filmmakers by providing a quotation from an e-mail they had received from Chiang Sung-hui. Rather than denounce the documentary, Chiang praised it and expressed gratitude to NHK.[40] The e-mail, which was written before Chiang was contacted and interviewed by Channel Sakura, seems to indicate that he liked it until anti-NHK activists convinced him otherwise.

NHK's official response to these complaints did not stop Channel Sakura and its allies from continuing to argue that NHK had misled and misrepresented the views of the Taiwanese interviewees.

The "Japan–Taiwan War"

Another problem that activists had with the NHK documentary was its use of a non-standard term for an armed conflict. When Taiwan was ceded from Qing China to Japan in 1895, Japan's arriving Occupation forces faced armed resistance from local military and militia forces that did not want to become a part of the Japanese Empire. The NHK documentary described the opposition to the Japanese military as fierce and widespread, occurring on a scale large enough to justify calling the event the "Japan–Taiwan War" (Nittai Sensō). It noted that the number of Japanese soldiers who died during the conflict was about 5,000.

This conflict is often referred to as the "Taiwan Heitei" (Suppression of Taiwan) in Japanese. A Japanese translation of the Chinese name "the War of the Yiwei Year" (Itsubi Sensō), is also used in Japan, a naming convention that emphasizes its place in the Chinese sexagenary cycle and not its participants. Activists saw NHK's adoption of the relatively unknown "Japan–Taiwan War" as a politically motivated decision. In their view, this was an attempt to damage Japan–Taiwan friendship by taking a small conflict against former Qing elites and guerillas and redefining it as a war against the Taiwanese nation and people. Channel Sakura's reporting on this controversy repeatedly reminded viewers that a reporter from the conservative *Sankei Shimbun* newspaper had found that Japan's National Diet Library did not contain a single publication using "Japan–Taiwan War" in its title.

There were also questions about whether the conflict was even large enough to be considered a "war" at all. While 5,000 Japanese soldiers died during the conflict, disease accounted for 4,642 deaths, compared to 164 Japanese combat deaths.[41] Protesters did not think that such a small-scale conflict could fairly be referred to as the "Japan–Taiwan War." These views were not exclusively limited to Japanese conservatives: Ka Tokuzō and Chiang Sung-hui both told Channel Sakura reporters that they felt the term was an exaggeration.[42]

Responding to these arguments, NHK explained that the term "Japan–Taiwan War" had first come into use following a 1995 academic symposium marking the 100th anniversary of the Sino-Japanese War.[43] It provided the titles of three history books that used the term, two published in 1997 and one published in 2007.[44] NHK also defended its description of the event as a foreign war by pointing to the retention of Japan's wartime-only Imperial General Headquarters until the conclusion of the Taiwan conflict and a telegram by Itō Hirobumi referring to the "foreign campaign" in Taiwan.[45]

On a Channel Sakura program that aired shortly after NHK's official response, Yūhara Masataka of the Friends of Lee Teng-Hui Association in Japan and Inoue Kazuhiko expressed disagreement with NHK's explanations. They acknowledged the existence of scholars that used the term "Japan–Taiwan War" but did not think that its use in a handful of books justified its use by a national broadcaster.[46] Throughout the protest campaign, Channel Sakura and allied groups continued to believe that NHK's usage of this term was based on an ideological desire to hurt Japan–Taiwan relations.

Taiwanese identity issues

As a coalition of groups that included many pro-Taiwanese independence activists, the anti-NHK protesters were also sensitive to any language that could be perceived as representing Taiwan as part of China and Taiwanese people as Chinese. There were a few examples of this in the NHK documentary that were presented by activists as proof of NHK's alleged anti-Japan and pro-China bias.

The first of these issues concerned the ethnic identity of the Taiwanese people. In describing the outbreak of war between Japan and China in 1937, the NHK documentary had stated that its 5 million inhabitants were Han Chinese and thus the "same ethnicity as the enemy." The protesters did not agree with the idea of labeling all of Taiwan as Han Chinese. Ka Tokuzō was most adamant about this issue, appearing multiple times on Channel Sakura programs to insist that Taiwanese people were of mixed ethnicity and should not be categorized as Han Chinese.[47]

Another issue was the documentary's use of the term "Chinese language" (chūgokugo) when describing the language spoken by Taiwanese people in the 1930s. It is a Japanese term that commonly refers to Mandarin Chinese, so the protesters interpreted that as the meaning NHK aimed to convey. The issue was so important that protesters distributed English-language fliers about it via the internet, which were then printed and passed out during street demonstrations (bold text kept as original):

> **Mandarin Chinese was spoken in Taiwan at the time under sovereignty of Japan???**
>
> It is absolutely a haphazard, failed remark. At the time under Japanese sovereignty, Taiwanese, Taiwan native tongues and Japanese were spoken in Taiwan.
>
> It was after the Second World War that Taiwanese began to use Mandarin Chinese, under the dictatorship by Chiang Kai-shek.[48]

The flier was factually correct – Mandarin Chinese was not spoken by most Taiwanese people before World War II. Its creator emphasized the difference between Taiwan and the mainland by describing Taiwan's adoption of Mandarin as a national language as a result of the undemocratic policies of an outsider.

NHK's official response denied that its filmmakers were saying that Taiwanese people spoke Mandarin Chinese in that period. Drawing upon the work of Waseda University professor Wakabayashi Masahirō, director of the Japan Association for Taiwanese Studies, NHK argued that the Min Nan and Hakka languages spoken in Taiwan at that time were dialects of the Chinese language.[49] It further argued that "Taiwanese language" (taiwango) usually refers to only the Min Nan language, so filmmakers opted for the more inclusive term "Chinese language." NHK also dismissed the claim that Taiwanese were not Han Chinese. Professor Wakabayashi defined Taiwan's non-aboriginal ethnic groups, which included Hakka, Min Nan, and other peoples who had originated on the Chinese mainland, as Han Chinese. Although NHK had cited one of the country's leading experts on Taiwanese politics and history, protesters were not convinced by these explanations.

Representing Taiwan's Aboriginal history: The Paiwan people and a "human zoo"

The anti-NHK protests benefited from the initial support of educated Taiwanese figures such as Ka Tokuzō and Chiang Sung-hui, but an arguably more significant contributor to the movement were representatives of a Taiwanese Aboriginal community. Members of the Paiwan ethnicity were displeased with how *A First-Rate Asian Power* portrayed them as pitiful victims when describing an event that they saw as a proud moment in their history.

The event was the Japan–British Exhibition held in London from May to October 1910. It was meant to showcase and introduce Japan and its empire to the citizens of Britain, Japan's imperial ally. Part of the exhibition consisted of mock villages showing traditional life within the Japanese empire. For the village display within the exhibition's Taiwan Pavilion, a group of 24 Paiwan aboriginals were paid to build a "Formosan Hamlet" and live there for the duration of the exhibition, entertaining visitors with cultural performances. The Paiwan people, who were known to practice headhunting, were advertised as a warrior tribe, as this quotation from the exhibition's official English guidebook indicates:

> [The Formosan Hamlet] was inhabited by specimens of "one of the fiercest and most intractable races on the globe," as a well-known traveler described the natives of Formosa. That was, of course, before the Japanese occupation of the island in 1891. These warlike dwellers of the mountain recesses of Formosa resided in their own peculiar native-built houses, and were seen at their occupations and sports. Their war dances were thrilling, while their mimic battles proclaimed them to be adept in the use of the spear, the bow, and the arrow.[50]

The above-quoted passage of the guidebook was briefly flashed on the screen in the NHK documentary, with the camera zooming in on the words "war dances" and "mimic battles." In both the beginning and middle of the documentary, a photo of the Paiwan villagers was displayed on screen, along with the text "human zoo" (ningen dōbutsuen). Supplemented by interview footage of French Historian Pascal Blanchard, who has used the term in his works on French colonialism, it was explained that by making a zoo-like "show" (misemono) of aboriginal culture, Japan was asserting its role as a civilizing imperial power. According to the documentary, this kind of "human zoo" was one way that Japan, emulating the European colonial empires, could display its superior status as a "first-rate power."

NHK traveled to Gaoshih village in Taiwan to interview the descendants of Chaibai Puiaion,[51] one of the men who worked in the Formosan Hamlet in 1910. Chaibai's daughter, Kao Hsu Yueh-mei, who was 75 years old in 2009, is shown for less than a minute in the documentary, reacting to a photo postcard of her father that had been sold as a souvenir in 1910. Saying that she was "sad" (kanashii), Kao Hsu added that she cannot say more because the topic was too heavy for her.

Channel Sakura and its allies were taken aback by the documentary's emphasis on Japan setting up a "human zoo." They were unfamiliar with the term and saw it as unfairly equating Japan's colonial rule with what they perceived as far more racist European empires.[52] Channel Sakura's reporters were dispatched to Taiwan in an effort to enlist the support of representatives of the Paiwan people. Their mission proved to be a remarkable success.

The people of Gaoshih village were apparently unaware that NHK planned to describe their ancestor's work in London as a "human zoo" and were highly receptive to Channel Sakura's arguments that the word was unfair and dehumanizing. From the perspective of these villagers, the problem was not so much that the documentary unfairly portrayed Japanese colonialism in a negative light but rather that their ancestors and traditional culture were being depicted as pitiful and sad. In their local memory, the 1910 exhibition was an event in which their ancestors proudly showed their culture to Britain, receiving respect as well as forging international friendships.

It was also revealed that the documentary had offended Kao Hsu Yueh-mei. She claimed that NHK had completely misrepresented her reaction to the postcard of her father. Her feelings of sadness were because she had no surviving photos of her father and was seeing his face for the first time in many decades. It was not, as NHK seemed to imply, a reaction to the fact that he had been in a "human zoo" (a term they had not used when speaking with her). Other members of the community, including the interpreter who had been present during NHK's filming and the elders of Gaoshih village, joined the protest movement.[53]

Channel Sakura's conducted several interviews with Kao Hsu in order to set the record straight and document her support for the anti-NHK protests. The interviews were conducted in Japanese, and despite some apparent communication difficulties, Channel Sakura's reporters concluded that the woman had really meant to say that she felt "nostalgic" (natsukashii) when she saw the photograph.[54] However, a later article, published by the *Taipei Times* in 2013, quoted her as complaining that the NHK documentary had said she was "nostalgic" for the colonial period (it had not) and that she meant to express "sadness."[55] Nonetheless, Kao Hsu and other representatives of the Paiwan community would strongly stick with the anti-NHK protest movement until the conclusion of their class-action lawsuit in 2016.

NHK's June 17, 2009, response to protesters' complaints included an explanation on why it used the term "human zoo." It argued that the term had been used in Europe at that time to describe displays of "savage" or "uncivilized" people by a "civilizing" colonial power and that Japan's display of the Paiwan people was modeled after such displays. To support its claim that the exhibition was modeled after the practices of Western colonial powers, NHK quoted from the prospectus of a 1903 exhibition in Osaka of Taiwanese and Ainu tribes. The prospectus stated in no uncertain terms that the event was based on displays put on by the "civilized western nations." It also included a quote from a Japanese newspaper article from 1910 that compared London's Formosan Hamlet to a zoo.[56]

The June 17 response did little to slow the momentum of the protest movement. The continued participation of Paiwan elders made it clear that this was not just a collection of right-wing nationalists and a few pro-Japanese Taiwanese. The protesters responded to NHK's explanation by arguing that there was no evidence that the term "human zoo" was ever used at that time, even in Europe. To question the claim that the London exhibition was meant to be a "human zoo," protesters pointed to the presence of a similar display at the 1910 exhibition that included ethnic Japanese people working in a mock farming village.

NHK's second official response, posted on July 22, demonstrated how seriously it took the protests. The new response, which was nearly the same length as NHK's July 17 response to several of the protest movement's complaints, was entirely devoted to addressing the "human zoo" issue. It traced the origins of the term "human zoo" back to 19th-century Germany and France. NHK noted that a zoo in Paris was turned into a display area for tribespeople in the 1870s. Records show the German term "anthropologisch-zoologische," the French term "exposition anthropozoologique," and the English term "anthropozoological exhibition" were used at that time to refer to anthropological displays of colonized tribal peoples. As an example of its more recent use in Japanese language scholarship, NHK pointed to a book by Tokyo University professor Yoshimi Shunya.

The document also provided a lengthier restatement of its argument that the exhibition was indeed based on similar European exhibitions. NHK added further information about the 1903 Osaka exhibition, as well as quotations from that era of a Japanese lawmaker who felt it had been demeaning to put fellow humans on display and a Japanese journalist who compared the London display to a zoo. The explanation stated that the opinions of the people put on display did not change the overall nature of the display. NHK also argued that the mock Japanese farming village's demonstrations of agriculture techniques were not comparable to the Formosan village display.[57]

On the issue of sadness versus nostalgia, NHK expressed confidence that it had not misrepresented Kao Hsu Yueh-mei's opinions. It provided an analysis of the Paiwan language that concluded that there were circumstances in which one word could express either sadness or nostalgia, but based on the context of conversations that had not been included in the final cut of the documentary, NHK's team concluded that Kao Hsu meant to say that she was sad. NHK admitted that its staff had not used the term "human zoo" when conducting the interview but had adequately explained the 1910 exhibition before asking her opinion about the photograph.[58]

NHK's explanations did not satisfy the Paiwan elders and Japanese protesters. The strength of the Paiwan elders' opposition to NHK might seem odd to readers, especially given NHK's evidence showing that the term "human zoo" was in fact widely used in academic discussions of these kinds of exhibitions. However, more recent scholarship has given more attention to the views of the colonial subjects themselves, something that has been left out of past studies. In particular, Kirsten L. Ziomek has conducted fascinating research into Japan's colonial exhibitions, which includes a whole chapter recovering the lost history of the Paiwan people who participated in the 1910 exhibition. Ziomek paints a far more complicated picture than NHK, in which the Paiwan people honored and celebrated the villagers who had traveled to London. Her research, which was published ten years after the NHK documentary aired, found that several of the participants were chiefs, a claim echoed by Paiwan representatives during the NHK protests:

> Those people who went to the exhibition were in fact the elites of these Paiwan villages. They were held in high regard by our people. It was unthinkable for the program to pervert it as though they were dancing like monkeys.[59]

Ziomek also found that Japanese officials had not wanted to include any village displays in the exhibition and only relented after considerable pressure from profit-minded British organizers. Japanese observers reacted negatively to the displays, especially to the display of a Japanese farming village, which they believed presented Japan as technologically and culturally behind the West. She convincingly argued that these international displays "caused concern at home that it reflected poorly on Japan's national status," and "should dissuade us from characterizing Japan as an imperial power eager to showcase its subjects."[60]

The lack of sensitivity in NHK's responses to Paiwan representatives has also been highlighted by Rong-Xuan Chu and Chih-Tung Huang, who conducted a critical discourse analysis of NHK's documentary and the official statements it delivered between 2009 and 2016. Their analysis found a "presence of insidious racial prejudice against the Paiwan people, combined with a lack of sensitivity towards indigenous peoples in general, both in the documentary and in the responses from NHK in the subsequent lawsuits." While not arguing that NHK was intentionally aiming to slander or insult the Paiwan people, they nonetheless wrote that "NHK's arguments have the potential to encourage negative views of both the plaintiffs and the Paiwan people, thereby risking the further marginalization of indigenous peoples in general."[61]

The two works of research mentioned above were not published until 2019, several years after the conclusion of the protests against the 2009 documentary, so activists could not use it to bolster their cause. However, the existence of this new research does help explain why anti-NHK activists saw the "human zoo" issue as so important to the 2009 protests.

By highlighting the issues mentioned in the preceding sections, Channel Sakura and its allies portrayed NHK as a dishonest and anti-Japanese organization. Through in-depth reporting that revealed the "fabrications" in NHK's documentary, Channel Sakura was showing its viewers that Japan's mainstream media could not be trusted. This was in contrast to the truth-telling and trustworthy reporters of Channel Sakura. Through the contribution of money to Channel Sakura and the participation in its grassroots protest campaigns, viewers were offered an opportunity to share in the responsibility for spreading the "truth" and saving Japan and Taiwan from nefarious foes.

Methods and tactics of the anti-NHK protests

Having introduced the issues protesters had with the documentary and the formation of a coalition of anti-NHK actors, I will next explain the methods of protest employed by Channel Sakura and its allies. Their use of a variety of methods, from internet-mediated information sharing to legal action, stand out as the actions of highly skilled challengers within a field of contestation. In contrast, NHK's responses were remarkably sluggish and technologically backward, sticking to very traditional methods such as uploading PDFs to their website and occasionally answering questions at formal press conferences.

Online video content

The distribution of information via online videos was a central feature of this protest campaign. As a satellite television station that also distributed free online content, Channel Sakura was a very important actor within this field. None of the other organizations that participated in the protest movement had their own television studio or access to high-quality video production techniques, so they relied on Channel Sakura to spread their message through this medium. Leaders of the pro-Taiwan groups frequently appeared as guests on Channel Sakura programs and linked to Channel Sakura videos to lend further support to the views they expressed on their websites and e-magazines.[62]

The use of free online video sharing is particularly noteworthy. Dozens of Channel Sakura videos containing detailed attacks on the NHK documentary were available on both YouTube and Nico Nico Douga. This distribution method was radically different from NHK and Japan's major private television networks, which at the time limited free online video content to breaking news videos, usually available only on a temporary basis.[63]

The fact that NHK only aired *A First-Rate Asian Power* on two occasions would typically mean that protesters and people filing complaints about the documentary would have needed to watch it on their television sets in order to formulate an opinion on its contents.[64] However, in the era of affordable broadband internet, anyone with internet access could go on YouTube at any time and view videos from Channel Sakura that provided detailed criticisms of the documentary. As I mentioned earlier in this chapter, some of the commentary programs were from people who had themselves missed the original broadcast of the documentary (and presumably had to watch a recorded copy).

Although NHK did not distribute *A First-Rate Asian Power* via YouTube, right-leaning netizens with little regard for copyright law went ahead and distributed it anyway. One unauthorized upload of the full-length version of documentary was available on YouTube beginning in April 2009. By December 2010, it had received over 72,000 views, a number that would grow to over 227,000 views by October 2020. The anonymous uploader put "NHK's Great Sin" in the title line of the video. The video description contained a warning about the "subliminal" images that could be found in the documentary. Another unauthorized copy of the documentary, also on YouTube, received over 75,000 views between its upload in February 2013 and October 2020. Like the other upload, its title and description directed viewers to the anti-NHK protest campaign.

The continued existence of these unauthorized uploads on YouTube displayed an incredible lack of initiative on the part of NHK. Uploading copyrighted documentaries without permission is a clear violation of YouTube's terms of use, and other TV channels have aggressively made use of these rules to swiftly report and remove violating content.[65] Under such circumstances, the continued presence of the above-mentioned videos on YouTube suggests that either NHK is unaware that this program is being distributed by third parties or perhaps those within NHK who did know about it were not in the proper bureaucratic position to file a formal copyright complaint with YouTube. Either way, it demonstrates how an incumbent organization within this field of contestation was unprepared or unwilling to make use of new technologies and methods. NHK did not seek public support via the internet through the free digital distribution of its documentary and did not make it available for purchase in DVD or digital format. This means that after its initial rebroadcast in May 2009 until the publication of this book in 2020, *A First-Rate Power in Asia* was only viewable via illegally uploaded copies that introduce it as a biased and anti-Japanese film.

In the months immediately following the airing of *A First-Rate Asian Power*, Channel Sakura uploaded anti-NHK videos several times a week, updating viewers on the latest developments in their movement. In addition to the earlier-mentioned interviews it filmed with Taiwanese people, there were frequent discussion panels about the content of the documentary. Panelists included members of the pro-Taiwan groups participating in the protests, conservative historians, and journalists.[66] Channel Sakura also frequently provided a platform for Tachibana Takashi, a former NHK employee–turned–activist who would later use his internet fame to successfully run for political office as the head of an anti-NHK political party, the Party to Protect the People from NHK.

Beyond its videos educating viewers about NHK's political bias, Channel Sakura produced videos aimed at promoting direction action and participation in protest activities. These included advertisements for protest marches, information seminars, and other offline protest events.[67] There were also after-action reports praising people who participated in offline protest events.[68] When a class-action lawsuit against NHK was prepared and filed, programs were also made calling on viewers to sign-on as plaintiffs.[69] Video programs also frequently promoted recently published anti-NHK magazine articles and books.[70]

Offline demonstrations

Online media fed into more traditional forms of offline protest, such as street marches, public speeches, and physically presenting protest letters to NHK.

The first of these took place on April 10, 2009, just five days after the first airing of *A First-Rate Power in Asia*. The Friends of Lee Teng-Hui Association in Japan formally delivered a protest letter to NHK, outlining its members' displeasure with various aspects of the documentary.[71] It was the first in a series of such protest letters, several of which received responses from one of the NHK executive producers responsible for the documentary. [72]

The pro-Taiwan groups and Channel Sakura also held several large protest marches near NHK's Tokyo headquarters. The first of these took place on May 16, 2009, with over 1,000 protesters marching to the NHK headquarters and submitting a letter of protest.[73] Many of those marching, including Mizushima Satoru, held signs calling for the complete dissolution of NHK. On the same day a small protest was also held in Taiwan, with a group of about 20 Taiwanese and Japanese holding signs and chanting slogans in front of NHK's Taipei branch office.[74]

A second major march took place on May 30, drawing about 1,000 protesters. In a break from earlier conduct, about 100 protesters temporarily entered the NHK building without permission.[75] The incident was alarming enough that NHK executives addressed it at a June press conference, stating that protesters' "behavior could have been disruptive and we shall consider what countermeasures to take to prevent any recurrence."[76]

A third major protest in Tokyo was held on June 20, drawing approximately 900 people.[77] Several subsequent protests, none of which compared to the scale of the first three large Tokyo demonstrations, were held in Tokyo, Osaka, Yokohama, Nagoya, Sapporo, and other parts of Japan.[78]

In July, August, and September 2009, several small events mixed community service and protest. Groups of Channel Sakura viewers gathered in the Shibuya area of Tokyo to clean-up litter on the streets while spreading public awareness of the protest movement.[79] A same kind of clean-up event was also carried out by a few Japanese protesters in front of the NHK branch office in Los Angeles.[80] In another event, viewers collected charity donations for Taiwanese typhoon relief.[81] During these events, participants wore t-shirts with anti-NHK slogans and had fliers on hand to spread the word about their protest movement to anyone who seemed interested. The events were promoted through YouTube and became subjects for the Channel Sakura's after-action news programs.

Although these actions took place offline, it is important to note that they were promoted beforehand through Channel Sakura's website and videos and through the e-magazine mailing lists of pro-Taiwan organizations. Photographs and video footage filmed at the offline protest events were also later shown on the internet through Channel Sakura and the websites of the pro-Taiwan groups. Although the offline protest activities ranged from dozens to about 1,000 participants, videos documenting their protests typically received thousands of views. This suggests a considerable number of people supported the protests from their computer screens.

The involvement of Japanese lawmakers

Several prominent Japanese lawmakers, most notably future prime minister Abe Shinzō, voiced support for the anti-NHK protesters through online media appearances and in their official duties as Diet members.

The first event of note took place on April 23, 2009, when members of the Machimura faction of the Liberal Democratic Party (LDP) brought up the topic of the documentary at a general meeting of the Diet. A *Sankei Shimbun* article quoted lawmakers Nakayama Nariaki, Inada Tomomi, Machimura Nobutaka, and Abe Shinzō as having voiced criticism of the documentary's portrayal of history.[82]

Several of these politicians, including Abe, were members of an LDP group called the Diet Member's League to Consider Japan's Future and History Education [Nippon no Zento to Rekishi Kyōiku wo Kangaeru Giin no Kai], which had been founded in 1997 to support conservative activists' efforts to create right-leaning history textbooks. As a group that involved itself in a variety of history-related disputes, it was receptive to the anti-NHK protest movement of 2009 and submitted its own letter of protest to NHK in late April 2009, demanding an explanation for allegedly biased and inaccurate points of the documentary.[83] On May 11, NHK sent an official response, defending the documentary.[84] A June 4 follow-up inquiry by League president Nakayama Nariaki received a similar response from NHK on June 6.[85] The arguments and wording of the letter were almost identical to the explanations that would later be posted to NHK's homepage.

On June 11, 2009, LDP lawmaker Furuya Keiji founded the Diet Members League to Consider the State of Public Broadcasting (Kōkyō Hōsō no Arikata ni tsuite Kangaeru Giin no Kai). The League consisted of 60 lawmakers from the Liberal Democratic Party (LDP), including former prime ministers Abe Shinzō and Mori Yoshirō.[86] On the same day the League was formed, Abe made a special appearance on Channel Sakura and spoke with Mizushima Satoru about the "problem of mass media," echoing many of the concerns that protesters had with the documentary.[87] Channel Sakura also aired video of the League's discussions.[88] Several weeks later Mizushima attended the June 25, 2009, meeting of the League, at which he was officially recognized for his reporting on the issue.[89]

Abe had stepped down as prime minister of Japan two years earlier, and although he held no cabinet position at the time of his Channel Sakura interview, the LDP was the ruling party at the time. Two months later, it would suffer a landslide defeat, so it may be tempting to say that the involvement of Abe and other LDP lawmakers in the anti-NHK protests could have contributed to the growing unpopularity of their party. However, it has been argued that Abe's involvement with this group and his appearances on Channel Sakura, together with other statements he made claiming that online media is more trustworthy than traditional mass media, was part of a successful "tightrope-walking populist strategy." By talking about media bias without denouncing NHK as traitors to Japan, Abe appealed to elements of the conservative right that had long held distrust toward NHK and other institutions that they believed to be anti-Japanese.[90] It might not be unfair to refer to this as dog-whistle politics – signaling implied support for a group's political goals without alienating the larger public.

Furuya Keiji also did not suffer negative political consequences from his founding and leading an anti-NHK lawmaker group. When Abe returned and formed his second cabinet as prime minister in 2012, Furuya was appointed Minister of State for Disaster Management, Minister for the Abduction Issue, and chairperson of the National Public Safety Commission. As of 2020, Furuya had been re-elected several times to the House of Representatives and continued to serve as president of the League.

Telephone and e-mail complaints to NHK

Anti-NHK campaigners frequently called on their supporters to make use of NHK's official viewer feedback channels, and many answered these calls. As a public broadcaster, NHK publishes public reports every month about viewer reactions to its programs, documenting the number of positive or negative comments received by each of the month's most popular programs. These reports show that the viewer response to *A First-Rate Asian Power* was extraordinary – it received thousands of viewer comments over a period of several months, far eclipsing all other NHK programs aired in 2009.

The first of these reports, featuring statistics from April 2009, noted that *A First-Rate Asian Power* received 2,924 viewer comments. This placed it at the top of the viewer response ranking for that month, more than the second, third, and fourth-ranked programs added together.[91] If comments had stopped at that point, it would have been the second-most responded-to NHK program of the 2009 fiscal year. However, viewer responses continued to come in for the next few months.[92]

As shown in Table 5.1, the viewer comments submitted to NHK via telephone and e-mail were at their highest immediately following the airing of the program on April 5, 2009. In May, the number of responses was 1,420, higher than any other program that aired that month on NHK. Given that the program was broadcasted once in April and once more in May, it is reasonable to assume

Table 5.1 Viewer Reactions to *A First-Rate Asian Power*

	Positive	*Negative*	*Inquiry*	*Other*	*Total*
April 2009	129	1,945	570	280	2,924
May 2009	26	981	194	217	1,420
June 2009	43	235	44	57	379
July 2009	–	–	–	–	141
Total	198	3161	808	554	4,864

Source: 2009 viewer reaction reports and viewer's voice newsletters published by NHK[94]

that many of these comments were from viewers who watched it on television. However, large numbers of responses continued to come for months, long after the program was no longer viewable on television. By the beginning of July, the number of viewer comments had reached an overall total of 4,824 – far more responses than any of the three documentaries in the *Japan Debut* series and more responses than any other program that year.[93] The data indicates that the responses were overwhelmingly negative.

In its April 2009 report, NHK highlighted the fact that the internet was influencing viewer responses. It included a headline in bold text announcing that many viewer comments had been received because *A First-Rate Asian Power* had become a popular topic online. The report included this quote from a comment sent to NHK by a 60-year-old man:

> *The Taiwanese people who were interviewed by NHK have appeared in internet videos. They are saying that NHK only aired the negative parts of their comments and completely left out all their positive comments.*[95]

The quote is a clear reference to Channel Sakura's investigative reports. Based upon the treatment this case received in NHK's official viewer reaction reports, it would appear that NHK was well aware that internet media was one of the major driving forces behind this protest movement.

The largest class-action lawsuit in postwar Japanese history

Just as in the 2001 NHK Affair, activists called on Japan's courts to rule whether an allegedly biased documentary was violating NHK's legal obligations to viewers and to the subjects it interviewed. In this case, rather than left-leaning activists filing a lawsuit, it was Japan's conservative right. It would be a class-action lawsuit, involving not only the subjects of the documentary seeking compensation for damages but also thousands of Japanese viewers demanding that their NHK subscription fees be returned.

The legal team was headed by Takaike Katsuhiko, a lawyer and the vice president of the Japan Institute for National Fundamentals, a conservative think-tank chaired by journalist Sakurai Yoshiko. Takaike had also been a leader of the successful conservative campaign that in 2005 convinced lawmakers to change the name of the national holiday marking Emperor Hirohito's birthday from "Greenry Day" to "Shōwa Day," in honor of the late emperor's reign name.[96] In addition to the NHK case, he was head attorney for three other notable lawsuits on behalf of conservative historical causes. The cases, together with the NHK case, represent a pattern of activist legal action, so I will discuss them briefly before providing more detail on the topic of NHK.

The first was a 2005 defamation case against journalist Honda Katsuichi on behalf of the families of two deceased Imperial Japanese Army soldiers. Honda had written articles describing how the two soldiers, Mukai Toshiaki and Noda Tsuyoshi, had engaged in a "100-Man Killing Contest" while fighting against the Chinese in 1937. The contest had originally been described in a 1937 Tokyo *Nichi Nichi Shimbun* article but largely faded from Japanese public memory until Honda wrote newspaper articles about it in the 1970s. The gruesome story was subsequently used to bring attention to the issue of wartime atrocities in China. Japanese conservatives claimed that the story was inaccurate wartime propaganda, and some Western historians, such as Bob Wakabayashi and Joshua Folger, lean toward this conclusion.[97] However, the lawsuit was dismissed in 2004 and once more on appeal in 2006. The preceding judge stated that the original article had contained "some false elements and exaggerations," but it could not be ruled a complete fabrication.[98]

The second lawsuit was filed in 2005 against Nobel laureate Ōe Kenzaburō. Like the 100-Man Killing Contest case, it was a defamation case claiming that an author had fabricated descriptions of a war atrocity. A surviving Imperial Japanese Army soldier and the family of one of his colleagues alleged that Ōe's 1970 essay, *Okinawa Notes*, contained a false account of Japanese soldiers ordering Okinawan civilians to commit suicide. The claim was rejected in 2008 by the Osaka District Court and Osaka High Court, and its final appeal was dismissed by the Supreme Court in 2011.[99] Unlike the other case, the judges in this case completely supported the author's claim that the war atrocities had taken place.[100]

The third lawsuit was a 2009 civil suit against Chinese film director Li Ying, creator of a 2007 documentary that negatively portrayed the Yasukuni Shrine. There are noticeable similarities between the complaints about this film and the complaints about *A First-Rate Power in Asia*. Like the NHK documentary, its creation had been funded by public money (in this case, a government-funded arts grant), and it also involved interviews with elderly people who later claimed to have been deceived about the purpose of the documentary. The lawsuit was filed on behalf of Koiwa Tōru, a man who alleged that Li violated his privacy by filming him without permission and using 90 seconds of the footage in the documentary. The lawsuit was settled out of court in December 2010, with an unspecified amount of damages paid to Koiwa.[101]

The common aim of these lawsuits, as filmmaker John Junkerman has argued, was "to discredit treatments of history that highlight the excesses of Japan's imperial past."[102] Despite the fact that some of these lawsuits did not result in favorable court rulings, they represented a sustained effort to put legal pressure on outspoken supporters of a progressive interpretation of Japanese history. Based on the failure rate of these lawsuits, they could arguably be categorized as strategic lawsuits against public participation (SLAPP) – aiming to silence political opponents through lawsuits that burdened the accused with the need to make a considerable investment of time and money to fight out in the courts.

This brings us to the 2009 lawsuit against NHK, which had similar ideological characteristics. This case, however, would be much larger in scale due to its class-action nature. Participants were recruited via Channel Sakura's programs and the e-mail lists of pro-Taiwan groups. They directed would-be plaintiffs to Channel Sakura's website, where lawsuit paperwork could be downloaded and filled out.[103] At the time of the first filing, nearly 8,400 people had submitted the paperwork, making it Japan's largest-ever class-action lawsuit in terms of the number of plaintiffs.[104]

The lawsuit accused NHK of violating its legal responsibility to create impartial and truthful documentaries. Using most of the previously mentioned points of dispute as examples, the plaintiffs claimed that NHK had represented "fabrications" as historical fact. They demanded that NHK give each plaintiff a compensation payment of 10,000 yen.[105]

As mentioned earlier in this chapter, participation in the lawsuit was not limited to Japanese citizens. Included in the instructions on how to submit lawsuit paperwork was an explanation about how non-Japanese could place their signature on documents instead of using a Japanese name seal. Although the exact breakdown of lawsuit participants was not reported by Channel Sakura or other media outlets, one news report stated that there are about 150 Taiwanese citizens among the plaintiffs.[106] The most visible of the non-Japanese participants were representatives of Taiwan's Paiwan ethnic group, who, with the assistance of Channel Sakura and pro-Taiwan independence groups, visited Japan on several occasions to speak with the press and voice their support of the lawsuit.[107]

Shortly after filing the lawsuit, Takaike's legal team appeared on Channel Sakura and stated that they believed the lawsuit would last several months to a year.[108] It would prove a much longer legal battle. The case worked its way to the Tokyo Regional Court, where a judge ruled against the plaintiffs in November 2012, completely rejecting the demand that NHK pay compensation. Forty-two of them appealed the decision, and the case went to the Tokyo High Court, where the judge ruled in November 2013 that only one person – Kao Hsu Yueh-mei, the daughter of a Paiwan man who had been a part of the "human zoo," should be paid 1 million yen in compensation because NHK's use of the term implied that her relative was like a zoo animal. The claims from all the other Paiwan representatives and the claims from all the Japanese plaintiffs were rejected.[109] Even though the courts had thrown out the claims of the thousands of other participants, anti-NHK activists celebrated the ruling as a major victory.

The victory, however, would be short-lived. The case was appealed to Japan's Supreme Court, which reversed the Tokyo High Court's ruling on compensation. The final ruling dismissed the claim that NHK's use of "human zoo" had defamed Kao Hsu or made viewers see the Paiwan people as animals.[110] In the end, all compensation claims were thrown out. It was a complete legal victory for NHK.

While the NHK case awaited appeal rulings, Takaike Kazuhiko launched another major class-action lawsuit against left-leaning media. The target this time was the *Asahi Shimbun*, which had published a series of articles about the "comfort women" issue in the 1980s and 1990s, quoting Yoshida Seiji, a man who is claimed to have forced Korean women into sexual slavery. Subsequent investigation of Yoshida's claims had found them to be likely fabrications, and the *Asahi Shimbun* later issued a formal retraction of the articles in 2014.[111] The retraction did not fully satisfy some members of the conservative right, and Takaike's class-action lawsuit sought financial compensation of 10,000 per plaintiff because the Asahi had "significantly hurt the international reputation of Japan and Japanese nationals, infringing on their personal rights and damaging their honor."[112] As in the anti-NHK case, Takaike used Channel Sakura to spread information about and distribute documents for participation in the lawsuit.[113] Over 25,000 people signed-on, making it even larger than the anti-NHK lawsuit. A July 2016 Tokyo District Court ruling ruled against the plaintiffs, determining that none of their reputations had been directly harmed by the newspaper's reporting.[114] Takaike did not appeal the ruling.

Takaike also represented another anti-NHK plaintiff in a lawsuit claiming that Japanese television owners had the right not to pay the public broadcaster's subscription fees. Rulings in favor of NHK were handed down in 2014 by the Tokyo High Court and upheld in 2013 by the Tokyo District Court. A final appeal to the Supreme Court also ended in failure, with a ruling defending the requirement that all television owners pay a subscription fee because it gave NHK financial independence that protected its programming from "influenced by state organizations and others."[115]

While ultimately unsuccessful, the existence of an ongoing lawsuit functioned as a form of de facto censorship for the director and others within NHK who were associated with the documentary, preventing them from speaking about the issue. Although NHK had an opportunity to post an official defense of the documentary on its website in early June 2009, after the lawsuit was filed later that month, public comments were limited for legal reasons. It is also likely that NHK avoided re-broadcasting or selling DVD copies of the documentary because of the ongoing legal proceedings.

Conclusion

In the 2009 anti-NHK protest campaign, Channel Sakura and a coalition of right-leaning groups recognized a chance to exert pressure within the field of contestation surrounding Japan's public broadcaster. The airing of *A First-Rate*

Power in Asia represented a chance for Japan's conservative right to mount a high-profile challenge to NHK that went outside the typical bounds of domestic protest against left-leaning media. *A First-Rate Power in Asia*'s subject matter and its treatment of Taiwanese interviewees allowed for the creation of a transnational protest movement, drawing upon the social connections provided by pro-Taiwan independence groups. Skilled social actors such as Inoue Kazuhiko and Mizushima Satoru of Channel Sakura, aided by the Friends of Lee Teng-Hui Association, made this possible.

Through its programs, Channel Sakura created a narrative that interpreted a left-leaning documentary about Japanese colonialism to be a sign of a devious anti-Japanese plot to destroy the bonds of friendship between Japan and Taiwan, benefiting mainland Chinese aims to deny Taiwan its freedom and punish Japan. This narrative was acceptable to the world view of both Japan's conservative right and Taiwan independence activists. In addition, they successfully recruited representatives of the Paiwan people to their cause, making the protests not just about satisfying nationalists but also about redressing insults to the dignity of indigenous people.

Channel Sakura and its allies also succeeded in using the internet to file unprecedentedly large class-action lawsuits against NHK, and later the *Asahi Shimbun*. Online media spread the word about the lawsuits, convincing thousands of people to take the time to fill out and file the necessary legal paperwork to join the lawsuits. Although the courts struck down the lawsuits, the appeals process kept NHK in courts for seven years after the airing of *A First-Rate Asian Power*.

The 2009 anti-NHK campaign resulted in a small shift within the field of contestation over NHK programming. NHK did not waver in its support of the documentary, but its defense of the filmmakers seemed weak in comparison to the aggressive campaign waged by Channel Sakura and its allies. The class-action lawsuit, the offline protests in front of NHK's offices, and the large number of viewer complaints filed with NHK put considerable pressure on NHK and its documentary filmmakers. The protest campaign made it clear that future attempts to make a documentary about the negative aspects of Japanese history would have the potential to trigger a very unpleasant situation for filmmakers and for NHK as a whole. This arguably weakens the position of NHK's documentary producers and their progressive supporters and strengthens the position of the right within this field.

The 2012 election of Abe Shinzō, a known opponent of NHK's progressive programming, also signaled a shift in the situation. Under Abe's leadership, political appointees with right-leaning historical views were put in charge of NHK's board. Momii Katsuto, an Abe ally who held the director generalship of NHK from 2014 to 2017, stirred controversy by telling in a press conference that NHK's coverage of territorial disputes should follow the position of the government: "We cannot say left when the government says right."[116] Other Abe appointees to NHK's board were novelist Hyakuta Naoki, an outspoken denier of Japan's wartime atrocities, and conservative essayist Hasegawa Michiko.[117]

As such, it has been argued that NHK's independence was significantly compromised under the Abe administration.[118] Ellis Kraus has recently written that the current situation at NHK is one in which government "influence, or one may say control, has become more explicit, assertive, and obvious."[119] In a study focusing on war-related programming in 2015, Philip Seaton argued that a decline in news reports and documentaries touching on Japan's war responsibility may signal that NHK is sliding toward becoming a "compliant" or "quasi-state" broadcaster. Among ten war documentaries that aired in August of that year, Seaton found that there were "only the briefest glimpses of any Japanese war responsibility issues."[120]

While there is reason to believe that NHK has lost some of its independence and engaged in self-censorship under the Abe administration, there were significant signs that its documentary filmmakers were pushing back. The NHK Special series of documentaries has continued to present views of history that are far from those of the conservative right. Some examples, available for digital viewing on NHK's On Demand service in mid-2020, were: a 2015 animated documentary about Okinawan children being brutalized and brainwashed into fighting alongside the Japanese military, a 2017 documentary about the atrocities of Unit 731, a 2018 documentary that described gruesome atrocities committed by Japanese soldiers in the battle of Luzon, a 2019 documentary about the private newspapers' role in promoting wartime nationalism and militarism, and a 2020 documentary featuring accounts of Okinawan civilians being murdered by Japanese soldiers.[121] Several of these, including the documentaries about Unit 731, Okinawan civilian deaths, and newspapers, were translated into English and distributed internationally by NHK World.

The next chapter will introduce a different campaign by Channel Sakura, one in which conservatives aimed to influence public remembrance of World War II in Okinawa. Unlike the NHK dispute, it ended in an unambiguous victory for Channel Sakura and its supporters.

Notes

1 Ellis S. Krauss, *Broadcasting in Japan: NHK and Television News* (Ithaca: Cornell University Press, 2000), 170–174.

2 Ellis S. Krauss, "NHK: The Changing and Unchanged Politics of Semi-Independence," in *Press Freedom in Contemporary Japan*, ed. Jeff Kingston (London: Routledge, 2017), 69–70.

3 Reiji Yoshida and Ayako Mie, "Momii's Rise Tests NHK's Reputation," *Japan Times*, February 2, 2014, http://www.japantimes.co.jp/news/2014/02/02/national/momiis-rise-tests-nhks-reputation/.

4 William Underwood, "NHK's Finest Hour: Japan's Official Record of Chinese Forced Labor," *Asia-Pacific Journal* 4, no. 8 (August 6, 2006), http://www.japanfocus.org/-William-Underwood/2187.

5 Philip A. Seaton, *Japan's Contested War Memories: The "Memory Rifts" in Historical Consciousness of World War II* (London: Routledge, 2007), 105.

6 Ibid., 104–105.

7 Shin'ichi Okada, 偏向NHKへの公開質問状 [An Open Letter to the Biased NHK] (Tokyo: Sanko, 1983), 4–6, quoted in Seaton, *Japan's Contested War Memories: The "Memory Rifts" in Historical Consciousness of World War II.*

8 Philip A. Seaton, "NHK, War-Related Television, and the Politics of Fairness," in *Press Freedom in Contemporary Japan*, ed. Jeff Kingston (London: Routledge, 2017), 173.

9 "Transcript of Oral Judgment, delivered in The Hague, The Netherlands, 4 December 2001," *Women's Caucus for Gender Justice*, last accessed September 2, 2020, http://www.iccwomen.org/wigjdraft1/Archives/oldWCGJ/tokyo/summary.html.

10 Yayori Matsui, "Statement of Protest to NHK by VAWW-NET Japan," *Corporate Watch in Japanese Mail List*, April 17, 2001, http://www.jca.apc.org/web-news/corpwatch-jp/150.html.

11 Ibid.

12 Gavan McCormack, "How the History Wars in Japan Left a Black Mark on NHK TV (Their BBC)," *History News Network*, February 7, 2005, http://hnn.us/article/9954.

13 Ikuhiko Hata, *Comfort Women and Sex in the Battle Zone* (Lanham: Hamilton Books, 2018), 220.

14 Norma Field, "The Courts, Japan's 'Military Comfort Women,' and the Conscience of Humanity: The Ruling in VAWW-Net Japan v. NHK," *Asia-Pacific Journal* 5, no. 2 (February 10, 2007), http://japanfocus.org/-Norma-Field/2352?rand=1395130360&type=print&print=1.

15 Ellis S. Krauss, NHK vs 日本政治 [NHK vs. Japanese Politics], trans. Michio Muramatsu and Junpei Gotō (Tokyo: Tōyō Keizai Shimpōsha, 2006), xv–vi.

16 Seaton, *Japan's Contested War Memories: The "Memory Rifts" in Historical Consciousness of World War II*, 108.

17 Michael Cucek, "Abe and Press Oppression," in *Press Freedom in Contemporary Japan*, ed. Jeff Kingston (London: Routledge, 2017), 78; and Yoshifumi Tawara, 安倍晋三の本性 [The True Nature of Abe Shinzō] (Tokyo: Kinyobi KK, 2016).

18 Jeff Kingston, *Contemporary Japan: History, Politics, and Social Change since the 1980s* (Chichester: Wiley-Blackwell, 2011).

19 Kamila Szczepanska, *The Politics of War Memory in Japan: Progressive Civil Society Groups and Contestation of Memory of the Asia-Pacific War* (London: Routledge, 2014), 91.

20 Tessa Morris-Suzuki, *The past within Us: Media, Memory, History* (London: Verso, 2005) and Koichi Nakano, "The Right-Wing Media and the Rise of Illiberal Politics in Japan," *in Press Freedom in Contemporary Japan*, ed. Jeff Kingston (London: Routledge, 2017).

21 From a flier titled "A Sinful Broadcast of NHK," last accessed December 11, 2010, http://loader.offmatrix.net/nhk/src/up_029.pdf.

22 One example of this nationalist literature is this Nanjing denial book: *Tadao Takemoto and Yasuo Ohara*, 再審「南京大虐殺」—世界に訴える日本の冤罪 [The Alleged Nanjing Massacre] (Tokyo: Meiseisha, 2000). Membership information retrieved from "役員名簿 « 日本会議" [List of Names (Nippon Kaigi)]. Nippon Kaigi, last accessed December 10, 2010, http://www.nipponkaigi.org/about/yakuin; and Jun Okamura, "Most of You Have Not Heard of Nippon Kaigi," *GlobalTalk 21* (Blog), January 02, 2008, http://son-of-gadfly-on-the-wall.blogspot.com/2008/01/most-of-you-have-not-heard-of-nippon.html.

23 "日本李登輝友の会" [Friends of Lee Teng-Hui Association in Japan], Wikipedia, last accessed December 10, 2010, http://ja.wikipedia.org/wiki/%E6%97%A5%E6%9C%AC%E6%9D%8E%E7%99%BB%E8%BC%9D%E5%8F%8B%E3%81%AE%E4%BC%9A.

24 "メールマガジン日台共栄" [Mail Magazine Japan-Taiwan Co-Prosperity], Melma!, last accessed December 10, 2010, http://www.melma.com/backnumber_100557/.

25 "1/4【永山英樹】ＮＨＫ「ＪＡＰＡＮデビュー」が削除したこと[桜H21/4/14]" ["Nagayama Hideki" What was removed from NHK's Japan Debut]. *Nihon Bunka Channel Sakura*, April 14, 2009, https://www.youtube.com/watch?v=uiO93BoNT1A
26 "1/2【ＮＨＫ・アジアの一等国】日台分断工作！？繰り返される" [1/2 "NHK – A First Rate Asian Power" Japan-Taiwan Split Due to Scheming Again]. *Nihon Bunka Channel Sakura*, April 11, 2009, https://www.youtube.com/watch?v=8aMHMTTjx9E
27 "【討論！】どうしたＮＨＫ？！「JAPANデビュー」問題" ["Controversy!" What's Wrong with the NHK?! The Japan Debut Issue]. *Nihon Bunka Channel Sakura*, April 16, 2009, https://www.youtube.com/watch?v=fvFR5QYr76o
28 Yao Liu, "A Study on Zainichi Taiwanese's National Identity: Focusing on the Name Rectification Movement," (Master's thesis, Seoul National University, 2018), http://hdl.handle.net/10371/143660.
29 Francesca Polletta, *It Was like a Fever: Storytelling in Protest and Politics* (Chicago: University of Chicago Press, 2006), 7.
30 "5/16【討論！】どうしたＮＨＫ？！「JAPANデビュー」問題" [5/16 "Controversy!" What's Wrong with the NHK?! The Japan Debut Issue]. *Nihon Bunka Channel Sakura*, April 16, 2009, https://www.youtube.com/watch?v=rpv59QLUFMs.
31 "1/5【台湾取材レポート】井上和彦・台湾取材で感じたこと" [1/5 "Taiwan News Report" Inoue Kazuhiko – Impressions While Reporting in Taiwan]. *Nihon Bunka Channel Sakura*, April 22, 2009, http://www.youtube.com/watch?v=8dqmJrgoSHQ.
32 Ibid.
33 Tokuzō Ka, 母国は日本 祖国は台湾 [Japan Is Where I'm Born, but Taiwan Is Where I'm From], (Tokyo: Sakura no Hana, 2005).
34 "【ＮＨＫ・ＪＡＰＡＮデビュー】井上和彦・台湾取材１２のポイント" [NHK – Japan Debut" Inoue Kazuhiko – 12 Points on Reporting in Taiwan]. *Nihon Bunka Channel Sakura*, April 27, 2009, http://www.youtube.com/watch?v=jMY9XIhhe58.
35 "【台湾取材レポート】蒋松輝氏インタビュー[桜 H21/4/21]" ["Taiwan News Report" Chiang Sung-hui Interview (Sakura Heisei 21/4/21)]. *Nihon Bunka Channel Sakura*, April 21, 2009, http://www.youtube.com/watch?v=tAL0FzMAwks.
36 Ariaki Nakayama, "再質問状(H21.6.4)に対するＮＨＫからの回答書" [Nakayama Nariaki – NHK's Response to the Question Posed on June 4, 2009]. *Nakayama Nariaki* (Homepage), last accessed December 9, 2010, http://nakayamanariaki.com/modules/bulletin/index.php?page=article&storyid=41.
37 "【直言極言】NHK、崩壊した嘘と隠蔽工作[桜H21/10/24]" ["Frank and Direct" NHK's Destroyed Lies and Cover-ups]. *Nihon Bunka Channel Sakura*, October 24, 2009, http://www.youtube.com/watch?v=P_JRu2MkScg.
38 Kazuhiko Inoue, "NHKスペシャル「JAPANデビュー」抗議噴出後に番組担当者が台湾再訪で行なったこと＝井上和彦" [NHK Special "Japan Debut" What Happened When the Responsible Parties of Program Rearrived in Taiwan After Protest]. *SAPIO, Shogakukan*, September 3, 2009, http://news.nifty.com/cs/magazine/detail/sapio-20090903-01/1.htm. A less dramatic version of the story appeared in August 2009 on Channel Sakura: "【永山英樹】ＮＨＫの大罪－明るみに出た隠蔽工作[桜 H21/8/11]" ["Nagayama Hideki" NHK's Great Sin – Uncovered Cover-up]. *Nihon Bunka Channel Sakura*, August 11, 2009, http://www.youtube.com/watch?v=Gx8GBhjQjTw. Although director Hamasaki is not mentioned by name in the SAPIO article, he was referred to by name by Tokuzō Ka in Channel Sakura interviews.

39 "ＮＨＫスペシャルで「発言ゆがめられた」柯徳三氏が死去" [Ka Tokuzō, Whose Words "Were Distorted" in an NHK Special, Has Died]. *Sankei Shimbun*, February 4, 2010; and "【台湾レポート】柯徳三氏の葬儀に参列して[桜H22/3/11]" ["Taiwan Report" At Ka Tokuzō's Funeral (Sakura Heisei 22/3/11)]. *Nihon Bunka Channel Sakura*, March 11, 2009, http://www.youtube.com/watch?v=OlozdWWhpa4.

40 Ibid.

41 Paul R. Katz, "Germs of Disaster: The Impact of Epidemics on Japanese Military Campaigns in Taiwan, 1874 and 1895," *Annales de Démographie Historique* (1996), https://doi.org/10.3406/adh.1996.1918.

42 "【ＮＨＫ・ＪＡＰＡＮデビュー】井上和彦・台湾取材１２のポイント" ["NHK – Japan Debut" Inoue Kazuhiko – 12 Points on Reporting in Taiwan]. *Nihon Bunka Channel Sakura*, April 27, 2009, http://www.youtube.com/watch?v=jMY9XIhhe58.

43 "シリーズ・JAPANデビュー　第1回「アジアの"一等国"」に関しての説" [Japan Debut Series: Regarding Episode 1 "A First Rate Asian Power"]. *NHK*, last accessed December 1, 2010, http://www.nhk.or.jp/japan/announce/090617.html.

44 The titles of the books are: Japanese Association of Modern East Asian History, 日清戦争と東アジア世界の変容 [The First Sino-Japanese War, East Asia, and How It Changed the World] (Kashiwa: Yumani Shobō, 1997), and Yukio Hiyama, 日清戦争 秘蔵写真が明かす真実 [The First Sin-Japanese War: The Truth Told Through Treasured Photographs] (Tokyo: Kodansha, 1997), and Komagome Takeshi, 東アジア国際政治史 [The History of East Asia in International Relations] (University of Nagoya Press, 2007).

45 "シリーズ・JAPANデビュー　第1回「アジアの"一等国"」に関しての説" [Japan Debut Series: Regarding Episode 1 "A First Rate Asian Power"]. *NHK*.

46 "【柚原正敬】「日台戦争」という戦争はあったのか？[H21/6/24]." ["Yuzuhara Masataki" Was There Really a War Against Taiwan? (Heisei 21/6/24)]. *Nihon Bunka Channel Sakura*, June 24, 2009, http://www.youtube.com/watch?v=8vOzE8F6eCE.

47 "5/8【台湾取材レポート】柯徳三氏インタビュー・1/3[桜　H21/4/21]" [5/8 "Taiwan News Report" Ka Tokuzō Interview – 1/3 (Sakura Heisei 21/4/21)]. *Nihon Bunka Channel Sakura*, April 21, 2009, http://www.youtube.com/watch?v=eXvmpZbfooA.

48 From a flier titled "TAIWANESE & JAPANESE; TRAMPLED UNDER FOOT BY JAPAN BROADCASTING," last accessed December 13, 2010. http://loader.offmatrix.net/nhk/src/up_032.pdf.

49 The quote is from Masahiro Wakabayashi, ed., もっと知りたい台湾 [Wanting to Know More about Taiwan] (Tokyo: Kōbundō, 1998).

50 Eri Obata, "The Display of Taiwan's Aborigines in the Japan-British Exhibition of 1910 as a Showcase of Japan's Colonial Power" (Master's Thesis, National Chengchi University, 2012), https://ah.nccu.edu.tw/retrieve/82513/400901.pdf.

51 The NHK documentary refers to him as "Chaibaibai." However, Taiwanese media sources and the postcard shown in the documentary spell his name as "Chaibai."

52 "1/4【台湾取材レポート】パイワン族の真実－前編[桜　H21/6/18]" ["Taiwan News report" The Truth Behind the Paiwan People – First Half (Sakura Heisei 21/6/18)]. *Nihon Bunka Channel Sakura*, June 18, 2009, http://www.youtube.com/watch?v=8vOzE8F6eCE.

53 Kuo Chu-chen and Lilian Wu, "Paiwan Tribe People Miffed after Losing NHK Discrimination Case," *Focus Taiwan*, January 22, 2016, https://focustaiwan.tw/society/201601220031.

54 "【NHKの大罪】これがＮＨＫ流の「真実の報道」なのか？[桜H21/6/20]" ["NHK's Great Sin" Is This What NHK's Version of "Reporting the Truth?)]. *Nihon Bunka Channel Sakura*, June 20, 2009, http://www.youtube.com/watch?v=R-Cg0362rZM.
55 Chen Yen-ting and Jason Pan, "Woman Sued NHK 'for Dignity,'" *Taipei Times*, December 2, 2013, https://www.taipeitimes.com/News/taiwan/archives/2013/12/02/2003578139.
56 "シリーズ・JAPANデビュー　第1回「アジアの"一等国"」に関しての説" [Japan Debut Series: Regarding Episode 1 "A First Rate Asian Power"]. *NHK*.
57 "シリーズ・JAPANデビュー　第1回「アジアの"一等国"」に関しての説明・追加" [Japan Debut Series: Regarding Episode 1 "A First Rate Asian Power – Addendum"]. *NHK*, last accessed December 1, 2010, http://www.nhk.or.jp/japan/announce/090722.html.
58 Ibid.
59 Yen-ting and Pan, "Woman Sued NHK 'For Dignity.'"
60 Kirsten L. Ziomek, *Lost Histories: Recovering the Lives of Japan's Colonial Peoples* (Cambridge: Harvard University Asia Center, 2019), 144–150.
61 Rong-Xuan Chu and Chih-Tung Huang, "Indigenous Peoples in Public Media: A Critical Discourse Analysis of the Human Zoo Case," *Discourse & Society* 30, no. 4 (2019): 395–411, https://doi.org/10.1177/0957926519837392.
62 One example from the Voice of Taiwan newsletter: "「台湾の声」【ＮＨＫ問題】報道動画と抗議活動案内（東京・岡山」）" [(Taiwan's Voice) "NHK Scandal" Explaining the Broadcast and Protest Activity (Tokyo, Okayama)]. *Voice of Taiwan Newsletter*, last accessed December 12, 2010, http://sv3.inacs.jp/bn/?2009100097078774001950.3407,
63 Examples included http://www.nhk.or.jp/news/ (NHK News), http://www.tv-asahi.co.jp/ann/ (ANN News), and http://www.news24.jp/ (NTV News).
64 "プロジェクトJAPAN：未来へのプレーバック。〔放送予定〕" [Project Japan: Playback to the Future (Planned Broadcast)]. *NHK*, last accessed December 11, 2010, http://www9.nhk.or.jp/japan/pjyotei/archive_2009.html/
65 "Guidelines and Requirements: Report a Copyright Violation," *YouTube*, last accessed December 15, 2010, http://www.google.com/support/youtube/bin/answer.py?hl=en&answer=113113.
66 An example can be found at: "1/4【桜プロジェクトＳＰ】ＮＨＫからの抗議状、そこから何が見えるのか？[H21/7/24]" ["Sakura Project SP" The NHK's Invitation for Discussion, and What's to be Gleaned from that]. *Nihon Bunka Channel Sakura*, July 24, 2009, http://www.youtube.com/watch?v=Nc6J-B-jGF8.
67 One example: "【高松&札幌】NHK「JAPANデビュー」に抗議する国民大行動[H21/7/2]" ["Takamatsu and Sapporo" Large Action by the People Against NHK's Japan Debut]. *Nihon Bunka Channel Sakura*, July 2, 2009, http://www.youtube.com/watch?v=LzEJHV_UEN8.
68 An example would include: "【NHKの大罪】6.13 NHK「ＪＡＰＡＮデビュー」に抗議する街頭宣伝行動in渋谷[桜 H21/6/16]" ["NHK's Great Sin" June 13, NHK "Japan Debut" Shibuya Street Protest in Shibuya Heisei 21/6/16)]. *Nihon Bunka Channel Sakura*, June 16, 2009, http://www.youtube.com/watch?v=_zAmlZ5n8BI.
69 "【NHK一万人集団訴訟】「第五回口頭弁論」報告[桜H22/11/19]" ["10.000-Person NHK Class-Action Lawsuit" Fifth Oral Proceedings Report (Sakura Heisei 22/11/19)]. *Nihon Bunka Channel Sakura*, November 19, 2010, http://www.youtube.com/watch?v=GFVKcPZQh2U.

70 "【プレゼント】NHK捏造事件と無制限戦争の時代[桜H21/11/13]" ["Presentation" NHK's Fabrications and the Era of Unlimited Warfare (Sakura Heisei 21/11/13)]. *Nihon Bunka Channel Sakura*, November 13, 2009, http://www.youtube.com/watch?v=i9PqFfZG0Vo; and "【プレゼント】撃論ムック最新刊「ＮＨＫの正体」[H21/7/4]" ["Presentation" Heated Discussion About the Newly Published Mook "The Truth Behind the NHK" (Sakura Heisei 21/7/4)]. *Nihon Bunka Channel Sakura*, July 4, 2009, http://www.youtube.com/watch?v=xNJmAT6RCnY. The books mentioned are: Kōyū Nishimura, 【撃論ムック】NHKの正体—情報統制で国民に銃を向ける、報道テロリズム[The Truth Behind the NHK – Information Terrorism, Pointing a Gun to the People through Information Control] (Tokyo: Oakla Publishing, 2009) and Genki Fujii, NHK捏造事件と無制限戦争の時代 [NHK's Fabrications and the Era of Unlimited Warfare] (Tokyo: Sōwasha, 2009).

71 "【NHK「JAPANデビュー」問題　これまでの経緯】" [NHK's Japan Debut Problem – The Facts So Far]. *Friends of Lee Tong Hui Association in Japan* (Homepage), last accessed December 9, 2010, http://www.ritouki.jp/2009NHK.html.

72 "1/4【柚原正敬】抗議声明回答報告と検証「台湾から見た日本」[桜H21/4/20]." [1/4 "Yuzuhara Masataka" Considering the Response to the Protest Letter "Japan As Seen From Taiwan" [Sakura Heisei 21/4/20]. *Nihon Bunka Channel Sakura*, April 20, 2009, http://www.youtube.com/watch?v=yP54Je4V1p0.

73 "ＮＨＫ反日報道に約１３００人が抗議 東京・渋谷" [Approximately 1300 People Protest NHK's Anti-Japanese Reporting – Tokyo, Shibuya]. *World Times*, May 17, 2009, http://www.worldtimes.co.jp/today/kokunai/090517-4.html.

74 "2/4【NHK抗議・台湾デモ】ＮＨＫは日本への愛情を傷つけた！[桜H21/6/2]" ["NHK Protest – Taiwan Demonstration" NHK Is Damaging the Love for Japan! (Sakura Heisei 21/6/2)]. *Nihon Bunka Channel Sakura*, June 2, 2009, http://www.youtube.com/watch?v=NR1uA-zfNpE.

75 "ＮＨＫ「台湾統治」番組 – 右派勢力の攻撃　狙いは" [NHK "Taiwan Governance" Program, Right-Wing Attack. The Aim ...]. *Akahata Shimbun*, August 13, 2009, http://www.jcp.or.jp/akahata/aik09/2009-08-13/2009081304_02_1.html.

76 "Summary of Press Conference (June, 2009)," *NHK*, last accessed December 13, 2010, http://www.nhk.or.jp/pr/english/toptalk/kaichou_e/k_e0906.htm#06, and "【NHK集団訴訟】8300件を越えた委任状とNHKからの抗議[H21/6/24]" ["NHK Class-Action Lawsuit" More Than 8300 Proxies and NHK's Protestations Heisei 21/6/24]. *Nihon Bunka Channel Sakura*, June 24, 2009, http://www.youtube.com/watch?v=Ekzrp2njurM.

77 "NHK「JAPANデビュー」問題　これまでの経緯" [NHK's Japan Debut Problem – The Facts So Far]. *Friends of Lee Teng Hui Association in Japan* (Homepage), December 9, 2010, http://www.ritouki.jp/2009NHK.html.

78 "【お知らせ】　NHK「JAPANデビュー」に抗議する国民大行動" ["Announcement" Large Action by the People against NHK's Japan Debut]. *Nihon Bunka Channel Sakura* (Homepage), December 9, 2010, http://www.ch-sakura.jp/topix/1041.html.

79 "【NHKの大罪】渋谷（ＮＨＫ）を掃除しよう！[H21/7/6]" ["NHK's Great Sin" Let's Clean Up Shibuya (the NHK)! Heisei 21/7/6]. *Nihon Bunka Channel Sakura*, July 6, 2009, http://www.youtube.com/watch?v=8vOzE8F6eCE.

80 "【NHKの大罪】「国民行動inロサンゼルス」報告[桜H21/8/26]" ["NHK's Great Sin" Civic Action in Los Angeles – Report (Sakura Heisei 21/8/26)].

Nihon Bunka Channel Sakura, August 26, 2009, http://www.youtube.com/watch?v=qQc4deQqqmQ.

81 "【台湾水害】台湾八八水害街頭募金活動と馬政権の対応[桜 H21/8/24]" ["Taiwan Flood" Taiwan Eight-Eight Flood Fund-Raising and the Ma Government's Reaction (Sakura Heisei 21/8/24)]. *Nihon Bunka Channel Sakura*, August 24, 2009, http://www.youtube.com/watch?v=8vOzE8F6eCE.

82 "安倍、町村氏らがＮＨＫ番組を批判「偏っている」" [Abe, Machimura Criticize NHK Program for "Bias"]. *Keizai Shimbun*, April 24, 2009.

83 "自民議連が「偏向番組問題」でＮＨＫに質問状" [LDP Caucus Sends Letter toNHK For Biased Program]. *Keizai Shimbun*, April 28, 2009.

84 Nakayama Nariaki, "平成２１年４月５日放送「ＮＨＫスペシャル シリーズ ＪＡＰＡＮデビュー第１回『アジアの一等国』」に対する公開質問状及び回答書" [Heisei 21/4/5 Broadcast – NHK Special – Japan Debut Series Part 1 "A First Rate Asian Power" Open Letter and Response]. *Nakayama Nariaki* (Homepage), last accessed December 9, 2010, https://web.archive.org/web/20120321061935/http://nakayamanariaki.com/modules/bulletin/index.php?page=article&storyid=32

85 Nakayama Nariaki, "再質問状(H21.6.4)に対するＮＨＫからの回答書" [Nakayama Nariaki – NHK's Response to the Question Posed on June 4, 2009]. *Nakayama Nariaki* (Homepage).

86 "自民党：公共放送を考える議員の会が発足総会" [LDP: Inaugural Meeting of Lawmakers Considering Public Broadcasting Association]. *Mainichi Shimbun*, June 12, 2009, and "「ＮＨＫ番組が偏向」＝自民有志が議連" ["NHK Program Biased" = LDP Volunteer Caucas]. *Jiji Press*, June 11, 2009.

87 "【安倍晋三】これからの日本とマスメディア問題[桜 H21/6/11]" ["Abe Shinzo" The Future Problems of Japan and its Mass Media (Sakura Heisei 21/6/11)]. *Nihon Bunka Channel Sakura*, June 11, 2009, http://www.youtube.com/watch?v=twjpMjtoBRk.

88 "【議連発足】公共放送のあり方について考える議員の会[H21/6/13]" ["Caucus Formed" Association of Lawmakers Considering Public Broadcasting Heisei 21/6/13]. *Nihon Bunka Channel Sakura*, June 13, 2009, http://www.youtube.com/watch?v=MZvRJzP-fFE.

89 "【第３回勉強会】公共放送のあり方について考える議員の会[H21/6/27]" ["Third Study Meeting" Association of Lawmakers Considering Public Broadcasting Heisei 21/6/27]. *Nihon Bunka Channel Sakura*, June 27, 2009, http://www.youtube.com/watch?v=XsPBaV7fEnY.

90 Fabian Schäfer, Stefan Evert and Philipp Heinrich, "Japan's 2014 General Election: Political Bots, Right-Wing Internet Activism, and Prime Minister Shinzō Abe's Hidden Nationalist Agenda," *Big Data* 5, no. 4 (2017), 294–309, https://doi.org/10.1089/big.2017.0049.

91 "視聴者対応報告" [Audience Response Report]. NHK, Report, April 2009, p. 6.

92 Translated from: "視聴者対応報告" [Audience Response Report]. NHK, Report, April 2009.

93 "視聴者対応報告" [Audience Response Report]. NHK, Report, January 2010.

94 "視聴者対応報告" [Audience Response Report]. NHK, Report, April 2009 and "視聴者対応報告" [Audience Response Report]. NHK, Report, May 2009. Data for July comes from a smaller newsletter: "お客さまの声" [Responses from Our Customers]. NHK, Report, July 2009. The newsletter does not provide statistics on what kind of viewer responses were received.

95 Translated from "視聴者対応報告" [Audience Response Report]. NHK, Report, April 2009, 6–7.

96 Shun Kawaguchi, "A Study on the Movement for the Establishment of Showa Day: Legislation Promoted by a Religious Group and a Conservative Society" (Master's Thesis, Seoul National University, 2017), http://s-space.snu.ac.kr/bitstream/10371/129330/1/000000141919.pdf.

97 Bob Tadashi Wakabayashi, "The Nanking 100-Man Killing Contest Debate: War Guilt Amid Fabricated Illusions, 1971–75," *The Journal of Japanese Studies* 26, no. 2 (2000), 307–340, https://doi.org/ 10.2307/133271; Bob Tadashi Wakabayashi, "The Nanking 100-Man Killing Contest Debate, 1971-75," In *The Nanking Atrocity, 1937-38: Complicating the Picture*, ed. Bob Tadashi Wakabayashii (Oxford: Berghahn Books, 2009); and Joshua A. Fogel, "The Nanking Atrocity and Chinese Historical Memory," in *The Nanking Atrocity, 1937-38: Complicating the Picture*, ed. Bob Tadashi Wakabayashi (Oxford: Berghahn Books).

98 Chris Hogg, "Victory for Japan's War Critics," *BBC News*, August 23, 2005, http://news.bbc.co.uk/2/hi/asia-pacific/4176272.stm.

99 Gavan McCormack and Satoko Oka Norimatsu, *Resistant Islands: Okinawa Confronts Japan and the United States* (Lanham: Rowman & Littlefield, 2012), 32.

100 Steve Rabson, "Case Dismissed: Osaka Court Upholds Novelist Oe Kenzaburo for Writing That Japanese Military Ordered 'Group Suicides' in Battle of Okinawa," *Asia-Pacific Journal* 6, no. 4 (April 2006), http://japanfocus.org/-Steve-Rabson/2716.

101 The only source for this claim is a website that has since been taken down. It is listed as: "関連事件等のお知らせ・解説 宗教法人礼拝山興亜観音による布告" [Announcements of Related Events: Commentary – Proclamation by Religious Organization Reihaizan Kōan Kannon], *Kōa Kannon* (Homepage), http://www.koakannon.org/jiken-sonota.html. A lack of post-2009 news articles about the case indicate that some sort of settlement was reached.

102 John Junkerman, "Li Ying's 'Yasukuni': The Controversy Continues," *Asia-Pacific Journal* 7, no. 31, (August 3, 2009), https://apjjf.org/-John-Junkerman/3198/article.html

103 "【NHK 訴訟】 一万人・集団訴訟 及び 名誉毀損訴訟" ["NHK Lawsuit" 10.000-Person Class-Action Lawsuit and Defamation Lawsuit]. *Nihon Bunka Channel Sakura* (Homepage), last accessed December 15, 2010, http://www.ch-sakura.jp/topix/1054.html.

104 "ＮＨＫ相手に８４００人が集団提訴　「ＪＡＰＡＮデビュー」歪曲報道で" [8.400-Person Class-Action Lawsuit Against the NHK Regarding Japan Debut Program Fabrication], Keizai Shimbun, June 25, 2010, and "ＮＨＫの台湾支配報道は「捏造」 歴史研究者ら８千人提訴" ["Fabrication" of NHK Report on Colonial Rule, 8000 Historians Raise Charges], Kyodo News, June 25, 2009, http://www.47news.jp/CN/200906/CN2009062501000527.html.

105 "【NHK 訴訟】 一万人・集団訴訟 及び 名誉毀損訴訟" ["NHK Lawsuit" 10.000-Person Class-Action Lawsuit and Defamation Lawsuit]. *Nihon Bunka Channel Sakura* (Homepage), last accessed December 15, 2010, http://www.ch-sakura.jp/topix/1054.html.

106 "ＮＨＫ相手に８４００人が集団提訴　「ＪＡＰＡＮデビュー」歪曲報道で" [8.400-Person Class-Action Lawsuit against the NHK Regarding Japan Debut Program Fabrication]. *Keizai Shimbun*, June 25, 2010.

107 "【ＮＨＫの大罪】パイワン族原告団来日記者会見 [桜H21/10/7]" ["NHK's Great Sin" Press Conference by Plaintiff Group of Paiwan People after Arriving in Japan (Sakura Heisei 21/10/7)]. *Nihon Bunka Channel Sakura*, October 7, 2009, http://www.youtube.com/watch?v=ZcI1gd8qPBw; and "【NHK集団訴

訟】パイワン族・華阿財氏来日[桜H22/5/14]" ["NHK Class-Action Lawsuit" The Paiwan People – Ka Azai Comes to Japan (Sakura Heisei 22/5/14)]. *Nihon Bunka Channel Sakura*, May 14, 2010, http://www.youtube.com/watch?v=l5wRU1fO-7M.

108 "1/2【ＮＨＫの大罪】ＮＨＫ集団訴訟弁護団に聞く[H21/6/15]" [1/2 "NHK's Great Sin" Asking Lawyer Association regarding the NHK Class-Action Lawsuit Heisei 21/6/15]. *Nihon Bunka Channel Sakura*, June 15, 2009, http://www.youtube.com/watch?v=Bu5iwQUIGM4.

109 Yen-ting and Pan, "Woman Sued NHK 'for Dignity.'" and Ryujiro Komatsu, "Court Orders NHK to Pay Taiwanese Woman for 'Human Zoo' Reference," *AJW by The Asahi Shimbun*, January 27, 2014, http://ajw.asahi.com/article/behind_news/social_affairs/AJ201311290059.

110 Chu-chen and Wu, "Paiwan Tribe People Miffed after Losing NHK Discrimination Case."

111 "Asahi Third-Party Panel Says Neglecting Erroneous Articles on 'Comfort Women' Coverage 'Betrayed Readers,'" *Asahi Shimbun*, December 22, 2014, http://www.asahi.com/ajw/articles/AJ201412220088.html.

112 Shusuke Murai, "Tokyo Court Rules against Conservative Group Suing Asahi over 'Comfort Women' Articles," *Japan Times*, July 28, 2014, https://www.japantimes.co.jp/news/2016/07/28/national/tokyo-court-rules-conservative-group-suing-asahi-comfort-women-articles/.

113 Michael Yon, "Japan: Lawsuits against Asahi Shimbun Newspaper," *Michael Yon JP* (Blog), February 27, 2015, http://michaelyonjp.blogspot.com/2015/02/blog-post_27.html.

114 Murai, "Tokyo Court Rules Against Conservative Group Suing Asahi over 'Comfort Women' Articles."

115 "Top Japan Court Finds Paying NHK Broadcast Fee 'Legal Obligation,'" *Kyodo News*, December 6, 2017, https://english.kyodonews.net/news/2017/12/340985196295-update2-top-court-finds-paying-nhk-public-broadcast-fee-legal-obligation.html.

116 William Pesek, "Abe Pulls Strings to Put NHK under His Thumb," *Japan Times*, February 7, 2014, https://www.japantimes.co.jp/opinion/2014/02/07/commentary/japan-commentary/abe-pulls-strings-to-put-nhk-under-his-thumb/.

117 "Journalists' Group Demands Resignation of NHK Top Officials," *Japan Press Weekly*, February 11, 2014, http://www.japan-press.co.jp/modules/news/index.php?id=6941.

118 Linda Sieg, "RPT-Japanese Media Self-Censorship Grows in PM Abe's Reign," *Reuters*, February 25, 2015, https://www.reuters.com/article/japan-media/rpt-japanese-media-self-censorship-grows-in-pm-abes-reign-idUSL4N0VY24P20150224.

119 Krauss, "NHK: The Changing and Unchanged Politics of Semi-Independence," 73.

120 Seaton, "NHK, War-Related Television, and the Politics of Fairness," 179–184.

121 "あの日、僕らは戦場で～少年兵の告白～" [That Day, On the Battlefield – Confessions of a Young Soldier –] NHK, aired August 11, 2015; "７３１部隊の真実～エリート医学者と人体実験～" [The Truth of Unit 731 – Elite Doctors and Human Experiments –]. *NHK*, aired on August 13, 2017; "祖父が見た戦場～ルソン島の戦い ２０万人の最期～" [The Battlefield my Grandfather Saw – The Battle of Luzon –]. *NHK*, aired on August 11, 2018; "沖縄 "出口なき"戦場 ～最後の１か月で何が～" [Okinawa "A Battlefield With no Exit" – What Happened in the Final Month –]. *NHK*, aired on August 2, 2020.

Bibliography

Akahata Shimbun. "ＮＨＫ「台湾統治」番組 – 右派勢力の攻撃 狙いは" [NHK "Taiwan Governance" Program, Right-Wing Attack. The Aim …]. August 13, 2009. http://www.jcp.or.jp/akahata/aik09/2009-08-13/2009081304_02_1.html.

Asahi Shimbun. "Asahi Third-Party Panel Says Neglecting Erroneous Articles on 'Comfort Women' Coverage 'Betrayed Readers.'" December 22, 2014. http://www.asahi.com/ajw/articles/AJ201412220088.html.

Chu, Rong-Xuan, and Huang, Chih-Tung. "Indigenous Peoples in Public Media: A Critical Discourse Analysis of the Human Zoo Case." *Discourse & Society* 30, no. 4 (2019): 395–411. https://doi.org/10.1177/0957926519837392.

Chu-chen, Kuo, and Wu, Lilian. "Paiwan Tribe People Miffed after Losing NHK Discrimination Case." *Focus Taiwan*, January 22, 2016. https://focustaiwan.tw/society/201601220031.

Cucek, Michael. "Abe and Press Oppression." In *Press Freedom in Contemporary Japan*, ed. Jeff Kingston, 76–90. London: Routledge, 2017.

Field, Norma. "The Courts, Japan's 'Military Comfort Women,' and the Conscience of Humanity: The Ruling in VAWW-Net Japan v. NHK." *Asia-Pacific Journal* 5, no. 2 (February 2, 2007). http://japanfocus.org/-Norma-Field/2352?rand=1395130360&type=print&print=1.

Fogel, Joshua A. "The Nanking Atrocity and Chinese Historical Memory." In *The Nanking Atrocity, 1937-38: Complicating the Picture*, ed. Bob Tadashi Wakabayashi, 267–284. Oxford: Berghahn Books, 2009.

Friends of Lee Tong Hui Association in Japan. "【NHK「JAPANデビュー」問題 これまでの経緯】" [NHK's Japan Debut Problem – The Facts So Far]. Homepage. Last accessed December 9, 2010. http://www.ritouki.jp/2009NHK.html.

Fujii, Genki. NHK捏造事件と無制限戦争の時代 [NHK's Fabrications and the Era of Unlimited Warfare]. Tokyo: Sōwasha, 2009.

Hata, Ikuhiko. *Comfort Women and Sex in the Battle Zone*. Lanham: Hamilton Books, 2018.

Hiyama, Yukio. 日清戦争 秘蔵写真が明かす真実 [The First Sin-Japanese War: The Truth Told Through Treasured Photographs]. Tokyo: Kodansha, 1997.

Hogg, Chris. "Victory for Japan's War Critics." *BBC News*, August 23, 2005. http://news.bbc.co.uk/2/hi/asia-pacific/4176272.stm.

Inoue, Kazuhiko. "NHKスペシャル「JAPANデビュー」抗議噴出後に番組担当者が台湾再訪で行なったこと＝井上和彦" [NHK Special "Japan Debut" What Happened When the Responsible Parties of Program Rearrived in Taiwan After Protest]. *SAPIO, Shogakukan*, September 3, 2009. http://news.nifty.com/cs/magazine/detail/sapio-20090903-01/1.htm

Japan Press Weekly. "Journalists' Group Demands Resignation of NHK Top Officials." February 11, 2014. http://www.japan-press.co.jp/modules/news/index.php?id=6941.

Japanese Association of Modern East Asian History. 日清戦争と東アジア世界の変容 [The First Sino-Japanese War, East Asia, and How it Changed the World]. Kashiwa: Yumani Shobō, 1997.

Jiji Press. "自民党：公共放送を考える議員の会が発足総会" [LDP: Inaugural Meeting of Lawmakers Considering Public Broadcasting Association]. *Mainichi*

Shimbun, June 12, 2009; and "「ＮＨＫ番組が偏向」＝自民有志が議連" ["NHK Program Biased" = LDP Volunteer Caucas]. June 11, 2009.

Junkerman, John. "Li Ying's 'Yasukuni': The Controversy Continues." *Asia-Pacific Journal* 7, no. 31, (August 3, 2009). https://apjjf.org/-John-Junkerman/3198/article.html.

Ka, Tokuzō. 母国は日本 祖国は台湾 [Japan Is Where I'm Born, but Taiwan Is Where I'm From]. Tokyo: Sakura no Hana, 2005.

Kannon, Kōa. "関連事件等のお知らせ・解説 宗教法人礼拝山興亜観音による布告" [Announcements of Related Events: Commentary – Proclamation by Religious Organization Reihaizan Kōan Kannon]. Homepage, http://www.koakannon.org/jiken-sonota.html.

Katz, Paul R. "Germs of Disaster: The Impact of Epidemics on Japanese Military Campaigns in Taiwan, 1874 and 1895." *Annales de Démographie Historique* (1996): 195–220. https://doi.org/10.3406/adh.1996.1918.

Kawaguchi, Shun. "A Study on the Movement for the Establishment of Showa Day: Legislation Promoted by a Religious Group and a Conservative Society." Master's Thesis, Seoul National University, 2017. http://s-space.snu.ac.kr/bitstream/10371/129330/1/000000141919.pdf.

Keizai Shimbun. "安倍、町村氏らがＮＨＫ番組を批判「偏っている」" [Abe, Machimura Criticize NHK Program for "Bias"]. April 24, 2009.

Keizai Shimbun. "自民議連が「偏向番組問題」でＮＨＫに質問状" [LDP Caucus Sends Letter to NHK For "Biased Program")]. April 28, 2009.

Keizai Shimbun. "ＮＨＫ相手に８４００人が集団提訴 「ＪＡＰＡＮデビュー」歪曲報道で" [8.400-Person Class-Action Lawsuit Against the NHK Regarding Japan Debut Program Fabrication]. June 25, 2010.

Kingston, Jeff. *Contemporary Japan: History, Politics, and Social Change since the 1980s.* Chichester: Wiley-Blackwell, 2011.

Komatsu, Ryujiro. "Court Orders NHK to pay Taiwanese Woman for 'Human Zoo' Reference." *Asahi Shimbun*, January 27, 2014. http://ajw.asahi.com/article/behind_news/social_affairs/AJ201311290059.

Krauss, Ellis S. *Broadcasting in Japan: NHK and Television News.* Ithaca: Cornell University Press, 2000.

Krauss, Ellis S. NHK vs 日本政治 [NHK vs. Japanese Politics]. Translated by Michio Muramatsu and Junpei Gotō. Tokyo: Tōyō Keizai Shimpōsha, 2006.

Krauss, Ellis S. "NHK: The Changing and Unchanged Politics of Semi-Independence." In *Press Freedom in Contemporary Japan*, ed. Jeff Kingston, 64–75. London: Routledge, 2017.

Kyodo News. "ＮＨＫの台湾支配報道は「捏造」 歴史研究者ら８千人提訴" ["Fabrication" of NHK Report on Colonial Rule, 8000 Historians Raise Charges]. June 25, 2009. http://www.47news.jp/CN/200906/CN2009062501000527.html.

Kyodo News. "Top Japan Court Finds Paying NHK Broadcast Fee Legal Obligation." December 6, 2017, https://english.kyodonews.net/news/2017/12/340985196295-update2-top-court-finds-paying-nhk-public-broadcast-fee-legal-obligation.html.

Liu, Yao. "A Study on Zainichi Taiwanese's National Identity: Focusing on the Name Rectification Movement." Master's thesis, Seoul National University, 2018. http://hdl.handle.net/10371/143660.

Matsui, Yayori. "Statement of Protest to NHK by VAWW-NET Japan." *Corporate Watch in Japanese*, April 17, 2001. http://www.jca.apc.org/web-news/corpwatch-jp/150.html.

McCormack, Gavan. "How the History Wars in Japan Left a Black Mark on NHK TV (Their BBC)." *History News Network*, February 7, 2005. http://hnn.us/article/9954.

McCormack, Gavan, and Norimatsu, Satoko Oka. *Resistant Islands: Okinawa Confronts Japan and the United States.* Lanham: Rowman & Littlefield, 2012.

Melma!. "メールマガジン日台共栄"[Mail Magazine Japan–Taiwan Co-Prosperity]. Last accessed December 10, 2010. http://www.melma.com/backnumber_100557/.

Morris-Suzuki, Tessa. *The Past within Us: Media, Memory, History.* London: Verso, 2005.

Murai, Shusuke. "Tokyo Court Rules Against Conservative Group Suing Asahi over 'Comfort Women' Articles." *Japan Times*, July 28, 2014. https://www.japantimes.co.jp/news/2016/07/28/national/tokyo-court-rules-conservative-group-suing-asahi-comfort-women-articles/.

Nakano, Koichi. "The Right-Wing Media and the Rise of Illiberal Politics in Japan." In *Press Freedom in Contemporary Japan*, ed. Jeff Kingston, 30–39. London: Routledge, 2017.

Nakayama, Ariaki. "再質問状(H21.6.4)に対するＮＨＫからの回答書 [Nakayama Nariaki – NHK's Response to the Question Posed on June 4, 2009]. Homepage.

Nakayama, Ariaki. "再質問状(H21.6.4)に対するＮＨＫからの回答書 [Nakayama Nariaki – NHK's Response to the Question Posed on June 4, 2009]. *Nakayama Nariaki* (Homepage). Last accessed December 9, 2010. http://nakayamanariaki.com/modules/bulletin/index.php?page=article&storyid=41.

Nakayama, Ariaki. "平成２１年４月５日放送「ＮＨＫスペシャル　シリーズＪＡＰＡＮデビュー第１回『アジアの一等国』」に対する公開質問状及び回答書" [Heisei 21/4/5 Broadcast – NHK Special – Japan Debut Series Part 1 "A First-Rate Asian Nation" Open Letter and Response]. Homepage. Last accessed December 9, 2010, https://web.archive.org/web/20120321061935/http://nakayamanariaki.com/modules/bulletin/index.php?page=article&storyid=32.

NHK. "視聴者対応報告" [Audience Response Report]. Report, April 2009.

NHK. "視聴者対応報告" [Audience Response Report]. Report, May 2009.

NHK. "お客さまの声" [Responses from Our Customers]. Report, July 2009.

NHK. "視聴者対応報告" [Audience Response Report]. Report, January 2010.

NHK. "プロジェクトJAPAN：未来へのプレーバック。〔放送予定〕" [Project Japan: Playback to the Future (Planned Broadcast)]. Last Accessed December 11, 2010. http://www9.nhk.or.jp/japan/pjyotei/archive_2009.html/.

NHK. "シリーズ・JAPANデビュー 第1回「アジアの"一等国 "」に関しての説" [Japan Debut Series: Regarding Episode 1 "A First Rate Asian Power"]. Last Accessed December 1, 2010. http://www.nhk.or.jp/japan/announce/090617.html.

NHK. "シリーズ・JAPANデビュー 第1回「アジアの"一等国"」に関しての説明・追加" [Japan Debut Series: Regarding Episode 1 "A First Rate Asian Power – Addendum"]. Last Accessed December 1, 2010. http://www.nhk.or.jp/japan/announce/090722.html.

NHK. "Summary of Press Conference (June, 2009)." Last Accessed December 13, 2010. http://www.nhk.or.jp/pr/english/toptalk/kaichou_e/k_e0906.htm#06.

NihonBunkaChannelSakura.“【NHK訴訟】一万人・集団訴訟及び名誉毀損訴訟” [“NHK Lawsuit” 10.000-Person Class-Action Lawsuit and Defamation Lawsuit]. Homepage. Last accessed December 15, 2010. http://www.ch-sakura.jp/topix/1054.html.

Nihon Bunka Channel Sakura. “【お知らせ】 NHK「JAPANデビュー」に抗議する国民大行動” [“Announcement” Large Action by the People Against NHK’s Japan Debut]. Homepage. Last accessed December 9, 2010. http://www.ch-sakura.jp/topix/1041.html.

Nippon Kaigi. “役員名簿 « 日本会議” [List of Names “Nippon Kaigi”]. Last accessed December 10, 2010. http://www.nipponkaigi.org/about/yakuin.

Nishimura, Kōyū. 【撃論ムック】NHKの正体—情報統制で国民に銃を向ける、報道テロリズム[The Truth Behind the NHK – Information Terrorism, Pointing a Gun to the People through Information Control]. Tokyo: Oakla Publishing, 2009.

Obata, Eri. “The Display of Taiwan’s Aborigines in the Japan-British Exhibition of 1910 as a Showcase of Japan’s Colonial Power.” Master’s Thesis, National Chengchi University, 2012. https://ah.nccu.edu.tw/retrieve/82513/400901.pdf.

Okamura, Jun. “Most of You Have Not Heard of Nippon Kaigi.” *GlobalTalk 21* (Blog), January 02, 2008. http://son-of-gadfly-on-the-wall.blogspot.com/2008/01/most-of-you-have-not-heard-of-nippon.html.

Pesek, William. “Abe Pulls Strings to Put NHK under His Thumb.” *Japan Time*, February 7, 2014. https://www.japantimes.co.jp/opinion/2014/02/07/commentary/japan-commentary/abe-pulls-strings-to-put-nhk-under-his-thumb/.

Polletta, Francesca. *It Was Like a Fever: Storytelling in Protest and Politics*. Chicago: University of Chicago Press, 2006.

Rabson, Steve. “Case Dismissed: Osaka Court Upholds Novelist Oe Kenzaburo for Writing That Japanese Military Ordered ‘Group Suicides’ In Battle of Okinawa.” *Asia-Pacific Journal* 6, no. 4 (April 1, 2008). http://japanfocus.org/-Steve-Rabson/2716.

Sankei Shimbun. “ＮＨＫスペシャルで「発言ゆがめられた」柯徳三氏が死去” [Ka Tokuzō, Whose Words “Were Distorted” In an NHK Special, has Died]. February 4, 2010.

Schäfer, Fabian, Evert, Stefan, and Heinrich, Philipp. “Japan’s 2014 General Election: Political Bots, Right-Wing Internet Activism, and Prime Minister Shinzō Abe’s Hidden Nationalist Agenda.” *Big Data* 5, no. 4 (2017): 294–309. https://doi.org/10.1089/big.2017.0049.

Seaton, Philip A. *Japan’s Contested War Memories: The “Memory Rifts” in Historical Consciousness of World War II*. London: Routledge, 2007.

Seaton, Philip A. “NHK, War-Related Television, and the Politics of Fairness.” In *Press Freedom in Contemporary Japan*, ed. Jeff Kingston, 172–185. London: Routledge, 2017.

Sieg, Linda. “RPT-Japanese Media Self-Censorship Grows in PM Abe’s Reign.” *Reuters*, February 25, 2015. https://www.reuters.com/article/japan-media/rpt-japanese-media-self-censorship-grows-in-pm-abes-reign-idUSL4N0VY24P20150224.

Szczepanska, Kamila. *The Politics of War Memory in Japan: Progressive Civil Society Groups and Contestation of Memory of the Asia-Pacific War*. London: Routledge, 2014.

Takemoto, Tadao, and Ohara, Yasuo. 再審「南京大虐殺」―世界に訴える日本の冤罪 [The Alleged Nanjing Massacre]. Tokyo: Meiseisha, 2000.

Takeshi, Komagome. 東アジア国際政治史 [The History of East Asia in International Relations]. University of Nagoya Press, 2007.

Tawara, Yoshifumi. 安倍晋三の本性 [The True Nature of Abe Shinzō]. Tokyo: Kinyobi KK, 2016.

Underwood, William. "NHK's Finest Hour: Japan's Official Record of Chinese Forced Labor." *Asia-Pacific Journal* 4, no. 8 (August 6, 2006). http://www.japanfocus.org/-William-Underwood/2187.

Voice of Taiwan Newsletter. "「台湾の声」【ＮＨＫ問題】報道動画と抗議活動案内（東京・岡山」）" [(Taiwan's Voice) "NHK Scandal" Explaining the Broadcast and Protest Activity (Tokyo, Okayama)]. Last Accessed December 12, 2010. http://sv3.inacs.jp/bn/?2009100097078774001950.3407,

Wakabayashi, Bob Tadashi. "The Nanking 100-Man Killing Contest Debate: War Guilt Amid Fabricated Illusions, 1971–75." *Journal of Japanese Studies* 26, no. 2 (2000): 307–340. https://doi.org/ 10.2307/133271

Wakabayashi, Bob Tadashi. "The Nanking 100-Man Killing Contest Debate, 1971–75." In *The Nanking Atrocity, 1937–38: Complicating the Picture*, ed. Bob Tadashi Wakabayashi, 115–148. Oxford: Berghahn Books, 2009.

Wakabayashi, Masahiro. もっと知りたい台湾 [Wanting to Know More About Taiwan]. Tokyo: Kōbundō, 1998.

Wikipedia. "日本李登輝友の会" [Friends of Lee Teng-Hui Association in Japan]. Last accessed December 10, 2010. http://ja.wikipedia.org/wiki/%E6%97%A5%E6%9C%AC%E6%9D%8E%E7%99%BB%E8%BC%9D%E5%8F%8B%E3%81%AE%E4%BC%9A.

Women's Caucus for Gender Justice. "Transcript of Oral Judgment, Delivered in The Hague, The Netherlands, 4 December 2001." Accessed September 2, 2020. http://www.iccwomen.org/wigjdraft1/Archives/oldWCGJ/tokyo/summary.html

World Times. "ＮＨＫ反日報道に約１３００人が抗議 東京・渋谷" [Approximately 1300 People Protest NHK's Anti-Japanese Reporting – Tokyo, Shibuya]. May 17, 2009. http://www.worldtimes.co.jp/today/kokunai/090517-4.html.

Yen-ting, Chen, and Pan, Jason. "Woman Sued NHK 'for Dignity'." *Taipei Times*, December 2, 2013. https://www.taipeitimes.com/News/taiwan/archives/2013/12/02/2003578139.

Yon, Michael. "Japan: Lawsuits against Asahi Shimbun Newspaper." *Michael Yon JP* (Blog), February 27, 2015. http://michaelyonjp.blogspot.com/2015/02/blog-post_27.html.

Yoshida, Reiji, and Mie, Ayako. "Momii's Rise Tests NHK's Reputation." *Japan Times*, February 2, 2014. http://www.japantimes.co.jp/news/2014/02/02/national/momiis-rise-tests-nhks-reputation/.

YouTube. "Guidelines and Requirements: Report a Copyright Violation." Accessed December 15, 2010. http://www.google.com/support/youtube/bin/answer.py?hl=en&answer=113113.

Ziomek, Kirsten L. *Lost Histories: Recovering the Lives of Japan's Colonial Peoples*. Cambridge: Harvard University Asia Center, 2019.

6 Conservative activism and historical remembrance of the Battle of Okinawa

The case of the 32nd Army headquarters

The 1945 Battle of Okinawa was the bloodiest battle of the Pacific War. Over the course of several months, the Imperial Japanese military conducted a desperate defense against American invaders, with the majority of its 80,000-man garrison dying in the process. The cost was even higher for Okinawa's civilian population. About 100,000 people – close to a fourth of Okinawa prefecture's prewar population – died. Wartime propaganda and postwar Japanese policies treated them as having voluntarily died alongside soldiers in defense of their nation, but many surviving Okinawans recalled cases of civilians pressured into committing suicide or being outright murdered by Japanese soldiers.

Okinawan accounts of widespread forced suicide and murder by the Japanese military have not been well received by one segment of Japanese society – the assertive conservative right. For decades Japan's right has striven to promote and preserve a historical narrative that downplays the negative aspects of Imperial Japan's colonialism and wartime conduct. To these conservatives, Japanese soldiers were heroic defenders of Okinawa and civilians were loyal subjects of the Japanese Empire who made noble sacrifices for their country. Differing historical interpretations, which depict the Okinawans as victims of Imperial Japan and its military, have been regarded as "anti-Japanese" propaganda.

In this chapter I explore one episode within the ongoing struggle over the remembrance of World War II in Okinawa – the fight over the wording of a historical signboard placed in front of the cave that once housed a Japanese Imperial Army headquarters. In 2011 and 2012, conservative activists successfully pressured local officials into deleting references to war atrocities from the signboard. This clear victory was largely due to the efforts of one organization – Nihon Bunka Channel Sakura (Japanese Culture Channel Sakura), an internet broadcaster that promoted the views of Japan's conservative right.

In the field of contestation over war memory in Okinawa, left-leaning Okinawan academics, activists, and the Okinawan media sought to give voice to local narratives of victimhood. Channel Sakura and its activists were challengers seeking to turn official remembrance in favor of their own viewpoints. Skilled social actors within Channel Sakura created a convincing series of video programs challenging the historical views of the Okinawan scholars and persuading numerous individuals to lodge complaints. The complaints prompted an official review of the signboard's content and eventually the deletion of passages that had offended the right.

The passages in question touched on two sensitive issues: the murder/suicide of Okinawan civilians and the so-called comfort women system of military brothels. To understand the context under which Channel Sakura carried out this campaign, I begin this chapter with background information on these two issues and the disputes surrounding them.

Responsibility for civilian deaths in Okinawa

Among the tens of thousands of Okinawan civilians who died in 1945, there are many documented cases of people who died of self-inflicted wounds. Using hand grenades or improvised weapons, it was alleged that they voluntarily took their own lives to avoid the "horror and shame of falling into American hands."[1]

This view of voluntarily death was in harmony with Japanese wartime propaganda that depicted civilians and the military coming together as one and dying in the defense of their island. Official postwar Japanese government policies also echoed this viewpoint. A 1952 compensation law for war-related losses stipulated that payments be issued to the bereaved family members of Okinawan civilians who could be categorized as having died while assisting the Japanese military.[2] This meant that people claiming that Japanese soldiers had murdered or forced their relatives to commit suicide would not receive compensation payments. Thus such deaths became a taboo topic for Okinawan war survivors.[3]

However, as years passed, increasing public attention was given to survivors' testimonies that highlighted forced suicide and murder by the Japanese military. For example, Marxist historian Ienaga Saburō's 1968 book *The Pacific War* and Ōe Kenzaburō's 1970 book *Okinawa Notes* contained descriptions of Okinawan civilians being ordered by the Japanese military to commit suicide. Ōe's book, based on interviews with Okinawan war survivors, stated that Japanese military officers ordered civilians on Zamami and Tokashiki Islands to commit suicide rather than be captured. Public sentiment in Okinawa gravitated toward the idea that the civilian population had been victims of the Japanese military, rather than willful participants who died while assisting the military. An understanding of the Battle of Okinawa that included and emphasized suffering at the hands of the Japanese military became "one of the most important building blocks for the construction of an Okinawan identity."[4]

This sentiment has influenced acts of violent and non-violent protest. When the then–Crown Prince Akihito and Crown Princess Michiko visited Okinawa in 1975 – the first imperial visit since the end of the war – someone threw a firebomb in their direction and nearly hit them. The attacker was a university student who blamed the emperor for Okinawan civilian war deaths.[5] Peaceful protests were also held against making Emperor Hirohito's birthday a national holiday, and a 1987 plan for Hirohito to visit Okinawan for a sports competition.[6]

By the 1980s, descriptions of military-ordered suicides and fratricide appeared in Japanese public school history textbooks. As with other claims of Japanese atrocities, the Okinawans' accounts of compulsory mass suicide became a target for Japan's assertive conservative right. It was seen by the right as another example of leftist groups distorting the past to portray Japan in a negative light. Akiko Naono has argued that the right preferred a narrative of "precious sacrifice," which depicts the war dead as choosing to fight and die for their country. This formed a "nationalist pedagogy" that "incites sentiments of love and loyalty to the nation through which the very act of the narrative performance interpolates a growing circle of national subjects." To protect this narrative, "Okinawa's compulsory mass suicide must be forgotten and instead remembered as consented and voluntary sacrifice."[7]

A major challenge to Okinawan historical views came in 1982 when right-leaning members of the Ministry of Education's textbook approval board ordered textbook publishers to remove descriptions of Japanese soldiers killing Okinawan civilians. The board claimed that the evidence supporting these claims, personal testimony from survivors, was not a reliable source of information. This sparked a wave of protest from Okinawa. The Okinawan Prefectural Assembly unanimously passed a resolution of protest demanding that the Ministry of Education reverse its decision. The vote was supported by Okinawan politicians of the ruling Liberal Democratic Party (LDP). The Ministry of Education backed down from its decision and restored the descriptions.

The following year, the Ministry of Education added the words "mass suicide" (shūdan jiketsu) to textbook descriptions of Okinawan civilian deaths. This wording implied that civilians voluntarily died instead of being forced to do so. Historian Ienaga Saburō sued the Ministry of Education over the wording change, and although he eventually lost the lawsuit, the Supreme Court ruling stated that the deaths could not fairly be described as voluntary. The decision caused more textbook publishers to include descriptions of non-voluntary Okinawan deaths.[8]

The comfort women issue

A major issue of dispute between Japan's conservative right and its opponents is the remembrance of the comfort women – the tens of thousands of women who worked in Japanese military brothels during World War II.[9] The existence of these women was not widely recognized until the 1990s and largely came to light due to the efforts of activists in South Korea and Japan. Interviews with surviving comfort women were used to make a case that Japan's state and military had systematically forced most of them work in brothels. The stories of the terrible abuse they endured at the hands of Japanese soldiers shocked the world.

To progressive activists, these women were "sex slaves" – kidnapped or coerced into sexually servicing the Japanese military. Activists and the surviving comfort women demanded that the Japanese state officially recognize and apologize for the comfort women system. In response to this pressure, the Japanese government conducted an official study in 1993 on the comfort women, concluding "that in many cases they were recruited against their own will, through coaxing, coercion, etc., and that, at times, administrative/military personnel directly took part in the recruitments."[10] It also established the Asian Women's Fund, a semi-private organization that delivered compensation payments and apology letters signed by the prime minister to surviving comfort women.

Japan's conservative right strongly disagreed with the official response of their government. In their view, the political left was distorting the truth about history. Nationalists argued that there was no systematic military participation in the coercion and kidnapping of Asian women. To emphasize their belief that most of the women had volunteered, they referred to the women as "prostitutes" or "camp followers" rather than as "sex slaves." If abuses had taken place during "recruitment" of the women, conservatives believed that most of those abuses were either isolated incidents of rogue soldiers or the work of private brokers. By passing responsibility away from the Japanese state and military leadership, they were depicting history in a manner that fits with their overall view of World War II: the Japanese Army was not involved in mass criminal actions.

Following Japanese government's recognition of the issue, descriptions of comfort women began to appear in Japanese junior high school history textbooks. The nationalist activist organization Tsukurukai (The Japanese Society for History Textbook Reform) was founded in 1996 as a direct response to the appearance of comfort women in history textbooks. Its founder, Fujioka Nobukatsu, was determined to see such references erased from all junior high school textbooks. He argued not only that it was "an absolute distortion of historical fact" that made Japanese schoolchildren dislike their own country but also that it hurt the image of Japan "all over the world."[11]

In addition to arguments based on perceived distortions of fact, Fujioka also objected to the inclusion of such a topic in junior high school textbooks because it was a sexual subject that was not suitable to be taught to young children. Fujioka and Tsukurukai aggressively lobbied politicians, school boards, and the Japanese public, arguing that comfort women should not be mentioned in any of the textbooks.

The first year of campaigning was unsuccessful. By 1997, all textbooks that passed that year's screening by the government contained mentions of comfort women in the context of the forced wartime mobilizations of Korean laborers.[12] However, by the early 2000s, Tsukurukai and its supporters began to see some success. Although Tsukurukai's own textbook was not popular, mainstream textbook publishers engaged in self-censorship to avoid the controversy and retain their market shares.[13] Only 20% of textbooks included descriptions of comfort women in 2002–2006. Tsukurukai had "precipitated a perceptible overall shift" toward their position on the acceptability of mentioning comfort women in textbooks.[14] After these successes, Tsukurukai moved on to targeting other issues, such as descriptions of Okinawan civilian deaths during the war.

History textbooks and reversals on Okinawan civilian suicides

In December 2006, during the first term of Prime Minister Abe Shinzō, a well-known supporter of the nationalist cause, Japan's Ministry of Education reversed its long-held position on the Battle of Okinawa. It ordered publishers to remove references to the Japanese military's involvement in Okinawan mass suicides. Instead of "being forced" (kyōsei sareta), the books were asked to state that civilians had been "cornered into" (oikomareta) committing killing themselves.[15]

As in 1982, the Okinawan Prefectural Assembly and local governments across Okinawa passed resolutions demanding that the textbook revisions be overturned. A protest march was organized, and over 100,000 people participated, making it the largest demonstration since Okinawa was returned to Japan in 1972.[16]

The Ministry reacted to the Okinawan pressure by slightly walking back its position. The phrase "civilians were forced by the Japanese army into committing mass suicides" was instead changed to "civilians were driven to commit mass suicides using hand grenades and other means distributed to them with the involvement of the Japanese army." The result dissatisfied Okinawan activists who had hoped for a complete reversal. However, it did represent a minor victory for the Okinawans against the right.[17]

The *Asahi Shimbun* ran an editorial in December 2007, questioning whether the first decision had been made due to the influence of Abe and arguing that the controversy had helped "attract unprecedented public attention" to the issue of mass suicides. The large protest rallies had also helped expose "serious flaws" in the Japanese government's textbook screening system.[18]

Other victories against the conservative right soon followed. As mentioned in Chapter 5, conservatives who filed a lawsuit aiming to discredit Ōe Kenzaburō's writings about civilian suicides had their case rejected in 2008 and 2011. The judges' decision that suicides had been ordered by the military further strengthened the position of progressive groups that fought to include such information in textbooks.

From the events of the 1990s and 2000s, Okinawa can be described as hostile territory for Japan's conservative right. In both 1982 and 2007 local assemblies, the prefectural assembly, and large numbers of protesters had mobilized to oppose attempted changes to history education that would have reflected the conservative viewpoints. If the local remembrance of World War II in Okinawa was a field of contestation, the activists of the right would most certainly be the challengers, fighting against progressive incumbents.

The remainder of this chapter focuses on a campaign by those conservative challengers, launched in 2011. The campaign was led by the activists of Channel Sakura, an internet broadcaster founded with the support of key members of Tsukurukai (as mentioned in Chapter 3).

The 32nd Army headquarters

In preparation for an expected American invasion of Okinawan, the Japanese Imperial Army build an extensive network of defensive fortifications, including tunnels and bunkers that would protect their forces from aerial and artillery bombardment. The 32nd Army, which was charged with the overall defense of Okinawa, centered a major network of defenses around Shuri Castle, in the southern part of the island. This included a system of tunnels and underground rooms that housed its headquarters.[19] The area saw some of the heaviest fighting of the battle. The castle, most of the tunnels, and the 32nd Army headquarters were destroyed, with many soldiers and civilians losing their lives in the process.

In the postwar era Shuri Castle was rebuilt, and the area around it turned into a public park, which has since become one of the most-visited tourist attractions in Okinawa prefecture. The ruined tunnels of the 32nd Army headquarters complex were off-limits to visitors, but in 1997 the Okinawa prefectural government launched preservations efforts with the aim of eventually opening the headquarters to the public. After considerable delays in the plan, the prefectural government decided in 2011 that it would erect a historical signboard near the entrance of the headquarters tunnels. A committee of five historical experts, chaired by Professor Ikeda Yoshifumi of the University of the Ryukyus, created and delivered a draft of the text for the signboard in November 2011.[20]

The draft, which was released to the public, included two sections that would prove controversial. The first of these was a sentence describing the people who had been present in the tunnels during the Battle of Okinawa. It listed officers, soldiers, Okinawan students drafted into military service, female nurses, and, of particular concern to nationalists, comfort women. The second was a phrase stating that in the vicinity of the caves there were cases in which "Okinawan civilians were seen as 'spies' and massacred by the Japanese military" (nihongun ni supaishi sare Okinawa jyūmin no gyakusatsu nado mo okorimashita). Both of these sections highlighted atrocities by the Japanese military, something that the conservative right did not want visitors to read about.

One day after the release of the draft, the conservative activists called for action against it. Channel Sakura produced a program informing its viewers that they needed to stop the Okinawan "leftists" who were "falsely accusing the heroic war dead" of war crimes. Channel Sakura president Mizushima Satoru and his co-host lamented that the many groups of schoolchildren who visit the park could read the signboard and become believers in fake "anti-Japanese" history.[21] It was all the more insulting to nationalists because a man they considered a military hero, General Ushijima Mitsuru, had taken his own life in those caves. Mizushima could not stand the idea that children would learn that Ushijima had spent the final days of his life in what could be seen as a brothel.[22] Although it was just a single signboard, the presence of the offending passages could influence the way that future generations viewed the actions of Japanese soldiers in the Battle of Okinawa. These leftists needed to be "absolutely stopped" from spreading their ideology across Okinawa and Japan.[23] As in Channel Sakura's other protest campaigns, the grassroots efforts of viewers were emphasized as necessary to stop the "anti-Japanese" left from distorting history.

Channel Sakura dispatched journalists to obtain survivor testimony that could be used to question the validity of its ideological opponents' historical claims. On November 24, 2011, it aired a special program interviewing Iha Naeko, who had served as a nurse inside the 32nd Army headquarters complex during the period described by the signboard. Iha was appalled by claims that comfort women had been present in the headquarters and countered that the only women present there were licensed nurses such as herself. She also strongly denied that the Japanese military had massacred Okinawan civilians in the area. Breaking into tears at several points in the interview, Iha stated that the kinds of "filthy things" mentioned in the signboard draft were an insult to the memory of the brave and honest people who died in the Battle of Okinawa. It was clear that she had great respect for the Japanese military, including General Ushijima, whom she referred to with the honorific "his excellency" (kakka). At the end of the interview, Channel Sakura's news anchors shared the e-mail address, phone number, and FAX number of the Okinawa prefectural government office that was in charge of reviewing the signboard draft.

Other Channel Sakura programs linked the historical views argued that the signboard represented a threat to Japanese national security. For example, a November 28 show focused on the Japanese Self-Defense Forces' policies to stop Chinese incursions in the waters near Okinawa prefecture devoted several minutes to the signboard. Retired Air Self-Defense Force Lt. General Satō Mamoru and host Inoue Kazuhiko argued that "leftist" Okinawans pushing for more descriptions of Japanese Army atrocities in textbooks and signboards were serving the interests of China and North Korea. Bad perceptions of the military fueled anti-base sentiment in Okinawa, weakening the overall defense of the country. Satō shared personal anecdotes about his conversations with elderly Okinawans who had expressed their respect for General Ushijima, saying that everyone who had been there knew the actual truth, as opposed to the "nonsense" reported by the Japanese mainstream media.[24]

Swift government action in favor of the Right

Channel Sakura's pressure campaign again the Okinawa prefectural government proved a success when the official wording for the signboard was announced in February 2012. References to comfort women and the killing of local residents had been completely removed from the text.[25] Local newspapers reported that the changes had been made after the prefectural government had received numerous protests. According to the Okinawa Times, a total of 82 complaints, many of them from people outside of the prefecture, had been received through telephone, e-mail, or fax. The Ryukyu Shimpo wrote that a "satellite television program" had been behind the complaints, a clear reference to Channel Sakura.[26]

Mizushima and his Channel Sakura co-hosts, who were used to mainstream media not mentioning the name of their organization when reporting on its achievements, celebrated the result as a victory.[27]

In addition to the changes mentioned above, it was decided that English, Chinese, and Korean translations would not be included in the sign for a reference to Okinawa as a "sacrificial stone" (sute-ishi). The term, which refers to a game piece sacrificed in order to attain victory in the game Go, was used in Imperial Japanese Army documents to describe an Okinawan fight-to-the-death as strategically necessary.[28] It is a term that has often been quoted by postwar Okinawans as proof that Imperial Japan and its military saw their island and its people as expendable.[29] Although the term was not specifically mentioned or targeted by Channel Sakura as something that needed to be removed, it is possible that political concerns, rather than translation difficulties, led to its removal from the foreign language texts on the signboard.[30]

The revision of the signboard draft did not go unnoticed and was strongly condemned by local activists, academics, and the local press. Members of the committee of experts who drafted the signboard text, including Professor Ikeda, publicly denounced the changes.[31] One committee member, Professor Arashiro Toshiki of Okinawa University, appeared on local television and responded to claims that the draft had not been based on evidence, stating that if the prefectural government had needed historical proof, he and the other committee members were on hand to readily provide it. No official had contacted him before the revision was announced.[32]

Editorials in Okinawa's two largest newspapers, the *Okinawa Times* and *Ryukyu Shimpo*, also criticized the decision and called on the prefectural government to officially explain why it had made the revisions.[33] Local activists, including an organization of volunteer tour guides and war survivors, held public study meetings to defend the historical accuracy of the original draft.[34] At one such event, held on March 17, 2011, Tokuyama Chōshō, who had been pressed into service as a 17-year-old soldier in 1945, told an audience of over 200 people that he had witnessed the very things that nationalists had pressured the government into deleting from the signboard.[35]

The censored signboard

Just days after local groups had started organizing against the signboard plan, the prefectural government printed and erected it on the grounds of Shuri Castle. The speed of its completion, which did not allow much time for public discussion or the organization of protests, could have been politically motivated. However, March was also the last month of the 2011 fiscal year, so bureaucratic concerns about spending already-allotted construction budgets may have also driven events.

The Okinawan prefectural government defended its decision in an official statement posted on its website on April 12, 2011. It denied claims that it was attempting to whitewash or hide atrocities committed by the Japanese military in

1945 by stating that the signboard was meant to inform visitors about the 32nd Army headquarters. It had conducted its own investigation regarding the housing comfort women and the massacre of civilians at the headquarters, concluding that there was no evidence to back up the descriptions found in the original draft. As proof of its own commitment to spreading the truth about both issues, it pointed out that the Okinawa Prefectural Peace Museum had detailed exhibits about both comfort women and the civilian massacres.[36]

There is some reason to believe, however, that the prefectural government was sympathetic to Channel Sakura's complaints. The signboard had been erected under a prefectural government headed by Governor Nakaima Hirokazu, a conservative politician who later came out as a public supporter of the historical revisionist organization Nippon Kaigi.[37] Prior to the signboard's completion, Shimoji Hiroshi, the prefectural official responsible for the signboard project, explained that the changes to the draft reflected the inability to confirm the truth of claims, rather than political bias:

> The Prefecture decided to delete some sections since we could not conclusively prove their veracity. Especially in regard to the sections on the presence of comfort women in the tunnels, there are some testimonies which confirm this and others that deny it. Therefore, since there are conflicting testimonies, we could not sufficiently determine the facts of the matter and, thus, we could not include this history on the marker.[38]

Shimoji explained that the decision had been his own, but he had obtained Governor Nakaima's approval before finalizing it.[39] Nakaima, when asked by an opposition lawmaker to explain the revision of its text, said that it was "common sense" for the signboard not to include information that "could not be confirmed."[40] One of Nikaima's harshest critics, author and activist Medoruma Shun, has argued that "using the right-wing protest that started with an appeal from Channel Sakura as an excuse, or in fact, as an opportunity, Governor Nakaima is actively trying to falsify accounts of the Battle of Okinawa."[41] Whether or not the ultimate decision may have been a result of the nationalist sympathies of Nakaima and others within the Okinawa prefectural government, Channel Sakura and its supporters had provided the impetus for the revisions. It was the result they had fought for.

Unlike many of Channel Sakura's activist campaigns during the period of my research, the case of the 32nd Army headquarters signboard was an unambiguous victory for the conservative right. In other cases, defeats or half-victories required lengthy explanations rationalizing the need to fight on and keep making financial contributions to the movement, but no one could question this successful outcome. Reflecting on the outcome, Mizushima Satoru told viewers that the result had been achieved thanks to "everyone's power" (minnasan no chikara de). The changes to the signboard showed how one could "truly feel" that Channel Sakura was spreading the historical truth and overturning the lies of the political left.[42]

Conclusion

Nakaima Hirokazu stepped down as governor of Okinawa in 2014, to be replaced by progressive governors Onaga Takeshi (2014–2018) and Tamaki Denny (2018–present). Under the terms of these new governors, local groups in Okinawa petitioned the government to reprint the 32nd Army headquarters signboard to re-include descriptions of war atrocities. Those calling for the change included peace activists and members of the committee of experts who created the original signboard draft text for the prefecture.

To bolster their claims in favor of the original draft, scholars presented survivor testimony contradicting the claims made by Iha Naeko. One survivor, Masako Shinjo Summers Robbins, also claimed to have been present at a military cave complex near Shuri Castle. Robbins had personally witnessed Japanese soldiers murdering Okinawan civilians and also saw local girls forced into "servicing" soldiers.[43] The *Okinawa Times* printed several articles in September 2016 drawing on Robbins' accounts, with headlines proclaiming that there had in fact been comfort women and civilian massacres at the 32nd Army headquarters.[44] Later that month, Robbins' written testimony was presented along with other evidence at a meeting between several former members of the expert committee.[45] They called on the prefectural government to re-adopt the wording they had originally suggested.

Despite the fact that the Okinawa prefectural government was under Governor Onaga, a man that Channel Sakura's programming depicted as a left-wing agent of the Chinese government,[46] requests for a change were rejected.[47] In the years since, progressive activists have called on the government to open the 32nd Army headquarters caves to the general public, and Governor Tamaki Denny responded in 2020 by creating a committee of civil engineers and other experts that will explore the feasibility of such a plan.[48] If the plan moves forward, the re-opening of the caves will create new opportunities for the political left and right to argue over the manner in which visitors are taught about the events of 1945. Given that progressive politicians are currently in power in Okinawa, it will likely be more difficult for the conservative right to influence the wording of any new official signage in the caves.

The 2011–2012 case of the 32nd Army headquarters signboard was just one battle of many in an ongoing conflict over the remembrance of World War II in Japan. In this field of contestation, the activists of the conservative right looked for both large and small opportunities to assert their views and influence the general public. This was a small opportunity to change one particular signboard, but it was a success. By noticing the opening, starting a protest campaign, and seeking out personal testimony from a war survivor who could support conservative claims, the skilled social actors within Channel Sakura convinced dozens of people to contact the Okinawan prefectural government and lodge complaints. The prefectural government, under an ideologically sympathetic governor, was receptive to these complaints and dismissive of progressive groups' counter-protests.

Even accepting that this was not a big victory, it was still an event that Channel Sakura used to create a sense of accomplishment for its supporters. Japan's conservative right portrays itself as an extreme underdog against powerful leftist and anti-Japanese forces, so any small adjustment in their favor, even if it is a piecemeal gain, can be cause for celebration. The result, even though small, was something that activists could point to as proof that victories are sometimes possible and that such victories are only possible when "everyone" joins together in a grassroots protest campaign.

Notes

1 Norma Field, *In the Realm of a Dying Emperor* (New York: Pantheon Books, 1991), 66.

2 Nobumasa Tanaka. "Desecration of the Dead: Bereaved Okinawan Families Sue Yasukuni to End Relatives' Enshrinement," trans. Steve Rabson. *Asia-Pacific Journal* 6, no. 5 (May 3, 2008), https://apjjf.org/-Nobumasa-Tanaka/2744/article.html.

3 Kyle Ikeda, *Okinawan War Memory: Transgenerational Trauma and the War Fiction of Medoruma Shun* (New York: Routledge, 2014), 29.

4 Hirofumi Hayashi, "Unsettled State Violence in Japan: The Okinawa Incident," in *State Violence in East Asia*, ed. N. Ganesan and Sung Chull Kim (Lexington, KY: University Press of Kentucky, 2013), 91–92.

5 "High Anxiety for Okinawa Governor over '75 Imperial Visit,'" *Japan Times*, November 23, 2012, http://www.japantimes.co.jp/news/2012/11/23/national/high-anxiety-for-okinawa-governor-over-75-imperial-visit/#.U_WGvfmSzB0.

6 Steven Rabson, "Okinawan Perspectives on Japan's Imperial Institution," *Asia-Pacific Journal* 6, no. 2 (February 1, 2008), https://apjjf.org/-Steve-Rabson/2667/article.html.

7 Akiko Naono, "Producing Sacrificial Subjects for the Nation: Japan's War-Related Redress Policy and the Endurance Doctrine," in *Toward a Sociology of the Trace*, ed. Herman Gray and Macarena Gómez-Barris (Minneapolis: University of Minnesota Press, 2010), 125–126.

8 Hayashi, "Unsettled State Violence in Japan: The Okinawa Incident," 91–92.

9 For the historical details of his issue, see: Toshiyuki Tanaka, *Japan's Comfort Women: Sexual Slavery and Prostitution during World War II and the US Occupation* (London: Routledge, 2007).

10 The full text of the 1993 Kono Statement can be found at: "Statement by the Chief Cabinet Secretary Yohei Kono on the Result of the Study on the Issue of 'Comfort Women,'" *Ministry of Foreign Affairs of Japan*, August 4, 1993, http://www.mofa.go.jp/policy/women/fund/state9308.html.

11 Nobukatsu Fujioka, "Education Issues, Comfort Women and the Creation of a New History Textbook," *Association for Advancement of Unbiased View of History from Association for Advancement of Liberal View of History*, February 25, 1999, http://www.jiyuushikan.org/e/education.html.

12 Chunghee Sarah Soh, *The Comfort Women: Sexual Violence and Postcolonial Memory in Korea and Japan* (Chicago: University of Chicago Press, 2008), 169–170.

13 Tawara Yoshifumi, "Comfort Women, Textbooks, and the Rise of 'New Right' Revisionism," in *Denying the Comfort Women: The Japanese State's Assault on Historical Truth*, ed., Rumiko Nishino, Puja Kim and Akane Onozawa (London: Routledge, 2018).

14 Philip A. Seaton, *Japan's Contested War Memories: The "Memory Rifts" in Historical Consciousness of World War II* (London: Routledge, 2007), 130–131.
15 Gavan McCormack and Satoko Oka Norimatsu, *Resistant Islands: Okinawa Confronts Japan and the United States* (Lanham: Rowman & Littlefield, 2012), 33–34.
16 Norimitsu Onishi, "Okinawans Protest Japan's Plan to Revise Bitter Chapter of World War II," *New York Times*, October 06, 2007, http://www.nytimes.com/2007/10/07/world/asia/07okinawa.html?pagewanted=all.
17 Steve Rabson, "The Politics of Trauma: Compulsory Suicides during the Battle of Okinawa and Postwar Retrospectives," *Intersections: Gender and Sexuality in Asia and the Pacific* no. 24 (June 2010), http://intersections.anu.edu.au/issue24/rabson.htm.
18 Asahi Shimbun Editorial, "Compulsory Mass Suicide, the Battle of Okinawa, and Japan's Textbook Controversy," trans. Kyoko Selden. *Asia-Pacific Journal* 6, no. 1 (January 1, 2008), https://apjjf.org/-Aniya-Masaaki/2629/article.html.
19 George Feifer, *The Battle of Okinawa: The Blood and the Bomb* (The Lyons Press, 1992), 69.
20 "OPG to Set up an Explanation Board about the Former 32nd Army Headquarters Shelter at Shuri," *Ryukyu Shimpo*, November 23, 2011. Accessed March 28, 2012, http://english.ryukyushimpo.jp/2011/11/30/4647/
21 "【沖縄戦】絶対阻止！英霊に濡れ衣を着せる沖縄左翼[桜H23/11/24]" ["Battle of Okinawa" Must Be Absolutely Stopped! The Okinawan Left Falsely Accuse the War Dead (Sakura Heisei 23/11/24)]. *Nihon Bunka Channel Sakura*, November 24, 2011, http://www.youtube.com/watch?v=P0coyjhk1EU.
22 "【伊波苗子】生き証人が語る、第32軍司令部壕の真実[桜H24/3/1]" ["Inami Naeko" A Living Witness Speaks, the Truth Behind the Commander Headquarters of the Thirty-Second Army (Sakura Heisei 24/3/1)]. *Nihon Bunka Channel Sakura*, January 3, 2012, https://www.nicovideo.jp/watch/so17121338.
23 "【沖縄戦】絶対阻止！英霊に濡れ衣を着せる沖縄左翼[桜H23/11/24]" ["Battle of Okinawa" Must Be Absolutely Stopped! The Okinawan Left Falsely Accuse the War Dead (Sakura Heisei 23/11/24)]. *Nihon Bunka Channel Sakura*, November 24, 2011, http://www.youtube.com/watch?v=P0coyjhk1EU.
24 "【佐藤守】南西航空混成団司令として見つめてきた沖縄[桜H23/11/28]" ["Satô Mamoru" Okinawa as Seen by a Commander of the Southwest Airlines Combined Brigade]. *Nihon Bunka Channel Sakura*, November 29, 2011, https://www.nicovideo.jp/watch/so16299095.
25 "「慰安婦」を削除　第３２軍司令部壕の説明板　県が方針決定" ["Comfort Women" Removed From Signpost Explaining the Thirty-Second Army Commander Headquarters]. *Ryukyu Shimpo*, February 24, 2012, http://ryukyushimpo.jp/news/storyid-187846-storytopic-1.html.
26 "文言削除　高まる批判" [Criticism of Deleted Wording Increases]. *Ryukyu Shimpo*, February 25, 2012, 28–29.
27 "【伊波苗子】生き証人が語る、第32軍司令部壕の真実[桜H24/3/1]" ["Inami Naeko" A Living Witness Speaks, the Truth Behind the Commander Headquarters of the Thirty-Second Army (Sakura Heisei 24/3/1)]. *Nihon Bunka Channel Sakura*, January 3, 2012, https://www.nicovideo.jp/watch/so17121338.
28 Rabson, "Okinawan Perspectives on Japan's Imperial Institution."
29 Nakazato Isao, "Okinawa as an Intersection of Colonialisms: Toward Creating a Place Open to and Interconnecting with Asia," *International Critical Thought* 3, no. 2 (2013), https://doi.org/10.1080/21598282.2013.787275.

30 "「慰安婦」を削除　第３２軍司令部壕の説明板　県が方針決定" ["Comfort Women" Removed From Signpost Explaining the Thirty-Second Army Commander Headquarters]. *Ryukyu Shimpo*, February 24, 2012, http://ryukyushimpo.jp/news/storyid-187846-storytopic-1.html.
31 "第３２軍壕説明板　検討委、県に記述削除の撤回求める" [Thirty-Second Army Headquarter Signage – Deliberative Committee Ask Prefecture to Retract Removal]. *Ryukyu Shimpo*, February 29, 2012, http://ryukyushimpo.jp/news/storyid-188070-storytopic-1.html.
32 "第32軍司令部壕説明板　委員会「削除は拙速」" [Thirty-Second Army Commander Headquarter Signage – Committee: "Removal Was Too Hasty"]. *Ryukyu Asahi Broadcasting*, February 29, 2012, https://www.qab.co.jp/news/2012022934096.html.
33 "「社説」−〔３２軍壕説明板設置〕県のやり方はおかしい" [Editorial – Thirty-Second Army Headquarter Signage: Prefecture Decision Raises Questions]. *Okinawa Times*, March 26, 2012, http://www.okinawatimes.co.jp/article/2012-03-26_31562/; and "３２軍壕記述削除　事実の明記は県の責務" [Thirty-Second Army Headquarter Signage Revision – Prefecture Has Responsibility to the Truth]. *Ryukyu Shimpo*, February 25, 2012, http://ryukyushimpo.jp/news/storyid-187895-storytopic-11.html.
34 "県強行設置に怒り　平和ガイドら「撤去を」　３２軍壕説明板" [Prefecture Decision Causes Anger – Peace Guide Asks for Retraction of Thirty-Second Army Headquarter Signage Revision]. *Ryukyu Shimpo*, March 26, 2012, http://ryukyushimpo.jp/news/storyid-189113-storytopic-1.html.
35 "第３２軍司令部壕、記述削除再検討を　アピール採択" [Thirty-Second Army Commander Headquarter, Revision to be Reconsidered – Appeal Accepted]. *Ryukyu Shimpo*, March 28, 2012, http://ryukyushimpo.jp/news/storyid-188791-storytopic-1.html.
36 "第32軍司令部壕説明板設置についての経緯と考え方" [The Details Surrounding the Thirty-Second Army Commander Headquarter Signage and How to Think of It]. *Okinawa Prefecture* (Homepage), April 12, 2012, http://www.pref.okinawa.jp/site/kankyo/heiwadanjo/heiwa/dai32.html.
37 "[沖縄]皇室と沖縄－沖縄、奉迎活動のご案内" [(Okinawa) The Imperial Household and Okinawa – Information on Okinawa Hôgei]. *Nippon Kaigi* (Homepage), June 30, 2014, http://www.nipponkaigi.org/tag/%E6%B2%96%E7%B8%84?cat=1&tag=89.
38 Meeting minutes of the Okinawa Prefectural Assembly, February 24, 2012. And Justin Aukema, "Cultures of (Dis)remembrance: War Memories at Shuri Castle," *Contemporary Society Bulletin* no. 13 (March, 2019).
39 "Accounts of 'Comfort Women' and 'Bloodshed' Erased from Okinawa Battle Monument," *Japan Press Weekly*, February 28, 2012, http://www.japan-press.co.jp/s/news/index.php?id=2805.
40 "県議会一般質問 第32軍司令部壕説明板で質疑" [Prefectural Assembly General Question, Thirty-Second Army Commander Headquarter Signage Questions]. *Ryukyu Asahi Broadcasting*, February 29, 2012, https://www.qab.co.jp/news/2012022934087.html
41 Shun Medoruma, "We Cannot Allow Governor Nakaima to Falsify the History of the Battle of Okinawa," *Asia-Pacific Journal* 10, no. 2 (2012), https://apjjf.org/2012/10/15/Medoruma-Shun/3738/article.html.
42 "【超限戦】沖縄・第32軍司令部壕跡説明文の捏造撃退[桜H24/3/26]" ["Unrestricted Warfare" Okinawa Thirty-Second Army Commander Headquarter Ruins Signage Fabrication Repelled (Sakura Heisei 24/3/26)]. *Nihon Bunka Channel Sakura*, March 26, 2012, https://www.youtube.com/watch?v=lRbs520bOe0.

43 Masako Shinjo Summers Robbins, "My Story: A Daughter Recalls the Battle of Okinawa," *Asia-Pacific Journal* 13, no. 4 (February 23, 2015), https://apjjf.org/2015/13/7/Masako-Shinjo-Summers-Robbins/4286.html.

44 "「ジュリ」が手記 「慰安婦」や兵隊と壕で生活" ["Comfort Women" and Soldiers Living Together in Army Headquarters According to Julie Notes]. *Okinawa Times*, September 2, 2016, https://www.okinawatimes.co.jp/articles/-/60339

45 "３２軍壕「慰安婦」文言復活を　沖縄タイムスの報道受け識者ら要請" [Thirty-Second Arm Headquarters "Comfort Women" Phrasing to be Restored – Experts Make Request After Okinawa Times Reporting]. *Okinawa Times*, September 27, 2019, https://www.okinawatimes.co.jp/articles/-/63885.

46 Julian Ryall, "Chinese Agent and Other Insults the Okinawa Governor Lives with for Opposing US Base," *South China Morning Post*, December 31, 2017, https://www.scmp.com/week-asia/geopolitics/article/2122311/chinese-agent-and-other-insults-okinawa-governor-lives.

47 "「慰安婦」「虐殺」文言の復活を　32軍壕説明板　沖縄県は見直しに難色" ["Comfort Women" and "Massacre" to Be Restored – Thirty-Second Army Headquarters Signage, Okinawa Prefecture Disapprove of Concession]. *Okinawa Times*, November 26, 2016, https://www.okinawatimes.co.jp/articles/-/72888.

48 "OPG to Form Committee of Civil Engineers and Other Experts to Look into Opening 32nd Army Underground Trenches to the Public," *Ryukyu Shimpo*, June 27, 2020, http://english.ryukyushimpo.jp/2020/07/05/32355/.

Bibliography

Asahi Shimbun Editorial. "Compulsory Mass Suicide, the Battle of Okinawa, and Japan's Textbook Controversy." Translated by Kyoko Selden. *Asia-Pacific Journal* 6, no. 1 (January 1, 2008). https://apjjf.org/-Aniya-Masaaki/2629/article.html.

Aukema, Justin. "Cultures of (Dis)remembrance: War Memories at Shuri Castle." *Contemporary Society Bulletin* no. 13 (March, 2019): 69–96. http://hdl.handle.net/11173/2853.

Feifer, George. *The Battle of Okinawa: The Blood and the Bomb*. Guilford, CT: Lyons Press, 1992.

Field, Norma. *In the Realm of a Dying Emperor*. New York: Pantheon Books, 1991.

Fujioka, Nobukatsu. "Education Issues, Comfort Women and the Creation of a New History Textbook." *Association for Advancement of Unbiased View of History from Association for Advancement of Liberal View of History*, February 25, 1999. http://www.jiyuushikan.org/e/education.html.

Hayashi, Hirofumi. "Unsettled State Violence in Japan: The Okinawa Incident." In *State Violence in East Asia*, ed. N. Ganesan and Sung Chull Kim, 75–104. Lexington, KY: University Press of Kentucky, 2013.

Ikeda, Kyle. *Okinawan War Memory: Transgenerational Trauma and the War Fiction of Medoruma Shun*. New York: Routledge, 2014.

Isao, Nakazato. "Okinawa as an Intersection of Colonialisms: Toward Creating a Place Open to and Interconnecting with Asia." *International Critical Thought* 3, no. 2 (2013): 183–197. https://doi.org/10.1080/21598282.2013.787275.

Japan Times. "High Anxiety for Okinawa Governor over '75 Imperial Visit'." November 23, 2012. http://www.japantimes.co.jp/news/2012/11/23/national/high-anxiety-for-okinawa-governor-over-75-imperial-visit/#.U_WGvfmSzB0.

McCormack, Gavan, and Norimatsu, Satoko Oka. *Resistant Islands: Okinawa Confronts Japan and the United States*. Lanham: Rowman & Littlefield, 2012.

Medoruma, Shun. "We Cannot Allow Governor Nakaima to Falsify the History of the Battle of Okinawa." *Asia-Pacific Journal* 10, no. 2, (2012). https://apjjf.org/2012/10/15/Medoruma-Shun/3738/article.html.

Ministry of Foreign Affairs of Japan. "Statement by the Chief Cabinet Secretary Yohei Kono on the Result of the Study on the Issue of 'Comfort Women.'" August 4, 1993. http://www.mofa.go.jp/policy/women/fund/state9308.html.

Naono, Akiko. "Producing Sacrificial Subjects for the Nation: Japan's War-Related Redress Policy and the Endurance Doctrine." In *Toward a Sociology of the Trace*, ed. Herman Gray and Macarena Gómez-Barris, 109–134. Minneapolis: University of Minnesota Press, 2010.

Nippon Kaigi. "[沖縄]皇室と沖縄－沖縄、奉迎活動のご案内" [(Okinawa) The Imperial Household and Okinawa – Information on Okinawa Hōgei]. Homepage, June 30, 2014. http://www.nipponkaigi.org/tag/%E6%B2%96%E7%B8%84?cat=1&tag=89

Okinawa Prefecture. "第32軍司令部壕説明板設置についての経緯と考え方" [The Details Surrounding the Thirty-Second Army Commander Headquarter Signage and How to Think of It]. Homepage, April 12, 2012. http://www.pref.okinawa.jp/site/kankyo/heiwadanjo/heiwa/dai32.html.

Okinawa Times. "「社説」–〔３２軍壕説明板設置〕県のやり方はおかしい" [Editorial – Thirty-Second Army Headquarter Signage: Prefecture Decision Raises Questions]. March 26, 2012. http://www.okinawatimes.co.jp/article/2012-03-26_31562/.

Okinawa Times. "「ジュリ」が手記　「慰安婦」や兵隊と壕で生活" ['"Comfort Women" and Soldiers Living Together in Army Headquarters According to Julie Notes]. September 2, 2016. https://www.okinawatimes.co.jp/articles/-/60339.

Okinawa Times. "「慰安婦」「虐殺」文言の復活を 32軍壕説明板 沖縄県は見直しに難色" ["Comfort Women" and "Massacre" to Be Restored – Thirty-Second Army Headquarters Signage]. *Okinawa Prefecture Disapprove of Concession*, November 26, 2016. https://www.okinawatimes.co.jp/articles/-/72888.

Okinawa Times. "３２軍壕「慰安婦」文言復活を　沖縄タイムスの報道受け識者ら要請 Okinawa Times" [Thirty-Second Arm Headquarters "Comfort Women" Phrasing to be Restored – Experts Make Request After Okinawa Times Reporting]. September 27, 2019. https://www.okinawatimes.co.jp/articles/-/63885.

Onishi, Norimitsu. "Okinawans Protest Japan's Plan to Revise Bitter Chapter of World War II." *New York Times*, October 06, 2007. http://www.nytimes.com/2007/10/07/world/asia/07okinawa.html?pagewanted=all.

Rabson, Steven. "Okinawan Perspectives on Japan's Imperial Institution." *Asia-Pacific Journal* 6, no. 2 (February 1, 2008). https://apjjf.org/-Steve-Rabson/2667/article.html.

Rabson, Steve. "The Politics of Trauma: Compulsory Suicides during the Battle of Okinawa and Postwar Retrospectives." *Intersections: Gender and Sexuality in Asia and the Pacific* 24 (June 2010). http://intersections.anu.edu.au/issue24/rabson.htm.

Robbins, Masako Shinjo Summers. "My Story: A Daughter Recalls the Battle of Okinawa." *Asia-Pacific Journal* 13, no. 4 (February 23, 2015). https://apjjf.org/2015/13/7/Masako-Shinjo-Summers-Robbins/4286.html.

Ryall, Julian. "Chinese Agent and Other Insults the Okinawa Governor Lives with for Opposing US Base." *South China Morning Post*, December 31, 2017. https://www.scmp.com/week-asia/geopolitics/article/2122311/chinese-agent-and-other-insults-okinawa-governor-lives.

Ryukyu Asahi Broadcasting. "県議会一般質問　第32軍司令部壕説明板で質疑" [Prefectural Assembly General Question, Thirty-Second Army Commander Headquarter Signage Questions]. February 29, 2012. https://www.qab.co.jp/news/2012022934087.html.

Ryukyu Asahi Broadcasting. "第32軍司令部壕説明板　委員会「削除は拙速」" [Thirty-Second Army Commander Headquarter Signage – Committee: "Removal Was Too Hasty"]. February 29, 2012. https://www.qab.co.jp/news/2012022934096.html.

Ryukyu Shimpo. "OPG to Set up an Explanation Board about the Former 32nd Army Headquarters Shelter at Shuri." November 23, 2011, last accessed March 28, 2012. http://english.ryukyushimpo.jp/2011/11/30/4647/

Ryukyu Shimpo. "「慰安婦」を削除　第３２軍司令部壕の説明板　県が方針決定" ["Comfort Women" Removed from Signpost Explaining the Thirty-Second Army Commander Dugout]. February 24, 2012. http://ryukyushimpo.jp/news/storyid-187846-storytopic-1.html.

Ryukyu Shimpo. "文言削除 高まる批判" [Criticism of Deleted Wording Increases]. February 25, 2012.

Ryukyu Shimpo. "３２軍壕記述削除　事実の明記は県の責務" [Thirty-Second Army Headquarter Signage Revision – Prefecture Has Responsibility to the Truth]. February 25, 2012. http://ryukyushimpo.jp/news/storyid-187895-storytopic-11.html.

Ryukyu Shimpo. "第３２軍壕説明板　検討委、県に記述削除の撤回求める" [Thirty-Second Army Headquarter Signage – Deliberative Committee Ask Prefecture to Retract Removal]. February 29, 2012. http://ryukyushimpo.jp/news/storyid-188070-storytopic-1.html.

Ryukyu Shimpo. "県強行設置に怒り　平和ガイドら「撤去を」　３２軍壕説明板" [Prefecture Decision Causes Anger – Peace Guide Asks for Retraction of Thirty-Second Army Headquarter Signage Revision]. March 26, 2012. http://ryukyushimpo.jp/news/storyid-189113-storytopic-1.html.

Ryukyu Shimpo. "第３２軍司令部壕、記述削除再検討を　アピール採択" [Thirty-Second Army Commander Headquarter, Revision to be Reconsidered – Appeal Accepted]. March 28, 2012. http://ryukyushimpo.jp/news/storyid-188791-storytopic-1.html.

Ryukyu Shimpo. "OPG to Form Committee of Civil Engineers and Other Experts to Look into Opening 32nd Army Underground Trenches to the Public." June 27, 2020. http://english.ryukyushimpo.jp/2020/07/05/32355/.

Seaton, Philip A. *Japan's Contested War Memories: The "Memory Rifts" in Historical Consciousness of World War II*. London: Routledge, 2007.

Soh, Chunghee Sarah. *The Comfort Women: Sexual Violence and Postcolonial Memory in Korea and Japan*. Chicago: University of Chicago Press, 2008.

Tanaka, Nobumasa. "Desecration of the Dead: Bereaved Okinawan Families Sue Yasukuni to End Relatives' Enshrinement." Translated by Steve Rabson. *Asia-Pacific Journal* 6, no. 5 (May 3, 2008). https://apjjf.org/-Nobumasa-Tanaka/2744/article.html.

Tanaka, Toshiyuki. *Japan's Comfort Women: Sexual Slavery and Prostitution during World War II and the US Occupation*. London: Routledge, 2007.

Yoshifumi, Tawara. "Comfort Women, Textbooks, and the Rise of 'New Right' Revisionism." In *Denying the Comfort Women: The Japanese State's Assault on Historical Truth*, ed. Rumiko Nishino, Puja Kim, and Akane Onozawa, 151–166. London: Routledge, 2018.

7 The Senkaku Islands, protest marches, and crowdfunded boat activism

On August 18, 2012, a small fleet of Japanese fishing boats left ports in Japan's Okinawa prefecture on an overnight journey to the Senkakus, a group of small uninhabited islands administered by Japan but claimed by China. On board the 20 boats were 152 Japanese right-wing activists and politicians, domestic and international journalists, and local fishermen. Shortly after arriving near the islands, several activists jumped from their boats and swam ashore to the islands, an action expressly forbidden by Japanese authorities. Their landing, which was filmed and widely publicized worldwide through social media and the press, was one of several key events that helped fuel a wave of mass anti-Japanese demonstrations and riots in over 80 Chinese cities.

This chapter explores the importance of non-state actors in the development of Japan's ongoing territorial dispute with China over the Senkaku Islands, zeroing in on the Japanese activists who organized and led the 2012 landing. Focus is placed upon Mizushima Satoru, one of the ten activists who swam ashore that day and the two organizations that he founded. The first was Nihon Bunka Channel Sakura (Japanese Culture Channel Sakura, commonly known as Channel Sakura), a conservative media organization that distributed video content via the internet. The second was Ganbare Nippon, a nationwide activist organization led by Channel Sakura's top figures. Following a collision between Japanese Coast Guard (JCG) patrol boats and a Chinese fishing trawler near the Senkakus in 2010, these organizations emerged as important actors in the field of contestation surrounding this territorial dispute. They transitioned from being mere reporters of the news to creating it – first through demonstrations in Japanese city streets and later through landings and fishing missions near the Senkakus. Recognizing the opportunities presented by structural shifts in 2010, they carried out an activist campaign that put pressure on the Japanese government, provoked protests from China, and helped provide shared meaning and a sense of accomplishment for their supporters.

The first part of this chapter details pre-2010 events to provide the background for more recent developments and how they can be considered as taking place within a field of contestation. The later part of the chapter will discuss events between 2010 and 2020 when an unsettling of the field created new opportunities for citizen activism. Special emphasis is placed on how Channel Sakura's internet videos explained the situation in a meaningful way to viewers and how skilled social actors within Channel Sakura and Ganbare Nippon used new and innovative tactics to exploit shifts in the field to their advantage. From this discussion, a picture emerges in which relatively small groups of highly motivated and organized activists can influence major international disputes.

Senkaku Islands – background

The Senkakus are a group of five small islands and three smaller rocks in the East China Sea. Of the islands, Uotsurijima (3.6 square kilometers) is the largest, followed by Kubajima (0.87 square kilometers), Minamikojima (0.32 square kilometers), and Kitakojima (0.26 square kilometers). The closest inhabited Japanese island to the Senkakus is Ishigaki Island, approximately 170 kilometers away. Taiwan is also less than 200 kilometers away, while the distance to the Chinese mainland is 400 kilometers. The islands are administered and controlled by Japan but are also claimed by Taiwan (the Republic of China – ROC) and mainland China (the People's Republic of China – PRC). Taiwan and China refer to the islands as the Daioyutai or Daioyu Islands.

Japan's territorial claim to the islands dates back to the end of the 19th century, a period when Japan was expanding as an imperial power. Although Japanese surveys conducted in 1880s found the islands to be uninhabited and "showed no particular trace of having been under the control of Qing China," no formal claim was announced due to concerns that doing so could result in diplomatic frictions.[1]

The islands were not formally annexed until January 1895. Although this took place during the Sino-Japanese War, Japan's government did not legally categorize the acquisition of the islands as a conquest of Chinese territory. Consequently, the islands were not mentioned among the territorial concessions that Japan received from China under the April 1895 Treaty of Shimonoseki.[2] From 1895 to 1945, the Senkaku Islands were administered as a part of Okinawa prefecture.

The economic value of the islands was acknowledged years before they were formally administered by Japan. Koga Tatsushirō, a wealthy and influential Japanese businessman in Okinawa, had sought since 1884 to utilize the islands.[3] Consequently, in 1896 Koga was granted a free 30-year lease to Uotsurijima, Kubajima, Kitakojima, and Minamikojima for the purpose of promoting their development.[4] Koga built a small village on Uotsurijima and set about exploiting the marine resource of the area. At the peak of local economic activity in 1909, 99 households consisting of 248 people lived on Uotsurijima.[5] Koga's business caught and killed huge numbers of fish and sea birds, inflicting enormous environmental damage on the islands. A once-striving population of hundreds of thousands of albatross and other sea birds was rapidly driven into virtual extinction.[6] As resources on the islands themselves became less, and motorized fishing boats from other islands took on a greater role in the area, the population of Koga's Senkaku village rapidly declined. Although Koga's son Zenji purchased

Uotsurijima and three other islands from the Japanese government in 1932, business activities were closed down in 1940 and the islands once again became uninhabited.[7]

The islands remained uninhabited until a tragic incident in the closing weeks of World War II. With Okinawa's main island falling to the American military, efforts were undertaken to evacuate Japanese civilians from outlying islands that had not yet been invaded, including Ishigaki Island. On June 30, two ships carrying about 200 people, many of them women, children, and the elderly, set out to Japanese-occupied Taiwan on a route that passed near the Senkaku Islands.[8] On the afternoon of July 3, just a few hours before their expected arrival in Taiwan, the ships were attacked and sunk by an American B-24 bomber. It is estimated that about 70 people died in the initial attack. A large group of survivors managed to reach Uotsurijima but lacked adequate food or provisions. Over the course of nearly 50 days, they desperately sought to survive on the meager resources of the island, eating tiny hermit crabs and grass.[9] About 70 people starved to death on Uotsurijima before a rescue ship arrived on August 18. An additional 20 people were so weakened that they died in the days after being rescued.[10] The mayor of Ishigaki City and several survivors of the incident returned to Uotsurijima in 1969 and erected a small memorial in memory of the Ishigaki residents who had perished there.[11]

From the end of the war until 1972, the Senkaku Islands were part of the American administered Ryukyu Islands. The US Navy used two of the islands for practice firing, paying rental fees to Koga Zenji and his family.[12] When the United States formally returned the Ryukyus to Japan in 1972, the Senkaku Islands were included in the transfer and once again became a part of Okinawa prefecture.

The emergence of a territorial dispute

Formal Chinese claims to the Senkaku Islands were announced in 1970, first by Taiwan and then by mainland China. Both parties claimed their ownership of the islands was based on pre-1895 historical evidence that demonstrated that the islands were a part of China. In their view, Japan unlawfully annexed the islands in 1895 as a part of its imperialist expansion. Japanese opponents of these claims have argued that both Chinese claims were influenced by a 1969 United Nations Economic Commission for Asia and the Far East (ECAFE) report that suggested the existence of oil and natural gas reserves in the seabed near the islands.

The territorial dispute did not prevent the normalization of diplomatic relations between mainland China and Japan in 1972, but it did rear its head in 1978 when the two nations were negotiating a peace and friendship treaty. Anti-treaty politicians in Japan, including Ishihara Shintarō of the Liberal Democratic Party (LDP)'s Seirankai faction, insisted that the Japanese government demand Chinese recognition of Japan's sovereignty over the islands.[13] On April 12, 1978, between 80 and 150 armed Chinese fishing boats appeared in the waters around the Senkakus. While many saw it as a Chinese show of dissatisfaction with the actions of Japan's anti-treaty politicians, it ended up backfiring and weakening pro-treaty forces. China then downplayed the presence of the boats and withdrew them within a few days.[14] The treaty was ultimately passed without official negotiations regarding the status of the islands. Chinese leader Deng Xiaoping explained that the two sides still held "different views" on the territorial dispute, so its resolution would be left to a "wiser" future generation that would "certainly find a solution acceptable to all."[15]

The issue was thus shelved at the governmental level in favor of pursuing "economic gains at the expense of their nationalist credentials."[16] Non-state actors, however, had different priorities and would seek to derail this arrangement from its very start.

State and non-state actors within a field of contestation

The beginning of an international territorial dispute in the 1970s birthed a field of contestation in which state and non-state actors sought to take advantage of structural shifts to improve the relative positions of their nations. In the period from the 1970s until the 2000s, the Japanese state held a major advantage as an incumbent actor, maintaining physical possession of the islands and resources such as the Japan Coast Guard, the Self-Defense Forces, access to media, financial resources, and so on.

The mainland Chinese state, on the other hand, was at a major disadvantage resource-wise and was not in a position to effectively overturn Japan's dominance in the field. As reflected by Deng's statement, China was willing to freeze the field and await a more favorable circumstance. In the early decades of the dispute, China was militarily and economically weaker than Japan, but that gap significantly lessened by the 2000s.

The Taiwanese state could also be described as a challenger, but following an international shift in diplomatic recognition to mainland China, good relations with Japan became more important than aggressively pursuing the territorial issue. The Japanese state, for its part, wanted to avoid the discussion of the Senkakus, as official recognition that any other country had a legitimate cause for disputing Japanese ownership would have weakened the Japanese state's position within the field.

State-level inaction prompted frustration and action from non-state actors in all of the involved nations. Japanese nationalist activists took it upon themselves to carry out activities that would assert Japan's ownership of the islands, while activists from Taiwan, Hong Kong, and mainland China sought to counter Japan's claims. Some of this activism took the form of traditional protest activities, such as street demonstrations and the publishing of nationalist literature. However, the most visible, and perhaps the most important actions, were landings on the islands. Japanese activists would land on the islands to erect flags, lighthouses, and memorials. Non-Japanese activists would seek to raise their own national flags and destroy or damage the physical structures placed by Japanese activists.

Boat activism and building lighthouses on the Senkaku Islands

The erecting of lighthouses was especially valuable to Japanese activists, who saw the creation of facilities that could then be passed over to Japanese government control as bolstering Japan's legal claim of "effectively controlling the islands."[17] Non-Japanese activists performed counter-landings to destroy or disable the "illegal" Japanese structures. On both sides the activists were acting in the place of states that were unwilling to take such actions. The lighthouse activism also highlighted how domestic groups could use the territorial issue to embarrass governments.[18] Through landings and counter-landings, activists hoped to compel the inactive governments to get involved in the dispute.[19]

The first activist landing on the Senkaku Islands took place in September 1970, during the period of American administration over the islands. The activists were a group of Taiwanese journalists, seeking to both express the Republic of China's territorial claim over the islands and compel their government to be more assertive. They planted a Republic of China flag on one of the islands and also carved "Long Live President Chiang" into a rock.[20] Ryukyu policemen "forcibly evicted" the journalists from the island and removed the flag.[21] It did not spark a major diplomatic incident.

Japanese nationalists began their activism in 1978 as a response to a perception that their own government had failed to adequately demonstrate Japanese sovereignty over the islands in response to the above-mentioned fleet of armed Chinese fishing boats. Their first landing took place on August 13, 1978, two days after Japan and the PRC signed the Treaty of Peace and Friendship. The activists had chartered a fishing boat from Miyako Island in Okinawa, carefully avoiding police and Japan Coast Guard patrols so that they could land and construct a makeshift lighthouse on Uotsurijima.

Anti-treaty politician Ishihara Shintarō was behind the landing. Ishihara was a prize-winning novelist who, in contrast to his friend Mishima Yukio, had chosen national electoral politics over violent paramilitary activism. Ishihara's memoirs detail how he organized the lighthouse-building expedition. Funds were raised from fellow conservative politicians within the LDP's Seirankai faction and private donors. Although Ishihara did not personally go to the islands, he helped recruit the men who did. One of the young men he recruited for the mission was Tōyama Rikkoku, grandson of the famous pre-war ultranationalist spymaster Tōyama Mitsuru. Other participants included a mixture of university students and right-wing activists. A former Imperial Japanese Army pilot and friend of Ishihara's provided a small aircraft that was used to drop provisions to the activists after they landed on Uotsurijima.[22] Interviewed years later, one activist believed Ishihara used his political influence to convince the Japan Coast Guard to leave the activists alone and allow them to complete their mission.[23]

One notable participant in Ishihara's expedition was Etō Toyohisa, a member and future leader of Nihon Seinensha (The Japan Youth Association – hereafter referred to as Seinensha). Seinensha was a uyoku group founded in 1969 by Kobayashi Kusuo, a top cadre of the Sumiyoshi-kai, one of Japan's largest yakuza syndicates.[24] Like other uyoku organizations, their members frequently dressed in military-style uniforms, making them stand out from less extreme citizen activists. From the 1970s until the 2000s, Seinensha would be the principal non-state actor involved in landings on the islands. According to its official homepage, their members were unsatisfied with the "weak-kneed" policies of the Japanese government and acted to protect Japan's claim to the Senkakus. They wrote that their actions were directly influenced by the "outrage" of Chinese incursions into the area and that their lighthouse "guarded the light of Japan."[25]

Seinensha landed on the islands several times over the following years: once in May 1979, once in March 1982, and again in June 1984. The missions were carried out to observe the state of the islands.[26] Goats were also released on Uotsurijima under the assumption that they could serve as an emergency food source if anyone was stranded there. The goat population gradually increased, and with it came the destruction of local vegetation. Ishihara Shintarō did not claim direct involvement in Seinensha's activism, but he did praise their work in upgrading and maintaining lighthouses.[27]

Seinensha members returned to Uotsurijima in 1988 to mark the 10th anniversary of the first lighthouse by upgrading it. They submitted an application to the Japanese government a year later, requesting that the lighthouse be granted the status of an official navigation indicator. After delays in the approval process, they returned to the islands in June 1990 to make further improvements to the quality of the lighthouse and ensure it would meet government regulations.[28] News reports suggesting that the application would be accepted prompted protests from mainland China and from Taiwanese politicians. A Taiwanese group attempted a landing on the islands, bringing along a news crew, who subsequently broadcasted the footage of the ships being turned back by the JCG. Anti-Japanese demonstrations followed, and the Japanese Foreign Ministry intervened in the process to force the rejection of Seinensha's application in April 1991.[29] Despite this setback, Seinensha returned to Uotsurijima in 1994 and 1995 to perform maintenance to the lighthouse.

Another small crisis took place in 1996 after Etō led Seinensha members to the islands and erected a solar-powered aluminum lighthouse on Kitakojima, again applying for Japanese government recognition.[30] China's Foreign Ministry lodged an official protest with the Japanese government, calling on Japan to respect the "shelving dispute" consensus.[31] Protests followed in Taiwan, Hong Kong, and mainland China. On September 26, 1996, an activist from Hong Kong drowned when trying to evade the Japan Coast Guard during a failed landing attempt. His death prompted another landing attempt a month later, this time by activists from Hong Kong and Taiwan. The activists succeeded in coming ashore at Uotsurijima on October 7, where they planted PRC and ROC flags. The flags were removed several days later by Japanese authorities. Prior to the landing, the Japanese government announced on October 4 that it had rejected Seinensha's lighthouse recognition application. When a Seinensha expedition was sent to the islands in December, they found that the lighthouse had been vandalized.

More landings followed in 1997. This time, it was conservative politicians and journalists instead of uyoku members. On April 27, Ishigaki City assemblyman Nakama Hitoshi and a *Sankei Shimbun* reporter landed on Uotsurijima.[32] A few weeks later, on May 6, House of Representatives lawmaker Nishimura Shingo also landed on Uotsurijima to fulfill an election campaign promise made during the 1996 crisis.[33] He was joined by Nakama Hitoshi, journalist Miyajima Shigeki, and filmmaker Inagawa Kazuo. It was the first time that an elected lawmaker of Japan's National Diet landed on the Senkaku Islands. Nishimura was not a member of the ruling party (the LDP), and the government officially denounced his visit. Official protests from China were answered with assurances that the Japanese government did not endorse Nishimura's actions and that Japan desired a continued "freeze" of the Senkaku situation.[34]

As in the past, activists from Hong Kong and Taiwan responded with their own attempt to land on the islands. In May 1997 activists arrived near the Senkakus with 30 small boats, facing off against JCG patrol vessels. Three of the boats ignored warnings from the JCG and entered Japanese territorial waters.[35] During the confrontation, the activists' boats collided with Japanese patrol vessels on several occasions, and two activists were captured after jumping onto a JCG patrol vessel. The activists were released without any charges filed against them, "in accordance with the decision taken by the relevant government authorities." Then, in September of 1997, Chinese activists attempted to charter an airplane that would fly them to the islands for a parachute landing. Engine trouble caused the airplane to make an emergency landing shortly after take-off from an airport in the Philippines, forcing a cancellation of the plan.[36]

Relative calm in the late 1990s to the early 2000s

The responses of the Chinese and Japanese governments to the boat activism of non-state actors clearly showed restraint and a willingness to prevent the dispute from harming other fields of relations between their nations. James Manicom has noted that official statements demonstrated noteworthy pragmatism in the face of attempted "provocations" from non-state actors. These statements condemned the landings and construction of lighthouses but also acknowledged that the landings had been against the policy of the Japanese government.[37] Chien-peng Chung has also argued that there is enough evidence to make an *indisputable* claim that the governments in Beijing, Taipei, and Tokyo were all

> engaging in tactic communication and behavioral convergence with one another, to signal the fact that they were trying their utmost to play down, if not suppress, the entire controversy by doing nothing to encourage and everything to restrain their domestic nationalist forces; and that they expected this goodwill to be reciprocated by the opposing governments.[38]

Within this field of contestation, the incumbent state actor and two challenging state actors decided to stick with the status quo for the time being. The Japanese activists – non-state actors within the field – tried the same kind of tactics they had employed in earlier decades but received no major response from the states involved. In November 1997, the Chinese and Japanese governments signed a new fisheries agreement, agreeing to establish jointly controlled maritime boundaries while leaving the waters around the Senkaku Islands untouched.[39]

Another right-wing organization, calling itself Nihonjin no Kai (Japanese Peoples' Association) landed on Uotsurijima in May 2001. They were accompanied by politician Nishimura Shingo. It was the only time that this organization visited the islands. One year later its members gained infamy when they founded Kenkoku Giyūgun (Nation Building Volunteer Corps), an armed nationalist organization, which was disbanded in 2003 after its key members were arrested for bomb threats and attacks on groups associated with North Korea. Nishimura later denied prior knowledge of the organization's criminal composition.[40]

Starting in 2002, Japan's national government began to rent the islands of Uotsurijima, Minamikojima, and Kitakojima from the family of businessman Kurihara Hiroyuki, who had purchased the Koga family land titles in 1991.[41] When landings by Japanese activists occurred in the 1990s, the Japanese government had cited the islands' private ownership as a reason why it could not ban Japanese citizens from coming ashore on the islands.[42] For example, after Seinensha's Kitakojima landing in 1996, Japan's Ministry of Foreign Affairs public stance was that "the islands are privately owned, the Japanese government cannot be directly involved … and we consider this building as just a physical building and not a lighthouse according to Japanese law."[43] After 2002 rental agreement, the government increasingly restricted access to the islands.[44] This was a new and significant shift in the Senkaku field of contestation, and Seinensha was blocked from carrying out further visits to the islands.

While the Japanese government restricted the activities of its own country's activists, Chinese government's action in the waters near the Senkakus increased. Throughout 1998 and 1999, Chinese surveying vessels were operating within the Japanese-claimed seas around the islands, refusing to recognize JCG orders to leave the area.[45] There were also a few cases of Chinese naval vessels operating near the islands.[46] Despite Japanese official protests, and a short-lived 2001 agreement that China would provide advanced notice of research activities carried out in "waters near Japan and in which Japan takes an interest," unannounced Chinese surveying missions continued. The situation gradually became one in which "Chinese vessels operated with relative impunity" in the waters around the islands.[47]

A multitude of factors in proximate fields led to increasing tensions between Japan and China, and Senkaku field of contestation was affected by those changes. The Japanese state's incumbent position in the field gradually weakened as China grew in economic and military power, becoming more assertive. Japanese prime minister Koizumi Junichirō took office in April 2001, and his subsequent visits to the controversial Yasukuni Shrine caused China to put a halt on meetings between the two countries' leaders while he remained in office. In a study of Chinese actions near the islands between 1978 and 2007, Krista Wiegand argued that increased Chinese activity near the islands from the late 1990s to the early 2000s could best be explained as "a dual strategy of issue linkage and coercive diplomacy." China used "militarized threats" such as increased patrols near the islands as "bargaining leverage to force changes in Japan's policies or actions regarding other disputed issues."[48] Wiegand identified linkages to Japanese government actions that were reaffirming the US–Japan security alliance in the late 1990s and to Koizumi's shrine visits in the 2000s.

Prior to 1996, ideational factors, namely the idea of asserting territorial sovereignty over the islands, were a main motivation for Seinensha activists. The islands were valued most of all because they were Japanese, making them a part of the sacred Japanese nation. They saw it as their mission to defend the sovereign territory of Japan. The economic or material advantages of controlling the islands were not particularly emphasized. However, after China declared an expansion of its Exclusive Economic Zone in 1996 and Chinese ships conducted more surveying missions in the area, there was a swing in nationalist thinking, with Seinensha and conservative politicians devoting more attention to the material and economic value of the East China Sea.[49]

March 24, 2004, saw the first-ever landing on the islands by mainland Chinese activists. Seven activists landed on Uotsurijima, planted two Chinese flags (a PRC and a ROC flag), and vandalized the lighthouse and shrine. It was also the first time that an activist landing party was formally arrested by Japanese authorities.[50] Before local authorities could file trespassing charges against the activists, Japan's national government intervened and they were quickly deported.[51] The swift action, which sent the Chinese activists home within 48 hours, reflected Prime Minister Koizumi's desire to prevent the issue from interfering with a planned visit by Japan's foreign minister to Beijing. Koizumi had "immediately asserted ownership over the decision-making process" over how to treat the activists, establishing an important precedent.[52] Beijing reacted with similar restraint, and there came to be an understanding that future landings by activists would result in deportation instead of arrests.

Japanese weekly magazine *Aera*, a part of the Asahi Shimbun company, printed a "scoop" article in October 2010 claiming that the restraint shown by both governments in 2004 was the result of "secret promises" between the LDP and the Chinese government. Unnamed sources stated that the Japanese side promised to prevent landings by Chinese activists on the islands but would not detain them unless they had committed a very serious offense. The Chinese side promised to prevent its activists from sailing in boats to the Senkakus. Subsequent events indicate that such promises may have indeed existed.[53]

On the non-state front of the 2004 incident, one Japanese uyoku group, Nihon Komintō, responded with violence to the Chinese landing and the Japanese government's deportation of the activists. In the early morning hours of April 24, a Nihon Komintō member rammed a loudspeaker bus into the gates of the Chinese consulate in Osaka. No one was hurt in the incident, but the gate to the consulate was badly damaged. Nakagama was arrested, and the Japanese government issued a formal apology to China.[54] Xinhua News Agency referred to the attack as "the most serious by a suspected Japanese right-winger against Chinese diplomatic facilities since the normalization of diplomatic relations in 1972." Japanese courts also treated this crime as a serious matter, and Nakagama was sentenced to seven years in prison.[55] Nihon Komintō, like Seinensha, was a uyoku group that dated back to the 1960s and had ties to organized crime. Other traditional Japanese uyoku groups have regularly held demonstrations near China's consulates and embassy, where large contingents of police are on hand to prevent them from inflicting harm. While demonstrations involving uyoku sound trucks are loud, Daiki Shibuichi has noted that "the degree of political influence of these events on Japanese foreign policy may be limited, which likely explains why the events go largely unreported."[56]

The island landing and consulate attack of 2004 did not become a major crisis for the two countries. However, the status quo would soon "unravel" as both governments began placing greater importance on the islands and their surrounding waters.[57]

The lighthouse that Seinensha built on Uotsurijima was granted official navigational beacon status by the Japanese government on February 9, 2005.[58] Seinensha's efforts to assert sovereignty seemed to have finally paid off, and they treated the decision as a major victory. While some considered this event an expression of a tougher stance toward China, others have argued that the government's decision was meant to prevent future escalation of the territorial issue.[59] Up until that point, Seinensha had used lighthouse maintenance as a justification for its attempts to land on the islands, with those landings provoking responses from abroad. By taking ownership of the lighthouse, the Japanese government was putting an end to Seinensha's boat activism. The Chinese government issued a very short statement of official protest over the decision but took no other meaningful action.[60]

The next few years passed without a major diplomatic incident involving the islands. One noteworthy event occurred in 2008 when a JCG patrol ship collided with a Taiwanese recreation fishing boat that had entered Japanese-claimed waters near the islands. The Taiwanese boat sank, and despite Japan's initial claims that the Taiwanese had rammed the Japanese ship, video evidence later proved that the JCG had been at fault in the collision. Japan issued a formal apology and paid compensation for the lost boast and fishing equipment.[61]

In 2009, Japan's Liberal Democratic Party was swept out of office and replaced by a new government under the Democratic Party of Japan (DPJ). The DPJ government pursued a closer relationship with China, and it initially seemed like there would be no major conflict with China. Yet despite the DPJ's stated intentions, a major crisis would destabilize the Senkaku field of contestation in 2010.

Channel Sakura and the Senkakus prior to 2010 crisis

In the first few years of Channel Sakura's existence, there was no major incident involving the Senkakus. During that period Channel Sakura focused its time and efforts on opportunities in other fields. Yet the Senkakus were still an issue of importance within the assertive conservative right. Some Channel Sakura programs introduced viewers to the value of the islands, both in a material sense and in an ideational sense.

For example, Professor Yamada Yoshihiko of Tokyo University of Marine Science and Technology discussed the state of the Senkakus with Channel Sakura's "Today's Self-Defense Forces" program in March 2009. Drawing on historical evidence, he claimed that the Japanese fishermen of Ishigaki Island had considered the Senkakus a valuable fishing area since the Edo Period. Yamada stated that the islands were far and difficult for small fishing boats to safely reach, even though they were a good source of tuna. Fishermen would benefit, he argued, if the Japanese government constructed facilities on the islands. There was also mention of how the government was renting the islands and would not allow people to land there. The importance of strengthening good relations with Taiwan, and with the Japan-friendly former Taiwanese president Lee Teng-Hui, was introduced as a way to take a stand against Chinese territorial claims. In this video one could observe the employment of a topic that would often appear in future Channel Sakura video programming about the Senkakus: the plight of the common fisherman. This narrative fit well with Channel Sakura's identity as a grassroots movement "by the Japanese people and for the Japanese people." Oil and mineral resources under the seabed were not completely ignored, but the hardworking Japanese fishermen were given more attention.[62]

The strategic value of the Senkakus – another important aspect of the dispute – could be observed in a "Today's Self-Defense Forces" episode that aired on September 14, 2009. Former Maritime Self-Defense Force officer Hirama Yōichi discussed the state of the Senkaku dispute under the DPJ's China-friendly policies. The DPJ was said to be threatening the US–Japan alliance with its plan to create an East Asian Community that would include China as a member state. Additionally, the DPJ government sought to alter previous basing agreements and reduce the US military presence in Okinawa. Hirama used the story of the Philippines pushing America to close its naval base in Subic Bay and the subsequent Chinese seizing of islands in the South China Sea as a warning to Japan: If America leaves, Japan could lose the Senkakus within six months. China would then have a foothold dangerously close to Ishigaki Island and the rest of Okinawa. In such a case, Japan would be like the Philippines – unable to draw upon American help in resisting aggressive Chinese actions. Not only would the Senkaku Islands be lost, Hirama argued, but Japan would also lose access to the seabed's strategically significant gas reserves.[63]

Past landings on the Senkakus were covered in a July 10, 2010, group discussion program about the "dangerous" situation in the Senkaku Islands. It included an impressively credentialed panel: retired Maritime Self-Defense Force Rear admiral Kawamura Sumihiko, retired Air Self-Defense Force lt. general Satō Mamoru, Japan Coast Guard Academy superintendent Miyake Norio, and Takubo Tadae of Nippon Kaigi. The panel held a detailed discussion of the growing military threat that China posed to Japan, including speculation about the methods China would employ to gain control of the Senkakus. Of particular note was General Satō recalling how the activists from Hong Kong and Taiwan were smart to bring many journalists along with them when they tried to land in 1996.[64] In the coming years, Channel Sakura would employ a similar tactic.

An interesting prediction came from Channel Sakura president Mizushima Satoru on a July 23, 2010, program. Although the program was meant to focus on Google Maps' policy of featuring both the Japanese and Chinese names for the islands, Mizushima mentioned a larger threat to Japan. He warned about a plan for an "invasion" of the Senkakus from mainland China, Taiwan, and Hong Kong. He called on the Japanese government to show the will to protect its nation, even if it meant developing nuclear weapons. Furthermore, if the politicians did not have the have the will to do it, then the people would need to rise up and defend the Senkaku Islands by establishing a "people's defense force" (minkan bōeitai). Three minutes into the video, Mizushima made a striking prediction. He mentioned that an international meeting of Chinese businesspersons would take place in Los Angeles on September 7, 2010, where participants would allegedly conspire to advance China's territorial claims to the islands.[65] Although the meeting in question proved to be unimportant, that particular date would indeed mark a major event in the Senkaku Islands dispute.

The 2010 boat collision incident

On the morning of September 7, 2010, a Chinese trawler collided with JCG patrol boats near the Senkakus. The captain of the trawler was detained and charged two days later with the crime of interfering with public servants in the execution of their duties. The Chinese government responded with demands for the release of the captain. Japan's DPJ government under Prime Minister Kan Naoto refused, stating that it would leave the decision in the hands of local prosecutors in Okinawa. China's response was harsh. Violent anti-Japanese street demonstrations occurred in Chinese cities, the Chinese government canceled ministerial-level meetings, exports to Japan of rare earth metals encountered sudden delays, and four Japanese employees of Fujita Corporation were arrested in China for allegedly filming a military installation. The pressure seemed to work, and on September 24, the prosecutors in Okinawa announced the release of the captain, citing diplomatic concerns.[66] The Kan administration was seen as caving in to Chinese demands while pushing responsibility for the decision onto a local official.[67]

The Kan administration had taken actions that broke with the status quo in the Senkaku field of contestation.[68] Whether or not one believes that there were secret promises between the LDP and the Chinese government, up until 2010 Japan had deported intruders instead of charging them with crimes.[69] Alternatively, it could be argued that China sensed its growing power relative to Japan and deliberately sought an escalation of the dispute, regardless of whether the trawler captain had been immediately deported without charges. Either way, it was a bad outcome for Kan and the DPJ. The Japanese government's handling of the dispute was widely criticized as weak, and public support for the Kan administration declined.[70]

Channel Sakura took advantage of the crisis, launching a grassroots campaign centered on the condemnation of what it saw as the Japanese government's weak-kneed response to China's aggression. A September 9 Channel Sakura news report described the collision as a deliberate political act by the Chinese government. They praised the JCG for detaining the captain, who was, according to Mizushima, likely an undercover Chinese naval officer. Mizushima explained the need to protest in front of the Chinese embassy to show that the Japanese people believed the territory belonged to their country.[71] Then, on September 10, Mizushima declared that Channel Sakura's activist co-organization, Ganbare Nippon, would be launching demonstrations to denounce Chinese "aggression" in the Senkakus. Denouncing the Japanese government's "cowardly" response and their unwillingness to take stronger actions displaying sovereignty over the islands, he reminded viewers of an article he had written for a Yasukuni Shrine newsletter in August. The article called readers to action under the headline "if the government can't fulfill its duty defend the country, then the people will."[72] This drew upon Channel Sakura's grant narrative of grassroots heroes rising up to save the country (detailed in Chapter 4). Ganbare Nippon held protests in Tokyo's Shibuya neighborhood and in front of the Chinese embassy on September 10 and 11, as well as in front of the DPJ party headquarters on September 13.[73]

Channel Sakura later uploaded video highlights from the September 10 and September 11 demonstrations. These included footage of Mizushima, Nagayama Hideki (Taiwan Research Forum), Kobayashi Tadashi (former chairman of Tsukurukai), and Umehara Katsuhiko (former mayor of Sendai). They also showed grassroots Ganbare Nippon volunteers as they diligently handed out fliers to passing pedestrians. The camera operator took special note of people who stopped to take photos of the demonstration, including several foreigners. At the end of the report, Channel Sakura news anchors discussed the importance of the demonstration, claiming that although most passing pedestrians would have less than 30 seconds to hear the speeches, just hearing the word "Senkaku" would make them aware of the issue.[74] Throughout September Channel Sakura regularly devoted its programs to the Senkaku issue and organized protests every weekend in Shibuya. Viewers were continually reminded of how the protests represented grassroots justice-seeking.

The release of the Chinese captain provided an opportunity to make a viral YouTube video. On September 25 Channel Sakura hit the streets of Tokyo's Kichijōji neighborhood to ask two hundred random people their views on the release of the captain. While a few people said they supported the government's decision and some did not have any opinion on the matter, the overwhelming majority of people shown in the video disagreed with the government's handling of the crisis. The video contained a short and simple introduction followed by 12 minutes of the pedestrians' responses. The final few minutes of the clip contained commentary from Ganbare Nippon executive secretary Miwa Kazuo, who compared the Japanese government's decision to someone caving in to extortion from a gangster. It was a simple video without a particularly extreme message, meaning that it could be easily shared online. Packaged in the form of comments from everyday people, its message could appeal to viewers outside of Channel Sakura's typical conservative audience. It proved one of Channel Sakura's most popular uploads of the year, receiving over 100,000 views in its first month online.[75]

The next phase of the activist campaign involved a major demonstration scheduled for October 2. Although their main march would take place in Tokyo, Ganbare Nippon chapters across Japan were called upon to organize regional demonstrations. Activists answered this call, and while others marched in Tokyo, they passed out fliers and delivered speeches in front of train stations in Akita, Utsunomiya, Yokohama, Kamakura, Nagoya, Fukushima, Matsuyama, Okayama, and Kumamoto cities. Mizushima called on anyone, even lone activists, to take to the streets and let people know that China was threatening the peace of Asia.[76] The Tokyo demonstration succeeded in attracting about 2,670 people, making it the largest demonstration organized by Ganbare Nippon to that date.[77] Ganbare Nippon organizers in Nagoya also succeeded in attracting about 400 people to their demonstration.[78] Retired Air Self-Defense Force general Tamogami Toshio, the nominal leader of Ganbare Nippon, stood at the front of the Tokyo march, alongside its primary organizer, Mizushima Satoru. The Tokyo demonstration attracted the attention of international media, such as the *Wall Street Journal*,[79] *Reuters*, and the *Globe and Mail*.[80] Channel Sakura noted that there was considerable attention from international outlets, but aside from the *Yūkan Fuji* newspaper, it was almost completely ignored by Japanese news media.[81]

Ganbare Nippon organized an even larger demonstration on October 16 in Tokyo, drawing between 2,800 and 3,200 participants.[82] Demonstrators carried some 600 Japanese flags as they marched, a visually impressive scene that was later shared with non-participants via Channel Sakura's recap videos.[83] Mizushima declared that so many "normal" people carrying the flag proved that Japan's national flag was no longer something reserved for fringe uyoku.[84] Comments were once again made about a lack of domestic media coverage, even though Mizushima claimed to have faxed announcements of the demonstration to every major Japanese newspaper and TV channel.[85] As in the case of the previous demonstration, international media was on hand to cover the event.[86]

More regional protests followed. Several days later, a demonstration organized by the Ganbare Nippon branch office in Kagawa drew about 300 people.[87] Then, on October 31, the Nagoya branch held a demonstration with about 640 participants.[88]

Meanwhile, anti-Japanese protests were held in China. The Chinese media covered Ganbare Nippon demonstrations, and images of the anti-Chinese protest signs were used to incite anger among Chinese nationalists.[89] The Chinese Foreign Ministry responded to the protests with a statement at an October 17 press briefing, expressing "grave concern" about what it considered a threat to the safety of its diplomatic missions and personnel.[90]

There were also examples of fake news spreading on the Chinese websites depicting the Ganbare Nippon demonstration as a gathering of militant uyoku extremists. Some Chinese internet users spread years-old photos of uyoku sound trucks and uyoku in military-style uniforms, claiming that they were images of the September and October 2010 protests held in Tokyo.[91]

Channel Sakura and Nihon Seinensha – working with uyoku?

Nihon Seinensha, a leading non-state actor in the Senkaku field of contestation from the 1970s until the early 2000s, did not play a major role in the 2010 protests. However, Seinensha did take notice of Channel Sakura's activism and sent them a gift: video footage taken during Seinensha's past landings on the Senkakus. Channel Sakura's treatment of the footage displayed apprehension about traditional uyoku groups.

On an October 14 special program about the footage, Mizushima seemed uncomfortable in mentioning the name of "Seinensha" – pronouncing it faster than any of the other words in his sentences. Nonetheless, he thanked them for providing the video. He reiterated the fact that Channel Sakura and Ganbare Nippon were a "citizen activist" group that was working for the sake of the Japanese people. He emphasized that "we" each have our "own way of thinking" and Channel Sakura's way of thinking was different from uyoku activism. By showing the world the video of Seinensha activists landing on the islands, Channel Sakura claimed to be displaying evidence that "we," the Japanese people, were practicing sovereignty of the islands. Mizushima reminded viewers that "we" needed to keep fighting to maintain that claim.[92]

Aside from about 20 seconds of one man in camouflage fatigues putting up a Japanese flag, almost nothing about the video clip from Seinensha looked like it came from a far-right uyoku group with underworld ties. In most of the footage shown by Channel Sakura, there were men wearing more normal blue-and-white work clothing. In the background, Japan Coast Guard ships were shown at anchor, taking no action against the activists.

However, searches on YouTube revealed that other, longer copies of Seinensha's video were available (showing landings made in 2001, 2002, and 2003).[93] The longer footage included groups of men wearing military-style uniforms and white headbands. Rather than being passive, the Japan Coast Guard was blaring out warnings over loudspeakers, informing the Seinensha activists that they were violating the law by landing on the island. Footage from 2004 showed Seinensha members verbally berating a silent line of shield-carrying coast guard officers who blocked access to their fishing boat and prevented them from carrying out a planned landing. The differences between the footage shown on Channel Sakura and the longer footage available elsewhere on YouTube suggest that Channel Sakura selectively aired footage that better fit the image of their preferred form of non-extremist activism. It would have been detrimental to their grassroots non-extremist identity to deliver too much praise to the alienating activism of the uyoku.

Sengoku38 and the leaking of the 2010 boat collision footage

Frustration with the Kan administration was further ignited by the news that the Japanese government had video footage of the boat collision but was withholding it from lawmakers and the public. A select group of lawmakers was allowed to see an edited portion of the video in the last week of September 2010, yet the government decided that the footage should not be released to the public. The situation took a dramatic turn on November 4 when the footage appeared on YouTube. Someone operating under the freshly created YouTube account "Sengoku38" had leaked the video without permission. A DPJ politician recognized the damage the leak would do to his party, stating that it was "totally different from presenting it to the public in an official manner, and it leads the people's further erosion of faith in Japan's government."[94] To make matters worse, Japanese media and viewers widely interpreted the footage as showing that the Chinese trawler intentionally rammed the JCG ships. To critics of the Japan's decision to bow to Chinese pressure and release the trawler captain, it proved that the government had shamefully failed to uphold the law.

Sengoku38's upload was traced to an internet café in Kobe, and the press reported that authorities had detained and were questioning an employee of the Japan Coast Guard. In a Channel Sakura report about the situation, Mizushima Satoru described the Kan administration's failure to release the video and the detention of Sengoku38 to be a "crime against the Japanese people." Mizushima's co-anchor added that the footage shared by Sengoku38 was clear enough for a child to see the Chinese captain was at fault. Not yet knowing the details of Sengoku38's situation, Mizushima nonetheless offered the full support of Ganbare Nippon, suggesting that its legal team in the anti-NHK lawsuit (discussed in Chapter 5) could also be used to defend Sengoku38.[95]

It soon came to light that Sengoku38 was Chief Mate Isshiki Masaharu, a 43-year-old JCG officer stationed in Kobe. Although authorities ultimately decided not to prosecute him, the JCG did punish Isshiki with a one-year suspension.[96] Isshiki applied and was granted an early discharge from JCG service, a decision that freed him to secure a book deal with Asahi Shimbun Publications. In "Why I Did It – the Confession of Sengoku38," released in February 2011, Isshiki justified his actions with harsh criticism of the Kan administration's lack of transparency:

> If this video qualifies as a national secret, then it will be possible to classify any unfavorable information as national secrets. If this was so, wouldn't it be like certain other countries in which rulers can get away with doing anything?[97]

Although the sentence didn't name the "certain other countries" (doko ka no kuni) he was referring to, it is rather clear that he was comparing that the Kan administration to communist China. Isshiki devoted much of the book to counter what he considered the Chinese government's dishonest propaganda. Given these kinds of opinions, it is not surprising that Isshiki later appeared as a guest on Channel Sakura programs. His first appearance on their channel was on September 7, 2011, the one-year anniversary of the boat collision incident.[98] He was invited back as a guest on several subsequent Channel Sakura programs, providing expertise on the JCG's role in protecting the Senkakus.[99]

Sengoku38's video leak was well-timed to perk interest in a November 6, 2010, protest rally that Channel Sakura had been promoting for weeks. Unlike the previous marches carried out under the banner of Ganbare Nippon, this event, held in Tokyo's Hibiya Park, was co-organized with several pro-Taiwan independence groups, as well as organizations that advocated independence for ethnic minority groups within China. It was given a grand title: The Meeting to Establish Solidarity for Freedom and Human Rights in Asia (also translated in some sources as "the Freedom and Peace for Asia Rally and Demonstration"). A Japanese language advertisement for the rally contained a message calling for action against "Chinese Imperialism":

> *The people of Asia who are threatened by Chinese Imperialism will join together to protect freedom and peace by holding the Meeting to Establish Solidarity for Freedom and Human Rights in Asia on November 6. We call on those with courage to join us!*[100]

Channel Sakura took the rare step of producing an English-language advertisement video, which contained the following description (the typos and misspellings were present in the original):

> *Condemn China's Invasion to Senkaku Islands!*
> *Condemn China's Militaristic Hegemony over Asia!*
> *Recapture Abduction Victims!*
> *Free Dr.Liu Xiaobo, The Novel Peace Winner!*
> *Solidarity of Asian Nations for Freedom and Human Rights!*
> *Rally Date: November 6th, 2010 from 1:00pm to 3:30pm*
> *Place: Hibiya Open-Air Concert Hall (Tokyo)*
> *Demonstration Parade: start at 3:45pm*
> *Street Speech: 5:30pm to 7:00pm at Yurakucho Station Open Space*
> *Guest Speakers for Rally*
> *Toshio Tamogami (former Chief of Staff, Japanese Air Force), Yuriko Koike (Chairperson of Executive Committee LDP), Hiroshi Yamada (former Suginami Mayor), Shingo Nishimura (former National Diet number), Masaaki Akaike (former National Diet number) Hideaki Kase, Kouichi Sugiyama, Shigeo Iizuka (Family member of Abduction victim), Huan Wenxiong (Taiwan), Ilham Mahamti (Uygur), Pema Gyalpo (Tibet), and other speakers from Mongolia, Manchuria, Indonesia, North Korea, Bangladesh, and etc.*
>
> *Hosted by:*
>
> - *Ganbare Nippon! National Action Commitee*
> - *Somo Zenkoku Chihogiinnokai (National Grass-Root Local Assembly Nembers) [sic]*
> - *Friends of Lee Tong-Hui Association in Japan*
> - *Taiwan Research Forum*

Participants gathered in front of a stage featuring banners in Japanese and English, declaring their support for peace, freedom, and human rights (see Figure 7.1). An impressive array of speakers took part in the event. Perhaps most noteworthy was Koike Yuriko, a mainstream politician who would be elected Governor of Tokyo in 2016. All of the individuals on the list had appeared on Channel Sakura in the past.

It was a remarkable success. Over 4,000 people attended, making it the largest right-wing street demonstration in postwar Japanese history.[101] To emphasize the international aspect of the demonstration, English-language announcements about their views were played over a loudspeaker as participants marched through the streets.[102] A recap video of the protest uploaded by Channel Sakura showed long lines of young people, including young mothers pushing baby carriages and people walking Hinomaru-wearing dogs, marching along the street. Onlookers were shown applauding them as they passed. Afterwards, Mizushima happily shared that Iran's PressTV, which had referred to Ganbare Nippon as a "right-wing" group when reporting on an earlier event, had instead used the word "conservative" to report about on this rally. Even NHK filed a report, referring to them as a "citizen's group" (shimin dantai). To Mizushima, the demonstrators were the "voice of the people" which had proven loud enough to attract media recognizing their movement.[103]

Figure 7.1 A photo of the November 6, 2010, rally in Hibiya Park. Flags of nations wronged by China, including those of Tibet and East Turkestan, are on display. (Public Domain, Wikipedia)

Mizushima had announced the event only one day beforehand.[118] Ganbare Nippon also held a protest on February 27 in front of the Chinese consulate, with about 400 people, including Mizushima, participating.[119]

Protest activities were planned for March 2011, but the Tōhoku earthquake and tsunami caused a temporary halt to the campaign. Like many organizations in Japan, Channel Sakura raised money and collected supplies to assist with disaster relief. They also created programs about the state of evacuees in temporary housing.

At the end of May 2011 Mizushima revealed photos of the fishing boat they had purchased, which would be named the Daiichi Sakura Maru. A few weeks later, Mizushima delivered an on-the-scene status report about the boat from Naha. He showed the viewers the interior of the boat they helped purchase, telling them that "we" (Mizushima and the viewers) would soon be going to Ishigaki Island and onward to the Senkakus. The mission would be carried to help defend the islands for the sake of the fishermen of Ishigaki. Landing on the Senkakus was not discussed. Instead, Mizushima stated that the plan would be to conduct fishing missions around the islands and film news reports. He wanted to perform activism that both would abide by Japanese law and support the fishermen of Ishigaki.

In celebration of the Daiichi Sakura Maru's upcoming voyage to the islands, a Channel Sakura viewer from Chiba prefecture donated a custom-made fishing flag (*tairyō bata*). The vibrantly colored flag featured waves splashing around Mount Fuji, with a sakura flower petal in one corner, the characters for "big catch" in another, and Daichi Sakura Maru in huge characters in its center. Mizushima shared his excitement about the flag with viewers by unwrapping and opening its box in front of the camera.[120] This performance was remarkably similar to unboxing videos that are popular on other YouTube channels, in which viewers and the creator share in the experience of opening the box of a new product.

Another program provided a detailed explanation of the purpose and meaning of Channel Sakura's fishing missions. Standing in front of the colorful fishing flag on July 1, Mizushima expressed his thanks to the viewer who donated money, flags, and other necessary materials. He talked about the beautiful Mt. Fuji and flower petal on the flag, both traditional symbols of the Japanese nation. Mizushima then lamented that the concept of having an obligation to defend your country did not exist in mainstream postwar Japanese society. However, "we," the people of Ganbare Nippon, were different. Ganbare Nippon was carrying out activism for the future, for "our" ancestors who created the 2,000-year-old country of Japan. Alleging that certain unnamed government officials had warned Ganbare Nippon not to bring a cameraman on their fishing trip, Mizushima blasted this attempted suppression of the people's "right to know" and the "freedom of the press." The most important way to defend Japan, he argued, would be to "protect the livelihood of the fishermen."[121] Thus, the boat's primary mission was to provide such protection for fishermen. Through this narrative, the activists and their supporters were depicted as collectively defending the basic rights of Japan and its people.

Fishing as territorial activism

The first activist fishing expedition was carried out on July 3, 2011. A Channel Sakura report that aired on July 7 deemed a resounding success. By carrying out the everyday activity of fishing in the area of the islands, they stated that they were reaffirming and defending the rights of Ishigaki's fishermen. A clear message was delivered to viewers: the Japanese government had failed to properly protect the fishermen, so it was up to Channel Sakura's grassroots movement to defend the country and its people. It was noted that this mission was only made possible thanks to everyone who watched Channel Sakura and made donations.[122] They also pointed to the fact that the Chinese government officially condemned their fishing mission as proof that their activities were exercising Japanese sovereignty over the islands.[123] That the JCG had blocked a Chinese activist boat from entering the same area days earlier served as an additional topic of celebration for Mizushima and his organization.[124]

A second fishing expedition was planned for October or November 2011. Mizushima emphasized beforehand that Ganbare Nippon's first fishing mission had honored a promise not to land on the islands. He also displayed photos of the islands, commenting on how beautiful they looked.[125] By stating that there would be no surprise landings on the island, Mizushima framed Channel Sakura and Ganbare Nippon's activism within the limits of the existing rules of the field of contestation. Setting a plan, submitting it to authorities, and following it without major deviation was the demonstration of his organization's willingness to not cross boundaries set by the Japanese state. This could have also been an attempt to gain recognition as a legitimate actor within the field. Since the start of Channel Sakura and Ganbare Nippon's activist campaigns, Mizushima had strived to differentiate himself from traditional uyoku organizations. They did not want to be seen as similar to lawbreaking extremist groups like Nihon Seinensha.

The second fishing expedition took place without major problems. Fish caught on the expeditions were brought to Tokyo and served to Diet lawmakers at a special luncheon in the National Diet building on November 15.[126] The flag of the Daiichi Sakura Maru, well-worn from the salty winds of two expeditions, was displayed on the wall of the room. Sushi chefs were brought in to prepare sashimi for the lawmakers. Over a dozen lawmakers from the LDP and DPJ attended the event. Among them was LDP lawmaker Kishi Nobuo, brother of former and future prime minister Abe Shinzō.

Through their support of a crowdfunding campaign that allowed the fishing missions to become a reality, Channel Sakura's viewers had "opened the road" to the Senkakus.[127] Between 2011 and the nationalization of the Senkaku Islands in 2012, nine successful missions were carried out.[128] Each mission was an affirmation of their belief that they were patriots protecting their country. The missions were recorded in detail and shared via the internet, bringing the virtual experience of visiting the Senkakus to thousands of supporters. Channel Sakura also allowed some viewers to directly participate in the fishing missions by selling tour packages that included airfare to Okinawa, hotel rooms, and a ride along on the fishing boat to one of the Senkaku Islands.

The nationalization of the Senkakus and more boat landings

The Senkaku field of contestation entered a new phase in April 2012 when plans to shift several of the islands from private to public ownership were announced in Washington, DC. The man who made this announcement was Ishihara Shintarō, who bankrolled the 1978 construction of a lighthouse on Uotsurijima and had since risen in the political world to become Governor of Tokyo. According to early press reports, it was not the first time that Ishihara had approached the Kurihara family and tried to purchase their land. However, because he made the previous offers as a private individual, they were unwilling to sell it. Now that the offer was being made on behalf of the Tokyo Metropolitan Government, the owners had changed their minds.[129] Purchasing the three largest islands, including Uotsurijima, would have allowed Ishihara to use his powers as governor to develop the Senkakus. Possibilities included the construction of port facilities or a police station.[130]

Rather than use tax revenue to make the purchase, Ishihara announced a fundraising campaign. Individuals who supported the plan were asked to send in contributions. Channel Sakura became an enthusiastic cheerleader for the campaign, producing videos calling on viewers to send money to Ishihara's Senkaku fund.[131]

The national government, which had been paying rental fees for the islands since 2002, had until the beginning of the 2013 fiscal year to take action and prevent the sale. The DPJ administration under Prime Minister Noda Yoshihiko decided to outbid Ishihara and nationalize the islands. The national government aimed to end the flare-up of the dispute by taking ownership of the Senkakus and preventing Ishihara from building facilities or using the islands for other purposes that could worsen relations with China. Foreign Minister Genba Koichirō stated that the purchase would ensure the "peaceful and stable maintenance and management" of the islands.[132]

The national government reportedly estimated the value of the three islands at around 500 million yen. However, Ishihara's fundraising campaign proved highly successful and the Tokyo Metropolitan Government collected more than 1.4 billion yen in contributions from the public for its bid. The central government was forced to counter with a higher offer of over 2 billion yen. The owners accepted the national government's offer, and Ishihara donated the 1.4 billion yen to the national government.[133]

Channel Sakura delivered glowing praise for Ishihara's push for change in the territorial dispute.[134] Viewers were told that the "anti-Japanese" mainstream media in Japan was carrying out a smear campaign to make Ishihara's plan appear like a waste of government resources and an unfair provocation. Ishihara needed to make his announcement in America, it was claimed, because the Western media would be on hand to report his remarks. This was because Japanese mainstream media could not be trusted to report the truth.[135] Such a claim reinforced the notion that Channel Sakura was one of the few media outlets in Japan that was trustworthy and willing to tell the people about important issues. Thus, its viewers were members of an exclusive group who had access to the truth and a responsibility to help spread the word to people who were being exposed to untruthful news reports from the mainstream media.

A Landing and counter-landing on Uotsurijima

Japanese boat activists had ambitious plans for summer 2012. Channel Sakura and Ganbare Nippon would turn their August fishing expedition into a large-scale ceremony to pray for the Japanese who had died on Uotsurijima in the closing weeks of World War II. Commemorating the tragedy of 1945 had taken on a major significance for activists, who saw such ceremonies as spiritually linking the physical territory of the islands to the Japanese people and nation. An application was made asking for government permission to land on the islands, but it was rejected by authorities. When reporting the rejection, Mizushima mentioned news articles about Hong Kong activists who planned a landing on the islands. He incorrectly predicted that a single foreign ship could easily be stopped by the Japan Coast Guard.[136]

The pro-China activists evaded the JCG and reached the islands on August 15, the anniversary of Japan's defeat in World War II. Seven activists from Hong Kong and Taiwan landed on Uotsurijima and raised flags as a means of "claiming our sovereign rights to the world." The activists, members of the same organization that had landed in 1996, were briefly detained by Japanese authorities and then deported. They were not charged with any crime.[137]

On the same day Mizushima and a group of Ganbare Nippon members were carrying out their annual march to the Yasukuni Shrine (a ritual discussed in Chapter 4). Mizushima delivered a short speech to a crowd of supporters, expressing his intent to travel to the islands and not mentioning any plan to make a landing.[138] An August 16 Channel Sakura news report portrayed the pro-China activists as sneakily taking advantage of a day when "people across Japan had been quietly gather to pray to the spirits of their ancestors and the heroic war dead." Mizushima denounced the DPJ government for quickly releasing the activists without taking the time to verify whether or not they were Chinese soldiers or spies.[139]

This landing marked a major change in the conditions of the Senkaku field of contestation. Pro-China activists had just performed an act that had increased their stature. Not only could the landing be seen as an assertion of China's sovereignty over the islands, but it was also a major embarrassment on a sacred day of remembrance for the Japanese right. Moreover, the Japanese government demonstrated an unwillingness to file any trespassing charges against the activists. If foreign activists could land on the island and not be punished, what about Japanese activists? It looked unlikely that the Japanese government would try to arrest and charge Japanese citizens for trespassing just days after it had let foreign activists get away with the same act. Mizushima and his fellow activists would take full advantage of this window of opportunity.

Events initially played out according to the plan that had been approved by authorities. Around 150 people gathered at Yonaguni and Ishigaki Islands on August 18 and boarded 20 fishing boats.[140] They included Ganbare Nippon and allied activists, conservative politicians, journalists from domestic and international media outlets, Shintō priests, and fishermen whose boats had been chartered for the journey. The politicians included Diet members from the Lawmakers Federation to Protect Japanese Territory (Nihon no Ryōdo wo Mamoru Tame Kōdō Suru Giin Renmei). Ganbare Nippon leader Tamogami Toshio was also present. The fleet arrived near Uotsurijima in the early morning of August 19 and a Shintō ceremony was held on one of the ships, offering prayers to dead of 1945.

Shortly after the ceremony Mizushima declared that he was going to swim ashore. With the help of Channel Sakura staff, he tied a rope around himself and jumped into the sea. After some minor difficulty with rough waves, he made it ashore.[141] The rope was then used to guide another nine people ashore: four from Ganbare Nippon/Channel Sakura and five politicians. The Ganbare Nippon members who joined Mizushima were Asano Kumi (Channel Sakura/Ganbare Nippon), Itō Sukeyasu[142] (Ganbare Nippon/retired Maritime Self-Defense Forces officer), and a Channel Sakura cameraman. The lawmakers were Kojima Yoshirō (Ibaraki Prefectural Assembly), Tanaka Yūtarō (Tokyo Suginami Ward Assembly), Kosaka Eiji (Tokyo Arakawa Ward Assembly), Wada Yūichirō (Hyogo Prefectural Assembly), and Suzuki Akihiro[143] (Tokyo Metropolitan Assembly). They spent two hours on the island, some of which was spent in offering prayer to the war dead. Channel Sakura representatives explored with their camera, documenting the existence of a small stream and taking note of the environmental degradation of the island. Their camera operator filmed plastic bottles and other garbage that had been swept ashore. The plastic bottles had Chinese labels, an indication that pollution from China was harming the islands.[144] JCG patrol ships were visible offshore, but the JCG did not take any action until the activists had returned to their own boats.[145] Rubber speedboats approached, and a team of JCG personnel briefly questioned them about the landing. No one was arrested.

Justifying the landing on Uotsurijima

Justifying his actions at a press conference on August 30, Mizushima claimed that the original and main intent of the trip to the islands was to carry out prayers for the war dead. Noting that their request to land had been rejected by authorities several days earlier, he insisted that he set off on his boat intending to honor the rules set by the government. His decision to jump into the water and swim ashore was a spontaneous action. He contrasted his actions with the landing carried out days earlier by the Hong Kong activists, referring to it as a Chinese military action. The pro-China landing party had included reporters from Phoenix TV, a station owned by individuals with ties to the Chinese Communist Party, thus making the reporters "paramilitary" agents of the Chinese state.[146]

Mizushima also portrayed his activists as environmentalists. The footage filmed by Channel Sakura represented a record of the environmental degradation on Uotsurijima. A lack of government management of the island had apparently led to a situation in which local flora and fauna were threatened. Moreover, Channel Sakura's videos were freely available for the public to view on YouTube and NicoNico Douga.[147] This was in contrast to the Japanese government, which Mizushima criticized for hiding information from the public.

Speaking to Channel Sakura viewers in an editorial video shortly after returning from Okinawa, Mizushima explained why he had broken with the procedure of only carrying out acts with prior government permission. He compared the Senkaku Islands to the yard of a neighbor's house. One usually will not enter the neighbor's property without permission. He raised a hypothetical question: what if you saw a crime happening in your neighbor's yard and your neighbor was deliberately doing nothing to stop it? Surely, Mizushima argued, such an emergency would call for entry into the neighbor's yard without permission. In this story, the neighbor represented the weak-kneed Japanese government, which was not doing enough to punish the Chinese, who had rammed its ships and landed on its islands. Channel Sakura, as a good neighbor, was standing up for the peace of the neighborhood.[148] From this description, Mizushima's decision to swim ashore almost sounded like it was a premeditated act, rather than a spur of the moment decision.

YouTube comments from viewers expressed praise and joy at Mizushima's landing on the island. For example, one user wrote, "Thinking of the importance of August 15th, one couldn't simply be quiet and do nothing!" Another stated their joy at the possibility of seeing video footage filmed by Mizushima and the landing party. Meanwhile, yet another added a simple, "I resolutely support Mizushima!"[149]

Whether it had been planned or was a decision made on that day, the landing on the Uotsurijima demonstrated that the Japanese government was unwilling to take strict measures against activists. Channel Sakura and Ganbare Nippon abruptly broke with their previous boat activism policy of firmly observing government-mandated rules. Their acts of disobedience took place within a window of opportunity in which it could be reasonably assumed that the Japanese authorities would be unwilling to arrest them. As skilled social actors, they used their social connections, monetary resources, and organizational skills to organize a small fleet of ships, bringing along politicians and the international media. The ability to gain the cooperation of politicians and media organizations was arguably thanks to the fact that their activists had built a reputation as law-abiding and peaceful, quite different from an uyoku group like Nihon Seinensha.

The landing was carried out in front of news cameras and reporters. Together with their own cameras and the ability to distribute video of their voyage to thousands of people via the internet, Channel Sakura's activists achieved a level of visibility that went far beyond the recognition that Nihon Seinensha achieved from the 1970s to the 2000s.

It was a limited window of opportunity, however. On subsequent fishing expeditions they did not attempt further landings. This was likely because the Japanese government began to take a stricter stance toward their fishing boats, fearing the impact of another landing.

China reacts

The formal shift in ownership Uotsuri, Kita-Kojima, and Minami-Kojima Islands from private businessman Kurihara Hiroyuki to the Japanese government occurred on September 11, 2012. Subsequent press reports revealed that Kurihara had been trying to sell the islands to the Japanese government since 2006 but had been offered land swaps instead of monetary payments. This was not satisfactory for Kurihara, who needed a large sum of cash to pay considerable debts. Kurihara then touched on the strategy of selling to Tokyo governor Ishihara Shintarō, who was willing to offer such cash. The subsequent bidding war between Ishihara and the national government allowed Kurihara to sell the islands for a very high price.[150] Involving an outspoken politician and his nationalist allies, however, made what could have been a quiet transfer of ownership into a major international news story.

Ishihara's fundraising campaign and the Japanese government's public attempt to outbid him were treated by China as major provocations. Channel Sakura and Ganbare Nippon added fuel to the fire. This could be seen in an "incident review" timeline posted on August 14 by the *Global Times*, a Chinese state media outlet, started on April 16, the day that Ishihara announced his plans to buy the islands. Events from the previous few years, such as the boat collision incident, were not included. The timeline contrasted measured warnings from the Chinese state with further provocations from Japan. The final provocation that prompted the landing mission by pro-China activists was the announcement that "Some 50 Japanese lawmakers plan to set foot on the Daioyu Islands on August 19 to hold a vigil for the victims of a refugee shipwreck during wartime on the islands."[151] This description, although inaccurate about the number of politicians involved and the prior certainty that they would land on the islands, was clearly referring to the event carried out by Ganbare Nippon.

Two waves of mass anti-Japanese protest erupted across China in 2012 – first in August, in response to the boat activism and indications that the Japanese government would nationalize the islands, and later in September, after the nationalization formally took place. Thousands of people marched in cities across mainland China, with some demonstrations turning into violent riots that destroyed Japanese cars and businesses.[152] The Japanese Foreign Ministry roughly estimated the riots, and the loss of business for Japanese firms may have amounted to more than 100 million USD in economic damage.[153]

It is frequently suggested in Japanese and Western news reports that the Chinese government encourages or allows anti-Japanese demonstrations when it wants to put diplomatic pressure on Japan or distract its people from domestic problems. However, there is considerable disagreement in scholarship on the Chinese state's role in the 2012 anti-Japanese demonstrations. It has also been argued that popular nationalism has placed considerable pressure on Chinese leaders to take a harder line against Japan. While there is little doubt that the Chinese state education system and state media helped spread anti-Japanese nationalism, China's elites now face the danger of having their nationalistic masses turn their anger to the government if it does not respond to Japanese "provocations."[154]

Although Chinese activists did not successfully land on the Senkaku Islands after 2012 until present, Chinese activities in nearby waters increased dramatically. The summer of 2012 marked a major change in China's stance toward entering seas claimed by Japan. Incursions by Chinese patrol boats and fishing craft that used to happen once every few months later became an almost weekly occurrence.[155] Japan Coast Guard and China Coast Guard patrol boats regularly engaged in tense stand-offs, demanding that their counterparts withdraw from the area. To date, these have not resulted in any loss of life, but the potential for such an event remains.

Japanese boat activism after 2012

Channel Sakura and Ganbare Nippon's first fishing mission organized after the 2012 landing was in March 2013. Several months earlier a national election had toppled the DPJ government, and a conservative LDP government led by Prime Minister Abe Shinzō had taken power. The activists of Ganbare Nippon had supported Abe's political ambitions. Abe appeared as a guest on Channel Sakura programs in September 2012, just weeks before the LDP presidential election that would return him to party leadership. However, Abe's new conservative government ended up enacting policies that heavily restricted the activities of non-state activists in the waters around the Senkakus.

The attitude of the Japan Coast Guard toward the Ganbare Nippon fishing trips became much stricter in 2013. Fishing boats, especially boats carrying activists, were regarded as an unwanted addition to the tense situation in the area. The Senkaku field of contestation had once again shifted to a new situation, in which Japanese and Chinese patrol ships were confronting each other around the Senkakus every month, but Japanese fishing boats were not welcome.

Prior to the March 2013 fishing mission, JCG officials warned Channel Sakura and Ganbare Nippon that their fishing boats would be required to maintain a distance of at least one nautical mile from the Senkakus. This was an order from above, meant to prevent a landing. The JCG also warned about the presence of three Chinese patrol vessels. The seas were quite rough that day and visibility was low, so despite the alleged presence of Chinese ships within three miles of their location, Channel Sakura's cameras could not obtain footage of them.

When activist fishing boats headed toward the islands for a mission in April 2013, JCG patrol boats shadowed the Daiichi Sakura Maru and repeatedly issued warnings about the one-mile restriction. Using a loudspeaker, Mizushima shouted back, insisting that his boats were not breaking any laws. The appearance of a Chinese patrol boat nearby convinced the activists to cut their mission short and head back to Ishigaki Island.[156]

Chinese patrol vessels were on the scene again when Mizushima conducted fishing missions in May and June 2013.[157] Subsequent NHK news reports were worded in a way that claimed the Chinese vessels had come in reaction to the presence of Japanese fishing boats. Mizushima criticized this style of reporting, arguing that it unfairly blamed the Japanese people for acts of aggression committed by China.[158] The Japanese state imposed further restrictions on their August fishing mission, with JCG aggressively placing its patrol boats in the path of the Ganbare Nippon ships. This was apparently done to prevent activists from entering an area deemed too close to the islands.[159] Channel Sakura's video compilations of these missions highlighted Mizushima standing on the deck of the Daiichi Sakura Maru with a megaphone, playing the Japanese national anthem, and taunting nearby Chinese patrol boats. JCG patrol boats and rubber speed boats circled around the activists, preventing the Chinese from reaching them but also driving away fish. Mizushima regarded this as the JCG intentionally interfering with peaceful fishing.[160]

Official interference reached a new level in July 2014. Channel Sakura reported that its activists had been completely blocked from carrying out a fishing mission. Following their regular procedure and applying for advance permission to carry out fishing activities around the Senkakus, they were shocked to receive a total rejection of their plan. Coast Guard officers then physically prevented them from boarding their fishing boats.[161] Rather than attempt an illegal fishing mission, the activists opted for weekly protests in front of government offices in Tokyo.

A brief reversal of the situation occurred in August 2014. Mizushima received a phone call from Fisheries Agency informing him that his organization would be allowed to conduct a fishing mission and an apology for the previous rejection, claiming that there had been a misunderstanding regarding the request. Ganbare Nippon conducted its 20th fishing expedition on August 12. Flanked by several JCG patrol vessels, they encountered three Chinese patrol ships. The JCG ships placed themselves in between the Daiichi Sakura Maru and the Chinese patrol ships, engaging in a stand-off as Japanese activists carried out some recreational fishing. When the activists finished, they played the Japanese national anthem over loudspeakers to emphasize that they were in Japanese territory. Channel Sakura cameras were on the scene to document everything so that it could be distributed for the world to see on YouTube. The presence of Chinese ships was depicted as a reason why "we" the Japanese people must support the continued efforts of Ganbare Nippon to engage in fishing near the Senkakus.[162]

The August 2014 fishing mission would prove to be the last successful attempt that included Ganbare Nippon activists and Channel Sakura camera crews until the present. As Chinese incursions into the area around the islands reached record numbers, Japan's Fisheries Agency rejected all of the activist's applications. In one video, recorded in October 2017, Mizushima lamented yet another rejection from the government, calling it an "unforgivable" action.[163] Most of his anger, as well as the anger of comments on the video, were aimed at the Fisheries Agency, rather than Prime Minister Abe. It was presumed that the rejected applications were due to the obstructionist attitudes of unelected bureaucrats who did not share the patriotic ideology of Mizushima and his fellow activists.

Serving Senkaku Sushi in Tokyo

Between June 2011 and June 2020, Channel Sakura attempted 24 fishing missions to the Senkakus, 18 of which reached the islands with activists on board. The last two missions, shown in Table 7.1, were only allowed to take place with crews of local fishermen. This meant that the Daiichi Sakura Maru could be used to fish in the area near the islands, but Channel Sakura staff and activists were barred from participation. Photos and video of these last two missions had to be filmed by locals, rather than Channel Sakura camera crews. These restrictions led to a shift in the focus of boat activism – rather than bring people to the Senkakus, activists would bring the Senkakus to the people – in edible form.

The catch from the June 2020 mission was made into "Senkaku sushi" and eating it would be a form of patriotic activism. Mizushima announced this plan

Table 7.1 Channel Sakura/Ganbare Nippon Fishing Missions to the Senkaku Islands[164]

1	June 22–23, 2011	2 ships
2	July 2–3, 2011	8 ships
3	November 1–2, 2011	3 ships
4	November 8, 2011	10 ships (turned back early due to bad weather)
5	November 12–13, 2011	11 Ships
6	January 1–2, 2012	3 ships
7	January 20–21, 2012	4 ships
8	June 9–10, 2012	14 ships (117 people)
9	June 25–26, 2012	4 ships
	August 15–18, 2012	Chinese activists land on Uotsurijima
10	August 18–19, 2012	20 ships (152 people), activists landed
11	March 17–18, 2013	3 ships
12	April 23–24, 2013	10 ships
13	May 25–26, 2013	4 ships
14	June 30–July 1, 2013	3 ships
15	August 17–18, 2013	4 ships
16	September 30–October 1, 2014	4 ships
17	November 23–24, 2013	6 ships
18	June 7, 2014	3 ships (kept at 20 nautical mile range from islands)
19	July 20, 2014	Forcibly canceled by the Fisheries Agency
20	August 12–13, 2014	3 ships (the last fishing mission)
21	October 4–5, 2014	6 ships (ceremony for war dead canceled due to Typhoon)
22	August 13–14, 2016	3 ships (ceremony for dead held 20 nautical miles away + Payaos fishing)
23	March 14–15, 2018	2 ships (local fishermen)
24	June 20–22, 2020	2 ships (local fishermen)

in a video filmed the day after the mission had returned to Ishigaki Island with 750 kilograms of fish. Appearing in the Channel Sakura studio flanked by two containers of fresh fish, he praised the bravery of local fishermen and explained the importance of catching and eating the fish. The Japanese government's failure to develop the Senkakus made it necessary for private citizens to prove their nation's "effective control" of the territory. Mizushima presented a chain of private acts that connected the islands to the rest of the nation: fishermen would go to the islands, they would catch the fish and bring it to market, the fish would be purchased by restaurants, restaurants would sell it to customers, and customers would then eat it. As the title of a special hour-length report on 2020 mission declared, the "power of the people" (minkan no chikara) was producing Japan's "only proof of effective control" over the islands.[165] The catch from the 2020 mission would first be served to politicians at Japan's National Diet building and then made available to ordinary citizens through the cooperation of several sushi restaurants.[166]

The president of Kanazawa Maimon Sushi, a nationwide chain of restaurants, provided chefs to prepare sushi for lawmakers and media attending the June 25 event.[167] Kanazawa Maimon Sushi helped with a similar event for lawmakers in 2011, but in 2020 several specific restaurants would serve Senkaku sushi to the general public. In particular, three restaurants in Tokyo were introduced by Channel Sakura as recipients of their catch. Viewers were encouraged to call the restaurants and request reservations to eat sashimi prepared from the fishing mission.[168]

The event at the National Diet building was presented as a great success. In a video message aired on Channel Sakura several days later, Mizushima thanked the politicians who supported the event. A list was placed on screen while the names of 18 Diet lawmakers who attended were read aloud, 11 from the House of Representatives and 7 from the House of Councilors. Every one of the attendees was a member of the ruling Liberal Democratic Party. Mizushima expressed specials thanks to Inada Tomomi for staying at the event from start to finish. In remarks delivered at the end of the event, Inada had claimed that she only intended to be there for about 15 minutes, but she had been so moved by content the presentation that she ended up staying over an hour. Inada stated that Mizushima's activism was carrying out the wishes of her late father, a fellow "social activist" (shakai katsudoka),[169] reminding viewers that her late father, Tsubakihara Yasuo, had been a long-time activist ally of Mizushima and leader of Ganbare Nippon's Kyoto chapter.[170] Turnout for the event was considerable, but unlike a similar event held in 2011, Prime Minister Abe's brother was absent. Mizushima had expressed a hope that the prime minister would be able to eat the Senkaku sushi,[171] but it appears to have not happened.[172]

The event also drew considerable attention from mainstream media outlets. Reporters were present from NHK, TBS, Fuji TV, Asahi TV, *Yomiuri Shimbun*, *Mainichi Shimbun*, *Sankei Shimbun*, *Jiji Press*, *Kyodo Press*, and *Yukan Fuji*. Several of these outlets subsequently aired and published reports about the event, but Channel Sakura's activists were unimpressed by the quality of most of the coverage. Several of the reports followed a familiar pattern of mainstream media reporting on their activism – mentioning the event but not including mention of Ganbare Nippon, Channel Sakura, or Mizushima Satoru. Several of the media outlets, most notably NHK, had sent reporters but never produced a report on the event. The *Asahi Shimbun* and *Tokyo Shimbun* – two left-leaning papers that were often targets of Channel Sakura's criticism – had not sent anyone. According to Mizushima, these media outlets had exercised their "freedom not to report" the truth. This situation was presented as ongoing proof of the poor quality of mainstream Japanese media and the need alternative outlets such as Channel Sakura.[173]

Conclusion

In this chapter, we explored Channel Sakura and Ganbare Nippon's activism regarding the Senkaku Islands dispute. Structural shifts within this field of contestation helped determine the kind of tactics employed by activists. Following the 2010 boat collision crisis, the activists of Channel Sakura and Ganbare Nippon perceived and acted upon destabilizations of the field. As skilled social actors, they drew upon the resources that were available and employed tactics based upon their conception of the rules of the field. Channel Sakura and Ganbare Nippon tried to conduct lawful and peaceful acts of protest, employing the language of grassroots activism, freedom, and democracy to justify the need to engage in collective action to "protect" the islands and their nation from Chinese incursions. On occasion, when the field was in a state of flux, lawbreaking acts of peaceful protest, such as the 2012 landing on Uotsurijima, were conducted without punishment from authorities. Events and their actions were explained in a way that helped forge a shared meaning for participants. Throughout the campaigns, they reminded viewers that grassroots support made everything possible. In doing so, they cast themselves and the viewers as patriots acting in place of a government that was not fulfilling its duty.

The preceding chapters told a story of an activist media organization that rose to prominence through the skilled use of digital media and the building of social ties. In the final chapter, I explore Channel Sakura's disastrous foray into electoral politics – which culminated in the 2016 arrest and conviction of Tamogami Toshio – a scandal that ended up seriously damaging the credibility of Mizushima and his media organization. We will also explore how new online media organizations have emerged on the Japanese right, challenging Channel Sakura's political and social influence.

Notes

1 Toshio Okuhara, "Territorial Sovereignty over the Senkaku Islands," *Japan Institute of International Affairs*, Rule of Law Series, March 2015, http://www2.jiia.or.jp/en/digital_library/rule_of_law.php.

2 Ibid.

3 Akitoshi Hiraoka, "明治期における尖閣諸島への日本人の進出と古賀辰四郎" [Koga tatsushirō and Japanese Incursion on Senkaku during the Meiji Era],

Human Geography 57, no. 5 (2005), 45–60, 59, https://www.jstage.jst.go.jp/article/jjhg1948/57/5/57_5_503/_pdf.

4 Serita Kentaro, "The Senkaku Islands," *Japan Institute of International Affairs*, Rule of Law Series, March 2015, http://www2.jiia.or.jp/en/digital_library/rule_of_law.php.

5 Makomo Kuniyoshi, "The Senkaku Islands in the Context of the History of the Modern Fishing Industry in Okinawa," *Japan Institute of International Affairs*, Rule of Law Series, March 2015, 13, http://www2.jiia.or.jp/en/digital_library/rule_of_law.php.

6 Ibid., 18.

7 Y. Nakauchi, "Issues Surrounding the Senkaku Islands and the Japan-China Relationship: A History from Japan's Territorial Incorporation to the Present Day and Contemporary Issues," *Japan Institute of International Affairs*, Rule of Law Series, March 2015, 3, http://www2.jiia.or.jp/en/digital_library/rule_of_law.php.

8 "無人島で飢餓地獄 ～ 軍から台湾疎開命令" [A Hell of Starvation on an Uninhabited Island – Taiwan Evacuation Order by the Army]. *Ryukyu Shimpo*, December 14, 1983.

9 " 不公正な補償に怒り ～「軍命」に一定の差別　遺族には見舞金" [Anger at Unfair Reparations – The Discrimination of "Military Orders," Living Relatives Compensated]. *Ryukyu Shimpo*, December 27, 1983.

10 "米軍機の機銃浴びる ～ 九死に一生を得た後に …" [Machine Gun Fire from American Plane – What Happened after Narrowly Avoiding Death]. *Ryukyu Shimpo*, December 15, 1983.

11 " 不公正な補償に怒り ～「軍命」に一定の差別　遺族には見舞金" [Anger at Unfair Reparations – The Discrimination of "Military Orders," Living Relatives Compensated]. *Ryukyu Shimpo*, December 27, 1983.

12 Koichi Sato, "China's Territorial Claims at Sea: The East China and South China Sea (Part I)," *Eurasia Border Review* 3, no. 1 (2012), https://eprints.lib.hokudai.ac.jp/dspace/bitstream/2115/50859/1/EBR3-1_002.pdf.

13 Reinhard Drifte, "The Japan-China Confrontation over the Senkaku/Diaoyu Islands – Between 'Shelving' and 'Dispute Escalation,'" *Asia-Pacific Journal* 12, no. 3 (2014).

14 Hanyi Shaw, *The Diaoyutai/Senkaku Islands Dispute: Its History and an Analysis of the Ownership Claims of the PRC, ROC, and Japan* (Baltimore: School of Law, University of Maryland, 1999), 16.

15 Quoted in Chi-kin Lo, *China's Policy Towards Territorial Disputes: The Case of the South China Sea Islands* (New York: Routledge, 1989), 171–172.

16 Koo in Min Gyo Koo, "The Senkaku/Diaoyu Dispute and Sino-Japanese Political-Economic Relations: Cold Politics and Hot Economics?," *Pacific Review* 22, no.2 (2009), 211, https://doi.org/10.1080/09512740902815342.

17 Shibuichi Daiki, "Contemporary Japanese Rightist Movements," PhD Diss., National University of Singapore, 2006, 183.

18 Min Gyo Koo, *Island Disputes and Maritime Regime Building in East Asia: Between a Rock and a Hard Place* (Dordrecht: Springer, 2009), 117.

19 M. Taylor Fravel, "Explaining Stability in the Senkaku (Diaoyu) Islands Dispute," in *Getting the Triangle Straight: Managing China-Japan-US Relations*, ed. Gerald L. Curtis, Ryosei Kokobun and Jisi Wang (Tokyo: Japan Center for International Exchange, 2010), 151.

20 Alexander Bukh, *These Islands Are Ours* (Stanford University Press, 2020) Kindle Edition, location 2976.

21 Unryu Suganuma, "Historical Justification of Sovereign Right over Territorial Space of the Diaoyu/Senkaku Islands: Irredentism and Sino-Japanese Relations,"

PhD diss., Maxwell School of Citizenship and Public Affairs, Syracuse University, 1996, 250.

22 Shintarō Ishihara, 国家なる幻影—わが政治への反回想 [An Illusion Called the Nation: Reflections on My Politics] (Tokyo: Bungei Shunju, 1999), 367–368.

23 “尖閣対談（上）　今だから話そう！　1978年　　　尖閣上陸作戦の全貌” [Senkaku Conversations (First Part); Now’s the Time to Talk! The Whole Story Behind the 1978 Senkaku Action]. *Seikai Ohrai Political Journal*, http://www.seikaiourai.jp/1208/120818.htm.

24 Shibuichi, “Contemporary Japanese Rightist Movements,” 2006; and Masayuki Hayashi, “The Emperor’s Legions: A History of Japan’s Right Wing,” *AMPO Japan-Asia Quarterly Review* 23, no. 2 (1988).

25 From the organization’s homepage: http://www.seinensya.org/.

26 Shibuichi, “Contemporary Japanese Rightist Movements,” 2006, 184.

27 Ishihara, 国家なる幻影—わが政治への反回想 [An Illusion Called the Nation: Reflections on My Politics], 369.

28 Ibid., 185.

29 Chien-Peng Chung, *Domestic Politics, International Bargaining and China’s Territorial Disputes* (London: RoutledgeCurzon, 2004), 41–45.

30 Mutsuko Murakami, “Center of the Storm Japan’s Rightists Shed Light on the Issue,” *CNN*, September 20, 1996, http://edition.cnn.com/ASIANOW/asiaweek/96/0920/nat1a.html.

31 Zhai Xin, “Shelving the Diaoyu Islands Dispute: A Tacit Consensus and the Abe Cabinet’s Policy Change,” *China Institute of International Studies*, January 20, 2014, http://www.ciis.org.cn/english/2014-01/20/content_6623684.htm.

32 “Politician Joins Activists in Landing on Senkaku Islands,” *Japan Times*, May 6, 1997, http://www.japantimes.co.jp/news/1997/05/06/national/politician-joins-activists-in-landing-on-senkaku-islands/ -.U9n-xfmSxe4.

33 James Manicom, *Bridging Troubled Waters: China, Japan, and Maritime Order in the East China Sea* (Washington: Georgetown University Press, 2014), 52.

34 Xin, “Shelving the Diaoyu Islands Dispute: A Tacit Consensus and the Abe Cabinet’s Policy Change.”

35 Hajime Hirose, “Japan’s Effective Control of the Senkaku Islands,” *Review of Island Studies,* June 10, 2013, https://www.spf.org/islandstudies/research/a00005.html.

36 Shaw, *The Diaoyutai/Senkaku Islands Dispute: Its History and an Analysis of the Ownership Claims of the PRC, ROC, and Japan*, 20.

37 Manicom, *Bridging Troubled Waters: China, Japan, and Maritime Order in the East China Sea*, 52.

38 Chung, *Domestic Politics, International Bargaining and China’s Territorial Disputes.*

39 Shaw, *The Diaoyutai/Senkaku Islands Dispute: Its History and an Analysis of the Ownership Claims of the PRC, ROC, and Japan,* 21.

40 David McNeill, “Murakami Ichiro and Ultra-Nationalist Intimidation in Japan,” *Asia-Pacific Journal* 2, no. 1 (July 2003), http://www.japanfocus.org/-David-McNeill/1750.

41 “Japan Says It Has Leased Disputed Island for Decades,” *Taipei Times*, January 9, 2003, http://www.taipeitimes.com/News/taiwan/archives/2003/01/09/0000190302.

42 “Press Conference by the Press Secretary,” *Ministry of Foreign Affairs of Japan*, October 4, 1996, http://www.mofa.go.jp/announce/press/1996/10/1004.html.

43 Quoted in Chung, *Domestic Politics, International Bargaining and China’s Territorial Disputes*, 48.

44 Maya Kaneko, “Ishigaki Fishermen Fret over Senkaku Encroachment,” *Japan Times*, December 8, 2010, http://www.japantimes.co.jp/news/2010/12/08/national/ishigaki-fishermen-fret-over-senkaku-encroachment/ - .U9m2KfmSxe4.

45 Paul O’Shea, “Sovereignty and the Senkaku/Diaoyu Territorial Dispute,” Working Paper, EIJS, Stockholm School of Economics, 2012.

46 Kerry Dumbaugh, David Ackerman and Richard Cronin, *U.S. China’s Maritime Territorial Claims: Implications for U.S. Interests* (Rept. Washington, DC: Congressional Research Service, 2001).

47 O’Shea, “Sovereignty and the Senkaku/Diaoyu Territorial Dispute.”

48 Krista E. Wiegand, “China’s Strategy in the Senkaku/Diaoyu Islands Dispute: Issue Linkage and Coercive Diplomacy,” *Asian Security* 5, no. 2 (2009), 189, https://doi.org/10.1080/14799850902886617.

49 James Manicom, “Sino-Japanese Cooperation in the East China Sea: Limitations and Prospects,” *Contemporary Southeast Asia* 30, no. 3 (2008), https://www.jstor.org/stable/41220523.

50 Zhouxiang Lu and Fan Hong, *Sport and Nationalism in China* (New York: Routledge, 2013), 150.

51 Staff Writer With AFP, “Japan Says It Has Leased Disputed Island for Decades,” *Taipei Times*, January 9, 2003, http://www.taipeitimes.com/News/taiwan/archives/2003/01/09/0000190302.

52 Sanaa Yasmin Hafeez, “The Senkaku/Diaoyu Islands Crises of 2004, 2010, and 2012: A Study of Japanese-Chinese Crisis Management,” *Asia-Pacific Review* 22 no. 1 (2015), https://doi.org/10.1080/13439006.2015.1038885.

53 Joshua Keating, “Japan’s Secret Foreign Policy,” *Foreign Policy*, October 18, 2010, https://foreignpolicy.com/2010/10/18/japans-secret-foreign-policy/; AERA, October 25, 2010, https://publications.asahi.com/ecs/detail/?item_id=12020.

54 “China Indignant at Japanese Right-Wing Attack on Consulate General in Osaka,” *People’s Daily Online*, June 25, 2004, http://english.peopledaily.com.cn/200404/23/eng20040423_141323.shtml.

55 “Japanese Man Jailed for Damaging Chinese Consulate,” *Xinhua News*, September 27, 2005, http://china.org.cn/english/2005/Sep/143521.htm.

56 Daiki Shibuichi, “Recent Trends in Political Extremism in Japan: A Decline in Physical Violence and a Rise in Extremism by Other Means,” *East Asia* 36 (2019), https://doi.org/10.1007/s12140-019-09306-w.

57 Manicom, *Bridging Troubled Waters: China, Japan, and Maritime Order in the East China Sea*, 52.

58 Norimitsu Onishi, “Japan and China Dispute a Pacific Islet,” *New York Times*, July 09, 2005, http://www.nytimes.com/2005/07/10/international/asia/10japan.html?pagewanted=all.

59 Manicom, *Bridging Troubled Waters: China, Japan, and Maritime Order in the East China Sea*, 52.

60 Andrew D. Taffer, “Threat and Opportunity: Chinese Wedging in the Senkaku/Diaoyu Dispute,” *Asian Security*, (2019), https://doi.org/10.1080/14799855.2019.1567493.

61 Ellis Krauss, “Crisis Management, LDP, and DPJ Style,” *Japanese Journal of Political Science* 14, no. 02 (2013), https://doi.org/10.1017/S1468109913000029.

62 “1/2【山田吉彦】石垣島から見た尖閣諸島をめぐる最新情勢[桜H21/3/27]” [1/2 “Yamada Yoshihiko” Latest Status of the Senkaku Islands as Seen From Ishigaki Island (Sakura Heisei 21/3/27)]. *Nihon Bunka Channel Sakura*, March 27, 2009, https://www.youtube.com/watch?v=6JQ5c6JwsKA

63 "【平間洋一】民主党政権における安全保障上の危機[桜　　H21/9/11]" ["Hirama Yōichi" The Dangers of the DPJ Government's Security Policy (Sakura Heisei 21/9/11)]. *Nihon Bunka Channel Sakura*, September 11, 2009, https://www.youtube.com/watch?v=VGi53F8usgc

64 "1/4【討論！】尖閣が危ない！危機の中の東アジアと日本[桜H22/7/10]" [1/4 "Discussion!" The Sankaku Islands Are in Danger! The Danger That East Asia and Japan Are Facing (Sakura Heisei 22/7/10)]. *Nihon Bunka Channel Sakura*, July 10, 2010, https://www.youtube.com/watch?v=lijP20j-uVA.

65 "【直言極言】尖閣列島が危ない！[桜H22/7/23]" ["Frank and Direct" The Sankaku Are in Danger! (Sakura Heisei 22/7/23)]. *Nihon Bunka Channel Sakura*, July 23, 2010, https://www.youtube.com/watch?v=ESjw-q_Y_Mg.

66 Martin Fackler and Ian Johnson, "Japan Retreats in Test of Wills With the Chinese," *New York Times*, September 24, 2010, http://www.nytimes.com/2010/09/25/world/asia/25chinajapan.html?pagewanted=all&_r=0.

67 Paul Jackson, "Prosecutor Diplomacy?" *Diplomat*, September 28, 2010, http://thediplomat.com/2010/09/japans-prosecutor-diplomacy-2/.

68 Sourabh Gupta, "Japan and China's Latest Spat over the Senkakus," *East Asia Forum*, September 23, 2012, http://www.eastasiaforum.org/2012/09/23/japan-and-chinas-latest-spat-over-the-senkakus/.

69 Tanaka Sakai, "Rekindling China-Japan Conflict: The Senkaku/Diaoyutai Islands Clash," *Asia-Pacific Journal* 8, no. 3, September 27, 2010, https://apjjf.org/-Tanaka-Sakai/3418/article.html.

70 Kosuke Takahashi, "China Signals V for Victory," *Asia Times Online*, October 5, 2010, http://www.atimes.com/atimes/Japan/LJ05Dh01.html.

71 "【日本解体の危機】尖閣侵略、女性天皇、靖国分祀[桜H22/9/9]" ["Japan in Danger of Being Torn Apart" Sankaku Invasion, Female Emperor, Yasukuni Division (Sakura Heisei 22/9/9)]. *Nihon Bunka Channel Sakura*, September 9, 2010, https://www.youtube.com/watch?v=Z_QAA6QEx40.

72 "【直言極言】守れ尖閣！目覚めよ国民！緊急国民行動[桜H22/9/10]" ["Frank and Direct" Defend Sankaku! Citizens, Open Your Eyes! Emergency Citizen Action (Sakura Heisei 22/9/10)]. *Nihon Bunka Channel Sakura*, September 10, 2010, https://www.youtube.com/watch?v=cEvEI8Zgi68.

73 "【国土防衛】遂に直接行動に出るか？中国の尖閣侵略[桜H22/9/10]" ["Territorial Defense" Finally Time for Direct Action? China's Invasion of Senkaku (Sakura Heisei 22/9/10)]. *Nihon Bunka Channel Sakura*, September 10, 2010, https://www.youtube.com/watch?v=v5j04kde6Z0.

74 "【頑張れ日本！】尖閣侵略阻止！民主党糾弾！緊急国民行動[桜H22/9/13]" ["Ganbare Nippon!" Prevent the Sankaku Invasion! Censure the DPJ! Emergency Civic Action (Sakura Heisei 22/9/13)]. *Nihon Bunka Channel Sakura*, September 13, 2010, https://www.youtube.com/watch?v=7Kx80n7jbXA.

75 "1/2【尖閣問題】日本の対応をどう思いますか？新宿・吉祥寺[桜H22/9/28]" [1/2 "Senkaku Problem" What Do You Think of Japan's Response? Shinjuku – Kichijoji (Sakura Heisei 22/9/13)]. *Nihon Bunka Channel Sakura*, September 28, 2010, https://www.youtube.com/watch?v=cJlrIQsRT_0.

76 "2/2【特別討論】徹底検証・尖閣問題の行方[桜H22/9/27]" [2/2 "Special Discussion" Thorough Inspection – Heading of the Senkaku Problem (Sakura Heisei 22/9/27)]. *Nihon Bunka Channel Sakura*, September 27, 2010, https://www.youtube.com/watch?v=oF8iWoDybG4.

77 "【街頭宣伝】10.2中国の尖閣諸島侵略糾弾！全国国民統一行動[桜H22/10/5]" ["Street Action" 10.2 Censure China for Its Invasion of Senkaku! Coordinated National Civic Action (Sakura Heisei 22/10/5)]. *Nihon Bunka*

Channel Sakura, October 5, 2010, https://www.youtube.com/watch?v=4ppJdqGfODE.

78 "【名古屋】10.2中国の尖閣侵略糾弾！全国国民統一行動[桜H22/10/8]" ["Nagoya" 10.2 Censure China for Its Invasion of Sankaku! Coordinated National Civic Action (Sakura Heisei 22/10/8)]. *Nihon Bunka Channel Sakura*, October 8, 2010, https://www.youtube.com/watch?v=6MlmWeoAio4.

79 Yuka Hayashi, "China Row Fuels Japan's Right," *The Wall Street Journal*, September 28, 2010. http://online.wsj.com/news/articles/SB10001424052748704791004575519662349329820.

80 "Rise of the Far-Right in Japan," *The Globe and Mail*, October 5, 2010. http://www.theglobeandmail.com/news/world/rise-of-the-far-right-in-japan/article1370255/.

81 "【街頭宣伝】10.2中国の尖閣諸島侵略糾弾！全国国民統一行動[桜H22/10/5]" ["Street Action" 10.2 Censure China for its Invasion of Senkaku! Coordinated National Civic Action (Sakura Heisei 22/10/5)]. *Nihon Bunka Channel Sakura*, October 5, 2010, https://www.youtube.com/watch?v=4ppJdqGfODE.

82 "【尖閣衝突事件】東京の中国大使館前で２８００人デモ、沖縄でも集会" ["Senkaku Collision" 2800 Person Demonstration in Front of the Chinese Embassy in Tokyo, Crowds Even in Okinawa]. *Sankei Shimbun*, December 16, 2010.

83 "【10.16尖閣デモ】中国大使館包囲！尖閣侵略糾弾！リレートーク[桜H22/10/18]" ["10.16 Senkaku Demonstration" Surround the Chinese Embassy! Censure China for Its Invasion of Senkaku! Relay Talk (Sakura Heisei 22/10/18)]. *Nihon Bunka Channel Sakura*, October 18, 2010, https://www.youtube.com/watch?v=dFA0cxbCeFE.

84 "【10.16尖閣デモ】中国大使館包囲！尖閣侵略糾弾！デモ行進[桜H22/10/18]" ["10.16 Senkaku Demonstration" Surround the Chinese Embassy! Censure China for the Invasion of Senkaku! Demonstration March (Sakura Heisei 22/10/18)]. *Nihon Bunka Channel Sakura*, October 18, 2010, https://www.youtube.com/watch?v=RyJj-p-lchohttps.

85 "【永山英樹】10.16尖閣デモに関するメディアの報道[桜H22/10/21]" ["Nagayama Hideki" 10.16 Senkaku Demonstration Media Portrayal (Sakura Heisei 22/10/21)]. *Nihon Bunka Channel Sakura*, October 21, 2010, https://www.youtube.com/watch?v=iUxj-md73bc.

86 "Japan Rallies Against China over Disputed Islands," *Reuters*, October 16, 2010, http://www.reuters.com/article/2010/10/16/us-japan-china-protests-idUSTRE69F0PH20101016.

87 "中国で再び反日デモ、香川県でも３００人規模の反中デモ" [Anti-Japan Demonstrations in Japan Again, 300 Person Anti-China Demonstrations in Kagawa]. *Searchina*, October 24, 2010, http://news.searchina.ne.jp/disp.cgi?y=2010&d=1024&f=politics_1024_001.shtml.

88 "漁船衝突事件で中国政府に抗議 名古屋でデモ" [Fisherman Boat Collision Cause Protests against Chinese Government – Nagoya Demonstration]. *Chunichi Shimbun*, November 1, 2010.

89 Lisa Liang, "Beijing Allows Anti-Japanese Sentiment to Flare in China Amid Massive Protests," *Christian Science Monitor*, October 18, 2010, http://www.csmonitor.com/World/Asia-Pacific/2010/1018/Beijing-allows-anti-Japanese-sentiment-to-flare-in-China-amid-massive-protests.

90 "Foreign Ministry Spokesperson Ma Zhaoxu's Remarks," *Chinese Embassy Website*, October 17, 2010, http://ma.china-embassy.org/eng/fyrth/t762394.htm.

91 Kai Pan, "Chinese Forwarding Photos of Anti-China Protests in Japan," *China/Divide*, October 2, 2010, http://chinadivide.com/2010/chinese-forwarding-photos-of-anti-china-protests-in-japan.html.
92 "さすが西村真悟！尖閣上陸[桜H22/10/14]" [As Expected of Nishimura Shingo! Senkaku Action (Sakura Heisei 22/10/14)]. *Nihon Bunka Channel Sakura*, October 14, 2010, https://www.nicovideo.jp/watch/sm12431260.
93 For example: "日本青年社 尖閣諸島灯台建設 保守管理 動画" [Nihon Seinensha, Senkaku Lighthouse Construction (Video)]. *Sakuranbo999*, April 4, 2010, https://www.youtube.com/watch?v=4fCy83BxZa8.
94 Kyung Lah and Jo Ling Kent, "Lawmaker: Leaked Video Shows Crash That Led to China-Japan Dispute," *CNN*, November 05, 2010, http://edition.cnn.com/2010/WORLD/asiapcf/11/05/japan.china.island.dispute/.
95 "【尖閣ビデオ】sengoku38氏への支援表明と海保職員殉職のデマ[桜H22/11/11]" [A Declaration of Support for Sengoku 38 and a Discussion of Rumors Concerning a Coast Guard Officer's Death]. *Nihon Bunka Channel Sakura*, November 13, 2010, https://www.nicovideo.jp/watch/sm12731981.
96 "Coast Guard Admits 17 Copied Collision Video," *Japan Times*, December 23, 2010, https://www.japantimes.co.jp/news/2010/12/23/national/coast-guard-admits-17-copied-collision-video/#.XxeaV54zaUk.
97 Masaharu Isshiki, 何かのために sengoku38の告白 [Why I did it – the Confession of Sengoku38] (Tokyo: Asahi Shimbun Publications, 2011), 101.
98 "【一色正春】尖閣事件から１年！領土を守る気概はあるのか？[桜H23/9/8]" ["Isshiki Masahara" 1 Year Since the Senkaku Incident! Is There Any Intention in Protecting Our Territory? (Sakura Heisei 23/9/8)]. *Nihon Bunka Channel Sakura*, September 8, 2011, https://www.nicovideo.jp/watch/1315470402.
99 "【一色正春】尖閣を守る海保の役割[桜H25/4/22]" ["Isshiki Masahara" The Coast Guard's Role in Protecting the Senkaku Islands (Sakura Heisei 25/4/22)]. *Nihon Bunka Channel Sakura*, April 22, 2013, https://www.nicovideo.jp/watch/so20677055; and "1/3【討論！】メディアが語らない中国尖閣侵略の現実[桜H25/10/5]" [1/3 "Discussion!" The Truth of the Chinese Invasion of Senkaku that the Media Won't Talk About (Sakura Heisei 25/10/5)]. *Nihon Bunka Channel Sakura*, October 5, 2013, https://www.nicovideo.jp/watch/1380885740.
100 "【更新版】11.6 自由と人権アジア連帯集会＆デモ[桜H22/10/27]" ["Updated Version" 11.6 Demonstration and Meeting to Establish Solidarity for Freedom and Human Rights in Asia (Sakura Heisei 22/10/27)]. *Nihon Bunka Channel Sakura*, October 27, 2010, https://www.youtube.com/watch?v=jO4q2eKSSU0.
101 "Anti-China Rally Held in Japan after Video Leak of Collision," *Sino Daily*, November 6, 2010, http://www.sinodaily.com/afp/101106161959.n8reemoh.html.
102 "【頑張れ日本】11.6自由と人権アジア連帯集会－デモ行進[桜H22/11/9]" ["Ganbare Nippon" 11.6 Demonstration and Meeting to Establish Solidarity for Freedom and Human Rights in Asia (Sakura Heisei 22/11/9)]. *Nihon Bunka Channel Sakura*, November 9, 2010, https://www.youtube.com/watch?v=U1YBM2AFY2s.
103 "【草莽崛起】11.6 自由と人権アジア連帯集会＆デモ ダイジェスト[桜H22/11/8]" ["Grassroots Uprising" 11.6 Digest to the Demonstration and Meeting to Establish Solidarity for Freedom and Human Rights in Asia (Sakura Heisei 22/11/8)]. *Nihon Bunka Channel Sakura*, November 8, 2010, https://www.youtube.com/watch?v=aqEYXWZIvnA.

104 "【11.13横浜】中国のアジア侵略・人権弾圧を阻止する抗議デモ[桜H22/11/15]" ["11.13 Yokohama" Demonstration to Prevent China's Asian Encroachment and Suppression of Human Rights (Sakura Heisei 22/11/15)]. *Nihon Bunka Channel Sakura*, November 15, 2010, https://www.youtube.com/watch?v=50VF-38SZIo.
105 "【11.20　大阪】中国糾弾！全国国民統一行動・デモ行進[桜H22/11/23]" ["11.20 Osaka" Censure China! Coordinated National Civic Action and Demonstration (Sakura Heisei 22/11/23)]. *Nihon Bunka Channel Sakura*, November 23, 2010, https://www.youtube.com/watch?v=onw1fmJcfdc.
106 "【頑張れ日本】12.5「中国による尖閣諸島侵略阻止！」デモin神戸[桜H22/12/9]" ["Ganbare Nippon" 12.5 "Prevent China's Invasion of the Senkaku Islands" Demonstration in Kobe (Sakura Heisei 22/12/9)]. *Nihon Bunka Channel Sakura*, December 9, 2010, https://www.youtube.com/watch?v=ERBEqaDsI9s.
107 "[尖閣事件]沖縄現地レポート・尖閣海域を守る沖縄県民の集い" ["Senkaku Incident" Okinawa Report – Gathering by the Okinawan People to Protect the Senkaku Sea Area]. *Nippon Kaigi* (Homepage), October 18, 2010, http://www.nipponkaigi.org/activity/archives/1519.
108 "【社会】民間団体「尖閣諸島を守ろう関西実行委員会」が中国政府に抗議するデモ行進" ["Society" Civil Organization "Kansai Action Committee to Protect the Senkaku Islands" Protests the Chinese Government with a Demonstration]. *Sankei News – Osaka*, October 22, 2010, http://sankei.jp.msn.com/politics/policy/101022/plc1010222252027-n1.htm.
109 "China Protests Japanese Visit to Disputed Islands," *Reuters*, December 10, 2010, http://www.reuters.com/article/2010/12/11/us-china-japan-islands-idUSTRE6BA0L320101211.
110 "3/3【頑張れ日本！】12.18渋谷　国民大行動・街頭宣伝活動[桜H22/12/20]" [3/3 "Ganbare Nippon!" 12.18 Shibuya Large Civic Action and Street Demonstration (Sakura Heisei 22/12/20)]. *Nihon Bunka Channel Sakura*, December 20, 2010, https://www.youtube.com/watch?v=LF24fBr2bJg.
111 "【仲間均&箕底用一】石垣市議尖閣上陸！[桜H22/12/21]" ["Nakama Hitoshi and Minosoko Yōichi" Ishigaki City Councilors Sets Foot on Senkaku! (Sakura Heisei 22/12/21)]. *Nihon Bunka Channel Sakura*, December 21, 2010, https://www.youtube.com/watch?v=qGx5mfn_xGA.
112 "【尖閣上陸】南小島上陸映像と秘密保全法[桜H23/1/6]" ["Setting Foot on Senkaku" Video of Southern Island and Secrecy Law (Sakura Heisei 23/1/6)]. *Nihon Bunka Channel Sakura*, January 6, 2011, https://www.youtube.com/watch?v=kSK4F84dKcc.
113 For more information on the concept of crowdfunding, consult: http://en.wikipedia.org/wiki/Crowdfunding.
114 "【ご報告】「尖閣防衛船」購入ご支援の状況[桜H23/2/3]" ["Announcement" Current Status of Contributions to Purchase Senkaku Defense Ship (Sakura Heisei 23/2/3)]. *Nihon Bunka Channel Sakura*, February 3, 2011, https://www.youtube.com/watch?v=HtIiHIF1dME.
115 "【ご報告】「尖閣防衛船」購入ご支援の状況[桜H23/2/10]" ["Announcement" Current Status of Contributions to Purchase Senkaku Defense Ship (Sakura Heisei 23/2/10)]. *Nihon Bunka Channel Sakura*, February 10, 2011, https://www.youtube.com/watch?v=aEoAdD7sIb0.
116 "【頑張れ日本】「尖閣防衛船」購入支援状況について[桜H23/2/24]" ["Ganbare Nippon" Regarding the Current Status of Contributions to Purchase Senkaku Defense Ship (Sakura Heisei 23/2/24)]. *Nihon Bunka Channel Sakura*, February 24, 2011, https://www.youtube.com/watch?v=_zluTeV5wCM.

117 "【ご報告】NHK名誉毀損裁判判決と尖閣防衛船購入[桜H23/4/28]" ["Announcement" NHK Slander Case Decision and the Purchase of the Senkaku Defense Ship (Sakura Heisei 23/4/28)]. *Nihon Bunka Channel Sakura*, April 28, 2011, https://www.youtube.com/watch?v=LdohTQeFR_0.

118 "【頑張れ日本】1.12　民主党言論封殺抗議！緊急国民行動[桜H23/1/13]" ["Ganbare Nippon" 11.2 DPJ Censorship Protest! Emergency Civic Action (Sakura Heisei 23/1/13)]. *Nihon Bunka Channel Sakura*, January 13, 2011, https://www.youtube.com/watch?v=hHBEyhxicm8.

119 "【頑張れ日本】2.27　尖閣・領事館、中国糾弾名古屋デモ[桜H23/3/3]" ["Ganbare Nippon" 2.27 Senkaku – Consulate, Censure China Nagoya Demonstration (Sakura Heisei 23/3/3']. *Nihon Bunka Channel Sakura*, March 3, 2011, https://www.youtube.com/watch?v=AReuvypuHDY.

120 "【尖閣防衛】草莽の志と共に、第一桜丸の大漁旗[桜H23/6/30]" ["Senkaku Defense" With the Grassroots Will of the People, the Big-Haul Flag of the Daiichi Sakura Maru (Sakura Heisei 23/6/30)]. *Nihon Bunka Channel Sakura*, June 30, 2011, https://www.youtube.com/watch?v=oqmKUQFjzSc.

121 "【直言極言】領土と歴史の防衛は国民の義務である[桜H23/7/1]" ["Frank and Direct" Defending Territory and History Is the Plight of the People (Sakura Heisei 23/7/1)]. *Nihon Bunka Channel Sakura*, July 1, 2011, https://www.youtube.com/watch?v=WjDQW-1d0U4.

122 "【草莽崛起】7.3　尖閣防衛、集団漁業活動報告　その２[桜H23/7/7]" ["Grassroots Uprising" 7.3 Senkaku Defense, Announcement Regarding Collective Action for the Fishing Industry Part 2 (Sakura Heisei 23/7/7)]. *Nihon Bunka Channel Sakura*, July 7, 2011, https://www.youtube.com/watch?v=0cygytMCrBs.

123 Li Xiaokun, "China, Japan Seek Better Ties Amid Sea Disputes," *China Daily*, July 5, 2011, http://www.chinadaily.com.cn/china/2011-07/05/content_12832991.htm.

124 "Taiwan Protests to Japan after Activist Boat 'barred,'" *Tengri News*, July 1, 2011, http://en.tengrinews.kz/unrest/Taiwan-protests-to-Japan-after-activist-boat-barred--2888/.

125 "【尖閣防衛】実効支配強化！集団漁業活動第２弾へ　[桜H23/9/23]" ["Senkaku Defense" Strengthen Effective Control! Collective Action for the Fishing Industry, Towards a Second Wave of Action (Sakura Heisei 23/9/23)]. *Nihon Bunka Channel Sakura*, September 23, 2011, https://www.youtube.com/watch?v=ZFz23pUHlXY.

126 "【守るぞ尖閣】11.15 尖閣の魚を食す会[桜H23/11/16]" ["Let's Defend Senkaku" 11.15 Association of Senkaku Fish Eaters (Sakura Heisei 23/11/16)]. *Nihon Bunka Channel Sakura*, November 16, 2011, https://www.youtube.com/watch?v=Sqw6Eor_CEY.

127 "【直言極言】尖閣問題から見える日本の主権[桜H23/7/22]" ["Frank and Direct" Japanese Sovereignty as Seen Through the Senkaku Problem (Sakura Heisei 23/7/22)]. *Nihon Bunka Channel Sakura*, July 22, 2011, https://www.youtube.com/watch?v=DWgIgYpL9Ec.

128 "【守るぞ尖閣】第18回　尖閣諸島集団漁業活動レポート[桜H25/11/28]" ["Let's Defend Senkaku" Report of the 18th Senkaku Collective Action for the Fishing Industry (Sakura Heisei 25/11/28)]. *Nihon Bunka Channel Sakura*, November 28, 2013, https://www.youtube.com/watch?v=-FJgbgsdKzM.

129 "Owner OK with Metro Bid to Buy Disputed Senkaku Islands," *Japan Times*, May 18, 2012, http://www.japantimes.co.jp/news/2012/05/18/national/owner-ok-with-metro-bid-to-buy-disputed-senkaku-islands/ - .U9ryX_mSzB0.

130 Jun Hongo, "Tokyo's Intentions for Senkaku Islets," *Japan Times*, April 19, 2012, http://www.japantimes.co.jp/news/2012/04/19/national/tokyos-intentions-for-senkaku-islets/.

131 "【守るぞ尖閣】東京都尖閣諸島寄附金口座ご案内[桜H24/4/30]" ["Let's Defend Senkaku" Guide to Donating to the Tokyo Senkaku Fund (Sakura Heisei 24/4/30)]. *Nihon Bunka Channel Sakura*, April 30, 2012, https://www.youtube.com/watch?v=p1kq8ez7lq8.

132 "Government's Senkakus Purchase Aims to End Dispute Flare-Up," *Asahi Shimbun*, September 6, 2012, http://ajw.asahi.com/article/views/editorial/AJ201209060033.

133 "Noda Government to Buy Senkaku Islands for 2 Billion Yen," Asahi Shimbun, September 5, 2012, http://ajw.asahi.com/article/special/isles_dispute/AJ201209050013.

134 "【守るぞ尖閣】東京都尖閣諸島寄附金口座ご案内[桜H24/4/30]" ["Let's Defend Senkaku" Guide to Donating to the Tokyo Senkaku Fund (Sakura Heisei 24/4/30)]. *Nihon Bunka Channel Sakura*, April 30, 2012, https://www.youtube.com/watch?v=p1kq8ez7lq8.

135 "【ニュースの読み方】東京都尖閣募金の意味[桜H24/5/9]" ["Reading the News" The Meaning Behind the Tokyo Senkaku Donation Fund (Sakura Heisei 24/5/9)]. *Nihon Bunka Channel Sakura*, May 9, 2012, https://www.youtube.com/watch?v=7YctvA4D_Eo.

136 "【尖閣】政府は上陸申請を却下、保釣連盟は … [桜H24/8/15]" ["Senkaku" Government Refuses to Grant Permission to Land, The Baodiao Federation … (Sakura Heisei 24/8/15)]. *Nihon Bunka Channel Sakura*, August 15, 2012, https://www.youtube.com/watch?v=ljbA1OnVHrY.

137 Chester Yung, "Hong Kong Activists Claim Success after Senkaku Landing," *Wall Street Journal*, August 15, 2012, http://blogs.wsj.com/chinarealtime/2012/08/15/hong-kong-activists-claim-success-after-senkaku-landing/.

138 "【HD】 H24.8.15 頑張れ日本 靖国神社内での演説 水島社長が尖閣に行きます" [(HD) Heisei 24.8.15 Ganbare Nippon – Speech at the Yasukuni Shrine – CEO Mizushima to Go to Senkaku]. *turbo911kai*, August 15, 2012, https://www.youtube.com/watch?v=NAFHEsDl4MMe.

139 "【尖閣不法上陸】活動家逮捕、メディアは強制送還へ世論誘導[桜H24/8/16]" ["Senkaku Illegal Landing" Activists Arrested, Media Manipulates Public Opinion with Calls for Repatriation (Sakura Heisei 24/8/16)]. *Nihon Bunka Channel Sakura*, August 16, 2012, https://www.youtube.com/watch?v=bvtYgdb9Gk8.

140 "Japan, China Islands Disputes Deepen with Landings, Protests," *Asahi Shimbun*, August 19, 2012, http://ajw.asahi.com/article/behind_news/social_affairs/AJ201208190016.

141 "1/3【守るぞ尖閣】魚釣島上陸レポート・低画質分割版[桜H24/8/23]" [1/3 "Let's Defend Senkaku" Report of Fishing Island Landing – Low-Quality Version (Sakura Heisei 24/8/23)]. *Nihon Bunka Channel Sakura*, August 23, 2012, https://www.youtube.com/watch?v=XSbWacm_mAg.

142 Itō swam ashore hours earlier to hike to the top of the island and plant a Japanese flag.

143 Suzuki gained international attention a few years later, after he apologized for making sexist remarks during a Tokyo assembly session: Will Ripley, "Tokyo Assembly Member Apologizes for Sexist Heckling of Female Colleague," *CNN*, June 24, 2014, http://edition.cnn.com/2014/06/23/world/asia/japan-sexism-heckling/.

144 "【守るぞ尖閣】魚釣島上陸レポート[桜H24/8/23]" ["Let's Defend Senkaku" Report of Fishing Island Landing (Sakura Heisei 24/8/23)]. *Nihon Bunka Channel Sakura*, August 23, 2012, https://www.youtube.com/watch?v=fe1GnttsGdY.

145 "3/3【守るぞ尖閣】魚釣島上陸レポート・低画質分割版[桜H24/8/23]" [3/3 "Let's Defend Senkaku" Report of Fishing Island Landing – Low-Quality

Version (Sakura Heisei 24/8/23)]. *Nihon Bunka Channel Sakura*, August 23, 2012, https://www.youtube.com/watch?v=ETyxLkYVqE0.

146 "【自由報道協会】8.28洋上慰霊祭と尖閣上陸に関する記者会見[桜H24/8/30]" ["Journalists Association of Japan" 8.28 Press Statement Regarding the Memorial Held on the Sea and the Senkaku Landing (Sakura Heisei 24/8/30)]. *Nihon Bunka Channel Sakura*, August 30, 2012, https://www.youtube.com/watch?v=cWC7ZKh2W68.

147 "【直言極言】頑張れ日本！全国行動委員会[桜H22/2/12]" ["Frank and Direct" Ganbare Nippon! National Action Committee (Sakura Heisei 22/2/12)]. *Nihon Bunka Channel Sakura*, February 12, 2010, https://www.youtube.com/watch?v=0wG1dgqBlL0.

148 "【直言極言】問題の本質、魚釣島への上陸を果たして[桜H24/8/24]" ["Frank and Direct" The Essence of the Problem, Landing on the Fishing Island (Sakura Heisei 24/8/24)]. *Nihon Bunka Channel Sakura*, August 24, 2012, https://www.youtube.com/watch?v=HQhgG8pmh0A.

149 Ibid.

150 Antoni Slodkowski, "How Debts and Double-Dealing Sparked Japan-China Islets Row," *Reuters*, November 12, 2012, https://www.reuters.com/article/us-china-japan-family/how-debts-and-double-dealing-sparked-japan-china-islets-row-idUSBRE8AA0EY20121111.

151 "Japan Urged to Ensure Safety of Diaoyu Activists," *Global Times*, August 14, 2012, http://www.globaltimes.cn/content/726875.shtml.

152 Ben Blanchard and Antoni Slodkowski, "Anti-Japan Protests Reignite across China on Occupation Anniversary," *Reuters*, September 18, 2012, http://www.reuters.com/article/2012/09/18/us-china-japan-idUSBRE88F00H20120918.

153 "China anti-Japan Protest Damage May Be over $100m," *Yahoo News*, November 14, 2012, https://sg.news.yahoo.com/china-anti-japan-protest-damage-may-over-100m-170824188.html.

154 Hafeez, "The Senkaku/Diaoyu Islands Crises of 2004, 2010, and 2012: A Study of Japanese-Chinese Crisis Management."

155 "Trends in Chinese Government and Other Vessels in the Waters Surrounding the Senkaku Islands, and Japan's Response," *Ministry of Foreign Affairs of Japan* (Homepage), October 2, 2020. https://www.mofa.go.jp/region/page23e_000021.html.

156 "【現地レポ】尖閣・操業不能海域、「我が海」を誇示する中国海警局[桜H25/4/25]" ["Report From the Groudn" Senkaku – Inoperable Waters, How the Chinese Waters Guard Flaunt "Our Seas" (Sakura Heisei 25/4/25)]. *Nihon Bunka Channel Sakura*, April 25, 2013, https://www.youtube.com/watch?v=BmFVHtEa00E.

157 "【守るぞ尖閣】中国公船団と遭遇、切迫する尖閣領海の現状[桜H25/5/28]" ["Let's Defend Senkaku" Encounter with China's Public Fleet and the Current State of the Impending Encroachment on Senkaku Territory (Sakura Heisei 25/5/28)]. *Nihon Bunka Channel Sakura*, May 28, 2013, https://www.youtube.com/watch?v=GaWbd5nDAc4.

158 "2/2【守るぞ尖閣】悠然たる中国公船、海保の敵は誰なのか？－南北小島編[桜H25/7/4]" [2/2 "Let's Defend Senkaku" The Calm of the Chinese Fleet, Who Are the Enemies of the Coast Guard? North and South Islands (Sakura Heisei 25/7/4)]. *Nihon Bunka Channel Sakura*, July 4, 2013, https://www.youtube.com/watch?v=YR50_QPve-Q.

159 "【職権とは】伊藤祐靖が見た尖閣の海Part６～命令と要請[桜H25/8/20]" ["On Authority" The Senkaku Seas According to Itō Sukeyasu Part & – Order and Request (Sakura Heisei 25/8/20)]. *Nihon Bunka Channel Sakura*, August 20, 2013, https://www.youtube.com/watch?v=CL6Evr27Ex4.

160 "【守るぞ尖閣】民間の力で唯一の実効支配を証明～石垣海人・尖閣漁業で大漁！安倍総理、二階幹事長、是非、尖閣の美味しい魚を食べてください！" [桜R2/6/22]" ["Let's Defend Senkaku" Prove Who Has Sole Effective Control with the Power of the People – Big Haul for Ishigaki Ama, Senkaku Fisheries! PM Abe, Nikai Chief Secretary, Try the Delicious Fish from Senkaku! (Sakura Reiwa 2/6/22)]. *Nihon Bunka Channel Sakura*, June 22, 2020, https://www.youtube.com/watch?v=lmrl36wWEZY.

161 "またも水産庁が不当妨害！一第２０回尖閣諸島漁業活動の顚末（附：チャンネル桜の緊急報道動画）" [Fisheries Agency Interferes Illegitimately Again! The Whole Story of the 20th Civic Action for the Senkaku Fisheries (PS: Sakura Channel Emergency Report Video)]. *Taiwan Is Japan's Lifeline!,* July 22, 2014, http://mamoretaiwan.blog100.fc2.com/blog-entry-2407.html; and "「頑張れ」出港再び阻止　「狙いうち」と反発" ["Ganbare" Stopped From Sailing Again, Targeted Attacks and Its Reaction]. *Yaeyama Nippo*, July 21, 2014, http://www.yaeyama-nippo.com/2014/07/21/%E9%A0%91%E5%BC%B5%E3%82%8C-%E5%87%BA%E6%B8%AF%E5%86%8D%E3%81%B3%E9%98%BB%E6%AD%A2-%E7%8B%99%E3%81%84%E3%81%86%E3%81%A1-%E3%81%A8%E5%8F%8D%E7%99%BA/.

162 "【守るぞ尖閣】中国公船三隻と対峙！尖閣漁業活動レポート[桜H26/8/14]" ["Let's Defend Senkaku" Confrontation with Three Ships from the Chinese Fleet! Report on Senkaku Fisheries Action (Sakura Heisei 26/8/14)]. *Nihon Bunka Channel Sakura*, August 14, 2014, https://www.youtube.com/watch?v=n0EyFZzxHHQ.

163 "【直言極言】事なかれ主義で領土を守れるか！水産庁が否定した尖閣防衛漁業活動[桜H29/10/13]" ["Frank and Direct" How Can You Protect Your Territory by Playing it Safe? Senkaku Fisheries Defense Action Rejected by Fisheries Agency (Sakura Heisei 29/10/13)]. *Nihon Bunka Channel Sakura*, October 13, 2017, https://www.youtube.com/watch?v=fa-0GZk3VQ4.

164 "【くにもり】「尖閣寿司」が食べられるお店、尖閣以上に危うい北海道の現状 他[R2/6/26]" ["Kunimori" Places Where You Can Eat Senkaku Sushi, The Even Worse Situation in Hokkaido (Reiwa 2/6/26))]. *Nihon Bunka Channel Sakura*, June 26, 2020, https://www.youtube.com/watch?v=dBpwuEpT4lM.

165 "【守るぞ尖閣】民間の力で唯一の実効支配を証明～石垣海人・尖閣漁業で大漁！安倍総理、二階幹事長、是非、尖閣の美味しい魚を食べてください！" [桜R2/6/22]" ["Let's Defend Senkaku" Prove Who Has Sole Effective Control with the Power of the People – Big Haul for Ishigaki Ama, Senkaku Fisheries! PM Abe, Nikai Chief Secretary, Try the Delicious Fish from Senkaku! (Sakura Reiwa 2/6/22)]. *Nihon Bunka Channel Sakura*, June 22, 2020, https://www.youtube.com/watch?v=lmrl36wWEZY.

166 "【守るぞ尖閣】尖閣の水揚げ鮮魚が到着！25日に議員会館で「尖閣の現在の映像」と「海の幸」をお披露目記者会見をします[桜R2/6/23]"　["Let's Defend Senkaku" Fresh Catch Arrives From Senkaku! Showing Videos of Senkaku as It Is Today and Presenting Its Seafood at the National Diet on the 25th (Sakura Reiwa 2/6/23)]. *Nihon Bunka Channel Sakura*, June 23, 2020, https://www.youtube.com/watch?v=c26QBwQ7yPU.

167 "【ch桜・別館】金沢まいもん寿司謹製「尖閣寿司」を堪能しながら、尖閣への航路を振り返る[R2/6/25]" ["Channel Sakura – Annex" Thinking Back on the Route to Senkaku While Enjoying Kanazawa Maimon Sushi's Quality Senkaku Sushi (Reiwa 2/6/25)]. *Nihon Bunka Channel Sakura*, June 25, 2020, https://www.youtube.com/watch?v=I5cgmTMFzKs.

168 "【くにもり】「尖閣寿司」が食べられるお店、尖閣以上に危うい北海道の現状 他[R2/6/26]" ["Kunimori" Places Where You Can Eat Senkaku Sushi, The Even Worse Situation in Hokkaido (Reiwa 2/6/26))]. *Nihon Bunka Channel Sakura*, June 26, 2020. https://www.youtube.com/watch?v=dBpwuEpT4lM.

169 "【完全版】尖閣漁業活動と中国船侵入状況報告の記者会見～尖閣諸島を護る我が国の積極的行動、周辺海域で捕れた魚のお披露目[桜R2/6/26]" ["Complete Version" Press Statement Regarding Action for Senkaku Fisheries and Report of Current Chinese Ship Encroachment – Pro-Active National Action to Defend the Senkaku Islands, Showcase of Fish Caught in the Senkaku Area (Sakura Reiwa 2/6/26)]. *Nihon Bunka Channel Sakura*, June 26, 2020, https://www.youtube.com/watch?v=yWLZgw-ouZw.

170 "【直言極言】尖閣民間防衛漁業活動に見る「報道しない自由」と「印象操作」[桜R2/6/27]" ["Frank and Direct" "Unfree Press" and "Fake News" as Seen Through the Senkaku Civil Defense Fisheries Action (Sakura Reiwa 2/6/27)]. *Nihon Bunka Channel Sakura*, June 27, 2020, https://www.youtube.com/watch?v=cHGR2-94HHA.

171 "【くにもり】尖閣へ日の丸船団出航！総理に尖閣まぐろを食べてもらおう！尖閣民間実効支配から東京、北海道まで～日本を縦断する侵略の赤い帯をぶった斬る国守衆~行動する草莽の力[R2/6/19]" ["Kunimori" Hinomaru Fleet Sets Sail to Senkaku! Prime Minister, Try the Senkaku Tuna! From Effective Private Control of Senkaku to Tokyo, Hokkaido – Kunimorishū Cuts Down the Red Thread Endangering the Whole of Japan – The Power of Grassroots Action (R2/6/19)]. *Nihon Bunka Channel Sakura*, June 19, 2020, https://www.youtube.com/watch?v=eHbIYXQpufw.

172 "【くにもり】「尖閣寿司」が食べられるお店、尖閣以上に危うい北海道の現状 他[R2/6/26]" ["Kunimori" Places Where You Can Eat Senkaku Sushi, The Even Worse Situation in Hokkaido (Reiwa 2/6/26))]. *Nihon Bunka Channel Sakura*, June 26, 2020, https://www.youtube.com/watch?v=dBpwuEpT4lM.

173 "【直言極言】尖閣民間防衛漁業活動に見る「報道しない自由」と「印象操作」[桜R2/6/27]" ["Frank and Direct" "Unfree Press" and "Fake News" as Seen through the Senkaku Civil Defense Fisheries Action (Sakura Reiwa 2/6/27)]. *Nihon Bunka Channel Sakura*, June 26, 2020, https://www.youtube.com/watch?v=cHGR2-94HHA.

Bibliography

AERA. October 25, 2010. https://publications.asahi.com/ecs/detail/?item_id=12020.

Asahi Shimbun. "Japan, China Islands Disputes Deepen with Landings, Protests." August 19, 2012. http://ajw.asahi.com/article/behind_news/social_affairs/AJ201208190016.

Asahi Shimbun. "Noda Government to Buy Senkaku Islands for 2 Billion Yen." September 5, 2012. http://ajw.asahi.com/article/special/isles_dispute/AJ201209050013.

Asahi Shimbun. "Government's Senkakus Purchase Aims to End Dispute Flare-Up." September 6, 2012. http://ajw.asahi.com/article/views/editorial/AJ201209060033.

Blanchard, Ben, and Slodkowski, Antoni. "Anti-Japan Protests Reignite across China on Occupation Anniversary." *Reuters*, September 18, 2012. http://www.reuters.com/article/2012/09/18/us-china-japan-idUSBRE88F00H20120918.

Bukh, Alexander. *These Islands Are Ours.* Stanford, CA: Stanford University Press, 2020.

Chinese Embassy Website. "Foreign Ministry Spokesperson Ma Zhaoxu's Remarks." October 17, 2010. http://ma.china-embassy.org/eng/fyrth/t762394.htm.

Chung, Chien-Peng. *Domestic Politics, International Bargaining and China's Territorial Disputes.* London: RoutledgeCurzon, 2004.

Chunichi Shimbun. "漁船衝突事件で中国政府に抗議 名古屋でデモ" [Fisherman Boat Collision Cause Protests Against Chinese Government – Nagoya Demonstration]. November 1, 2010.

Daiki, Shibuichi. "Contemporary Japanese Rightist Movements." PhD dissertation, National University of Singapore, 2006. https://scholarbank.nus.edu.sg/handle/10635/15241.

Drifte, Reinhard. "The Japan-China Confrontation Over the Senkaku/Diaoyu Islands--Between 'Shelving' and 'Dispute Escalation.'" *Asia-Pacific Journal* 12, no. 3 (2014).

Dumbaugh, Kerry, Ackerman, David, and Cronin, Richard. U.S. China's Maritime Territorial Claims: Implications for U.S. Interests. Rept. Washington, DC: Congressional Research Service, 2001.

Fackler, Martin and Johnson, Ian. "Japan Retreats in Test of Wills with the Chinese." *New York Times*, September 24, 2010. http://www.nytimes.com/2010/09/25/world/asia/25chinajapan.html?pagewanted=all&_r=0.

Fravel, M. Taylor. "Explaining Stability in the Senkaku (Diaoyu) Islands Dispute." In *Getting the Triangle Straight: Managing China-Japan-US Relations*, ed. Gerald L. Curtis, Ryosei Kokobun, and Jisi Wang, 144–164. Tokyo: Japan Center for International Exchange, 2010.

Global Times. "Japan Urged to Ensure Safety of Diaoyu Activists." August 14, 2012. http://www.globaltimes.cn/content/726875.shtml.

Gupta, Sourabh. "Japan and China's Latest Spat over the Senkakus." *East Asian Forum*, September 23, 2012. http://www.eastasiaforum.org/2012/09/23/japan-and-chinas-latest-spat-over-the-senkakus/

Hafeez, Sanaa Yasmin. "The Senkaku/Diaoyu Islands Crises of 2004, 2010, and 2012: A Study of Japanese-Chinese Crisis Management." *Asia-Pacific Review* 22 no. 1 (2015): 73–99. https://doi.org/10.1080/13439006.2015.1038885.

Hayashi, Masayuki. "The Emperor's Legions: A History of Japan's Right Wing." *AMPO Japan-Asia Quarterly Review* 23, no. 2 (1988): 26–31.

Hiraoka, Akitoshi. "明治期における尖閣諸島への日本人の進出と古賀辰四郎" [Koga Tatsushirō And Japanese Incursion on Senkaku During the Meiji Era]. *Human Geography* 57, no. 5 (2005): 45–60, 59, https://www.jstage.jst.go.jp/article/jjhg1948/57/5/57_5_503/_pdf.

Hirose, Hajime. "Japan's Effective Control of the Senkaku Islands." *Review of Island Studies*, June 10, 2013. https://www.spf.org/islandstudies/research/a00005.html.

Hongo, Jun. "Tokyo's Intentions for Senkaku Islets." *Japan Times*, April 19, 2012. http://www.japantimes.co.jp/news/2012/04/19/national/tokyos-intentions-for-senkaku-islets/.

Ishihara, Shintarō. 国家なる幻影—わが政治への反回想 [An Illusion Called the Nation: Reflections on My Politics]. Tokyo: Bungei Shunju, 1999.

Isshiki, Masaharu. 何かのために Sengoku38の告白 [Why I Did It – the Confession of Sengoku38]. Tokyo: Asahi Shimbun Publications, 2011.

Jackson, Paul. "Prosecutor Diplomacy?" *Diplomat*, September 28, 2010. http://thediplomat.com/2010/09/japans-prosecutor-diplomacy-2/.

Japan Times. "Politician Joins Activists in Landing on Senkaku Islands." May 6, 1997. http://www.japantimes.co.jp/news/1997/05/06/national/politician-joins-activists-in-landing-on-senkaku-islands/ – .U9n-xfmSxe4.

Japan Times. "Owner OK with Metro Bid to Buy Disputed Senkaku Islands." May 18, 2012. http://www.japantimes.co.jp/news/2012/05/18/national/owner-ok-with-metro-bid-to-buy-disputed-senkaku-islands/ – .U9ryX_mSzB0.

Japan Times. "Coast Guard Admits 17 Copied Collision Video." December 23, 2010. https://www.japantimes.co.jp/news/2010/12/23/national/coast-guard-admits-17-copied-collision-video/#.XxeaV54zaUk.

Kaneko, Maya. "Ishigaki Fishermen Fret over Senkaku Encroachment." *Japan Times*, December 8, 2010. http://www.japantimes.co.jp/news/2010/12/08/national/ishigaki-fishermen-fret-over-senkaku-encroachment/ – .U9m2KfmSxe4.

Keating, Joshua. "Japan's Secret Foreign Policy." *Foreign Policy*, October 18, 2010. https://publications.asahi.com/ecs/detail/?item_id=12020.

Koo, Min Gyo. *Island Disputes and Maritime Regime Building in East Asia: Between a Rock and a Hard Place*. Dordrecht: Springer, 2009.

Krauss, Ellis. "Crisis Management, LDP, and DPJ Style." *Japanese Journal of Political Science* 14, no. 2 (2013): 177–199. https://doi.org/ 10.1017/S1468109913000029.

Lah, Kyung, and Kent, Jo Ling. "Lawmaker: Leaked Video Shows Crash That Led to China-Japan Dispute." CNN, November 05, 2010. http://edition.cnn.com/2010/WORLD/asiapcf/11/05/japan.china.island.dispute/.

Liang, Lisa. "Beijing Allows Anti-Japanese Sentiment to Flare in China Amid Massive Protests." *Christian Science Monitor*, October 18, 2010. http://www.csmonitor.com/World/Asia-Pacific/2010/1018/Beijing-allows-anti-Japanese-sentiment-to-flare-in-China-amid-massive-protests.

Lo, Chi-kin. *China's Policy Towards Territorial Disputes: The Case of the South China Sea Islands*. New York: Routledge, 1989.

Lu, Zhouxiang, and Hong, Fan. *Sport and Nationalism in China*. New York: Routledge, 2013.

Manicom, James. "Sino-Japanese Cooperation in the East China Sea: Limitations and Prospects." *Contemporary Southeast Asia* 30, no. 3 (2008): 455–478.

Manicom, James. *Bridging Troubled Waters: China, Japan, and Maritime Order in the East China Sea*. Washington: Georgetown University Press, 2014.

McNeill, David. "Murakami Ichiro and Ultra-Nationalist Intimidation in Japan." *Asia-Pacific Journal* 2, no. 1 (July 2003). http://www.japanfocus.org/-David-McNeill/1750.

Ministry of Foreign Affairs of Japan. "Press Conference by the Press Secretary." October 4, 1996. http://www.mofa.go.jp/announce/press/1996/10/1004.html.

Ministry of Foreign Affairs of Japan. "Trends in Chinese Government and Other Vessels in the Waters Surrounding the Senkaku Islands, and Japan's Response." October 2, 2020. https://www.mofa.go.jp/region/page23e_000021.html

Murakami, Mutsuko. "Center of the Storm Japan's Rightists Shed Light on the Issue." CNN, September 20, 1996. http://edition.cnn.com/ASIANOW/asiaweek/96/0920/nat1a.html.

Nippon Kaigi. "[尖閣事件]沖縄現地レポート・尖閣海域を守る沖縄県民の集い" ["Senkaku Incident" Okinawa Report – Gathering by the Okinawan People to

Protect the Senkaku Sea Area]. Homepage, October 18, 2010. http://www.nipponkaigi.org/activity/archives/1519.

Okuhara Toshio. "Territorial Sovereignty over the Senkaku Islands." *Japan Institute of International Affairs, Rule of Law Series*, March 2015. http://id.nii.ac.jp/1658/00000052/.

Onishi, Norimitsu. "Japan and China Dispute a Pacific Islet." *New York Times*, July 09, 2005. http://www.nytimes.com/2005/07/10/international/asia/10japan.html?pagewanted=all.

O'Shea, Paul. "Sovereignty and the Senkaku/Diaoyu Territorial Dispute." Working Paper, EIJS, Stockholm School of Economics, 2012.

Pan, Kai. "Chinese Forwarding Photos of Anti-China Protests in Japan." *China/Divide*, October 2, 2010. http://chinadivide.com/2010/chinese-forwarding-photos-of-anti-china-protests-in-japan.html.

People's Daily Online. "China Indignant at Japanese Right-Wing Attack on Consulate General in Osaka." June 25, 2004. http://english.peopledaily.com.cn/200404/23/eng20040423_141323.shtml.

Reuters. "Japan Rallies Against China over Disputed Islands." October 16, 2010. http://www.reuters.com/article/2010/10/16/us-japan-china-protests-idUSTRE69F0PH20101016.

Reuters. "China Protests Japanese Visit to Disputed Islands." December 10, 2010. http://www.reuters.com/article/2010/12/11/us-china-japan-islands-idUSTRE6BA0L320101211.

Ripley, Will. "Tokyo Assembly Member Apologizes for Sexist Heckling of Female Colleague." CNN, June 24, 2014. http://edition.cnn.com/2014/06/23/world/asia/japan-sexism-heckling/

Ryukyu Shimpo. "無人島で飢餓地獄 ～ 軍から台湾疎開命令" [A Hell of Starvation on an Uninhabited Island – Taiwan Evacuation Order by the Army]. December 14, 1983.

Ryukyu Shimpo. "米軍機の機銃浴びる ～ 九死に一生を得た後に…" [Machine Gun Fire from American Plane – What Happened After Narrowly Avoiding Death]. December 15, 1983.

Ryukyu Shimpo. "不公正な補償に怒り～「軍命」に一定の差別　遺族には見舞金" [Anger at Unfair Reparations – The Discrimination of "Military Orders," Living Relatives Compensated]. December 27, 1983.

Sakai, Tanaka. "Rekindling China-Japan Conflict: The Senkaku/Diaoyutai Islands Clash." *Asia-Pacific Journal* 8, no. 3 (September 27, 2010). https://apjjf.org/-Tanaka-Sakai/3418/article.html.

Sankei News – Osaka. "【社会】民間団体「尖閣諸島を守ろう関西実行委員会」が中国政府に抗議するデモ行進" ["Society" Civil Organization "Kansai Action Committee to Protect the Senkaku Islands" Protests the Chinese Government with a Demonstration]. October 22, 2010. http://sankei.jp.msn.com/politics/policy/101022/plc1010222252027-n1.htm

Sato, Koichi. "China's Territorial Claims at Sea: The East China and South China Sea (Part I)." *Eurasia Border Review* 3, no. 1 (2012): 19–31. https://eprints.lib.hokudai.ac.jp/dspace/bitstream/2115/50859/1/EBR3-1_002.pdf.

Searchina. "中国で再び反日デモ、香川県でも３００人規模の反中デモ" [Anti-Japan Demonstrations in Japan Again, 300 Person Anti-China Demonstrations in Kagawa]. October 24, 2010. http://news.searchina.ne.jp/disp.cgi?y=2010&d=1024&f=politics_1024_001.shtml.

Seikai Ohrai Political Journal. "尖閣対談（上） 今だから話そう！ 1978年尖閣上陸作戦の全貌" [Senkaku Conversations (First Part); Now's the Time to Talk! The Whole Story Behind the 1978 Senkaku Action]. http://www.seikaiourai.jp/1208/120818.htm.

Shaw, Hanyi. *The Diaoyutai/Senkaku Islands Dispute: Its History and an Analysis of the Ownership Claims of the PRC, ROC, and Japan*. Baltimore: School of Law, University of Maryland, 1999.

Shibuichi, Daiki. "Recent Trends in Political Extremism in Japan: A Decline in Physical Violence and a Rise in Extremism by Other Means." *East Asia* 36 (2019): 23–36. https://doi.org/10.1007/s12140-019-09306-w.

Sino Daily. "Anti-China Rally Held in Japan after Video Leak of Collision." November 6, 2010. http://www.sinodaily.com/afp/101106161959.n8reemoh.html.

Slodkowski, Antoni. "How Debts and Double-Dealing Sparked Japan-China Islets Row." *Reuters*, November 12, 2012. https://www.reuters.com/article/us-china-japan-family/how-debts-and-double-dealing-sparked-japan-china-islets-row-idUSBRE8AA0EY20121111

Staff Writer With AFP. "Japan Says It Has Leased Disputed Island for Decades." *Taipei Times*, January 9, 2003. http://www.taipeitimes.com/News/taiwan/archives/2003/01/09/0000190302.

Suganuma, Unryu. "Historical Justification of Sovereign Right over Territorial Space of the Diaoyu/Senkaku Islands: Irredentism and Sino-Japanese Relations." PhD dissertation, Maxwell School of Citizenship and Public Affairs, Syracuse University, 1996.

Taffer, Andrew D. "Threat and Opportunity: Chinese Wedging in the Senkaku/Diaoyu Dispute." *Asian Security*, 2019. https://doi.org/10.1080/14799855.2019.1567493.

Taipei Time. "Japan Says It Has Leased Disputed Island for Decades." January 9, 2003. http://www.taipeitimes.com/News/taiwan/archives/2003/01/09/0000190302.

Takahashi, Kosuke. "China Signals V for Victory." *Asia Times Online*, October 5, 2010. http://www.atimes.com/atimes/Japan/LJ05Dh01.html.

Tengri News. "Taiwan Protests to Japan after Activist Boat 'Barred.'" July 1, 2011. http://en.tengrinews.kz/unrest/Taiwan-protests-to-Japan-after-activist-boat-barred--2888/.

Wiegand, Krista E. "China's Strategy in the Senkaku/Diaoyu Islands Dispute: Issue Linkage and Coercive Diplomacy." *Asian Security* 5, no. 2 (2009): 170–193. https://doi.org/10.1080/14799850902886617.

Xiaokun, Li. "China, Japan Seek Better Ties Amid Sea Disputes." *China Daily*, July 5, 2011. http://www.chinadaily.com.cn/china/2011-07/05/content_12832991.htm.

Xin, Zhai. "Shelving the Diaoyu Islands Dispute: A Tacit Consensus and the Abe Cabinet's Policy Change." *China Institute of International Studies*, January 20, 2014. http://www.ciis.org.cn/english/2014-01/20/content_6623684.htm.

Xinhua News. "Japanese Man Jailed for Damaging Chinese Consulate." September 27, 2005, http://china.org.cn/english/2005/Sep/143521.htm.

Yahoo News. "China Anti-Japan Protest Damage May Be over $100m." November 14, 2012. https://sg.news.yahoo.com/china-anti-japan-protest-damage-may-over-100m-170824188.html.

Yung, Chester. "Hong Kong Activists Claim Success After Senkaku Landing." *Wall Street Journal*, August 15, 2012. http://blogs.wsj.com/chinarealtime/2012/08/15/hong-kong-activists-claim-success-after-senkaku-landing/.

8 Epilogue

The case studies in the previous chapters examined campaigns that mainly took place between 2009 and 2014, but several major developments have taken place in the years afterward. In this chapter, I will briefly discuss three of them: Nihon Bunka Channel Sakura's foray into electoral politics, the emergence of rival alternative media outlets, and the influence of new overseas right-wing populism.

Tamogami Toshio and electoral politics

Channel Sakura celebrated the 10th anniversary of its founding on August 15, 2014. Mizushima Satoru, Matsuura Yoshiko, and other leaders of the organization declared that the past decade has been very successful and told viewers that it had all been thanks to their grassroots support.[1] However, all was not well behind the scenes. A major scandal was brewing – one that would split Channel Sakura's supporter base.

The scandal involved Tamogami Toshio, a Channel Sakura contributor and the nominal head of Ganbare Nippon, Channel Sakura's activist wing. As I discussed in Chapter 7, Tamogami had taken on an important leadership role in Channel Sakura's activism during the 2010–2012 protests over the Senkaku Islands dispute. It was hoped that a nationally prominent figure like Tamogami could represent their movement by winning a major political office. With the encouragement of Channel Sakura's activists, Tamogami put himself forward as a candidate for the February 2014 Tokyo gubernatorial election.[2]

The 2014 election

Mizushima Satoru temporarily stepped down as president of Channel Sakura and devoted his time to a new role – Tamogami's campaign director. Mizushima and Tamogami remained in their leadership posts within Ganbare Nippon, drawing upon its members to provide grassroots support for the campaign. A special section of Ganbare Nippon's website was devoted to providing YouTube links to Tamogami's gubernatorial speeches.[3] Channel Sakura programs called on viewers to donate money or time to promote Tamogami's campaign.

Although Tamogami had hoped for an endorsement from the conservative Liberal Democratic Party (LDP), Japan's ruling party instead backed former health minister Matsuzoe Yōichi, a candidate who was not an outspoken nationalist. Tamogami nonetheless stated during the campaign that his policy ideas were closely aligned with those of LDP leader and prime minister Abe Shinzō.[4] Public endorsers of Tamogami included former governor Ishihara Shintarō, novelist Hyakuta Naoki, Dewi Sukarno.[5]

The fact that Japan's main conservative party had endorsed another candidate meant that Tamogami's campaign had almost no hope of victory. Although Channel Sakura and its activists frequently voiced support for Abe and other nationalistic politicians within the LDP, the party's conduct during the 2014 race was another matter. Mizushima believed that the LDP was using underhanded tactics to damage the Tamogami campaign. An example of this took place on Sunday, February 2, one week before the election. Tamogami was scheduled to deliver a speech in Tokyo's busy Ginza district, but when volunteers arrived to set up for the speech, they discovered that Matsuzoe campaign vans were occupying the area. When asked to move, Matsuzoe campaign officials refused, stating that the Tamogami campaign event was not scheduled to begin for another 30 minutes. In an exchange that was filmed and uploaded to YouTube, Mizushima used a loudspeaker to angrily denounce the bad manners of the rival campaign and engaged in an argument with a Matsuzoe campaign official. The official, claiming that Mizushima was in the wrong, eventually agreed to move the van with 15 minutes to spare until the Tamogami speech.[6]

Polls leading up to the race placed Tamogami in a distant fourth place, with support from only 6–7% of voters.[7] Unscientific online polling, which was treated as less reliable, recorded higher levels of support.[8]

A Channel Sakura video uploaded on the morning of election day commemorated Tamogami's final campaign speech, held outdoors during a heavy snowstorm. Scenes of Tamogami delivering the speech were interspersed with shots of the faces of adoring supporters who had gathered to hear him despite the inhospitable weather. One couple held a large sign that read "WE ♡ TAMO."[9]

Polls were correct in predicting that Tamogami would come in fourth place, but his vote total greatly exceeded predictions. Tamogami received 610,865 votes, which came to 12.5% of voters. Two exit polls indicated that Tamogami received 24% or 27% of votes from people in their twenties, second only to governor-elect Matsuzoe.[10] It was a surprising result, although it should be noted that voters in their twenties had a much lower turnout than other age groups.[11]

An election night Channel Sakura special report, aired before the full results were known, acknowledged Tamogami's defeat, thanked the many viewers who had volunteered for the campaign, and pledged that this was not the end of their struggle. Mizushima, who would soon return as president of Channel Sakura, declared that getting more than 10% of the votes was a huge accomplishment worthy of celebration. He blamed the loss on large organizations that opposed grassroots politics – namely the LDP and Soka Gakkai.[12]

Some of Tamogami supporters were angry with the result and blamed the loss on Mizushima's lack of political experience. In a Channel Sakura report aired on February 12, host Mitsuhashi Takaaki spent nearly 10 minutes addressing various "rumors" and attacking Mizushima's campaigning were being spread on Twitter. Mitsuhashi denied that Mizushima had told Tamogami to refuse an endorsement from the LDP and denied that their campaign had refused the advice of professional consultants. The people spreading these claims were then declared to be similar to dishonest Korean netizens – a harsh comparison for a group with such a negative view of Korea.[13] The loss was also spun as not a total defeat for their cause. Other Channel Sakura videos argued that it was an impressive vote total for a candidate who did not have the organizational support of a major party.[14]

Domestic and international media outlets reacted with surprise at Tamogami's performance. A *Time* magazine article claimed that the election had "galvanized the country's ultra-nationalists."[15] Michael Cucek predicted that Tamogami's political career was going to take off:

> This election was a fundraising and membership drive for Tamogami. We should expect that his rallies, which were merely attracting thousands, will now attract tens of thousands.[16]

Tamogami's political career did appear to be taking off but very slowly. He stepped down from his position as a leader of Ganbare Nippon and became a member of Ishihara Shintarō's new Party for Future Generations. A bid to represent Tokyo's 12th District in the December 2014 general election was again unsuccessful, with Tamogami again coming in fourth place, behind the Japan Communist Party.[17] It was not all bad news, though. He did receive 18.5% of votes, indicating that there was a considerable portion of the electorate that still supported him.

Tamogami's arrest and conviction

Fundraising would be Tamogami's downfall. Tamogami's fund management organization had raised some 130 million yen in 2014, far more than it spent on its political campaigning. Between the February gubernatorial election and the December general election, approximately 50 million yen seemingly vanished from the organization's books. Mizushima, who had not been directly in charge of managing the funds, brought this discrepancy up with Tamogami, who allegedly stated that Mizushima was mistaken in his assessment.[18]

The failure to account for the missing money, much of which had been donated by Channel Sakura's grassroots supporters, greatly distressed Mizushima. After failing to receive a satisfactory response from those involved, he decided to go public with his accusations. On the February 17, 2015, episode of Sakura Project, Mizushima announced to viewers that he believed potential fraud had taken place and that he had spoken to other media outlets about it.[19] In reporting the disappearance of the money, Mizushima stated that neither he nor the numerous

Channel Sakura contributors who had volunteered as campaign staff had received a single yen from the campaign. He was not sure what had happened to the money, and Tamogami had denied responsibility for what happened, but it was clear that a large amount of money was missing. As leaders of the campaign, Mizushima stated that both he and Tamogami had a responsibility to disclose the truth about the scandal.

Tamogami's response was to deny direct knowledge of the missing money and blame campaign officials responsible for managing donation funds. He also alleged that Mizushima had requested that the leftover money be illegally transferred to Ganbare Nippon after the February election.[20] This accusation was joined by other statements from Tamogami supporters that questioned Mizushima's credibility and motives. Mizushima responded by calling Tamogami a dishonest traitor to the conservative cause.[21] Channel Sakura's videos on the scandal, which reported Mizushima's allegations as truth and Tamogami's as lies, were characterized as an unfair smear campaign.[22] A rift emerged within Channel Sakura's viewer base, with some believing that Mizushima was making spurious claims that harmed the conservative cause.

Japan's justice system sided with Mizushima. On April 16, 2015, Tamogami was arrested and charged with embezzlement of funds and making illegal payments to campaign staff.[23] Prosecutors argued that Tamogami had approved the payment of leftover election funds to several senior campaign staff. Under Japanese law, this kind of payment was considered illegal bribery. In May 2017 the Tokyo District Court delivered a guilty ruling and sentenced Tamogami to 22 months in prison, suspended for five years.[24] Mizushima praised the decision but expressed regret that authorities had seemingly given up determining what had happened to other large portions of the missing campaign funds.[25]

Tamogami, who pled not guilty to the charges, continued to insist that he had not broken any laws. Having received a suspended sentence, the Japanese equivalent of probation, he was free to continue his life as a public figure. He would do so on other conservative media outlets, some of which maintained their own popular rival YouTube channels to Channel Sakura.

Rival alternative media outlets on YouTube

During its first ten years of uploading content to YouTube, Channel Sakura stood out as the leading conservative political channel on the site. In more recent years, other conservative organizations and individuals have launched their own independent channels, with many equaling or surpassing Channel Sakura's viewership (502,000 subscribers).

The lower cost of high-quality cameras, coupled with audiences that do not expect professional sets or high production values, made it possible for conservative pundits to launch their own personal YouTube channels, free from editorial control. Some of these pundits, such as economist Mitsuhashi Taakaki (256,000 subscribers), maintained independent channels while regularly appearing on Channel Sakura. Others, such as Watanabe Tetsuya, host programs for both

Channel Sakura and the conservative YouTube channel Bunkajin TV, founded in 2017 (345,000 subscribers).[26]

More numerous, however, are pundits who do not appear as regular guests on Channel Sakura and have gravitated toward rival media outlets. Sakurai Yoshiko, president of the Japan Institute for National Fundamentals, and magazine editor Hanada Kazuyoshi host programs on Genron TV, founded in 2012 (139,000 subscribers). Other popular conservative pundits, such as KAZUYA (740,000 subscribers), Kent Gilbert (53,000 subscribers), Kurayama Mitsuri (193,000 subscribers), and Fujii Genki (251,000 subscribers), have become regulars on DHC Television (706,000 subscribers).

While ideologically on the side of the nationalist cause, DHC Television is in some ways the antithesis of Mizushima Satoru's vision of grassroots media. It is a media outlet firmly under the control of the billionaire owner of DHC Corporation, Yoshida Yoshiaki, who uses its programs to heavily promote his political views, as well as the supplements and cosmetics his companies produce.[27] Since 2015 it has produced two major programs, *News Joshi* a weekly news/variety show, and *Tora no Mon News*, a live weekday morning news show. *News Joshi*, which is filmed in a professional studio and includes mainstream actresses and celebrities as guests, has production values that rival major broadcast networks. This kind of high-budget programming was beyond the capability of any other conservative YouTube channel, including Channel Sakura. Many conservative journalists who once hosted programs on Channel Sakura moved to DHC, including Otani Miki, Inoue Kazuhiko, and Orimoto Kaori.

DHC Television also welcomed Tamogami Toshio onto its programs as an expert on military and historical issues. These appearances have occurred both before and after the guilty verdicts in his trials. These appearances on DHC prompted Channel Sakura to produce programs reminding their viewers that the Tamogami court ruling was fair and that DHC was incorrectly portraying Tamogami as the victim of a political trial. The two media outlets also exchanged faxes complaining about their respective coverage of the Tamogami case.[28] Another point of contention was DHC's addressing of Tamogami as "your excellency" (kakka) in its programs, which Mizushima considered laughable given the man's status as a "proven criminal."[29]

The emergence of popular alternatives, the departure of key contributors to other channels, and the presence of an unfriendly rival channel all arguably led to a decline in Channel Sakura's relative importance on Japan's nationalist right. While it once functioned as the go-to media outlet for many conservative activists and pundits, it is now one of several possible choices, noticeably lagging behind DHC. Viewership of Channel Sakura videos, however, has not noticeably declined. There is in fact a case to be made that it has grown in popularity. It was quite common for some of its programs in 2020 to receive hundreds of thousands of views on YouTube, something that was rare in the early 2010s. In addition, its subscriber count has continued to climb, gaining several hundred new subscribers each week.[30]

Overseas right-wing populism and Channel Sakura

When I first began my research on this topic, the emergence of right-wing populist movements in Europe and the United States, and the accompanying electoral successes of Brexit and Donald Trump were almost inconceivable. While these developments have led to increased interest in academic research on the political right, they have not produced major changes to Channel Sakura's activism.

Numerous small cosmetic changes, such as the use of the terms "fake news" and "antifa" have taken place, but the core message remains the message that they inherited from the 1990s activism of the assertive conservative right. Distrust of mainstream media has been a constant in their movement, regardless of whether or not it was referred to as "fake news." Channel Sakura's street demonstrations continued to be held in the same manner they have been held for over a decade, without major changes in tactics or increases in demonstration turnout. The success of populists abroad does not seem to have helped boost a similar movement in Japan, at least as far as Channel Sakura is concerned.

Some of this consistency can be explained by Channel Sakura's stable leadership. Mizushima Satoru was the president of Channel Sakura and the central figure in most of its programming throughout the entire period covered in this book. If Mizushima, who turned 71 in 2020, were to retire from his position, it is conceivable that Channel Sakura could undergo major changes, provided that it can survive without his leadership.

Rather than boost Japan's right, the success of right-wing groups abroad may actually threaten the survival of Japanese organizations that utilize the internet to spread information and mobilize protest campaigns. Increased perception abroad about the dangers of right-wing ideology is having an impact on Japan. YouTube and Twitter, two major social media platforms utilized by Channel Sakura and its supporters, are based in the United States, meaning that their policies are influenced by political conditions in America. In the wake of Donald Trump's election victory and increased media attention to the racism of the "alt-right," YouTube came under fire for allowing racists and extremists to flourish on its platform. In response to pressure from media and advertisers, YouTube announced new community guidelines in 2017 that led to the removal of many right-wing videos and channels. In 2018 I argued that a lack of overt expressions of racist language or overt incitements of hatred toward entire groups made it possible for Channel Sakura to spread its message without censorship from YouTube.[31]

YouTube's community guidelines continued to evolve, and in 2020 Channel Sakura faced the possibility of a complete ban of its content. Mizushima Satoru's infamous 2007 documentary, "The Truth about Nanjing," was removed from YouTube in early 2020. Although Mizushima characterized it as the unfair targeting of a video that criticized the Chinese government, it was more likely due to its clear violation of a rule enacted in 2019 that banned "denying well-documented violent events."[32] This prompted Channel Sakura to create a second YouTube channel in June 2020, which it called its "annex," to be used in the event that the main channel is banned.[33] Past crackdowns have occasionally spared second channels, but there are also instances of stricter bans. When YouTube banned the American conspiracy theorist Alex Jones in 2019, Jones and his co-hosts were completely banned from the platform and prohibited from creating new channels.[34] If Channel Sakura were targeted in a similar manner, it would need to seek out an alternative video hosting platform with looser rules regarding hate speech and history denial.[35] However, no alternative platform in 2020 could compare to the popularity and accessibility of YouTube.

Closing thoughts

As the threat of social media censorship looms over Channel Sakura, there are other factors at play that could ensure its continued survival. First and foremost is its adaptability to change, which I have documented in the previous chapters of this book. Mizushima Satoru and other activists have built a cohesive organization that has consistently noticed and taken advantage of small opportunities to move forward while maintaining a base of loyal supporters who provide it with regular donations. Leaders, donors, and viewers were all part of a "grassroots revolution," one that could shrug off frequent failures as the unavoidable consequence of just underdogs struggling against a society that had not yet awakened to the "truth" of their movement. Even in the face of a split between two leading figures – Mizushima and Tamogami – a large number of supporters remained loyal to Mizushima and Channel Sakura, and its viewer numbers have slowly but steadily grown.

Domestic and international political factors also favor the continuation of Channel Sakura and similar organizations. The LDP, Japan's conservative ruling party, has not faced a major rival since it shattered the DPJ in the 2012 general election. With no viable alternative on the horizon, nationalist politicians within the LDP, many of whom regularly cooperate and support Channel Sakura, are likely to remain in office. It would be no exaggeration to suggest that these politicians, together with non-state actors like Channel Sakura, have contributed to Chinese and Korean perceptions of a Japan unwilling to atone for its historical wrongs. Channel Sakura's boat activism near the Senkaku Islands, which has not gone unnoticed abroad, has added to tensions between Japan and China (see Chapter 7). Since many of Channel Sakura's campaigns have centered around mobilizing negative feelings toward China and Korea, worsened relations with those countries will provide new reasons for activists to continue their struggle. While there is little to suggest that they will rise into a mass movement of millions and dominate Japan, I believe that the cases presented in this book show that small conservative activist groups have played and will continue to play a significant role in Japan's domestic and international handling of historical and territorial issues.

Notes

1 "【水島総】井尻先生の復帰と、10年の歩みを振り返って[桜H26/8/18]" ["Mizushima Satoru" Ijiri-sensei's Return – Thinking Back on the Past Ten Years

(Sakura Heisei 26/8/18)]. *Nihon Bunka Channel Sakura*, August 18m 2014, https://www.youtube.com/watch?v=1ZTw7YQ5lNs.

2 "田母神会長を都知事選出馬へ要請！熱い思いを語る水島総幹事長14.1.3「謹賀新年　靖国神社の英霊と共に！」②" [Tamogami Enters Gubernatorial Race! Mizushima Satoru Speaks with Passion 14.1.3 "Happy New Year Together with the War Dead at Yasukuni Shrine!" 2]. *Iwata Makoto*, January 3, 2014, https://www.youtube.com/watch?v=qXsvR1wfIEM.

3 "田母神会長・東京都知事選動画" [Tamogami – Tokyo Gubernatorial Election Videos]. *Ganbare Nippon!*, September 30, 2020, https://web.archive.org/web/20140706012040/http://www.ganbare-nippon.net/tamogami.html.

4 Ayako Mie, "Tamogami Finds Right-Wing Niche," *Japan Times*, February 4, 2014, https://www.japantimes.co.jp/news/2014/02/05/national/politics-diplomacy/tamogami-finds-right-wing-niche/.

5 "「平手打ちしたデヴィです」と田母神氏応援" ["My name is Dewi, from That Slap I Gave" Speaks in Support of Tamogami]. *Nikkan Sports*, January 23, 2014, https://www.nikkansports.com/entertainment/news/f-et-tp0–20140123–1247875.html.

6 "都知事選街頭演説 選挙妨害 ｶﾞﾁﾊﾞﾄﾙ 田母神 vs 舛添 銀座4丁目 平成26年2月2日(日)" [Gubernatorial Election Street, Election Disrupted in Ferocious Battle – Tamogami vs Masuzoe, Ginza 4-Chome, Heisei 26/2/2 (Sunday)]. *Clean Up Japan*, February 2, 2014, https://www.youtube.com/watch?v=1tTjt-FEkL4.

7 "都知事選投票率55％で宇都宮60万、舛添230万、細川250万予測" [Gubernatorial Election Turnout at 55% – Predictions: Utsunomiya, 600.000 Vote; Masuzoe, 2.30.000 Vote; Hosokawa 250.000 Votes]. *Shūkan Post*, January 20, 2014; and Alexander Martin, "Polls Show Ex-PM Hosokawa's Tokyo Governor Bid Not Gaining Traction," *Wall Street Journal Japan Real Time*, January 27, 2014.

8 Ayako Mie, "Tamogami Finds Right-Wing Niche," *Japan Times*, February 4, 2014, https://www.japantimes.co.jp/news/2014/02/05/national/politics-diplomacy/tamogami-finds-right-wing-niche/.

9 "【東京都知事選挙】2.8　田母神としお候補、雪の秋葉原・最後の訴え[桜H26/2/9]" ["Tokyo Gubernatorial Election" 2.8 Toshio Tamogami in Snowy Akihabara – Final Appeal (Sakura Heisei 26/2/9)]. *Nihon Bunka Channel Sakura*, February 9, 2014, https://www.nicovideo.jp/watch/1391907960.

10 Masaaki Kameda, "Tamogami Finds Some Support in Younger Generation," *Japan Times*, February 10, 2014, https://www.japantimes.co.jp/news/2014/02/10/national/politics-diplomacy/tamogami-finds-some-support-in-younger-generation/.

11 Tsunehira Furuya, 若者は本当に右傾化しているのか [Have the Young Really Gone to the Right?] (Tokyo: Aspect Co., 2014), 85–93.

12 "【アーカイブ】2014年東京都知事選挙開票特番[桜H26/2/11]" ["Archive" 2014 Gubernatorial Election Result Special (Sakura Heisei 26/2/11)]. *Nihon Bunka Channel Sakura*, February 11, 2014, https://www.nicovideo.jp/watch/so22862174.

13 "【東京都知事選挙】三橋貴明より、デマと口撃に淫する人達へ[桜H26/2/12]" ["Tokyo Gubernatorial Election" Takaaki Mitsuhashi Speaks to Those Spreading Lies and Attacks]. *Nihon Bunka Channel Sakura*, February 12, 2014, https://www.nicovideo.jp/watch/so22871135.

14 "【東京都知事選】田母神としお候補の戦いを振り返って[桜H26/2/14]." *Nihon Bunka Channel Sakura*, February 14, 2014, https://www.nicovideo.jp/watch/so22885003.

15 Kirk Spitzer, "This Is the Extreme Right Wing Japanese Politician Who Has a Lot of People Worried," *Time Magazine,* February 13, 2014, https://world.time.com/2014/02/13/toshio-tamogami-japanese-right/.

16 Ibid.
17 Robert J. Pekkanen and Steven R. Reed, "From Third Force to Third Party: Duverger's Revenge?," in *Japan Decides 2014*, ed. Robert J. Pekkanen, Steven R. Reed and Ethan Scheiner (London: Palgrave Macmillan, 2016), 68, https://doi.org/10.1057/9781137552006_6.
18 Hiroyuki Seto, 田母神裁判傍聴記 [Record of the Tamogami Trial] (Tokyo: Seirindō, 2017), 21–23.
19 "【水島総】田母神俊雄事務所の使途不明金問題について[桜H27/2/17]" ["Mizushima Satoru" Regarding the Missing Funds at Tamogami Toshio's Office (Sakura Heisei 27/2/17)]. *Nihon Bunka Channel Sakura*, February 17, 2015, https://www.nicovideo.jp/watch/so25598282.
20 Mitsuhashi Takaaki, " 第３８回「耳が汚れる話」" [Part 38 "A Dirty Story"]. *Gekkan Mitsuhashi*, February 26, 2015, http://keieikagakupub.com/38news/%E7%AC%AC%EF%BC%93%EF%BC%98%E5%9B%9E%E3%80%8C%E8%80%B3%E3%81%8C%E6%B1%9A%E3%82%8C%E3%82%8B%E8%A9%B1%E3%80%8D/.
21 "【直言極言】田母神金銭スキャンダル、草莽崛起と南洲翁遺訓の原点に[桜H27/2/20]" ["Frank and Direct" Tamogami Funds Scandal, At the Root of Grassroots Uprising and Manshū ôi Kun (Sakura Heisei 27/2/20)]. *Nihon Bunka Channel Sakura*, February 20, 2015, https://www.nicovideo.jp/watch/so25618809.
22 Hiroyuki Seto, 田母神裁判傍聴記 [Record of the Tamogami Trial], 13, 55, 122.
23 Jonathan Soble, "A Champion of Japan's Right Wing Is Jailed over Campaign Payments," *New York Times*, April 14, 2016, https://www.nytimes.com/2016/04/15/world/asia/japan-toshio-tamogami.html.
24 "Ex-ASDF Chief Tamogami Found Guilty over Illegal Payments to Campaign Staff," *Kyodo News*, May 22, 2017, https://japantoday.com/category/crime/Ex-ASDF-chief-Tamogami-found-guilty-over-illegal-payments-to-campaign-staff.
25 "【特番】田母神事件報告～最高裁上告の悪足掻き[桜H30/3/28]" ["Special" Tamogami Incident Report – Supreme Court Final Appeal a Useless Attempt at Resistance (Sakura Heisei 30/3/28)]. *Nihon Bunka Channel Sakura*, March 28, 2018, https://www.nicovideo.jp/watch/so32960370.
26 Subscriber figures for this chapter were collected on September 30, 2020.
27 Austin Smith, "Taking a Stand Online: An Examination of DHC's Corporate Socio-Political Involvement," Master's thesis, Waseda University, 2019.
28 "【田母神横領買収事件】DHCシアターへ通告、イエロージャーナリズムへの反省を求む[桜H28/4/11]" ["Tamogami Embezzlement Scandal" DHC Sister Notification, Yellow Journalism Requires a Good Look at Itself]. *Nihon Bunka Channel Sakura*, April 11, 2016, https://www.nicovideo.jp/watch/so28617826.
29 "【田母神事件報告】それでも「軍人」か？刑事被告人の欺瞞と嘘[桜H30/6/29]" ["Tamogami Incident Report" A Soldier Nevertheless? The Lies and Deceit of the Accused]. *Nihon Bunka Channel Sakura*, June 29, 2018, https://www.nicovideo.jp/watch/so33440397.
30 "SakuraSoTV," *Social Blade*, last accessed September 30, 2020, https://socialblade.com/youtube/channel/UC_39VhpzPZyOVrXUeWv04Zg/monthly.
31 Jeffrey J. Hall, "Japan's Right-Wing YouTubers: Finding a Niche in an Environment of Increased Censorship," *Seoul National University Asia Review* 8, no. 1 (2018), https://doi.org/10.24987/SNUACAR.2018.08.8.1.315.
32 "YouTube to Ban 'Hateful,' 'Supremacist' Videos," *Phys.org*, June 5, 2019, https://phys.org/news/2019–06-youtube-speech-guidelines-prohibit-videos.html.
33 【ch桜・別館】水島総から別館開設のお知らせ[桜R2/6/3]" ["Channel Sakura – Annex" Announcement by Mizushima Satoru of the Construction of an Annex

(Sakura Reiwa 2/6/3)]. *Nihon Bunka Channel Sakura*, June 3, 2020, https://www.youtube.com/watch?v=-xOiC2hi-ic.

34 Bill Chapel, "YouTube, Apple and Facebook Ban Infowars, Which Decries 'Mega Purge,'" *NPR*, August 6, 2018, https://www.npr.org/2018/08/06/636030043/youtube-apple-and-facebook-ban-infowars-which-decries-mega-purge.

35 Milo Trujillo, Maurício Gruppi, Cody Buntain and Benjamin D. Horne, "What Is BitChute? Characterizing the 'Free Speech' Alternative to YouTube," *arXiv*, April 4, 2020, https://arxiv.org/abs/2004.01984.

Bibliography

Chapel, Bill. "YouTube, Apple and Facebook Ban Infowars, Which Decries 'Mega Purge.'" *NPR*, August 6, 2018. https://www.npr.org/2018/08/06/636030043/youtube-apple-and-facebook-ban-infowars-which-decries-mega-purge.

Clean Up Japan. "都知事選街頭演説 選挙妨害 ｶﾞﾁﾊﾞﾄﾙ 田母神 vs 舛添 銀座4丁目 平成26年2月2日(日)" [Gubernatorial Election Street, Election Disrupted in Ferocious Battle – Tamogami vs Masuzoe, Ginza 4-Chome, Heisei 26/2/2 (Sunday)]. February 2, 2014. https://www.youtube.com/watch?v=1tTjt-FEkL4.

Furuya, Tsunehira. 若者は本当に右傾化しているのか [Have the Young Really Gone to the Right?]. Tokyo: Aspect Co., 2014.

Ganbare Nippon! "田母神会長・東京都知事選動画" [Tamogami – Tokyo Gubernatorial Election Videos]. September 30, 2020. https://web.archive.org/web/20140706012040/http://www.http://ganbare-nippon.net/tamogami.html.

Hall, Jeffrey J. "Japan's Right-wing YouTubers: Finding a Niche in an Environment of Increased Censorship." *Seoul National University Asia Review* 8, no. 1 (2018): 315–347. https://doi.org/10.24987/SNUACAR.2018.08.8.1.315.

Iwata Makoto. "田母神会長を都知事選出馬へ要請！熱い思いを語る水島総幹事長14.1.3 「謹賀新年　靖国神社の英霊と共に！」②" [Tamogami Enters Gubernatorial Race! Mizushima Satoru Speaks with Passion 14.1.3 "Happy New Year Together With the War Dead at Yasukuni Shrine!" 2]. January 3, 2014. https://www.youtube.com/watch?v=qXsvR1wfIEM.

Kameda, Masaaki. "Tamogami Finds Some Support in Younger Generation." *Japan Times*, February 10, 2014. https://www.japantimes.co.jp/news/2014/02/10/national/politics-diplomacy/tamogami-finds-some-support-in-younger-generation/.

Kyodo News. "Ex-ASDF Chief Tamogami Found Guilty over Illegal Payments to Campaign Staff." May 22, 2017. https://japantoday.com/category/crime/Ex-ASDF-chief-Tamogami-found-guilty-over-illegal-payments-to-campaign-staff.

Martin, Alexander. "Polls Show Ex-PM Hosokawa's Tokyo Governor Bid Not Gaining Traction." *Wall Street Journal Japan Real Time*, January 27, 2014.

Mie, Ayako. "Tamogami Finds Right-Wing Niche." *Japan Times*, February 4, 2014. https://www.japantimes.co.jp/news/2014/02/05/national/politics-diplomacy/tamogami-finds-right-wing-niche/.

Nikkan Sports. "「平手打ちしたデヴィです」と田母神氏応援" ["My Name Is Dewi, from That Slap I Gave" Speaks in Support of Tamogami]. January 23, 2014. https://www.nikkansports.com/entertainment/news/f-et-tp0–20140123–1247875.html

Pekkanen, Robert J., and Reed, Steven R. "From Third Force to Third Party: Duverger's Revenge?" In *Japan Decides 2014*, ed. Robert J. Pekkanen, Steven R. Reed, and Ethan Scheiner, 62–71. London: Palgrave Macmillan, 2016. https://doi.org/10.1057/9781137552006_6.

Phys.org. "YouTube to Ban 'Hateful,' 'Supremacist' Videos." June 5, 2019. https://phys.org/news/2019–06-youtube-speech-guidelines-prohibit-videos.html.

Seto, Hiroyuk. 田母神裁判傍聴記 [Record of the Tamogami Trial]. Tokyo: Seirindō, 2017.

Shūkan Post. "都知事選投票率55%で宇都宮60万、舛添230万、細川250万予測" [Gubernatorial Election Turnout at 55% – Predictions: Utsunomiya, 600.000 Vote; Masuzoe, 2.30.000 Vote; Hosokawa 250.000 Votes]. January 20, 2014.

Smith, Austin. "Taking a Stand Online: An Examination of DHC's Corporate Socio-Political Involvement." Master's thesis. Waseda University, 2019.

Soble, Jonathan. "A Champion of Japan's Right Wing Is Jailed over Campaign Payments." *New York Times*, April 14, 2016. https://www.nytimes.com/2016/04/15/world/asia/japan-toshio-tamogami.html.

Social Blade. "SakuraSoTV." Last accessed September 30, 2020, https://socialblade.com/youtube/channel/UC_39VhpzPZyOVrXUeWv04Zg/monthly.

Spitzer, Kirk. "This Is the Extreme Right Wing Japanese Politician Who Has a Lot of People Worried." *Time Magazine*, February 13, 2014. https://world.time.com/2014/02/13/toshio-tamogami-japanese-right/.

Takaaki, Mitsuhashi. "第３８回「耳が汚れる話」" [Part 38 "A Dirty Story"]. *Gekkan Mitsuhashi*, February 26, 2015. http://keieikagakupub.com/38news/%E7%AC%AC%EF%BC%93%EF%BC%98%E5%9B%9E%E3%80%8C%E8%80%B3%E3%81%8C%E6%B1%9A%E3%82%8C%E3%82%8B%E8%A9%B1%E3%80%8D/.

Index

For Product Safety Concerns and Information please contact our EU
representative GPSR@taylorandfrancis.com
Taylor & Francis Verlag GmbH, Kaufingerstraße 24, 80331 München, Germany

www.ingramcontent.com/pod-product-compliance
Ingram Content Group UK Ltd.
Pitfield, Milton Keynes, MK11 3LW, UK
UKHW020006200926
475702UK00015B/2508
9780367558437